Medicine and the Body

Medicine and the Body

Simon J. Williams

SAGE Publications
London • Thousand Oaks • New Delhi

First published 2003

SAGE Publications Ltd
6 Bonhill Street
London EC2A 4PU

SAGE Publications Inc
2455 Teller Road
Thousand Oaks, California 91320

SAGE Publications India Pvt Ltd
B-42, Panchsheel Enclave
Post Box 4109
New Delhi 100 017

British Library Cataloguing in Publication data

A catalogue record for this book is
available from the British Library

ISBN 0 7619 5638 7
ISBN 0 7619 5639 5 (pbk)

Library of Congress Control Number: 2002109395

Typeset by M Rules
Printed in Great Britain by Cromwell Press Ltd, Trowbridge, Wiltshire

For Ruth

Contents

Acknowledgements

Some of the chapters in this book are *substantially reworked* versions of previously published work. Chapters 1, 5 and 7 are based on articles in *Sociology of Health and Illness* (Williams 2001a, 2000, 1999a, respectively); Chapter 3 draws on arguments which first appeared in *Sociology* (Williams 1998a); Chapter 6 draws from an article on sleep in *Health* (Williams 2002); and Chapter 8 is an update on arguments first published in *Social Science and Medicine* (Williams 1997). I am grateful for permission to 'reproduce' this material from the above sources. Thanks also to Sharon Boden for typing and commenting on some of the chapters in the book, and to Bryan Turner for his constructive comments on the submitted manuscript. Thanks are also due to Chris Rojek and those at Sage for sticking with me and to Justin Dyer for some sharp-eyed copy-editing! The book, I hope, does everyone justice, save the errors, which I dutifully bear.

Body is one great reason, a plurality with one sense, a war and a peace, a flock and a herdsman. (Nietzsche, *Thus Spake Zarathustra*)

Introduction:
Medical Sociology in the New Millennium

This is a book about the body, medicine and health, and the sociological agendas these raise, with emotions at the heart of the matter: the animating principle, so to speak. What is the body? Where do its boundaries lie? How are bodies thought, lived, experienced and expressed, in sickness and in health? What of relations between the body and medicine, health and healing? Do emotions provide the 'missing link' between nature and culture, biology and society, structure and agency, the public and the private? And what of ethics: what role bodies? Medical sociology, given the very nature of its subject matter, is well placed to address, if not (fully) answer, these embodied questions and emotion-laden issues, and it is to an exploration of these very matters that this book is devoted.

The origins, nature and status of medical sociology, to be sure, have been much debated over the years, with or without explicit reference to bodies. Medical sociology, for example, according to conventional accounts,[1] was in large part a child of the post-Second World War era, moving from its early status as a sub-discipline in-the-service of medicine (a sociology *in* medicine), to a more fully fledged, autonomous sociology *of* medicine (or a sociology of health and illness):[2] one able to critically reflect upon matters of health and illness, within and beyond the formal health care arena, championing voices hitherto silenced by medicine (*qua* dominant profession) along the way. Others, however, challenge any such interpretation, tracing the roots of (medical) sociology much further back, thereby recovering its 'secret' history of the body in the process. Turner (1992, 1995), for example, reminds us of Foucault's contention that sociology had its origins in nineteenth-century medical practices such as medical surveys. This in turn suggests not simply that sociology and medicine are inextricably bound together, but that 'modern medicine is in fact applied sociology, and sociology is applied medicine' (Turner 1995: 6; see also Claus 1983 on the development of European medical sociology). The history of medical sociology, from this alternative viewpoint, is itself an 'outline of certain conceptual developments' with respect to three key issues, namely 'nature, society and embodiment', raising a series of pertinent ontological and epistemological questions in doing so (Turner 1995: 6). To the extent, moreover, that medical sociology confronts the ontological question 'what is disease', which in its current form translates into the question 'what is the body?', these relations cannot be overstated (Turner 1995: 6).

Whatever its roots or points of origin, medical sociology, by all accounts, is now a thriving sub-field of inquiry, spanning a diverse array of themes and issues, from ongoing medicalization debates to the tracking and tackling of health inequalities, images, representations and experience of health and illness, to the dilemmas of high-technology medicine, challenges to professional power and dominance (including new social movements), to the changing (global) dynamics of health care in the new millennium. In many countries, Cockerham (1995) comments, medical sociology is either the largest or one of the largest specialty groups. The European Society for Medical Sociology, for instance, is a 'large and active professional society, as are the medical sociology sections of the American, British and German Sociological Associations' (1995: xi). Australian medical sociology, likewise, has flourished in recent years, with signs of similarly healthy take-off in countries such as Japan. Medical sociology, then, appears to be in good shape, with a growing membership world-wide. It has also now secured a place in the interdisciplinary medical curriculum (see, for example, GMC 2002a).

Parsons, of course, theoretically speaking, stands out as a key figure here in all this, given his classic sociological formulation of illness as social deviance, channelled through the institutional mechanism of the sick role.[3] Foucault too, as noted above, has been particularly influential in recent years, giving rise to a promising array of studies in health and beyond with the body at the very centre of discursive discussion and debate. Today, however, it is probably fair to say that the sociology of health and illness comprises a wide range or an eclectic mix of theoretical perspectives and positions, from interactionism to political economy, phenomenology to postmodernism and post-structuralism (see, for example, Gerhardt 1989). Feminisms too, it should be stressed, have contributed much to these agendas, shedding important light on issues of gender and patriarchy, health and healing, across the public/private divide – challenging, along the way, claims to previous corporeal neglect.

Tensions remain, nonetheless, not simply concerning this eclectic theoretical mix, but also regarding various funding crises, institutional dilemmas and the push towards more evaluative health service research, including so-called 'evidence-based medicine' (Sackett et al. 1997) and various quality assurance initiatives – themselves linked to the changing nature and status, if not McDonaldization (cf. Ritzer, 1995), of contemporary medical practice, with changes of a similar kind currently sweeping through the academy (Turner 1992: 139–42, 154–8). A sociology of the body, Turner ventures, is crucial in responding to these dilemmas. The sociology of the body, he argues, elaborating on the above points, provides an organizing principle in medical sociology and a much needed method for integrating existing approaches. This in turn creates promising new interdisciplinary linkages and fruitful avenues of future embodied inquiry, including renewed attention to such fundamental, existentially charged issues as pain and suffering, disability and death (1992: 169–70). What this amounts to then, for Turner at least, is nothing short of a 'theoretical defence' of medical sociology and its disciplinary integrity, given the tensions raised above and the broader relations between medicine and sociology of which they are a part (1992: 169).

These corporeal calls and issues, of course, whilst particularly pertinent and pressing for medical sociology and medical anthropology, are themselves part and parcel of a broader upsurge of interest in body matters in recent years, both inside and outside the academy. From Turner's pioneering statement in *The Body and Society*, currently in its second edition (1996/1984), to Grosz's *Volatile Bodies* (1994), and from Martin's *Flexible Bodies* (1994) to Crossley's *The Social Body* (2001), these corporeal lines of development and debate can be traced: developments themselves underpinned by the ideas of thinkers as diverse as Foucault, Merleau-Ponty, Schilder, Mauss, Elias, Goffman, Bourdieu and Douglas, to name but a few. We even now have a journal, *Body & Society* (co-founded and co-edited by Featherstone and Turner in 1995), specifically devoted to these issues, itself providing a forum for a number of key debates in recent years, including special issues devoted to such timely topics as cyberbodies/cyberpunk/cyberspace, body modification and the commodification of bodies.

One consequence of these developments, as I have commented elsewhere (Williams and Bendelow 1998a), is that the body is everywhere and nowhere today. The old adage that the more closely we approach things the less clear they become seems particularly apposite in this case. The body, for instance, has been variously described as: an effect of power/knowledge (cf. Foucault); the site of lived experience (cf. Merleau-Ponty); a metaphorical treasure trove (cf. Douglas); a form of capital and distinction (cf. Bourdieu); a product of the civilizing process (cf. Elias); an interactional or dramaturgical resource (cf. Goffman); even a leaky, fluid, uncontainable entity (cf. Irigaray). Many bodies, as this suggests, now roam the sociological landscape, some more ethereal than others. Fortunately, however, as alluded to earlier, this deafening chorus of cries to bring the body back in is now giving way to a new, more critical call which seeks to 'question' this current state of play, reopen debates about the role of biology, and move towards a more 'integrative' phase of theorizing. The emphasis here is not simply on rereading old sociological themes in a new corporeal light – one which itself questions the charge of previous sociological neglect[4] – but on mapping out new ways of thinking and research agendas which challenge former divisions such as mind and body, nature and culture, biology and society. There is also now, thankfully, a growing corpus of theoretically informed empirical research pertaining to the body in everyday life (Cunningham-Burley and Backett-Milburn 2001; Nettleton and Watson 1998).

As with the body, so too with emotions. Sociological interest in emotions has likewise mushroomed in recent years, over-spilling its former sub-disciplinary boundaries or confines in the process, so to speak.[5] Landmark texts here include Hochschild's *Managed Heart* (1983), Denzin's *On Understanding Emotion* (1984) and Scheff's *Microsociology: Discourse, Emotion and Social Structure* (1990). Like the body through which they flow, a sociological focus on emotions has opened up a whole new way of 'seeing' the world (Hochschild 1983), raising a series of important agendas along the way. Again, in doing so, we confront here the problems of former divisions of the reason and emotion, male and female, public and private variety.

A related set of questions also arise at this juncture. Are we, for example, talking here about a sociology *of* the body (one in which the body becomes an object of sociological scrutiny and debate), or an *embodied* sociology (one which takes seriously the lived embodiment of its practitioners, as well as those we seek to study) (Frank 1991a). Any such concerns, of course, will include, if not incorporate emotions. Some, indeed, have gone further, calling for nothing short of a 'passionate sociology' (Game and Metcalfe 1996), with emotions at the heart of the sociological enterprise, thereby connecting us to the world in a fully *embodied* fashion. Whatever one's take on these issues, the body it is clear, in its manifold corporeal guises, is alive and kicking in (medical) sociology today, without of course precluding death and dying.

It is against this backdrop of embodied themes and issues, themselves, as we have seen, rapidly unfolding, that the present book is located. The aims are simple, namely to draw together in the scope of a single volume my work on the body and medicine, emotion and health, over the past five or so years, in the context of these broader debates on embodiment, and to comment upon other key areas and issues which I take to be central to these evolving agendas, in the sociology of health and illness and beyond. The focus and emphasis, in doing so, is very much on embodiment, although I shall not stick rigidly to this term or issue on each and every occasion. These embodied agendas in turn are used, along the way, to critically reassess the merits of various constructionist positions and to find other, more promising (realist) ways of bringing the biological (back) into sociological discussion and debate: not simply, that is to say, another body of knowledge, however important such insights might be.

This, it should be stressed at the outset, is not a textbook as such, if by that one means a basic introductory textbook, with handy bite-sized chunks of knowledge in nicely presented boxes for students to snack on in these McDonaldized times. Nor am I attempting to be comprehensive in coverage, itself a Herculean task in an era of information overload. My focus instead is more selective. Readers expecting to find a book brimming over with facts and figures pertaining to this or that aspect of health, medicine or disease may be disappointed, for example. Others looking for bodily insights into institutions such as clinics, hospitals, waiting rooms, wards, training courses, community arrangements, national health organizations, will also (in all likelihood) find much to bemoan or condemn. The book nonetheless does, I hope, on its own terms of reference, flag up a series of pertinent corporeal agendas and debates, both old and new alike, which demonstrate, at one and the same time, the intimate links and fruitful relations between sociological theory and medical sociology. I have also, despite the McDonaldized caveats and disclaimers above, attempted to make it a text which speaks directly to the reader, in a clear, accessible manner, without unnecessary jargon, thereby conveying complex ideas in a digestible form.

The book takes off in Chapter 1 with a revisiting of the biomedical model and some of the tensions and dilemmas surrounding sociological critiques of it. In particular I return to Strong's (1979a) charge of sociological imperialism, assessing its strengths and weaknesses, and updating the insights contained therein in the light of certain current developments in the field; questions, that is to say, concerning the 'limits' of the sociological enterprise itself with particular reference to social constructionism. This in turn entails a bringing of the biological body back into sociological discussion and debate in new, non-reductionist ways.

The next chapter focuses squarely on issues of health, tracing a variety of bodily themes and issues in the process, from the Bourdieuesque notion of bodily 'capital' to Martin and Haraway's analysis of 'flexible/immunological' bodies, and from Crawford's 'dilemmatic' bodies to the alleged rise of 'holistic/effervescent' bodies. In these and other ways, a thinking of health through bodies is attempted, including comments on the very nature of boundaries themselves.

One of the key areas and staple diets of medical sociology over the years has been the study of inequalities in health. Chapter 3 picks up on these issues at a critical moment: one in which health inequalities, politically speaking, are back on the agenda in the UK through New Labour's pledge to tackle the 'widening gap'. The chapter in this respect, drawing on a range of sources (including Wilkinson's work on income distribution and *relative* deprivation), explores the crucial role emotions play in such body–society relations – the translation, that is to say, of key features of social structure into the health and illness of the emotionally embodied agent. These issues in turn are placed, towards the end of the chapter, in the context of other important recent debates, namely neo-materialist critiques and reinvigorated agendas regarding the role of neo-liberalism and the deeper (class) relations this entails. This, it is argued, underlines the complexity of contemporary inequalities, their cross-cutting axes, and the need to go beyond either/or debates through the elaboration and extension of social causation approaches, broadly conceived, including flows of 'capital' and their (realist) dynamics.

The next chapter, following on from these previous concerns with social structure and health, examines the issue of health across the lifecourse with particular reference to childhood and ageing, or 'growing up' and 'growing old'. Again issues of embodiment are brought to the fore: first, through an emphasis on children as embodied agents and active constructors of their world; and, secondly, through a focus on the positive and negative scenarios surrounding the prospects of ageing in which new biocultural forms of 'destabilization' are said to be occurring.

Chapter 5 returns us to more long-standing sociological concerns to do with chronic illness and disability. Taking my lead from Bury's (1982) pioneering notion of biographical disruption, I seek to critically explore the strengths and weaknesses of this tried and trusted concept, including the fact that illness cannot unproblematically be read in this way if meaning and context are taken seriously. The notion of biographical disruption as chronic illness is also explored alongside the positive as well as the negative dimensions of illness, however counter-intuitive this may at first appear.

The next chapter leads nicely on from these themes. Here I explore an issue which is very dear to my heart, perhaps to us all: the dormant matter and neglected sociological issue of sleep. Debates surrounding the (prospective) medicalization or healthization of sleep are considered before then proceeding to more familiar corporeal terrain regarding the mortal body in late/postmodernity. In doing so, points of continuity and contrast between these particular dimensions of embodiment are discussed and debated.

Chapter 7 takes up the issue of mental health, providing a vehicle for the further exploration of emotional themes and issues to do with reason and emotion, the body and society, and the 'colonization' of emotions by various forms of expertise. It also provides some speculative comments, in the light of these issues, on the very nature of the term mental health: a contradiction in terms perhaps?

One of the key issues surrounding bodies today is the remarkable array of 'options' (I use both this and subsequent terms advisedly) at our disposal, in this hi-tech era, for *repairing* or *restoring*, *modifying* or *transforming*, *altering* or *enhancing*, even perhaps *replacing* or *transcending* them. These issues, and the corporeal dilemmas they raise, are traced through a series of biotech/medically related issues in Chapter 8, including the notion of *plastic* bodies, *bionic/interchangeable* bodies, (genetically) *engineered* bodies and *digital/virtual* bodies. This, in turn, raises a broader series of issues on the very nature of medicine in late/postmodernity, and its relations to a new global era of biocapitalism/bioprospecting: debates, as we shall see, which remain pressing yet, by their very nature, uncertain.

The final chapter explores a series of underlying issues which pulse their way throughout the book as a whole. These concern notions of caring bodies and the ethics of embodiment. Issues covered here include the emotional tensions and (psycho-)dynamics of medical encounters, the dilemmas of consumerism, gender and the emotional division of labour in health care, together with the search for an ethics of embodiment and the future of health and healing in the twenty-first century.

A brief conclusion serves to round the book off, highlighting a series of future issues, including global health agendas and the threat of a new era of bio-terrorism, for which medical sociology, it is argued, is again well placed to contribute as we face the 'challenges ahead'.

Whatever one makes of it, the book, I hope, taken as a whole, is yet another testimony and contribution to the vibrant agendas of medical sociology or the sociology of health and illness in the new millennium. No mere flight of fancy or fashion, embodiment, in short, provides a profitable relay between mainstream theory and the sociological study of medicine, health and illness, demonstrating once again the symbiotic relations between the two.

Notes

1 See, for example, Gerhardt (1989), Scambler (1987), Stacey and Homans (1978), Straus (1957), Williams et al. (1998, 2000).

2 Whilst, in general, I will adhere to the latter term in this book, I shall not religiously follow it.

3 Strictly speaking, of course, as Turner (1995) notes, writers such as Parsons cannot properly be regarded as medical sociologists, given their mainstream theoretical concerns. See Gerhardt (1989), however, for a somewhat different line here.

4 Marx, Weber, Durkheim and Simmel all in fact, directly or otherwise, addressed bodily matters. See, for example, Williams and Bendelow (1998a) for a discussion of the body in classical sociology.

5 Kemper, for example, traces the beginnings of American sociological interest in emotions back to the 'watershed year' of 1975, arguing that, by the brink of the 1980s, the sociology of emotions was truly 'poised for developmental take-off' (1990: 4). The British Sociological Association sociology of emotions study group is also growing fast, in keeping with a broader sociological interest in emotions in recent years, within and beyond any such groupings.

1

The Biomedical Body: Reductionism, Constructionism and Beyond

In this opening chapter I want to take another look at what, for some seasoned readers, may seem like old, familiar, well-trodden turf: the medicalization debate, that is to say, both past and present. My aim, in doing so, is not simply to throw the 'limits' of biomedicine (yet again) into critical relief, reductionist or otherwise, but to turn the glare of the spotlight on the 'limits' of sociology itself, particularly its constructionist variants, together with broader 'imperialist' debates. Consideration of these issues raises associated questions of crucial importance concerning the nature and status of the biological, within and beyond the sociology of health and illness. It is with these issues in mind that the chapter proceeds in four main ways: firstly, through a revisiting of the biomedical model, including its historical emergence and the so-called 'orthodox' medicalization debate; secondly, through a re-examination of the social constructionist and postmodern challenge to the biomedical body; thirdly, through a critical account of the place and function of these sociological critiques themselves, and the 'limits' they display; and finally, as a kind of meta-theoretical theme, through a rethinking of the nature and status of the biological within and beyond the sociology of health and illness: one which steers a cautious path between the Scylla and Charybdis of (biological) reductionism and (social) constructionism alike.

Some caveats and disclaimers are perhaps in order at the outset, lest the tone and content of the chapter be misconstrued. Social constructionism, it should be emphasized – which comes in many shapes and sizes – is simply *one*, albeit an influential, strand of sociology. It cannot therefore be equated or conflated with the sociological enterprise as a whole. Sociology cannot, moreover, in any real sense, be seen as an 'imperialist' enterprise, unless we are prepared to equate critique with territorial 'take-over', which again is untenable. The 'limits' of sociology nonetheless, con-structionist or otherwise, are important to face up to – a comment which applies to all disciplines for that matter. Herein lines the rationale or warrant for the line taken in this particular chapter; a reflexive form of sociological housekeeping, perhaps, as a guard against our own self-conceit and deceptions. It is with these caveats and dis-claimers in mind that we proceed.

The 'limits' of biomedicine: '(de)medicalizing' the body?

What is biomedicine? Is biomedicine neutral and value-free? What are its limits? Have our bodies and lives become 'medicalized' through its influence? And what role should sociology play in these and related debates? These are some of the questions which have exercised the minds and bodies of medical sociologists over the years, in more or less (dis)passionate ways. They also provide a useful starting point for the themes and issues discussed in this chapter. First, however, a few preliminary words on changing theories of the body and disease are required as an historical backdrop to the issues which follow.

Changing theories of the body and disease – a brief history

In many respects, Porter comments, the 'medical history of humanity' in Europe (from Greco-Roman antiquity onwards) can be depicted as a series of stages which, broadly speaking, involved the systematic replacement of transcendental explana-tions, positing instead a natural basis for disease and healing (1997: 9). Prior to the 'age of reason', for example, supernatural beliefs about malevolent spirits, ideas about evil and divine intervention, and practices of sorcery and witchcraft were highly influential in Christian Europe, retaining a 'residual shadow presence' ever since in certain sects and segments of lay and popular culture (Porter 1997: 9). Other, more 'naturalistic' beliefs and approaches, in contrast, provided a somewhat firmer basis or grounding for the medical history of humanity to root and flourish. Greek medicine, for instance, in this more 'naturalistic' mould, emphasized the 'microcosm/macro-cosm' relationship in which the healthy body was seen to be in tune via humoral theories of *'balance'* and the regulation of lifestyle. From Hippocrates in the fifth cen-tury ʙᴄ to Galen in the second century ᴀᴅ, humoral medicine stressed the

> analogies between the four elements of external nature (fire, water, air and earth) and the four humours or bodily fluids (blood, phlegm, choler or yellow bile, and black bile) whose balance determined health. The humours found expression in the temperaments and complexions that marked an individual. The task of regimen was to maintain a balanced constitution, and the role of medicine was to restore the balance when disturbed. Parallels to these views appear in classical Chinese and Indian medical traditions. (Porter 1997: 9)

These medical teachings of antiquity remained 'authoritative' until the eighteenth century, including what by modern-day standards may be seen as an intimate physician–patient relationship (Porter 1997: 10). 'Bedside medicine', at this time, involved an 'open-ended model' of bodily processes founded, crucially and characteristically, upon 'extrapolation from the patient's self report of the course of their illness' (Jewson 1976: 228). The 'sick man', therefore, in Jewson's terms, was at the centre of medical cosmology at this time, comprising a unique or peculiar combination of physical, emotional and spiritual factors, incorporated in the symptom complex: one in which mind and body, psyche and soma were integrated as a 'conscious human totality' (1975: 227).

The emergence of biomedicine, however, changed all this in a more or less irrevocable way. Important historical precursors here included Vesalius's anatomical atlas *De Humani Corporis Fabrica* (1543) and Harvey's discovery of the circulation of the blood in *De Motu Cordis* (1628), both of which challenged former Galenic wisdom, thereby paving the way for the subsequent development of a new, more 'scientific', hospital-based form of medicine from the late eighteenth century onwards. Within this new form of 'Hospital Medicine', the accurate diagnosis and classification of cases came to the fore, based on the four great innovations of structural nosology, localized pathology, physical examination and statistical analysis (Jewson 1976: 229). Disease, therefore – aided and abetted by nineteenth-century inventions and discoveries such as Laennac's stethoscope in 1819, Pasteur and Koch's landmark work on micro-organisms in the 1860s, and Röntgen's X-Rays in 1896 – came to be seen as an objective entity, in which external symptoms correlated with internal lesions within the organs and tissues of the body, in contrast to former generalized notions of disturbances of the body as a whole in bedside medicine. The corporeal surfaces and spoken words of the patient, therefore, gave way to hidden underlying causes, based on detailed physical or clinical examination. Thus, as Jewson puts it, the sick man effectively 'disappeared' through the advent of Hospital Medicine, later to be microscopically or micro-organismically transformed, via Laboratory Medicine, into a collection of cells, with medical practice itself, effectively, becoming an 'appendage to the laboratory' (1976: 230).

In the short run, it is fair to say, biomedical knowledge and understanding far outstripped its curative potential (Porter 1997). Developments such as the introduction of sulfa drugs and antibiotics in the twentieth century, nonetheless, helped marry this advancing knowledge basis with tangible strides forward in medicine's own socalled 'battle' against disease and premature mortality (Porter 1997: 10). The new genetics, in similar fashion, promises to more or less radically transform the fortunes of medicine, for better or worse, in a new 'molecular' era where DNA is clearly no acronym for DO NOT ALTER (see Chapter 8).

The biomedical model, to be sure, has engendered much (heated) discussion and debate within and beyond medical sociology circles, not least concerning its reductionist focus, the 'machine metaphor' through with it operates, and the infamous

Cartesian mind/body dualism upon which it is premised, so named after the seventeenth-century French philosopher René Descartes, whose famous dictum '*Cogito ergo sum*' (I think therefore I am) drove a wedge between mind and body.[1] As for the key features of this biomedical model, Mishler (1989), in a much cited paper, lists four characteristics – (i) disease as a deviation from 'normal' biological functioning; (ii) the doctrine of specific aetiology (specific diseases are caused by specific micro-organisms); (iii) the generic or universal nature of disease, regardless of culture, time and place; (iv) the 'scientific neutrality' of medicine – which serve, in effect, as a foil for the sociological imagination itself. Each, that is to say, is open to sociological scrutiny and debate (see the following two sub-sections).

How, then, have sociologists responded to or engaged with these 'core' features of biomedicine, and what have their critiques entailed?

The 'efficacy' and medicalization debates

It is possible to identify two main, overlapping, lines of critique here, the first (more within biomedicine's own terms of reference) concerning its 'efficacy', the second pertaining to a broader social and cultural critique of modern medicine's dominance and its (il)legitimate spheres of influence. The former so-called 'efficacy' debate will not concern us much here, suffice it to say that McKeown's (1976) well-rehearsed critique of the limited historical role of medicine vis-à-vis other environmental measures and improved living standards in the decline of infectious diseases[2] has itself been superseded by the push, echoing Cochrane's *Efficacy and Efficiency* (1972), towards evidence-based medicine (Sackett et al. 1997) – medicine, that is to say, based on the 'best' available evidence (the gold standard being randomized controlled trials)[3] – together with a more 'open debate' on medical errors and accountability (see Chapter 9).

Porter's somewhat ironic remark that 'medicine's finest hour is the dawn of its dilemmas' (1997: 718) is indeed apposite in this context. As Renée Fox comments, in her revisiting of 'medical uncertainty':

> shifts in multidimensional ways, long-standing sources and manifestations of uncertainty have been reactivated, accentuated, or modified and new ones have formed. It is with extensive uncertainty about its state of knowledge and accomplishments, its future directions and limitations, and with a mixture of confidence and insecurity, that modern Western medicine is approaching the twenty-first century. (2000: 422)

These tensions, dilemmas and debates in turn, feed into the second broader set of sociological issues concerning the social and cultural critiques of modern medicine and its 'expansionist' tendencies. Again a number of overlapping lines of thought and points of criticism may be identified here. Mishler (1989), for example, returning to the 'core' features of the biomedical model identified above, takes issue with each of these specific assumptions. 'Deviant for whom?' he asks, with respect to the first criteria of 'normal' biological functioning. The doctrine of specific aetiology is likewise problematic – no one-to-one correspondence can be assumed between pathological agent X and disease Y – as is the notion that manifestations of disease are somehow transhistorical and transcultural. The key issue upon which much sociological debate has turned, however, concerns the very notion that medicine, as a 'scientific' enterprise, stands 'outside' social relations. In contrast, it is held, medicine is an institution of social control. Parsons (1951) may have been the first to grasp this issue, in his classic formulation of the 'sick role' (see Chapter 9). It was left to others, nonetheless, to fully formulate the sociological critique at stake here, of which the so-called 'medicalization thesis' is a prime expression. 'Medicine's monopoly', Freidson states, 'includes the right to create illness as an official social role' (1970: 206). Zola, in similar fashion, notes how medicine, in 'nudging aside' if not 'incorporating' the more traditional institutions of law and religion, is becoming the 'new repository of truth, the place where absolute and often final judgements are made by supposedly morally neutral and objective experts' (1972: 487). This, he argues, is a largely 'insidious' and often 'undramatic' accomplishment by 'medicalizing' daily life; a process in which the labels 'healthy' and 'ill' become 'attached' to an ever-increasing part of human existence (1972: 487). Manifestations of this 'attaching' or medicalizing process, Zola claims, are evident in at least four concrete ways: (i) through the expansion of what in life is deemed relevant to the good practice of medicine; (ii) through the retention of near absolute control over certain technical procedures; (iii) through the retention of near absolute control over certain 'taboo' areas; and (iv) through the expansion of what in medicine is deemed relevant to the good practice of life (1972: 488).

Perhaps the most radical formulation of these issues is provided by Illich (1975), whose thesis on the 'medicalization of life' and the associated issues of medical nemesis has engendered much discussion and debate over the years. The medical establishment, Illich boldly proclaims, has become a 'major threat to health'. By transforming 'pain, illness and death from a personal challenge into a technical problem, medical practice expropriates the potential of people to deal with the human condition in an autonomous way and becomes the source of a new kind of un-health' (Illich 1974: 918). These debates surrounding the so-called 'iatrogenic' consequences of modern medicine – be it clinical (medical complications/drug side-effects, for example), social (the artificial need for medical products) or structural (the undermining of peoples' autonomy and competence) – are well rehearsed.[4]

Suffice it to say that Illich himself is open to criticism on a number of counts. Navarro (1975, 1980), for example, from a neo-Marxist perspective, takes issue with both the explanations and solutions proposed by Illich to these iatrogenic problems, *qua* medical nemesis. Illich's resentment of the industrialization of all fetishism (including medicine), Navarro asserts, ends up fetishizing the very process of industrialization itself (1975: 359–60). The professional power and dominance of medicine, moreover, is an illusion, with medicine itself labouring under capitalism, the interests of which it represents and reproduces in numerous ways. Power relations within the bourgeois order, from this perspective,

> were the ones which determined the forms and nature of medicine. It led to scientific inquiry where the aim of that inquiry was the discovery of the cause or micro-organism, and the instrument of that inquiry was the microscope. By focusing on the microcausality of disease, however, science ignored the analysis of the macrocausality, i.e. the power relations in society. (Navarro, 1980: 541)

These contentions find echoes in Taussig's (1980) own elegant writings on processes of reification and the consciousness of the patient. Drawing upon Marx's analysis of the commodity and Lukács's application of this approach to the objectification of social relations, Taussig highlights a situation in which *human relations* embodied in signs, symptoms and therapy are denied, thereby mystifying these very relations and reproducing political ideology in the guise of a science of physical 'things'. Medical practice, from this viewpoint, is an important way of maintaining the 'denial as to the social facticity of things', instead taking on a 'life of their own' severed from the 'social nexus' within which they are embedded (Taussig 1980: 5). It is not therefore, contra Illich, that patients lose their autonomy. Rather what happens, Taussig maintains, is that a contradictory situation arises (given the modern clinical reductions of biomedicine), in which the 'patient swings like a pendulum between alienated passivity and alienated self assertion' (1980: 9).

Neo-Marxist critiques, as this suggest, develop lines of argument which extend far beyond the initial terms of reference of the medicalization thesis as formulated by writers such as Freidson, Zola and Illich. Feminist critiques too, of course, add a further dimension to these debates, throwing into critical relief the ideological construction and technological control of women's bodies, which the rise of medicine has entailed. From the 'cultural warping' (Haire 1978) and 'captured womb' (Oakley 1984) of childbirth (see also Wolf 2001), to debates over women, misogyny and mental illness (Showalter 1985; Ussher 1991), and from the construction of male and female bodies in medical textbooks (Lawrence and Benedixen 1992; Martin 1987) to debates over menstruation (Bransen 1992), hormone replacement therapy (Griffith 1999), obesity (Riessman 1989) and the new reproductive technologies (Denny 1996), the medicalization of women's bodies and (reproductive) lives has been a more or less abiding theme in various strands of feminisms. The personal, from this stance, is very much the political: 'our bodies, ourselves' (Boston Women's Health Book Collective 1973).

The medicalization thesis, as this suggests, has opened up a critical series of questions concerning the role and function, place and limits of biomedicine, interfacing with a variety of related perspectives which draw upon and extend these insights in their own distinctive ways. Recent additions to this growing corpus of research and writing include debates on chronic fatigue syndrome (Broom and Woodward 1996), repetitive strain injury (Arksey 1998), not to mention Gulf War syndrome (Bury 1997; Showalter 1997). Even so-called 'alternative' or 'complementary' therapies, it seems, on closer inspection, turn out to involve both de-medicalizing and re-medicalizing tendencies (Armstrong 1986; Lowenberg and Davis 1994) (see Chapters 2 and 9).

It is easy, perhaps, within all this, to lose sight of what precisely medicalization is, or is not (a much used and abused term it seems), including who precisely is involved at what level. Conrad (1992), in a useful review of research and evidence, highlights a number of important points to bear in mind here, not least concerning conceptual and definitional issues, questions of medical *and* lay involvement, and the need to distinguish between de-professionalization and de-medicalization. As regards the first of these issues, medicalization, Conrad argues, consists of 'defining a problem in medical terms, using medical language to describe the problem, adopting a medical framework to understand a problem, or using a medical intervention to "treat" it' (1992: 211). This, in turn, may occur on at least three distinct levels: (i) the *conceptual* (when medical vocabulary or models are used to define/order a 'problem'); (ii) the *institutional* (when organizations use a medical approach to tackle or control a particular problem); (iii) the *interactional* (when doctors and patients meet face-to-face in medical encounters and treatments are prescribed). As for the second set of issues, this is a socio-cultural process, Conrad stresses, 'that *may or may not* involve the medical profession, lead to medical social control or medical treatment, or be the result of *intentional expansion by the medical profession* (1992: 211, my emphasis). Sub-cultures, groups and individuals, moreover, like doctors themselves, may vary in their 'readiness to apply, accept or reject medicalized definitions' (Conrad 1992: 211; see also Cornwell 1984). Debates on de-medicalization, in keeping with these points, must therefore bear in mind that medicalization is an *interactive* process, that de-professionalizing a problem does not necessarily lead to its de-medicalization, and that whilst 'medicalization has significantly outpaced demedicalization, it is important to see this as a *bi-directional* process' (Conrad 1992: 226, my emphasis; see also Fox 1977).

The recent 'Viagra' debate throws many of these issues into critical relief. On the one hand, this looks like grist to the medicalization theorists' mill. By mid-May 1998, for example, the hype surrounding this drug had propelled weekly sales in the US to a staggering 278,000 new prescriptions, some predicting that by the year 2011 sales will top $1 billion a year. 'Forget mind-altering drugs', one new specialist in 'vitality medicine' is reported to have said, 'the new vogue is penis-altering drugs. Erectile dysfunction is coming out into the open' (*Sunday Times Magazine* 1998: 48). On the other hand, however, there appears to be genuine concern, at least in certain segments of the medical profession, about the 'recreationalization' of the drug in the US, extending far beyond the realm of the impotent male, to the maximization of sexual function and pleasurable performance for men and women alike. The growing list of side-effects and adverse reactions associated with the drug compounds these problems and fuels these concerns. Whilst some medics, in this respect, *qua* expert-entrepreneurs, appear to have capitalized on this 'expanding market' – collaborating closely with the pharmaceutical giant Pfizer, who are marketing the drug – others have called for what they term, somewhat paradoxically, a 're-medicalization' of the drug, limiting it to clear-cut clinical cases of sexual impotence (*Sunday Times Magazine* 1998). Downward financial pressures by other corporate concerns, such as private health insurers in the US, presage these developments, adding yet another tier to an already complex picture of criss-crossing trends and counter-trends, both *internal* and *external* to medicine itself.

The medicalization critique, to summarize, speaks more or less forcefully to the role of medicine in society as an institution of social control: issues which may or may not be the direct result of *intentional* expansion by the medical profession or the active collaboration of the lay populace. This very critique, however, has itself been extended, if not superseded, in recent years through the new discursive imperatives of Foucauldian thought and the linguistic twists and turns of postmodern scholarship: arguments which take us far beyond the traditional terms of reference of these medicalization critiques, as discussed above.

The social constructionist challenge: political anatomy and the (de)territorialized body (without organs)

The medicalization critique, of course, has always involved a form of social constructionism (Conrad 1992; Schneider 1985; Spector and Kitsuse 1977). This, however, took on altogether new dimensions from the early 1980s through a variety of Foucauldian scholarship. Thus a new, more thoroughgoing 'medicalization' critique emerged, in which former acknowledgement or acceptance of an underlying 'natural' or 'biophysical' reality was itself thrown in doubt, if not abandoned altogether.

Both approaches, Lupton (1997a) comments, agree in broad terms that medicine (as a dominant institution in Western societies) has come to play an increasingly important role in everyday life, shaping, for better or worse, the way we think about and indeed 'live' our bodies. For Foucauldians, however, the so-called 'orthodox' medicalization thesis has its 'limits', resting on a number of 'inconsistencies' and 'paradoxes'. The move toward 'de-medicalization', for example, may paradoxically be interpreted as a 'growing penetration of the clinical gaze into the everyday lives of citizens, including their emotional states, the nature of their interpersonal relationships, the management of stress and other "lifestyle" choices' (Lupton 1997a: 107). Medicalization, from this latter viewpoint, involves not simply new forms of 'surveillance' but also the 'fabrication' of new subjectivities, from the so-called 'health-promoting self' (Glassner 1989; Lupton 1995) to the 'dying patient' (Armstrong 1987) and the 'whole person' (Armstrong 1986).

Perhaps most importantly for our purposes, the traditional disease–illness distinction – a key point of departure for medical sociologists in the past (Freidson 1970) – has now given way to a more or less wholesale view of the body and disease as socially constructed entities: an ethereal matter in which the matter of bodies is no real matter at all, or perhaps more accurately, a discursive matter via the productive effects of power/knowledge. The seemingly 'solid', 'visible' body, Foucault proclaims, 'is only one way – neither the first nor the most fundamental – in which one spatializes disease. There have been and will be other distributions' (1973: 3). It is not therefore simply a question of

> stripping away medicine as a dominant frame of reference to reveal the 'true' body, as most orthodox critics would argue. From the Foucauldian perspective, 'demedicalizing' the body, or viewing it through alternative frames of reference that are not medical, may well lead to different, but not more 'authentic' modes of subjectivity or embodiment. (Lupton 1997a: 107)

Armstrong, himself a qualified medic, has been a key figure or disciple of this Foucauldian message within the sociology of health and illness, applying and developing these insights in a variety of ways. Foucault, Armstrong (1983) confesses, helped remove the blinkers from his eyes in ways which, as a neophyte medical student, had never before occurred to him: a sort of conversion which challenged the very notion of the solid, stable, invariate reality of the body and disease. Whilst Foucault's (1973) problematic was the birth of the 'clinical gaze' in France from the late eighteenth-century onwards, Armstrong instead charts the subsequent transformation of this clinical gaze in twentieth-century Britain through new medical techniques in which patient views and the psychosocial spaces *between* bodies come to the fore. The appearance of these new techniques, in turn, gave rise to new 'objects' or areas of inquiry centred on issues such as the doctor–patient relationship, neuroses, chronic illness and the 'normal' child, together with new forms of medical specialism or expertise, including developments in general practice, psychiatry, the emergence of paediatrics, and geriatric and community medicine. The human sciences, moreover, have also contributed to these shifting perceptions of the body and social identity: 'separate components of an overall apparatus of power which has as its object and its effect a particular political anatomy' (Armstrong 1983: 113). All in all what this amounts to, Armstrong insists, is a situation in which the human body has been subjected to a

> more complex, yet perhaps more efficient, machinery of power which, from the moment of birth (or more correctly, from the time of registration at an ante-natal clinic) to death, has constructed a web of investigation, observation and reordering around individual bodies, their relationships and their subjectivity, in the name of health. (1983: 112)

'Surveillance Medicine', we are told, has now eclipsed 'Hospital Medicine' (Armstrong 1995), a transition symbolized, in the current era of health promotion, by the strategic shift to a spatio-temporal calculus of risk factors, crystallized in the moral pursuit of health through lifestyles.[5] The regulation of bodies, in these and other ways, is primarily achieved through new forms of 'governmentality' – what Foucault (1988a) later come to term 'technologies of self' – or the imperative of health (Lupton 1995), themselves all the more effective through the subjectivities they fabricate and the modes of self-surveillance they spawn. Whilst it may seem difficult, in short, given these latter day perspectives, to take a definitive stance on issues of medicalization, awareness of these very difficulties, Lupton assures us, is itself an 'important outcome that emerged from the entrée of Foucauldian perspectives into the debate' (1997a: 108).

These 'relativizing' currents, alongside the broader questioning of medical 'truth' and 'progress' they entail – what Bury (1986) refers to as the 'abyss of relativism' – have in turn paved the way for a variety of postmodern currents and perspectives on medicine, the body and health. As a theoretical position, postmodernism rejects modernist truth claims and grand/master narratives such as the Enlightenment project (of which Marxism is a part), pointing instead to the *contingent* or *relative* nature of all knowledge about the world and its socially constructed character. This, in turn, involves the *deconstruction* of former modernist dualisms such as mind/body, reason/emotion, fact/value, and a critique of the rational, autonomous, stable or coherent self. Modernist notions of certainty, containment and control (not to mention progress) are therefore abandoned in favour of fluidity and flux, fragmentation and multiplicity, the local and the specific, becoming and otherness. In doing so, important new spaces are said to open up for voices and (multivocal) subjectivities hitherto silenced or denied through prevailing forms of power/knowledge (see Scambler 2002 for a useful account of the material, cultural-aesthetic, rational and methodological elements of postmodernism).

Nicholas Fox (1999), for example, a forceful exponent of this postmodern viewpoint, condemns the modernist underpinnings of existing sociological and medical approaches to the body, in sickness and in health.[6] Postmodernism, he claims, *promises* to 'open up' the discourses which 'fabricate' our bodies and territorialize us, through various forms of disciplinary expertise, in the name of health and illness. The discourses of medicine and its 'collaborators' within the modernist human sciences, it is claimed, seek to 'territorialize us as "organisms"' – *bodies-with-organs* (Deleuze and Guattari 1984, 1988), doomed to face the ministrations of these disciplines – to "health", "beauty" to a "full and active life", to patience in the face of the failure of senses and memory, to accept, to *be*, never to become other' (Fox 1999: 6). Biomedicine, in other words, constrains and closes down other, more promising options, possibilities, choices, rendering us, in effect, (fixed) bodies with organs vis-à-vis other, more nomadic, deterritorialized, postmodern forms of subjectivity and embodiment which, Fox claims, take us 'beyond' health (see Chapter 2).

These are issues we shall return to more fully in subsequent chapters. Suffice it to say, at this point, that these latter postmodern perspectives, in keeping with other strands of Foucauldian scholarship, have added a radical new dimension to the socially constructed nature of medical knowledge, and its so-called 'fabrications' or 'territorializations' of the body and disease, health and illness. They also, Fox stresses, carry a somewhat more positive or optimistic message than much of Foucault's (early) disciplinary work and writings, pointing to the possibilities of *resistance*, and the opening up of new de-territorialized 'lines of flight'. So much for the pros then, what about the cons?

The 'limits' of sociology: an 'imperialist' enterprise?

Here we arrive at what, in this chapter, provides the flipside of the arguments presented so far; the limits, that is to say, of sociological critiques themselves, old and new alike. A number of points, both general and specific, may be made in this respect. First, we have the question of the sociological portrayal of the biomedical model itself. All too often it seems, caricatures of the biomedical model (such as Mishler's [1989], cited above) have provided the foil or point of departure for the advancement of sociological critiques and counter-claims. Medical 'irritation', in this respect, as Strong comments, rests on an awareness of the 'factional nature of medicine and on the fact that the model when considered as an intellectual theory, *did not survive the nineteenth-century* in this pure and simple form' (1979a: 211, my emphasis). It is, Kelly and Field remark, actually

> very hard to find this medical model in practice. Few practitioners, and no textbooks of any repute, subscribe to uni-directional causal models and invariably interventions are seen in medical practice as *contingent and multi factorial* and ultimately based on assessments and probabilities. Disease taxonomies, aetiologies and therapeutics are used in medical practice as ideal-types, *constantly subject to revision*. Patients (and sociologists) may wish to believe in simply physical causes and simple cures, but *medicine tends to be much more holistic than medical sociology traditionally gives it credit for.* (1994: 35, my emphasis)[7]

This, of course, may not seem a fair criticism, particularly when latter day constructionist perspectives themselves highlight these very shifts to new, more complex forms of biographical or surveillance medicine, including lifestyles and the psychosocial dimensions of health and illness (see also, in a different vein, Baszanger's [1998] illuminating analysis of the development of pain medicine from the laboratory to the clinic). Underlying elements or tendencies towards reductionism, moreover, cannot be dismissed so easily, despite these and other apparent 'shifts' in medical thinking.[8] This may all be true. The underestimation, neglect or dismissal of medicine's own successes, however, remains a characteristic feature of many such critiques; happier, it seems, to debit than to credit medicine's balance sheet. A healthy scepticism of course, as Conrad and Schneider (1980: 77) note, is undoubtedly important in evaluating professional claims – medicine, after all, is a 'moral enterprise' (Freidson 1970) if not a 'conspiracy against the laity' (Shaw 1946/1911). Medicine nonetheless, its iatrogenic elements notwithstanding, is a crucial resource which has contributed much to improvements in the quality of life of the Western population over the past century. Again Kelly and Field's comments are instructive here:

> To deny the effectiveness of modern medical procedures such as coronary artery bypass, renal dialysis, hip replacement, cataract surgery, blood transfusion, the pharmacology of pain relief and the routine control of physical symptoms in restoring or improving the quality of life for those suffering from chronic illness is to *deny the validity of the everyday experiences of the lay public in modern Britain*. In stressing the limitations and costs of medical interventions, the physical and social contributions of modern medicine are all too frequently ignored. (1994: 36, my emphasis)

Discussion of these issues, in turn, highlights two other important factors which any adequate sociological critique must bear in mind. First, medicine itself is not composed of a body of like-minded individuals. Instead it is split into a variety of specialisms and factions, with much in-house fighting to boot. There are, moreover, professional, corporate and state constraints to medical expansionism, whether or not these accord with the wishes or desires of particular doctors at whatever level. The second issue concerns the lay populace itself, in the era of late or postmodernity, who are far from simply passive victims of medicalization. A number of possibilities in fact suggest themselves, including active resistance as well as collaboration with these very processes (see, for example, Williams and Calnan 1996a, 1996b).

But which sociologists really worth their salt, it might reasonably be retorted, hold to such simplistic or caricatured views anyway? Sociologists, both old and new, have surely taken many of these points and issues on board in developing their critiques (as Conrad's [1992] review and update on the medicalization thesis, discussed above, clearly demonstrates). This, to a point, is fair enough. Let me, however, take up the related charge of *sociological imperialism*. Strong (1979a), for example, over twenty years ago now, raised this tricky question in his classic paper on 'sociological imperialism and the profession of medicine': the dangers, that is to say, inherent in the thesis of medical imperialism itself, which is not simply 'exaggerated' but 'self-serving'. Medical sociology and its 'ally' public health, Strong claims, have a 'vested interest' in the diminution of the medical empire as it is currently constituted, building their own little empire in the process. The social model of health and illness which they themselves advance, moreover, is in fact a far better vehicle for medical imperialism than the much abused biomedical model. Herein lies the irony for Strong of a thesis designed to curb, if not counter, the problem of medical expansionism.

Much water has indeed flowed under the bridge since this time, as we have seen, but have these and related sociological conundrums, we may ask, abated or worsened? Is the charge of sociological imperialism redundant or wrong-headed, or is it as relevant today as ever it was? Certainly there are problems with Strong's thesis. Conrad and Schneider, for example, take issue with a number of points, including Strong's setting up of an 'overly simplistic either/or–win/lose situation' (1980: 77). Two key points, for our purposes, arise here. First, there is Strong's conflation of medical *imperialism* with *medicalization*, the former implying some 'intent to dominate and control', the latter a more 'descriptive term' that does not necessarily 'attribute motive or intent'. The allegation of sociological imperialism, likewise, is ultimately *irrelevant* to an evaluation of the medicalization argument from this counter-viewpoint. Instead it must be 'evaluated for its own merits and shortcomings, not on the motives attributed to those who offer it' (1980: 76). Sociology, we may add, cannot seriously be seen as a rival to medicine, given its relatively powerless position and its absence of any clients or territory to claim. At best it provides critique, but with different interests, investments and issues at stake. The second overlapping issue, returning to an earlier point, concerns various levels of medicalization (that is, *conceptual, institutional* and *doctor–patient interaction*). In limiting himself to the latter, it is claimed, Strong 'misses the considerable amount of medicalization which is not manifested on the level of doctor–patient interaction' (1980: 76).

These are important points to raise, particularly with respect to the disentangling of alleged imperialist motive or intent from processes of medicalization and their independent evaluation. The question of professional limits, sociological or otherwise, nonetheless remains: issues, I venture, which become all the more important in the light of subsequent developments in these medicalization, *qua* constructionist, critiques. Let me turn, therefore, to a more critical engagement with these latter day Foucauldian perspectives and postmodern developments, set against the backdrop of the criticisms raised above.

The constructionist challenge, as we have seen, has added an altogether new twist to former medicalization debates, undermining the traditional disease/illness distinction, and liquidating notions of 'discovery' or 'progress' in the process. In doing so, the earlier (weaker) versions of constructionism upon which the so-called 'orthodox' medicalization critique rested have been replaced with newer (stronger) claims in which the body and disease are credited, more or less wholesale, to the socio-cultural side of the balance sheet, *qua* discursive entities: *fabrications* or *inventions*, that is to say, rather than *discoveries*. The search for 'truth', 'authenticity' and 'progress', therefore, gives way to the seemingly certain claim there are no certainties and that all knowledge is relative. These positions, to repeat, have their merits. It is possible nonetheless, qualifications apart, to raise a number of critical points and issues.

First, what we have here is a prime example of the 'epistemic fallacy' (Bhaskar 1998): the conflation, that is to say, of epistemological and ontological matters, or, in more common parlance, *what* we know and *how* we know it with what there *is* to know. The world, like the body within it, has become conflated or equated with our discursive constructions or renderings of it: a 'writing out', in effect, through this very process of 'writing in'. Constructionists, of course, may reasonably object that the 'extra-discursive' features of body and world are not denied. They can only be known, however, in this or that way through particular frames of reference or con-figurations of power/knowledge. Constructionists, moreover, Conrad reminds us, are 'more concerned with the *aetiology of definitions* than the aetiology of the behaviour or condition in question' (1992: 212, my emphasis). This again is fair enough. All too often, however, the slide from this perfectly reasonable, weaker claim to stronger endorsements of the constructionist line proves tempting if not irresistible; one in which the discursive and the extra-discursive are collapsed anew with no attempt to theorize these issues *both ways*, so to speak. What this amounts to, in the final analysis, is not so much the overcoming of biological reductionism as its *inversion* through a new form of reductionism or 'discourse determinism' in which all is reduced to the social *qua* power/knowledge. In doing so, the biological is itself writ-ten out or rendered unimportant, except as yet another ('rival') body of power/knowledge. An infinite regress it seems.

Craib (1997) adds a further twist or sting to the tale – drawing upon Strong (1979a) amongst others in support of his case – through his own more general, if somewhat ironic, observations on the 'limits' of social constructionism as a string to the sociologists' bow. Constructionism, he (playfully) suggests, with his psy-chotherapist's hat on, is a form of 'social psychosis'. Sociologists, from this viewpoint, particularly those of a social constructionist persuasion, find it difficult to recognize or accept the limitations of their discipline (the so-called [Kleinian] 'depressive position'), a prime reason being the absence of any real territory or clients to claim. Social constructionism, in this respect, offers a potential way out of this (depressing) conundrum, convincing its advocates that the world can indeed be explained ('away') in precisely these terms, including the 'rival' knowledge claims of other disciplines and the lives they 'fabricate', 'regulate', 'monitor' and 'transform'. The 'manic psychosis' of sociology *qua* constructionism, from this viewpoint, is one which

> rejects, or better 'ejects' threatening knowledge and then re-internalises it as the object of sociological knowledge, passive and unthreatening. Once this is done *it is not possible to discover anything very new*; from our omnipotent position we already know what is happening – we have an imagery of scripts or discursive prac-tices, of the imaginary and the symbolic, and all we have to do is apply them to redescribe the world. We cannot discover anything new. (Craib 1997: 14, my emphasis)

We have indeed come full circle here. Armed with the 'firm belief' that 'firm bodies of knowledge' do not exist, nor for that matter the matter of bodies them-selves, *some* sociologists, through the 'manic psychotic' tendencies of social constructionism, have themselves fallen prey to a diagnostic label, however playfully or ironically applied. The 'remedy', Craib (1997) suggests, is relatively simple and straightforward. Firstly, we must accept, in the spirit of Strong's critique, our limits and limitations, and acknowledge that other disciplines, like biology, do indeed have important things to contribute to our own *partial* knowledge of the world and our place within it – forcing us perhaps, along the way, to revise or rethink our own theories accordingly. Secondly, we must face up to the fact that, in doing so, we (or *some* of us at least) *may* have to be somewhat more 'humble' in our claims, if not 'mature' or 'balanced' in our theorizing (1997: 14).

To these observations, echoing earlier points and issues, we may add the fact that sociological critiques, in the absence of any viable alternatives, all too easily neglect or problematize the crucial role which biomedicine plays in our lives as a *critical resource*. As Bury puts it, the deep involvement of medicine

> in reorganising the disruptive experience of chronic illness, in reordering its arbitrary and threatening characteristics, inevitably involves issues of social control. That medical sociology should seek to explore this is important but to suggest, as some writers do that the experience of pain, illness and even death can be faced without recourse to such codes is patently false. (1982: 179).[9]

Again the question of limits looms large, be it the limits of biomedicine or the limits of sociological critiques themselves. Where, then, do we go from here? One important issue, clearly, concerns a return to and rethinking of the biological itself, in sociology and beyond.

Bringing the biological body back in: a question of 'balance'?

Already we have glimpsed, in the pages of this chapter, the problems of biological reductionism and social constructionism alike: the latter itself a form of reductionism. Underpinning these issues lies that thorny old question of the nature and status of the biological itself, both in past and present sociological thinking. It is not the time or place to go into a detailed history of the trials and tribulations of the biological in sociology, except perhaps to say that the former has in large part provided a foil for the latter: a defence of the autonomy of sociology and its social subject matter *sui generis*, given various forms of biological reductionism, including sociobiology (Wilson 1975) and the current dubious claims of evolutionary psychology (see Higgs and Jones 2000 and Rose and Rose 2000 for a sustained critique of the latter). This equation of the biological with reductionism, of course, is itself yet another caricature or distortion both of biological *processes* themselves and of various strands of thought within and beyond the biological *sciences* themselves. The choices, Benton reminds us,

> no longer have to be seen (in reality they never did) as limited to an intellectual imperialist, politically conservative biological reductionism on the one hand and an idealist or dualist anthropocentricism, on the other. The state of biological science is fluid, there are numerous competing conceptualisations within biology, and

there are several well-articulated alternatives to reductionist materialism available for use as philosophical means in the attempt to re-think the biology/society relationship. (1991: 18, my emphasis)

Reductionist readings or renderings of the biological, therefore, have their limits, masking as much as they reveal about biological processes themselves and various alternative ways of theorizing these issues, in the biological sciences as elsewhere.

How, then, precisely, do we go 'beyond' the biological without leaving it 'out' altogether? What, to put it differently, does it take to mount an adequate and effective challenge to reductionism which overcomes these either/or debates in a satisfactory manner? A number of more or less promising answers to these questions can be advanced, albeit tentatively or provisionally. Perhaps the first issue to tackle returns us to the epistemic fallacy mentioned above. We cannot, that is to say, collapse or conflate the (ontological) nature and status of the biological with the (epistemological) ways in which we 'know' it, however important the latter might be in 'mediating' or 'constructing' our relations *with* and understandings *of* the former. We live, as Rose (1997) puts it, in 'one world', but with many ways of 'knowing it'. To the extent, then, that we may speak of differing levels or strata of world, and our location with them, these in part are

> *ontological*, and relate to scale and complexity, in which successive levels are nested one within another . . . each level appears as a holon – integrating levels below it, but merely a subset of the level above it. In this sense, levels are fundamentally irreducible . . . However, to some extent – and this is where the confusion enters – the levels are *epistemological*, relating to different ways of knowing the world, each in turn the contingent product of its own discipline's history. The relationship between such epistemological levels . . . is best described in the *metaphor of translation* . . . problems arise when one attempts to apply concepts and terms applicable at one level to phenomena on another level . . . the power of metaphor is such that we always run the danger of confusing it with reality. (Rose 1997: 304–5, my emphasis)

Translated into the parlance or register of critical realism – in which irreducibility and emergence in 'open' (rather than 'closed' experimental) systems is acknowledged and adequately theorized[10] – this is a viewpoint in which

> biological, chemical and physical powers are *necessary conditions* for the existence of the social world but the latter has properties – particularly . . . communication, interaction and discourse, which are *irreducible* to or *emergent* from these ontological strata. If we couple this stratified ontology with a critical realist analysis of causation, in which . . . *the existence of a causal power is not uniquely and deterministically linked to a particular outcome*, then it becomes possible to see that the acknowledgement of a biological (and other physical) sub-stratum of social life need not be seen as denying variety and agency at the social level . . . without an appreciation of *emergence* and the *open* nature of biological and social systems . . . unsatisfactory resolutions of the relationship between the biological and the social are inevitable. (Sayer 1997: 479–80, my emphasis)

It is possible, then, as this suggests, to recognize the complexity of the world, and the biological and social relations therein, through non-reductionist principles of irreduciblity and emergence in 'open' systems. In doing so, moreover, a 'weak' version of social constructionism may be readily accommodated or endorsed – one which no longer conflates epistemological and ontological matters, or what we know and how we know it with what there is to know.

A second key point, embedded in this first set of issues, concerns the need to conceive of the biological in more 'balanced' terms, not solely or simply as a constraint but also as an *enabling* set of powers and capacities. My biological constitution may indeed set limits on what I can achieve or do. I cannot, for instance (unaided at least), fly or breathe underwater. I do nonetheless, *qua* human being, possess an extraordinary range of power and potentialities, endowments and dispositions, skills and capacities – from bipedalism to tool and language use – which equip me for life in society, including the devising of technological means to alter or otherwise enhance these very powers and capacities still further. We are indeed, as organic bodies, part of nature, the animal/human distinction itself being in many ways problematic. Human beings nonetheless, Elias (1991) remarks, represent something of an 'evolutionary breakthrough': a process of 'symbol emancipation', as he puts it, in which the balance between *learnt* and *unlearnt* behaviours tilts ever more heavily towards the former, as social developments 'take off' without the need for further evolutionary changes or breakthroughs at the biological level. Elias, however, is himself open to criticism, particularly in his neglect of biological matters post-symbol emancipation (Dickens 2000; Shilling 1993).[11] The main point nonetheless, one which goes far beyond the merits of Elias's own particular stance on these matters, is to counter the all too common view that recourse to the biological is ever solely or simply a question of 'constraint'.

A third key point, in challenging past 'naturalistic' views and ideologies, concerns the fact that, far from legitimating social hierarchies, recourse to the biological may itself provide the basis for a profound *critique* of existing social arrangements, including oppressive social practices and crimes against humanity. Again this point may be approached from a variety of angles. Connell, for example, in his deliberations on gender and power, draws attention to the manner in which the social emphasis on difference *negates, transcends* and *transforms* natural similarity – an effect that is necessary, he emphasizes, 'precisely because the biological . . . cannot sustain the gender categories' (1987: 81). Sayer (1997) too, in a critical realist vein, draws attention to the crucially important role which recourse to various biologically based powers and capacities of human beings, *qua* organic bodies, plays as part of a critique of oppressive social practices. Without recourse to these powers and capacities, needs and dispositions, he argues – echoing the views of others such as Soper (1992) and Nussbaum (1992) – it is difficult if not impossible to say what exactly oppression is oppressive *of* or does damage *to*.[12] A critical social science, in this respect, if it is to fulfil its true emancipatory promise or potential, demands and necessitates an engagement with these very issues and levels of analysis (see also Dickens 2001).

A fourth key point, underpinning much of the foregoing discussion, concerns the *processual* nature of the biological, as a moving, pulsing, animating, dynamic life force, rather than an innate or static entity. Rose, again, provides eloquent testimony to this point, sketching, in the process, the importance of thinking in terms of *organisms* (rather than molecules), the *autopoetic* principles of our lifelines – the capacity, that is, of organisms to sustain themselves – and the complex, *developmental trajectories* this entails (see also Birke 1999). This trajectory is not

> determined by our genes, nor partitioned into neatly dichotomous categories called nature and nurture . . . Rather it is an autopoetic process, shaped by the *interplay of specificity and plasticity* . . . This autopoetic interplay is in a sense captured by that old paradox of the Xeno – the arrow shot at a target, which at any instant of time must be both somewhere and in transit to somewhere else. Reductionism ignores the paradox and freezes life at a moment of time. In attempting to capture its *being* it loses its *becoming*, turning processes into reified objects. This is why reductionism always ends by impaling itself on a mythical dichotomy of materialist determinism and non-materialist free will. Autopoiesis, self-construction, resolves these paradoxes. (Rose 1997: 306, my emphasis)

The argument here, to summarize, involves a number of key points and issues in attempting to rethink the biological within and beyond sociology. This includes: (i) a clear, non-conflationary, thinking through of *epistemological* and *ontological* matters; (ii) a more balanced view of biological *enablements* as well as *constraints*; (iii) a recognition of the *critical* potential of the biological in exposing rather than legitimating oppressive social practices; (iv) an appreciation of the *processual*, *dynamic*, *developmental* nature of our lifelines, *qua* human organisms, which simultaneously encompass both *being* and *becoming* (thereby countering the 'gene's-eye' view of the world in the process and, as we shall see in the next chapter, the dispersal or dissolution of bodies into codes/information). It is insights such as these, I venture, which may go some way toward giving the biological that, albeit cautious, welcome 'back in' which Benton (1991) called for over a decade ago now. In doing so, in an era where developments such as the new genetics loom large, the limits of biological reductionism and (strong) social constructionism alike are exposed and overcome. One can but hope.

Conclusions

The general thrust or guiding theme of this opening chapter, simply stated, has been about 'limits'. First, we have the limits of biomedicine itself, including debates as to its 'efficacy', its (self-acknowledged) paradoxes and uncertainties, together with sociological critiques of its medicalizing tendencies, intentional or otherwise. This latter critique, in turn, has been extended in new ways in recent years through a variety of Foucauldian and postmodern scholarship. These more recent developments, as we have seen, take the constructionist underpinnings of former 'orthodox' medicalization critiques much further, questioning the very nature and status of the body and disease as anything other than discursive entities: power/knowledge's most productive effect, in effect. The charge of biological reductionism is therefore countered, yet paradoxically inverted, through these new forms of social constructionism or discourse determinism: the reduction of body and world, that is to say, to the subtle play of power/knowledge.

Herein lies the second key limit identified in this chapter, the flipside of the first, concerning the limits of sociological critiques themselves, particularly those of the (strong) constructionist variety. Issues of 'balance', if not 'imperialism', arise here, their import, it seems, increasing rather than diminishing with the passage of time. Underpinning these issues, I have argued, lie age-old problems as to the nature and status of the biological within and beyond sociological theory, including the spectre of reductionism. Bringing the biological back into our sociological theorizing need not, however, entail a slide into these former reductionist traps. An adequate theory indeed, be it biological or sociological, has no truck with the limits of reductionism. Other potentially fruitful ways forward instead suggest themselves, as we have seen, including a commitment to principles of *irreduciblity* and *emergence*, whereby the complex intertwining of biological and social processes is emphasized in 'open' (non-determinist) rather than 'closed' systems. A weak form of constructionism, moreover, is quite compatible with this viewpoint: one which knows it own limits, and avoids the epistemic fallacy in doing so. In these and other ways, polemically or otherwise, the call has been for a new 'balance' in our theorizing about the world and our place within it, including an (albeit cautious) welcome 'back in' of the biological (Benton 1991). The 'return of the repressed' perhaps, but one, it seems, which is long overdue given the weight and legacies of constructionist thought.

These are issues we shall return to, in various guises, throughout the pages which follow. The chapter therefore sets the scene for the book a whole, including, of course, its own limits.

Notes

1   This, in truth, is not wholly accurate. Descartes did, in fact, operate with a limited form of mind–body interaction. To all intents and purposes, however, his work is very much cast in this dualistic mould. Interaction, moreover, still implies a dualism, given that two separate substances are 'interacting'.
2   See also Szreter 1988 on the role of public health.
3   For a critical discussion of evidence-based medicine, see Hunter (1996), for example.
4   Illich is not alone in his strong condemnation of medicine. George Bernard Shaw (1946/1911) had some equally caustic things to say in *The Doctor's Dilemma*, the greatest satire on the medical profession, it is claimed, since Molière's *Maladie imaginaire*.

5 Conrad also draws a distinction here between medicalization and healthization. Whilst medicalization proposes biomedical causes and interventions, healthization in contrast, 'proposes lifestyle and behavioural causes and interventions'. One, in short, turns the 'moral into the medical, the other turns health into the moral' (Conrad 1992: 223). See Chapter 6 for a discussion of this distinction in relation to sleep.

6 Whilst Fox is cited here as an example of this postmodern approach to health, there are of course many others, some, as we shall see later, holding more promise than others for the concerns and issues addressed in this book.

7 Haraway makes a similar point, in this vein. '"Science says"', she notes, 'is represented as a univocal language. Yet even the spliced character of the potent words "in science" hints at a barely contained and inharmonious heterogeneity' (1991: 204).

8 The question therefore, in part, becomes the differential weight accorded these factors and the potential for reductionism by default if not design.

9 Charlton (1993) goes further, arguing that the playful deconstructions of postmodernism are really only an option for the healthy rather than the sick. When the 'chips are down', he claims, as in illness they surely are, recourse to modern medicine is an eminently preferable option to the relativizing, deconstructive spirit of postmodernism.

10 Critical realism is a position stemming from the work of Bhaskar (1998) and others which acknowledges the reality of the world independently of the ways we know it, including deep underlying structures and non-observable mechanisms, with generative properties, which operate in 'open' rather than 'closed' (experimental) systems. Critical realism, therefore, refuses to collapse or conflate *ontological* and *epistemological* issues – what we know and how we know it (epistemology) with what there is to know (ontology) – whilst emphasizing, at one and the same time, the critical potential, in identifying these underlying structures and mechanisms, for transformation and change (see also Archer 1995, 2000).

11 Critical realists, Sayer (1997) notes, must necessarily embrace a *dual conception* of nature, one which stresses *continuity* with the human organism, the other which stresses the *distinctiveness* of the latter. See also Archer (2000) on human being and its embodied dimensions.

12 Sayer (1997), in fact, endorses what he terms a moderate non-determinist essentialism here. For a fuller account of these issues, in a critical realist vein, see Sayer (2000).

2

What Is Health? Thinking through the Boundaries of the Body

We need only reflect that it is quite meaningful to ask someone 'Do you feel ill?', but it would be quite absurd to ask someone 'Do you feel healthy?' Health is not a condition that one introspectively feels in oneself. Rather, it is a condition of being involved, of being in the world, of being together with one's fellow human beings, of active and rewarding engagement with one's everyday tasks. (Gadamer 1996: 113)

A key question to confront at an early stage in this book concerns the very notion and nature of health. Medical sociology, it is fair to say, has traditionally been concerned with matters of illness *qua* 'deviance' rather than health: an imbalance which has only recently been redressed. Parsons' (1951) early formulation of illness as deviance and the sick role, for example, alongside subsequent debates within the interactionist paradigm over the labelling of deviance (Gerhardt 1989), are classic cases in point. Whether illness can be seen as deviance, of course, given its prevalence within the community and the potential for conformity to the sick role, is a moot point (Pflanz and Rhode 1970).

Turning away from these traditional debates, however, what of health? How are we to theorize and understand health in the current era? What dilemmas and contradictions does health symbolize and evoke? And what does this tell us about the very nature and boundaries of bodies themselves? This chapter seeks to address, if not answer, some of these questions. The aim, in doing so is less a detailed exposition, still less a comprehensive review, of the vast lay concepts literature[1] – much of which, again, has been preoccupied with ideas about illness and disease causation as opposed to health – than a focus on various perspectives and debates on health and the boundaries of the body in late/postmodernity: an era of unprecedented social transformation and change. Within this late/postmodern landscape, as we shall see, a variety of 'bodies', or, perhaps more correctly, perspectives on and dimensions of embodiment, appear, themselves part and parcel of the complex, if not contradictory, nature of health and healthism in late/postmodernity.

Capitalizing on bodies: habitus, health and lifestyles

Our starting point, on this corporeal trail of health, concerns Bourdieu's insights into what, in effect, amounts to health as 'capital': a perspective which casts a critical light on issues of class, health and the struggle for social distinction through associated notions of habitus, capital and field. Bourdieu, in this respect, provides one more or less promising explanation for the relationship between class, health and lifestyles, forged within the practical logic of everyday life. This, in turn, goes some way toward explaining the conundrum, for health educators and promoters alike, of the 'gap' between knowledge and action, and the readiness to adopt so-called 'healthier' practices.

Already, however, a number of terms have been introduced which themselves require further explanations en route to a fuller Bourdieuesque appreciation of 'tasteful' bodies and health as 'capital'. First, the notion of habitus.[2] Habitus, for Bourdieu, in keeping with his emphasis on practical logic and the desire to transcend the sterile objectivism–subjectivism divide, pertains to an 'acquired system of generative dispositions', which is objectively adjusted to the particular conditions in which it is constituted (Bourdieu 1977: 95). It is through the habitus that the 'structure which has produced it governs practice', engendering in turn 'all the thoughts, all the perceptions, and all the actions consistent with those conditions, and no others' (1977: 95). The habitus, as this suggests, is a 'structuring structure', a 'socialized subjectivity' which gives rise to and serves as the classificatory basis for individual and collective practices. As such, it provides individuals with class-dependent, predisposed, yet seemingly 'naturalized' ways of thinking, feeling, acting and classifying the social world and their location within it.

These dispositions and generative principles are literally and metaphorically embodied in human beings. For Bourdieu, indeed, the very ways in which people treat and relate to their bodies reveal the 'deepest dispositions of the habitus' (1984: 190). This in turn is further underlined through his associated notion of 'bodily hexis', which relates directly to forms of body posture, deportment, style and gait – the socially inscribed manner, that is to say, in which individuals 'carry themselves' (1984: 218). Bodily hexis, according to Bourdieu, is 'political mythology realized, *embodied*, turned into permanent dispositions, a durable manner of standing, speaking, and thereby of feeling and *thinking*. . . The principles em-bodied in this way are placed beyond the grasp of consciousness, and hence cannot be touched by voluntary, deliberate transformation, cannot even be made explicit' (1977: 94). The power of the habitus and bodily hexis, as this suggests, stems from the largely unthinking nature of practice and habit, rather than from consciously learned rules and principles (Jenkins 1992: 76): a 'practical logic', that is to say, based on the 'logic of practice'. Whilst habitus is meant to function as an 'open system of dispositions', there is indeed a 'relative irreversibility' to the process (Bourdieu and Wacquant 1992: 133). As the 'unchosen principle of all choices', habitus is largely determined by the social and economic conditions of its constitution (Bourdieu and Wacquant 1992: 136).

Here we encounter the other two concepts mentioned above, namely capital and field. The habitus, together with the trajectories and strategies which are produced, is operative within the context of various *'fields'*. Fields, Bourdieu explains, have their own internal logics and dynamics, themselves characterized by the struggles of various agents concerned with maintaining or improving their position vis-à-vis the particular forms of *'capital'* at stake. A field, therefore, is a structured system of social positions. It is also a structured system of force or power relations in the sense that positions occupied within the said field stand in relations of domination, subordination, homology, to one another by virtue of the access they afford or deny to goods or resources, conceived as capital. Capital, in this respect, pertains to any of the following: *economic* capital, *cultural* capital (legitimate knowledge of various sorts), *social* capital (various kinds of relations with significant others) and *symbolic* capital (prestige and social honour). The body too becomes a form of capital, referred to either as 'physical capital' or more generally under the rubric of 'cultural capital'. Like habitus, Bourdieu stresses, capital does not exist or function except in relation to a field (Bourdieu and Wacquant 1992: 101). As a space of potential or active forces, a field, then, by definition, is also a 'field of potential struggles aimed at preserving or transforming the configuration of these forces' (Bourdieu and Wacquant 1992: 101). Herein lies the dynamic elements in Bourdieu's theory of habitus, capital and field.

As for matters of health, the application of Bourdieu's analysis to the class and lifestyles debate is suggestive on a number of fronts. Whether one is looking at concepts of health in particular or health-related practices in general (see, for example, Blaxter 1990; d'Houtaud and Field 1984; Radley 1989), it is the (class-related) habitus – itself expressive of bodily tastes and dispositions – together with the volume and composition of capital within particular social fields, which is at work here: a relationship, that is to say, between *position* and *disposition*. Stated succinctly, what we have here is the following formula: '[(habitus) (capital)] + field = practice' (Bourdieu 1984: 101).

The power of Bourdieu's position, as this suggests, lies in its ability to explain the relative durability of differing forms of health-related behaviour, or practice, addressing both structure and agency in the process. This, in turn, brings to light the manner in which the very pursuit of health and the cultivation of lifestyles are themselves caught up in various (class-related) struggles for social recognition or 'distinction'. This, for example, includes the 'symbolic violence' which the dominant classes exercise over the 'vulgar' bodily forms and practices of the working classes: the latter, it is held, possessing a more *instrumental* versus *expressive* relation to their bodies. Bourdieu too serves to remind us that whilst economic factors (capital in his terms) are clearly an important part of the health and lifestyles equation, 'taste' and the underlying body-schemas the habitus engenders (themselves expressions of these broader factors and relations) are equally important to consider. The habitus, Bourdieu argues, engenders a 'taste for the necessary', adjusting 'subjective expectations to objective probabilities'. As such, it steers people into food choices, exercise and sporting activities, and the like, which are *broadly congruent with their underlying bodily schemas*. Even when different classes and class fractions pursue similar activities, the meaning and function of these, Bourdieu maintains, is likely to differ considerably. With respect to sport, for instance:

> It would not be difficult to show that the different classes do not agree as to the effects expected from bodily exercise, whether on the outside of the body, such as visible strength of prominent muscles which some prefer, or the elegance, ease and beauty favoured by others, or inside the body, health, mental equilibrium etc . . . Class habitus defines the meaning conferred on sporting activity, the profits expected from it; and not the least of these profits is the social value accruing from the pursuit of certain sports by virtue of the distinctive rarity they derive from their class distribution. (Bourdieu 1978: 835–6)

Bourdieu's analysis of health as 'capital', therefore, has its merits, linking lifestyle 'choices' via the bodily habitus to the broader economic, cultural, social and symbolic dynamics of which they are a part (see also Chapter 3). It also, however, has its drawbacks. Bourdieu, for instance, has been charged with stripping agency of any real agency, with habitus tending to operate in a largely unthinking fashion 'behind actors' backs' (Jenkins 1992).[3] Lifestyles, moreover, as writers such as Giddens (1991) stress, may well be 'routinized', but the routines followed are reflexively open to change, amidst a pluralization of options and choices in late modernity. This, in turn, raises broader questions to do with the merits of a class-based analysis itself in an era of rapid social change (see Chapter 3). What we have here nonetheless, these critiques notwithstanding, is a more or less promising view of health as 'capital', which in turn may be capitalized upon in relation both to inequalities in health in general, and to health across the lifecourse in particular (see Chapters 3 and 4).

Ambivalent/dilemmatic bodies: the disciplines and delights of health

If Bourdieu's analysis takes us so far, but not perhaps quite far enough with respect to the enigma of health (Gadamer 1996), then Crawford (1984, 2000), in many respects, provides the missing ingredients, shedding further corporeal light on the tensions and contradictions, dilemmas and dramas, routines and rituals inherent in the health-related habitus of middle-class Americans: a 'baroque modern' habitus, in Mellor and Shilling's (1997) terms, which confirms and refutes its Protestant roots.

On the one hand, Crawford notes, it is possible to interpret the very pursuit of health in daily life as organized around the disciplinary practices and imperatives of corporeal 'control'. Health promotion encourages and cajoles, exhorts and commands us to adopt a 'healthy' lifestyle with strong echoes of the Protestant work ethic: a rationally disciplined or calculative way of life which itself is intimately bound up with the reflexive project of self (cf. Giddens 1991). Risk therefore replaces sin, whilst 'working out' becomes the modern day passport to health and success in all walks of life. The boundaries between the ascetic and aesthetic, in this context, become blurred. Disciplining the body, from this viewpoint, is as much about the cultivation of 'outer' appearance through youthful corporeal ideals as it is to do with 'inner' concerns for physiological functioning or optimal 'fitness' (Featherstone 1991). The adage 'no pain, no gain', and the motto 'looking good, feeling great', similarly suggest that the emotional payoffs of these reflexive strategies of body maintenance may themselves be more or less pleasurable if not euphoric (as the endorphin buzz testifies). Monaghan (2001), for example, speaks clearly to these issues in his ethnographic study of the vibrant physicality of body-building and the erotics of the gym. The 'addictive' potential of body-building, he argues, should not blind us to the sensual pleasures and pragmatic benefits of anaerobic exercise, just like those associated with other aerobic forms of activity. Particularly within today's fitness-orientated culture, it seems, the 'active/strong/disciplined/self-controlled body' – itself often 'chemically/nutritionally/pharmaceutically enhanced' – has become a 'central site for sensual embodied pleasure and the construction of subjectivity'. Without doubt, Monaghan asserts, 'popular gym culture is the domain where experiential and emotional bodies (irrespective of class, age and gender) come to the fore', opening up important possibilities to experience 'hidden visceral processes and vibrant physicality' (2001: 351).

Discipline, then, may harbour its own embodied pleasures. The fears and anxieties of health as 'control', nevertheless, are equally important to stress, providing, at best, a mixed bag of possibilities. Take coronary heart disease (CHD), for example. The risks of CHD, we are told, are associated *inter alia* with a variety of hereditary, lifestyle and environmental factors, much of which we are encouraged to do something about. So, as a 41-year-old man who falls well within the remit of various well-person check-ups and health screening devices, I should get my cholesterol levels measured, my blood pressure monitored, watch my weight, eat sensibly, reduce saturated fats, take regular exercise, avoid or reduce my exposure to stressors of various sorts, stay off the cigarettes, drink red wine (not too much mind), and so on. Risk profiling in this context, and its subsequent reduction or prevention through remedial measures, becomes a watchword or a way of life, particularly for those of us (un)fortunate enough to be labelled the 'worried well': a middle-class sport or pastime *par excellence*.

The rational disciplines of health as control, as this and countless other examples suggest, are fuelled if not premised, in part at least, on a series of fears and anxieties in risk society, including the limits of expertise itself. Whilst rational control, through the disciplined, tightly bounded body/self, may bring some degree of comfort here, the proliferation of risks in contemporary society means that one cannot rest easy (for long). We should, in fact, continually be on guard in order to reflexively monitor or manage, reduce or prevent the latest health 'scare', from the purity of body fluids in the era HIV/AIDS (Kroker and Kroker 1988) to the dangers of GM food, and from the BSE crisis to the threat of meningitis and multi-resistant super-bugs, not to mention the apocalyptic prospect of bioterrorism (Williams 2001c).

This, of course, is not to suggest that everyone is running around anxious and panic-stricken about their bodies and health in 'risk society' or 'reflexive modernity' (Beck 1992; Giddens 1991). Davison and colleagues (1991, 1992), for example, have drawn attention to the 'healthy' degree of scepticism within the lay populace, given official pronouncements on risk reduction or preventive policies. On the one hand, many of the factors that went into the assessment of coronary candidacy, in this study of lay thinking/epidemiology in South Wales at least, appeared to be linked to those highlighted in contemporary health promotion programmes – especially regarding smoking and weight control. On the other hand, examples were readily given of individuals who provided living testimony to the limits of official wisdom and contemporary risk profiling. This, quite literally, was embodied in the figure of 'Uncle Norman', an overweight, red-in-the-face folk hero who lived to a ripe old age despite his heavy drinking and smoking habits (Davison et al. 1992: 682). To this, moving to the opposite extreme, we may add the 'lithe jogger' and 'healthy' if not 'happy' eater, who drops down dead of a heart attack at the age of 50. A prevention paradox emerges here, as these authors suggest, in which lay epidemiological reasoning, based on traditional notions of fatalism, luck and chance, exposes the limits of current expertise based on probabilistic reasoning. Lay epidemiology, in short, 'readily accommodates official messages concerning behavioural risks within the important cultural fields of luck, fate and destiny'. This, in turn, constitutes both a 'rational way of incorporating potentially troublesome information, and a potential barrier to the aims of health education' (Davison et al. 1991: 1; see also Williams and Calnan's [1994] study of GPs' perspectives on coronary heart disease prevention).

It is precisely at this point that the other of Crawford's two dominant modalities of health looms large: the cultural mandate of health as 'release'. An economy based solely or simply on the disciplinary imperatives of control, Crawford comments, would be 'ruinous'. Consumption *qua* playful, fun-loving, pleasurable 'release' is equally crucial therefore to the health and wealth of late capitalism. To let go, to relinquish these tightly bounded, rationally set controls, to indulge one's whims and passions, to pursue one's desires and wishes, these and other manifestations of cultivated or civilized release, both real and imagined, are central to consumer culture: a Romantic ethic, in Campbell's (1987) terms, as the modern day complement to Weber's Protestant work ethic.[4] The trick of consumer culture, it seems, rests precisely on these (false) promises and (illusory) ideals of the good life, including the imaginative fantasies and projections of consumers themselves, as the guarantee of ever-renewed consumption (Falk 1994).

Health, through this modality, is about the pursuit of well-being via the corporeal pleasures of release: a relaxing or relinquishing of former disciplinary mandates in more or less satisfying or gratifying ways. Too heavy an emphasis on health as control, too great a reliance on the disciplines of the flesh, is indeed, from this viewpoint, self-denying if not self-defeating. A slavish adherence to a rigorously set, expert-approved, 'healthy' lifestyle, in other words, is itself 'unhealthy'. The language of will-power, self-control and careful regulation, therefore, gives way to one of well-being, contentment, relaxation, enjoyment and 'the good life': a view summed up, playfully perhaps, by the axiom 'if it feels good it can't be all bad' (Crawford 1984: 81).

It is in this context, as I have argued elsewhere (Williams 1998b, 1999b), that the transgressive dimensions of health are glimpsed, or, perhaps more correctly, that health as a potential site of corporeal transgression can be discerned (see also Crawford's [1999] reply). The so-called 'hedonism' of modern day consumption *qua* release is not, however, the hedonism of old – a far cry, indeed, from the grotesque realism of Rabelaisian carnival culture, in medieval times, with its over-brimming abundance of festive corporeal excess (Bakhtin 1968). What we have here instead, as Campbell's (1987) deliberations on the Romantic ethic and the spirit of consumerism suggest, is a new (late) modern version of 'rational hedonism': a civilized, calculative, cultivated, yet playful, form of consumer bliss, based on the 'controlled decontrol of emotions' (cf. Elias and Dunning 1986) and the pleasurable tensions it evokes. The history of corporeality, Falk remarks, is not merely about the 'disciplining' of the body or the 'destruction of its sensuality', any more than it is about the 'great emancipation' of the body's potential, but a paradoxical combination of the two (1994: 66). As borders multiply, as regulations become ever tighter, corporeal transgression itself becomes ever more complex, subtle and sophisticated – though primarily, Falk argues, in the *experiential* as opposed to the *expressive* realms (1994: 65).

Translated into the contemporary dilemmas of health, what we have here is something akin to a ritual dance, played out in the moral contexts of everyday life, the aim of which is to 'resolve', 'balance' or 'bridge', however precariously, these seemingly contradictory mandates of control and release. 'A healthy lifestyle', indeed, as Lupton and Chapman's (1995) study of media coverage and lay responses to the cholesterol controversy suggests, may well 'be the death of you': 'everything in moderation' is seen instead as the favoured way of managing this confusion and controversy surrounding diet. As Crawford puts it, in the American context:

> The still mysterious but imaginatively rich relations of mind and body are incorpo-
> rated into a script which, in endlessly playing out the moral tensions between
> denial and pleasure, must remain improvisational. Both denial and pleasure, the
> achievements of work and pleasurable fulfilments are essential to the perceived
> well-being of contemporary Americans. The dual conditions of a 'healthy' economy
> are replicated in two expressions of 'healthy' disposition. Like the ambivalence
> generated by opposing economic mandates, middle-class Americans *want both* the
> 'health' promised by a medicalized regime of self-control and the 'health' of pleas-
> urable escapes from the 'stress' of renunciations. (2000: 227)

In these and other ways, in short, health provides a potent metaphor for the contradictions of life and living in late capitalism: dilemmas, it seems, which are first
and foremost the problem and privilege of the contemporary (American) middle
classes (a sign of distinction perhaps?).

Flexible/immunological bodies

Whilst Crawford's dominant cultural mandates of health as control and release capture important facets of life and living in late capitalism, other writers push these
themes further, pointing to the emergence of new discourses and forms of power
which are changing our very conception of bodies and their 'productive' relations
with other bodies in the late/postmodern era. Martin (1994, 2000), for example,
using data from her own ethnographic fieldwork in America, discusses an emerging
conception of bodies which, she argues, has the potential to lead to new forms of
discipline and control. People in all walks of life, she observes, are coming to see
their bodies not as a set of 'mechanical parts', but as 'complex, non-linear systems'.
This, in turn, is underpinned, in part at least, by an enormous

> cultural emphasis on the immune system, which has moved to the very centre of
> the way ordinary people now think of health. Many people are reaching for a way
> of imaging a *fluid, ever-changing body*, a body containing turbulence and instabil-
> ity, in constant motion, a body that is the antithesis of a rigid, mechanical set of
> parts. This new body is also in a delicate relationship to its environment, a complex
> system nested in an infinite series of other complex systems. (Martin 2000: 123, my
> emphasis)

From the science lab, through AIDS organizations, to the corporate capitalist
boardroom, the immune system, it is claimed, is permeating the ways we think
about health and work: discourses which imply a 'dramatic departure' from the
taken-for-granted conception of health and the body which prevailed even a decade
ago. This shift, Martin stresses, is happening for 'good reason'. It 'dovetails well', in
fact, with 'changes in the kind of person and worker regarded as desirable – indeed,
necessary, if one is to survive – in the fiercely competitive and rapidly transforming
corporate world' of late capitalism (2000: 125). The immune system, from this

viewpoint, has begun to function critically as the new key to health and the marker of 'differential survival' for the twenty-first century (2000: 125). The body at stake through these new discourses, moreover, becomes a kind of 'training ground', in which 'educating' or 'nurturing' the immune system, from vaccination to dirt exposure, exercise, stress avoidance and other 'healthy' practices – and the 'immune system machismo' which frequently accompanies it – becomes increasingly important. This, in other words, is an era of flexible bodies, conceived as complex systems, designed to 'fit' into the complex, flexible, workaday world of late capitalist imperatives and controls (2000: 128–38): a new kind of 'balance' indeed, which extends and develops Crawford's insights in important new ways (see also Tauber's [1997] illuminating study of 'the Immune Self').[5]

Haraway (1991) too raises similar immunological themes, albeit in a more postmodern vein, in her 'leaky' deliberations on cyborgs and the reinvention of nature. Since the mid-twentieth century, she argues, biomedical discourses have been 'progressively organized around a very different set of technologies and practices, which have destabilized the symbolic privilege of the hierarchical, localized, organic body' (1991: 211). What this amounts to, she argues, is a new biopolitics of postmodern bodies: a 'translation', that is to say,

> of Western scientific and political languages of nature from those based on work, localization, and the marked body to those based on *codes, dispersal, networking, and the fragmented postmodern subject* . . . the body ceases to be a stable spatial map of normalized functions and instead emerges as a *highly mobile field of strategic differences*. The biomedical-biotechnical body is a *semiotic system, a complex meaning-producing field*, for which the *discourse of immunology*, that is, the central biomedical discourse on *recognition and misrecognition*, has become a *high stakes practice in many senses*. (1991: 211, my emphasis)[6]

We can refrain, at this point, from a detailed discussion of the merits of Haraway's analysis, except to say that the prime aim, in keeping with her cyborg manifesto and postmodernism in general, is to reimagine and rethink 'natural' bodies in ways that 'transform the relations of same and different, self and other, inner and outer, recognition and misrecognition into gendered maps for inappropriate/d others', and in doing so to 'acknowledge the permanent condition of fragility, mortality and finitude' (1991: 3–4).

Dangers lurk nonetheless in this current configuration of possibilities. Could it be, for example, returning to Martin, that this new emphasis on 'flexible' bodies and immunological discourses, postmodern or otherwise, provides the opportunity for new forms of discrimination to emerge? HIV/AIDS, for example, is a case in point, ushering in what some have described as a new era of 'body McCarthyism' based on the purity of body fluids (Kroker and Kroker 1988), together with a 'fetishization' of the HIV test as a way of regulating bodies (Lupton et al. 1995). What we have here, Crawford (1994) argues, is a new 'cultural politics' for reconstructing the 'healthy' self/'unhealthy' other, in conformity with intensified mandates of control and heightened concerns and anxieties about the robustness/flexibility of one's immune system. A new 'inflexible form of flexibility' may well be emerging here, Martin warns, extending far beyond a concern with HIV/AIDS, whereby some 'rigid' folk will fall by the wayside in a neo-Social, Darwinian stampede based on the survival of the fittest. These new 'flexible' bodies, in short, are also 'highly constrained': 'they cannot stop moving, they cannot stabilize or rest, or they will fall off the 'tightrope' of life and die' (2000: 143–4). Not quite so flexible, then, as things may seem.

Nomadic bodies (without organs): 'beyond' health?

Talk of the biopolitics of postmodern bodies in turn brings us face to face with the corporeal agendas of other writers within this genre, including calls to go 'beyond' the very boundaries of health as conventionally understood, nomadically or otherwise. Frank (1991a), for example, seeks to recover in Parsons' (1951, 1964) own formulation of health, illness and the sick role, a postmodern health role. Health, from this deconstructive viewpoint, is not something which resides 'in' the body, but that which circulates or flows *between* bodies. As a communicative medium of exchange, health is based on the *teleonomic* capacity of bodies – the capacity or propensity, that is, to undertake successful goal-oriented action – within an interactive system (see, for example, Parsons 1978). Health, then, conceived in this way, provides a bridge between any one organic body and its environment: a property of 'neither the body nor the environment, but that which exists between them' (Frank 1991b: 207). To this postmodern Parsonian conception of *health as medium*, Frank argues, we should add the following:

> From Michel Foucault, we add that health is a medium of imposed bodily discipline. From Jean Baudrillard, we question whose teleonomy is involved; thus the second modification is 'teleonomy mediatized'. From Jürgen Habermas, we understand that the nature of health as a medium is to be 'non-discursive'. Finally in Pierre Bourdieu we return to Parsons' notion of circulation to suggest health as 'physical capital' . . . These modifications are in no sense discrete from one another, but, as Parsons would be the first to recognize, they interpenetrate. (1991b: 207)

Nicholas Fox goes further in this postmodern direction, 'beyond health' in fact. The 'Anti-Oedipal' writings of Deleuze and Guattari (1984, 1988), as noted in Chapter 1, provide a key point of reference here, particularly their emphasis on the *productive* nature of desire and the *Body-without-Organs* (BwO) – a term originally coined by Antonin Artaud (1988) to denote a philosophical and political surface of intensities, investments and flows, as opposed to the anatomical body with organs. It is in this context, Fox argues, given the biomedical *territorialization* of the body-without-organs (as an anatomical body with organs), that the notion of so-called *arché-health* arises, with the postmodern *nomad*, as opposed to the modernist *detective*, at its heart. *Arché-health*, we are told, is a process of

> *becoming*, a de-territorializing of the BwO, a resistance to discourse, a generosity towards otherness, *a nomadic subjectivity*. It is not intended to suggest a natural, essential or in any way prior kind of health, upon which other healths are super-imposed, it is not supposed to be a rival concept, indeed the reason for using this rather strange term is its homage to Derrida's notion of *arché-writing*, which is not writing but that which supplied the possibility of writing, that is, the system of dif-ference upon which language is based: *différance* – that which differs and is deferred. (2000: 342, my emphasis, except the last)

Arché-health then, to deconstruct and decipher this arcane language, is a process of *becoming*, which by definition defies definition. As such, it can never become the object of scientific investigation without falling back into the territorialized dis-courses of health and illness. An absent/presence indeed.

We have, to be sure, traversed new terrain here, promisingly or otherwise, wan-dering nomadically in the boundless postmodern realms of *arché-health*. Again, however, echoing points raised in Chapter 1, a series of questions arise in relation to this latter strand of postmodern thinking.[7] To what extent, for example, are former binarized modes of thought and practice really overcome in this way, given that Fox's analysis itself proceeds through a series of juxtapositions, including bodies with and without organs, territorialization versus deterritorialization, the detective and the nomad, and so on? Can biomedical territorializations of the body with organs, moreover, simply be written off or dismissed in this way (and if so at what cost)? To this we may add the nagging doubt as to whether or not this very commitment to difference and the endless process of becoming other – a politics of 'disembodiment' in Fox's (1999: 133–4) terms – is itself a route to political 'indifference', thereby undermining or compromising more collective or identity-based political struggles. Finally, we must surely ask whether recourse to such inscrutable language, itself somewhat elitist or exclusionary, is really necessary or desirable in order to make the simple (yet important) point that: (i) biomedical readings of the body have their limits; (ii) the world is complex and diverse; and (iii) new ways of relating to and caring for one another which respect this complexity and diversity may profitably be found (see also Scambler's [2002] assessment of the pros and cons of postmod-ernism). From here it is only a short step to the last of our corporeal examples of health in late/postmodernity.

Holistic/effervescent bodies: the sacred and the profane

No discussion of the shifting boundaries and contested meanings of health in late/postmodernity would be complete without recourse to so-called 'holistic' health, and the movement to back it up. As part and parcel of a broader health consciousness or 'healthism' discussed above, this includes a diverse array of healers and an even larger group of adherents (some more zealous than others), including individuals who have turned many of its principles into a 'new way of life' and a more 'ecologically informed' vision of the world (Coward 1989; Crawford 1980).[8] Healing methods range from homeopathy to meditation, naturopathy to biofeedback, massage to acupuncture, nutritional therapies to movement or dance therapy, osteopathy to faith healing and iridology. Health and illness, from this perspective, are never solely or simply physical matters but also mental and spiritual ones. Holistic health, in this respect, becomes a new '"way of being", an interrelation or balance of body, mind and spirit, a concern with "high-level wellness", "super health" or "joy of life"' (Crawford 1980: 366). Emotions, as this suggests, play a crucial role. Perhaps more than anything, Coward notes, it is attention to emotional states and personality predispositions, coupled with life forces and vital energies, which informs the idea of 'whole person' treatment (1989: 71).

People may indeed be turning to these therapies in their droves (or at least certain segments of the lay populace), but again this supposed 'challenge' to biomedical hegemony and the 'warm embrace' with Mother Nature it entails – one which echoes theories of humoral 'balance' way back in the Middle Ages – may be more apparent than real (see Chapter 9). Whatever the therapy, *personal* responsibility and lifestyle change is invariably placed high on the agenda, thereby deflecting attention away from the wider political economy of health and illness – a 'privatization', in effect, of the struggle for generalized 'well-being' (Berliner and Salmon 1980; Crawford 1980). To this we may add the problematic use of the term 'natural' and the fact that, despite an emphasis on the unity of mind and body, an underlying hierarchical form of dualism remains (with mind accorded primacy over body in the 'healing' process). 'Holistic health' also, as noted in Chapter 1, contains important elements of both 'de-medicalization' and 're-medicalization'. On the one hand, as Lowenberg and Davis (1994) note, the locus of causality is firmly restored to the individual and status differentials between providers and clients are seemingly minimized, thereby suggesting a process of de-medicalization. On the other hand, the exponential expansion of the 'pathogenic sphere' and remit of the holistic health movement (that is, lifestyle modification, mind–body continuity) simultaneously suggests a drastic increase in the medicalization of life in late Western society (see also Armstrong 1986). Seen in this light, the 'liberatory' potential of 'complementary' therapies and 'holistic health' takes on a more troubling hue, as important elements of 'continuity' with biomedicine and consumer culture are instead thrown into critical relief (Sharma 1996). This, coupled with the more general questions of 'authenticity' it raises – the search, that is, for 'authenticity' in an 'inauthentic age' (cf. Meštrović 1997) – means that the 'dilemmatic' aspects of health are once again symbolically expressed and ritualistically 'resolved' within these 'new' (health-conscious) movements.

Discussion of these issues, in turn, connects up with broader (more wild or fanciful) claims regarding the 'resensualization' or 're-enchantment' of society. Writers such as Michel Maffesoli, for instance, celebrate what is seen to be the contemporary shift from Promethean to Dionysian values in Western culture. What this amounts to, in sociological terms, is a shift from the Weberian Protestant ethic (of productivist modernity) towards a society, or, more precisely, a form of *'sociality'*, governed by the Durkheimian logic of emotional renewal and collective effervescence: themes which echo, in spirit if not content, Bataille's championing of the sacred over the profane, the heterogeneous over the homogenous (Evans 1997).

We are, Maffesoli claims, living at a decisive moment in the history of modernity, one in which the 'rationalization of the world' is being displaced if not replaced by a parallel 're-enchantment of the world'. This is a process in which 'emotional renewal' comes to the fore. In contrast to writers such as Giddens and Beck, therefore, Maffesoli stresses what he takes to be an age characterized by the 'decline of individualism' and a 'return of the tribes': a form of 'sociality' based on a new 'culture of sentiment' and multiple forms of 'being together' (or *'proxemics'*). The 'sacred canopy' has all but collapsed, on this reading, only to be replaced by a looser, more shifting or fluid series of alliances and sensual solidarities which, taken together, spell a resurgence of the 'sacred' in a multitude of disparate, vibrant, effervescent ways (see also Chapter 9).

For Maffesoli this 'underground centrality' of sociality – the antithesis of arid Apollonian culture or Promethean instrumental rationality – bestows strength, vitality and effervescence to social life as an antidote to the cultural 'crisis' of individualism. From New Age movements and alternative therapies to the 'relativization of the work ethic', and from networks of 'amorous camaraderie' to the importance of dress and cosmetics, the emblematic figure of Dionysus, he claims, is giving rise to what Weber termed ' "emotional cults" as opposed to the atomization characteristic of bourgeois or aristocratic dominance' (Maffesoli 1996: 156). As a 'fusion realm' or 'communalized empathy', sociality constitutes all those forms of 'being together' which, for the past few decades, have been transforming society. 'Loosing one's body' either literally or metaphorically within the collective body, Maffesoli claims, is a 'characteristic feature of the emotional or affective *community* that is beginning to replace our utilitarian "society"' (1996: 154). The 'divorce induced by objectivity', in short, is slowly but surely

giving way to the intuition of experience. . . we are moving towards 'experiential communication' [and a] . . . 'fundamental compassion' – defined in the true sense of the term . . . To take the most obvious examples, astrology, *macrobiotic food, ecological movements, alternative medicines*: the importance of nature, regional loyalties and the stress on 'locality' all show that the *'keep your distance' stance, which was common to epistemologies and social practices alike, is giving way to a more 'participatory' mode of being.* (Maffesoli 1996: 150, my emphasis)

Maffesoli, to be sure, is open to criticism on a number of counts, not least concerning his over-felicitous view of any such resurgence of the 'sacred' (see, for example, Evans 1997; Mellor and Shilling 1997). Again we return here to the problems as well as the promises of postmoderninsm. Holistic, if not effervescent, bodies, nonetheless, are very much part and parcel of the broader discourses and debates on health at the dawn of the new millennium: the 'sacred' and 'profane' indeed.

Conclusions

What conclusions may be drawn, given the diverse themes and issues addressed in this chapter? The answers, surprisingly enough, are quite simple. Health, as we have seen, is a contested notion and an elusive phenomenon: one glimpsed, through the perspectives discussed, as 'capital', as 'control'/'release', as 'flexibility/immunity', as a 'nomadic' pursuit, and/or an 'holistic/effervescent' possibility. This, to repeat, is to imply not a series of mutually exclusive bodies, but a variety of (complementary/competing) perspectives and discourses on health in late/postmodernity. Health, it seems, is many things to many people, with a huge 'industry' to back it up, much of which itself appears quite 'unhealthy'.

The boundaries of the body, in this respect, are themselves thrown into critical relief. Herein lies the other main conclusion to draw in this chapter, concerning the *risks* as well as *opportunities*, *problems* as well as *possibilities* embedded in notions of flexibility, fluidity and flows: vehicles perhaps – even when they feel like 'liberation' – for new forms of domination and oppression in the global era (cf. Martin 1994). Holding on to some sort of boundaries therefore, including the very integrity of bodies *qua* organisms in the face of their 'dispersal' into codes or information, may well be important, in health as elsewhere (Birke 1999). The (ritual) dramas of health, meanwhile, roll on.

Notes

1   Classic studies here, for example, include the following: Blaxter (1983, 1990); Calnan (1987); Cornwell (1984); Herzlich (1973); Williams (1990). Studying lay concepts, it is argued, is important for the following reasons: (i) lay people draw upon this knowledge to make sense of signs and symptoms; (ii) lay knowledge may influence health- and illness-related behaviours and patterns of help seeking; (iii) lay perspectives are important in the evaluation of health care and medical technology (Calnan 1987). To this we may add their importance for health promotion. Lay concepts, moreover, as this chapter attests, tell us much about relations between nature and culture, body and society, including the moral dimension of health and illness, both past and present. We may also question just how 'lay', lay concepts are in fact, in conditions of late/postmodernity (Bury 1997; Shaw 2002; Williams and Calnan 1996a, b).

2 The term 'habitus', it should be stressed, has a long, illustrious history in Western thought, featuring in the works of thinkers as diverse as Aristotle, Mauss and Elias. Bourdieu, in this respect, appropriates rather than coins the term in his theorization of these matters.

3 For a detailed discussion of the links between habitus, reflexivity and the social body, see Crossley (2001), who himself goes some way toward rescuing Bourdieu from his critics in doing so.

4 See Boden and Williams (2002) for a critical discussion of Campbell's thesis in relation to recent sociological work on embodiment and emotion.

5 In the same sense that our personal identity remains a philosophical problem, Tauber argues, so our current theories of immune identity – involving the identification and integrity of self – seek answers to these age-old philosophical questions. *Self*, as a metaphor, Tauber states, has 'achieved an unassailable status in immunology, not because it is a precise scientific term, but because it resonates with our understanding of core identity, which in actuality is a most nebulous concept' (1997: 7–8). Tauber moreover, echoing Martin, notes how metaphor serves to project immunology well beyond the confines of the laboratory to the broader culture, making its own particular contribution to understanding ourselves.

6 See also Haraway's (1997) more recent work on the Biomedical TechnoService Complex™, and Chapter 8 of this volume. Montgomery (1991) too provides an interesting discussion of these issues in his analysis of the biomedical transition from combat to *codes*.

7 Other (more embodied) strands of postmodern thought, as we shall see in subsequent chapters, provide somewhat more promising ways forward. I do not therefore wish to write postmodernism off completely here, simply to provide a critical point of commentary on some of its 'wilder', more fanciful, if not 'excessive', claims regarding medicine, health and the body.

8 Sharma (1996), however, takes issue with some of these broader claims made by authors such as Coward, stressing instead a series of more pragmatic reasons for these trends.

3

'Structuring' Bodies: Emotions, Inequalities and Health

Much has been written about inequalities in health over the years, within and beyond the confines of medical sociology. This, perhaps, is not surprising, given the lives cut short and the unnecessary suffering inflicted by these inequalities. Inequalities in health indeed, both past and present, provide a key index and graphic testimony of socio-structural arrangements and the cohesion of society: inequalities, quite literally, experienced and expressed through the health and illness of each and every one of us *qua* embodied agents. This chapter takes a closer look at these issues with particular reference to the embodied relations between emotion, social structure and health. The emphasis, in doing so, as in other chapters, is less on a detailed or comprehensive review of this vast literature and its manifold debates than on a *selective* focus on the *experience* and *expression* of inequalities in health, using emotions as a guiding embodied theme.

In the first part of the chapter, a brief sketch of the current state of play concerning contemporary inequalities in health is provided as a backdrop to the emotion-centred themes and issues which follow. The question of what precisely emotions are is then addressed, before concentrating more fully, via so-called 'psychosocial' pathways, on the experiential and expressive role emotions play in the health and illness of existentially embodied agents. This, in turn, provides the basis for some further reflections on issues of biography, time and place, together with a revisiting of neo-materialist critiques of these and related lines of inquiry, including debates on the role of 'neo-liberalism'. The complex, multi-dimensional nature of contemporary inequalities, and their 'deeper' relations and intersections, is therefore a key theme, itself elaborated on more fully in the latter part of the chapter, in keeping with the need to go beyond either/or debates in which bio-logical and social, material and psychosocial explanations are played off against one another.

What, then, is the current position regarding contemporary inequalities in health, and how have these (persistent) patterns been explained?

Patterns, paradigms and puzzles: a preliminary sketch of health inequalities today

Inequalities in health are no new phenonema. Engels (1987/1844), for example, in a bold statement, likens 'the condition of the working class in England' to 'social murder' by the bourgeoisie. The combination of poor sanitary and environmental conditions, together with poor nutrition and long, arduous, health-risking forms of labour, he shows, resulted in a general 'enfeeblement' of working class bodies, including women and children, which aged prematurely and died early. In Liverpool, for example, in 1840, the average life span of the upper classes, gentry and professional men was 35 years; that of businessmen and the better-placed handi-craftsmen, 22 years; and that of operatives, day-labourers and serviceable classes in general, just 15 years. These chilling statistics, Engels stresses, were not uncommon: Chadwick's *The Sanitary Conditions of the Labouring Population of Great Britain* (1965/1842) contained a wealth of similarly stark facts and figures. 'A whole gener-ation wrecked, afflicted with disease and infirmity,' Engels concludes, 'purely to fill the purses of the bourgeoise' (1987/1845: 183–4).

Improvements (in health) have indeed occurred since this time, yet inequalities remain. A landmark here, following the optimism of the British post-war Welfare State, was the Black Report (1979), in which inequalities in health were, once again, thrown into stark relief. The class gap in health, it appeared, was evident for most causes of disease across the lifecourse, for men and women alike. The evi-dence and recommendations of the Black Report, needless to say, struck a dissonant note with the in-coming Conservative administration, but eventually found a wider audience through its independent publication (Townsend and Davidson 1980). These findings, in turn, have been supplemented and updated through a variety of other reports and policy documents, including *The Health Divide* (Whitehead 1988), the more recent Independent Inquiry into Inequalities in Health (see Box 3.1),[1] and Shaw et al.'s *The Widening Gap* (1999). To this we may add the recent ESRC Health Variations Programme (Graham 2000a), together with New Labour's attempt to put *inequalities* in health back on the political agenda – under the former Conservative administration one could only refer to health *vari-ations* – in the shape of policy documents such as *Saving Lives: Our Healthier Nation* (Secretary of State for Health 1999). The Acheson Report, for example, reminds us that

BOX 3.1: HEALTH INEQUALITIES IN BRITAIN TODAY: AN UNHEALTHY GAP?

Key findings from the Acheson Report (1998: 10–25), include the following:

- *Death rates* have fallen for men and women across all social groups, but far more amongst those at the top than the bottom of the social scale: a shift from a two-fold to a three-fold differential among class V (unskilled) men, compared to class I (professional) men, from the early 1970s to the early 1990s.

- This pattern holds for most of the *major causes* of disease, including coronary heart disease, stroke, lung cancer, suicide amongst men, and respiratory disease and lung cancer amongst women.

- By the late 1980s, men at the top of the social scale could *expect to live* on average to 75 years, those at the bottom to 70 years. For women the differential was 80 years compared to 77 years. Life expectancy at age 65 was also considerably better for those in higher social classes.

- *Infant mortality rates*, whilst decreasing, are also lower amongst babies born into higher social classes, with no evidence that the differential has decreased over the past two decades

- Socio-economic differentials for many measures of *morbidity* are substantial: the likelihood of having a limiting long-standing illness in 1996, for instance, rose from 17 per cent for men aged 45–64 in the professional classes to 48 per cent of the unskilled. Mental health also varies markedly by social class, particularly for neurotic disorders (such as anxiety, depression, phobias) amongst women, and alcohol and drug dependency amongst men.

- These differentials, in turn, are anticipated by widening gaps in *income, poverty, wealth* and *unemployment* (see Shaw et al. 1999, for example). Countries such as Sweden, in contrast, where income distribution is much more egalitarian, show much less steep class gradients. Japanese life expectancy has likewise increased dramatically during the past few decades as its income differentials have narrowed (Wilkinson 1996).

[i]nequalities in health exist, whether measured in terms of mortality, life expectancy or health status; whether categorised by socio-economic measures or by ethnic group and gender. Recent efforts to compare the level and nature of inequalities in international terms indicated that Britain is generally around the middle of comparable Western countries, depending on the socio-economic and inequality indicators used. Although in general disadvantage is associated with worse health, the patterns of inequalities vary by place, gender, age, year of birth and other factors, and differ according to which measure of health is used. (1998: 10)

Shaw and colleagues in similar fashion warn us that social class differences in infant mortality, despite overall declines, are clear and widening, as is the life expectancy gap between social classes. Geographical differences in mortality too are increasing (see also Shaw et al. 2002). These gaps, it is stressed, have 'real, lethal meaning for large groups of people living in Britain today' (Shaw et al. 1999: 107). This, moreover, has been anticipated by a widening gap on a number of other socio-economic measures of well-being associated with factors such as income, poverty, wealth and unemployment (Shaw et al. 1999: 107).

A number of explanations have been proposed for these widening gaps, including those (following the Black Report) associated with: (i) measurement issues, biases and the social construction of official statistics (*artefact* explanations) (Bloor et al. 1987); (ii) health-related social mobility (health *selection* explanations whereby the healthy move up and the unhealthy move down the social scale) (Blane et al. 1993; Illsley 1955; West 1991); (iii) lifestyles (*cultural* and *behavioural* explanations) (Blaxter 1990); and (iv) *material/structural* factors, favoured by the Black Report and advocates of neo-materialist explanations (Shaw et al. 1999, 2002). Macintyre (1997), for example, in reviewing research and evidence since the Black Report, notes how the Report accepted the 'hard' version of a materialist/structural explanation – in which material, physical conditions of life associated with class structure are seen to be the complete explanation for class gradients in health – but rejected the hard versions of the other three explanations. It did not, however, reject the 'soft' version of these latter explanations, and there now appears to be some concession that they are not necessarily alternatives. As she states:

The 'selection versus causation', 'artefact versus real differences' and 'behaviour versus material circumstances' distinctions can thus be seen to be politically and conceptually important but are becoming *false antitheses* if treated as being mutually exclusive: the same applies to new distinctions such as those between *material and psychosocial* factors, and between early life and adult life influences on inequalities. (1997: 740)[2]

The key issue for our purposes, however, set against the backdrop of these debates, concerns the newly emerging body of work regarding *psychosocial* explanations for the 'afflictions of inequality' and for 'unhealthy societies' in general: explanations which link hierarchies, health and human evolution in promising new sociological ways (Wilkinson 1996, 2000a). It is income *inequality* rather than simply low income, Wilkinson argues, which is now the key factor in determining poor health: a case of *relative income* rather than *absolute income* in rich, developed countries of the contemporary Western world. Income inequalities, from this stance, influence national mortality rates primarily by determining the strength and impact of *relative deprivation* on health. A nation's health, that is to say, reflects the way resources are *distributed* and not simply the existence of different levels of income between socio-economic groups. Relative differences in income, moreover, are seen to undermine social cohesion in differing societies by increasing the *stress* of the disadvantaged and damaging *self-esteem*. The emphasis, therefore, given the corrosive effects of income inequalities and associated social hierarchies, is placed upon so-called 'psychosocial' factors – feelings, for example, of stress, a sense of lack of coherence or control, and associated emotions such as anxiety or fear, anger or resentment – rather than the (direct) material effects of poverty. As Wilkinson states:

> The importance of income distribution implies that we must explain the effect of low income on health through its social meanings and implications for social position rather than through the direct physical effects which material circumstances might have independently of their social connotations in any particular society. This is not to say that bad (or even non-existent) housing and inadequate diet do not affect the health of a minority (though still a large number) of people in developed societies: they clearly do. What it means is that the direct material effects of factors such as these are not the main explanations of why national standards of health are related to income distribution. Nor does this mean that we shall ignore the health of the poorest in society. The poor suffer psychosocial effects of deprivation as well as its direct material effects. Indeed, it is *important to recognise that as well as the greatest material deprivation, those at the bottom of the social hierarchy also suffer the greatest social, psychological and emotional deprivation*, and this may well have a greater impact than the more direct effects of material deprivation. (1996: 176, my emphasis)

As for the 'sociobiological translation', whereby social factors are translated into biological processes (cf. Tarlov 1996), most of the main psychosocial influences on health, Wilkinson maintains, can be seen as sources of *stress* that are likely to cause physiological arousal of some sort (2000a: 36–7). Cortisol, for example, is a key 'stress hormone', with a range of biological and physiological effects within the body. Sustained stress too may damage the mechanisms by which insulin controls glucose levels in the blood, and/or disrupt aspects of immune system functioning, thereby rendering us more susceptible or vulnerable to illness and disease of many kinds (2000a: 39–40).

The psychosocial perspective, to summarize, takes up a familiar social causation type of explanation, locating the genesis of social inequalities in health in the varying environment of social positions. Rather than material shortages and/or negligent behaviour, however, the emphasis instead is placed upon psychological stress, relative deprivation and the psychosocial afflictions of inequality (Elstad 1998: 600).

Aetiologically speaking, the health-damaging effects of psychosocial stress, following Elstad, may in turn be subdivided into two somewhat different pathways: firstly, a *direct* effect on disease development; and, secondly, an *indirect* route when stress is expressed through health-damaging behaviour such as excessive alcohol use, smoking, accident-prone behaviour, conscious or subconscious self-destructive acts, and so forth (1998: 600–1). The term psychosocial 'perspective', in this respect, is used advisedly. It is, Elstad comments, more a related set of approaches than a unified theory, drawing from the following four main sources: (i) the social stress approach; (ii) the related self-efficacy approach; (iii) the newer sociology of emotion; and (iv) the social cohesion approach (1998: 600).[3]

What, then, of the sociology of emotion? What particular light does it shed on these debates? And how might these very insights be carried forward, so to speak, into a more fully *embodied* (experiential and expressively rich) approach to inequalities in health? Any such discussion, however, must first address the very nature of emotions themselves.

What are emotions? Sociological themes and issues

Emotion indeed is a moving or slippery target, itself the subject of much discussion and debate. What is fair to say, however, given a variety of differing perspectives and viewpoints, is that emotion is a complex, *multi-dimensional, multi-faceted human compound*, including *irreducible* biological and cultural components, which arises or emerges in various socio-relational contexts. As a thinking, moving, feeling 'complex' (rather than a static, unidimensional 'thing'), emotion is *embodied* through and through (Denzin 1984), the animating principle of sociality and selfhood, conceived in intersubjective, intercorporeal, communicative terms (Crossley 1998). The importance of *body-image* – itself socio-culturally contingent (cf. Schilder 1950) – to the ways in which we think and feel, experience and express our emotions further underlines this embodied viewpoint (see, for example, Williams 2001b). As multi-dimensional, multi-faceted complexes, the experience and management of the emotionally embodied self operates at differing levels, including highly reflexive or calculative strategies, habituated or routinized practices linked to the habitus and associated body-techniques (cf. Bourdieu 1984 and Mauss 1973/1934), as well as other, more unconscious responses (Craib 1995; Lupton 1998a: 168).

Emotions, as this suggests, are endlessly elaborated, like colours on a painter's palette, across culture, time and place, including fundamental social processes of *socialization, management, differentiation* and *change* (Gordon 1990). The irreducible biological dimensions of emotion, from this viewpoint, are best conceived in 'open' rather than 'fixed' terms. No emotion, Elias (1991) reminds us, is ever an 'entirely unlearnt response'. This in turn links the emotional experiences and expressions of embodied individuals, through the social *habitus* and associated *body techniques*

(Lyon 1997), to key features of social structure such as power and status. It is a question not simply of the *social structuring of emotion*, however, but of the *emotional structuring of society*. Emotion, in other words, conceived in spatio-temporal terms, is both socially *responsive* and socially *efficacious* (Barbalet 1998), providing a key index of the social bond (Scheff 1990). From Collins' (1990) pioneering work on emotional energy (EE) and the micro-foundations of social structure, to Hochschild's (1983) insights into emotional labour and the 'managed heart', and from Barbalet's (1998) analysis of class and resentment, to a variety of other recent work on emotion in organizations (Fineman 2000a), these emotion-laden micro–macro relations can be traced. A close rereading of classical sociology, moreover, sheds further emotional light on these dynamic social relations, from the trials and tribulations of alienated labour in capitalist society (Marx), to the instrumental demands of bureaucratic rationality (Weber), and from the sacred fires of collective effervescence (Durkheim), to the bored and the blasé outlook of metropolitan man (Simmel).

The emphasis here, as before, is on putting minds back into bodies, bodies back into society, and society back into the body. Emotion, to repeat, *qua* processual embodied phenomena, cannot be reduced to innate biology. Nor can it be subsumed as a 'special' (disembodied) case of cognition or language, culture or symbol (Lyon 1998). Rather, the *socio-relational genesis*, *multi-dimensional nature* and *irreducible features* of emotion take us far beyond traditional either/or debates, blurring a series of (disciplinary) borders or boundaries along the way (Lyon 1996, 1998). The micro and macro levels of sociological investigation, in this respect, are not simply connected anew; they are quite literally reanimated in fully embodied ways.

Experiencing and expressing inequalities in health: the emotional body

Let me take the opportunity at this point to recap on the arguments advanced so far. Psychosocial factors, it has been suggested, following Wilkinson, play a key part in the contemporary patterning of health. This in turn, it is argued, fleshing the 'psychosocial' out more fully (as indeed one should), throws emotion into critical relief, viewed in *embodied*, socio-relational terms which translate more or less readily into matters of health and illness through the afflictions of inequality. Emotions, embodiment and health, therefore, interpenetrate in complex ways, providing a key index of prevailing social arrangements, including socio-economic, power and status differentials.

It is to sources within and beyond the sociology of emotion, however, that we must turn to fully flesh out the embodied implications of these issues. Freund (1990), for example, provides a promising lead here in his work on the 'expressive' body. The expressive body, he argues, provides a 'common ground' for the sociology of emotion and the sociology of health and illness. A central part of understanding human emotions, from this *lived* perspective, is to see them as 'existential modes of being' involving a fusion of physical and psychic states of a pleasant or unpleasant kind (cf. Buytendijk 1950). These different modes of emotional being, in effect, are differing ways of feeling *empowered* or *disempowered*, which themselves are very much linked to people's material and psychosocial conditions of existence throughout their embodied biographies. It is indeed at this very juncture, Freund ventures, that '"[e]xternal" social structural factors such as one's position in different systems of hierarchy and various forms of social control can influence the conditions of our existence, how we respond and apprehend these conditions of existence and our sense of embodied self. These conditions can also affect our physical functioning' (1990: 461).

A person's social position and status, from this viewpoint, will determine the resources at their disposal in order to define and protect – through 'status shields' (cf. Hochschild 1983) and various other forms of self care (cf. Goffman 1959, 1967) – the boundaries of the self and thereby counter the potential invalidation by significant others. Status shields, as the term suggests, protect us from attacks on self; their absence is a structural source of feeling powerless which is more likely to occur among lower social status persons and to be inflicted by those in power. Being in an extremely powerless social status therefore 'increases the likelihood of experiencing "unpleasant" emotionality or emotional modes of being' (Freund 1990: 466).

From this it follows, Freund argues, that less powerful people face a 'structurally in-built handicap' in managing social and emotional information. This, in turn, may contribute to existential fear, anxiety and neuro-physiological perturbations of many different sorts (as discussed earlier). In particular, the 'dramaturgical stress' of social roles and relationships (Goffman 1959), and problems of ontological insecurity (cf. Laing 1965), may engender a form of what Freund, borrowing from Kelly (1980), refers to as 'schizokinesis'. Schizokinesis, he explains, involves a split between that which is shown and consciously experienced, and that which occurs somatically. Freund poses two important sociological questions here: how 'deep' can the social construction of feelings go, and can emotion work eliminate the responses of an 'unconsciously knowing body'? The implications of his argument seem to suggest, echoing the points raised earlier, that society affects physiological reactivity deep within the recesses of the human body, knowingly or not. As continued emotional and other kinds of distress alter physiological reactivity, neurohormonally related functions such as blood pressure and raised basal cortisol levels may markedly increase in response to a stressor without being consciously experienced.

Further support for these contentions comes from a variety of studies: from Lynch's (1985) work on the recalcitrant language of the (broken) heart and Lyon's (1994) embodied insights into the relationship between emotion and respiration, to the biological effects of status hierarchies amongst baboons (Sapolsky 1991) and civil servants (Brunner 1996; Marmot et al. 1978, 1991); and from the (un)anticipated consequences of unemployment, job insecurity and a lack of control over one's working conditions (Alfredsson et al. 1982; Karasek and Theorell 1990; Mattison et al. 1990; Siegrist et al. 1990), to the beneficial (health) effects of social support at home and in the community (Cohen and Syme 1985; Thoits 1995). These findings, in turn, have been reinforced by research within the life-events paradigm which has documented, with ever increasing precision, the complex relationship between social factors, cognitive-emotional responses and the onset of a variety of physical and mental conditions. Brown and Harris (1989a), for example, building on their earlier work (1978) on the 'depressogenic' links between *provoking agents* (severe life-events and long-term difficulties), *vulnerability factors* (such as lack of a close confiding relationship) and the onset of clinical depression, distinguish between two main sources of emotion: those arising from everyday activities of a largely routinized, taken-for-granted nature, and those deriving from plans and purposes, motives and commitments. Both, of course, are inextricably related. It is from this latter, more complex level of human emotionality, nonetheless, Brown and Harris suggest, that the power and force of life-events derive, changing more or less radically one's plans and purposes, motives and commitments, with a series of deleterious consequences for health (1989a: 442).[4]

These and many other examples, returning to Freund, point to a subtle and sophisticated form of socially 'pliable' biology which accords emotional modes of being a central role in linking the health and illness of the existential-phenomenologically embodied agent with wider structures of power and domination, civilization and control in society. Hierarchical roles, from this viewpoint,

> shape the conditions in which one lives. This position influences access to resources. It may also determine the forms of emotional-social control to which one is subject as well as the severity of impact these controls have on the person . . . Such a process may mean internalising the emotional definitions that others impose on what we are and/or 'should be'. The physiological aspects of such processes are of interest to those studying emotions. However, these physical aspects may also be seen as examples of ways in which controls are sedimented and fixed in the psycho-soma of the person. Physiological aspects of social control can also act as a form of feedback that colours the tone of existence. This feedback can *indirectly* serve social control functions. For instance, conditions that create depression . . . construct an emotional mode of being where the motivation to resist is blunted. (Freund 1990: 470)

It is here, then, at this existential nexus, that the 'mindful' (Scheper-Hughes and Lock 1987), emotionally 'expressive' body is located: one forged in and through a social habitus and associated body techniques, which in turn is more or less active in the context of power and status, conflict and control.

As for the broader relations within which such processes occur, ours is an era, Sennett (1998) comments, of new corporate initiatives where risk, flexibility and the endless process of reinvention replace previous modes of organization, including the personal, enduring character and career that went with them a generation ago: an era, that is to say, based on the principle of 'no long term'. On the one hand, Sennett concedes, such dynamism may be positive. On the other hand, he argues, it can prove destructive, engendering fear and insecurity and eroding a sustained sense of purpose, integrity of self and trust in one another. What this amounts to, in Sennett's view, is nothing short of a 'corrosion of character', with a variety of deleterious consequences for individuals and communities alike. Sennett's observations, as this suggests, cast further light on the personal consequences of work, and the feelings this engenders, in the disorientating world of the new flexible capitalism: issues which echo some of the points raised previously in Chapter 2. A 'regime which provides human beings with no deep reasons to care about one another', he concludes, 'cannot long preserve its legitimacy' (1998: 148) – nor, we might add, the health of its citizens!

Time and biography, place and space

Implicit if not explicit in much of the discussion so far are an interrelated cluster of issues to do with time and biography, place and space: issues in which embodiment again looms large. Blaxter (2000), for example, notes how questions of time are crucial to the conceptualization, understanding and explanation of inequalities in health across the lifetime of both individuals and generations. A distinction is drawn here between *social* time, *calendar* time and *personal* time, the latter itself intimately bound up with issues of biography. It is obvious, Blaxter argues, that

> biography and health are always intertwined, and that subjective time is not the same as either calendar or socio-historical time. A real lifetime is measured subjectively in social periods – infancy, schooldays, family formation, work, retirement – rather than calendar years: periods of life which may be determined by social roles but are particular to individuals . . . In creating and recounting biographies . . . people add up periods of time which may not be juxtaposed in calendar time: the genesis of this problem was this, then something else contributed, then this outcome followed . . . These definitions of biotemporal orderliness provide structure to life and health. To suffer physical events outside their proper time is disconcerting. This 'proper' time is personally and socially constructed, and is not incorporated into the sort of structural regularities represented by Standardized Mortality Ratios analysed according to RG [Registrar General's] social class. To a considerable extent, it is constructed by family and intergenerational biographies as well as personal ones. (2000: 41–2)

Personal time, as this suggests, concerns the way in which individuals perceive 'their own lives in the context of historical time, in the light of class situations of the past and class rhetorics of the present' (2000: 43). One of the key features of social disadvantage, for instance, is that time accelerates the perceived ageing process, engendering feelings of temporal deprivation. The emphasis, in this respect, is very much on (class) *trajectories* and their *dynamic* links to health over time, thereby moving away from more static or snapshot views (see also Wadsworth 1991, 1997).

Talk of time and biography, in turn, inevitably raises issues of space, themselves inextricably bound together across the biographically embodied lifecourse. Freund (1998), for example, in his more recent work, has usefully extended and refined his earlier analysis of the expressive body (discussed above) through a focus on spatial metaphors, informational preserves and the 'geography' of emotions. In doing so, the issue of emotional communication is raised anew, in the context of *psychosomatic* space, *intra-psychosomatic* space – by which Freund means 'internal conversations' which 'past-urize' and 'futurize' the dramatic encounters of our everyday lives in our imaginations (1998: 278) – and *social-physical* space. Dramaturgical emotional relationships, from this viewpoint, can themselves be portrayed topographically as a 'map' of relationships occurring both within the embodied self and between the embodied self and others:

> Located in a sociophysical place, the feelings that underlie emotions are experienced positionally – that is, in terms of merging and establishing boundaries in one's relationships with others. The structures of feelings are shaped by activities occurring within the context of socially organized emotional 'spaces' ... Dramaturgical strategies of impression management, the reading of what others either intentionally or 'unconsciously' make visible to us, are part of this 'topography' that affects our conscious and unconscious subjective relationship to self and others. The display and concealment from others (and from oneself) of emotions and the use of dramaturgical space interact with emotional modes of being and psychosomatic space. (Freund 1998: 271)

The degree of homology between psychosomatic, social and physical space is of course, as Freund himself acknowledges, an open question. The spatial metaphors used here, nonetheless, enrich the connections between individual performance, emotional communication and conduct, and the social and cultural context within which they occur, conceived in embodied terms. This, in turn, through the status hierarchies and power dynamics these processes index, carries important implications for health.[5]

To these embodied discussions and dramaturgical enactments of the 'geography' of emotions, we may add a broader series of debates concerning issues of area or place, and questions (very much on the political agenda today) as to whether or not 'social capital' is a good investment for public health. This, of course, returns us to matters already touched on in this and the previous chapter, including Bourdieu's notion of 'capital', Wilkinson's appeal to socially cohesive societies, and Sennett's deliberations on community (that 'dangerous pronoun "we"') as a remedy for the ills of work. Social capital, without doubt, is a hotly contested term these days. Debates abound, moreover, as to its merits for public health.[6] Popay, for example, argues that social capital must be conceptualized as a dynamic process involving people living in places, which in turn includes its subjective, experiential dimensions (2000: 401). The question as to whether or not aspects of social capital are *compositional, contextual* or something altogether different, she argues, must recognize the crucial light which *subjective* experiences of area, or perhaps more appropriately 'place', shed on these very matters and their links to health. Narratives of the relation between social capital and health inequalities, from this viewpoint, provide a deeper, richer, more meaningful picture which takes us far beyond existing compositional and contextual debates. These narratives, Popay states,

> 'challenge' the research endeavour that concerns itself with the arguably 'artificial' pursuit of separation between the composition and context of an area . . . narratives tell a story of close and compelling linkages between people and the places they live in. To the extent that these relations are the 'stuff' of social capital, they suggest that social capital is neither contextual nor compositional but rather generated, accessed and/or used at the interface between people and places. (2000: 401)

The social capital debate, in short, looks set to continue for some time to come. Seen in this light, nonetheless, the underlying issues to which it speaks, of people and places, time and biography, are of more or less abiding importance, in (public) health and beyond.

The neo-materialist debate: a question of either/or?

Much has been made in this chapter, via Wilkinson, Freund and others, of psychosocial factors and the emotional dimensions of contemporary inequalities in health. What, however, of material factors? Wilkinson, for example, as noted earlier, has been strongly criticized by those who advocate a more or less hard line neo-materialist explanation for the 'widening gap' in health.

The emphasis on psychosocial pathways, Lynch and colleagues (2000a) argue, raises several conceptual and empirical problems. Interpretation of the links between income inequality and health, they assert, must begin with the *structural* causes of inequalities, and not just focus on *perceptions* of that inequality. Reducing health inequalities and improving public health in the twenty-first century, from this viewpoint, requires strategic investment in neo-material conditions via a more equitable distribution of public and private resources. The metaphor of airline travel, it is suggested, helps us to appreciate both the limits of psychosocial factors and the direct impact of material conditions on health. Differences in neo-material conditions between first and economy class, Lynch et al. argue, may produce inequitable health outcomes after a long flight. Within a psychosocial framework, these are seen as a product of negative emotions engendered by perception of relative disadvantage amongst economy class passengers. Under a neo-materialist explanation, in contrast, 'people in economy class have worse health because they sat in cramped space and an uncomfortable seat, and they were not able to sleep' (2000a: 1203–4).

Criticisms, as noted earlier, have also been levelled against the notion of social capital as a good investment strategy for public health, including the dangers of collective victim blaming and the fact that strong social networks can be *coercive* and a source of *strain* rather than support (Muntaner and Lynch 1999). To maximize its importance for public health, it is argued, social capital must be seen as a product of broadly defined social relations rather than a primarily psychosocial construct (Lynch et al. 2000b: 406; see also Baum 2000). The vision of social capital, in other words, should embrace

> structural as well as interpersonal social relations . . . Our societies are divided by economic, racial, ethnic and gender inequalities that receive institutionalised political, legal and corporate sanctions. If we understand social capital as a society-wide capacity for inclusiveness, human rights, social justice, and full political and economic participation, then indeed public health should invest. (Lynch et al. 2000b: 407–8)

These, to be sure, are important issues to raise. The key point, however, to repeat, is that we are no longer dealing here (if ever we were) with *either/or* explanations. Things indeed are far more complex than that. Viewed across the lifecourse, health inequalities instead, in the words of the ESRC Health Variations Programme co-ordinator, are the outcome of 'cumulative differential exposure to adverse material conditions and to behavioural and psychosocial risks' (Graham 2000b: 15). When it comes to the health effects of low social status, for example, it is not too difficult, Wilkinson remarks, to find 'possible material factors that may, and often do, have direct effects on health'. This, nonetheless, is not the end of the story. There is abundant evidence, as we have seen, of additional 'very important psychosocial pathways through which people's circumstances affect their health' (Wilkinson 2000b: 412).

As for issues of social capital, an important factor underpinning this upsurge of interest, Wilkinson stresses, comes not from ignoring income distribution, but precisely from the opposite direction: from trying indeed to 'understand why income distribution is important to health' (2000b: 411). Approaches to social capital are not therefore an argument against trying to reduce social divisions based on inequalities in income distribution; quite the contrary. It is likely, moreover, that reducing income differentials also reduces the dangers of discrimination against minorities (Wilkinson 2000b: 412): that is to say, that societies which fail to reduce income inequalities will be more likely to display tendencies towards discrimination and victimization of vulnerable groups. By *'reducing inequality*, we *increase cohesion* partly by reducing some of what fuels these social divisions' (Wilkinson 2000b: 412). Issues of equality and social cohesion, in these and other respects, are placed high on the political agenda, providing governments with practical steps and realistic possibilities for improving important aspects of life and living in contemporary society. This, in turn, promotes not only more healthy societies, but also more egalitarian, internally cohesive ones (Wilkinson 1996: 184–5).

The psychosocial perspective, in summary, echoing Elstad (1998), should be viewed as an *enrichment* of the *social causation* explanation: one which needs developing further when studying health, by considering *both* material and psychosocial environments and their *mutual interaction*. It is important, moreover, to distinguish here between an *'extreme'* formulation of these issues – one which lays claim to psychosocial pathways as *the* most decisive influences on health in present day Western societies – and a less drastic (more endorsable) possibility, which acknowledges the *relevance* of psychosocial links without dismissing the *direct* consequences of material deprivation. One may reasonably suggest, therefore, that the role of the psychosocial perspective will 'not be to institute a paradigm shift, but rather to extend and enrich the social causation explanation for health inequalities' (Elstad 1998: 613).

Something old, something new? The cross-cutting axes (and 'deeper' relations) of inequality

Where, then, does this leave us in relation to class debates? What, moreover, of gender and ethnicity? Taking each of these issues in turn, the relationship between mainstream theoretical debates over the future of class inequalities – broadly speaking, the class *restructuring* versus the class *demise* debate (Crompton 1998; Pakulski and Waters 1996; Scott 2000) – and ongoing research into inequalities in health has at best been somewhat tenuous (until quite recently). There has, in other words, been a tendency to turn theoretical debates into methodological ones, such that we are 'not really sure what exactly the inequalities in health we observe through our research actually mean' (Annandale 1998: 121–2). To the extent that class has been theorized at all, moreover, it has tended to be in its somewhat *'weaker'* form of late, referring 'not to a collective identity, but to a range of inequalities . . . along a number of axes which are unlikely to align to a form of strong collective economic or social identity' (Annandale 1998: 101). Wilkinson's work, for example, as we have seen, alerts us to a complex pattern of inequalities – including not only *income* inequalities, but also *status* inequalities (including inequalities within and between gender and ethnic minority groups) and *power* inequalities (authoritarian hierarchies, non-democratic organizations, and the like) – all of which have a fundamental influence on the content of social relations and social interactions, and hence health (Elstad 1998: 610).

Others, however, have recently reasserted a *stronger* formulation of class relations, in health as elsewhere (Higgs and Scambler 1998; Navarro 1994, 2002; Scambler and Higgs 1999; Westergaard 1995). The recent neo-liberalism debate, for example, is a case in point (Coburn 2000a, 2000b): a further *elaboration* of the neo-materialist debate, in effect, with *class relations* to the fore. Wilkinson's (neo-Durkheimian) work in particular, and neo-positivist research on health inequalities in general, is again taken to task here for abandoning the search for causes and underlying generative mechanisms too soon. Not enough attention, in other words, has been paid to the *social context* of factors such as income inequality. From this viewpoint, it is a question not so much of inequality leading to low social cohesion and poor health, but of 'neo-liberalism' – a more or less thorough adherence, in rhetoric if not reality, to the virtues of the market-orientated society (Coburn 2000a: 139) – producing 'both higher income inequality and lower social cohesion and, presumably, either lowered health status or a health status which is not as high as it might otherwise have been' (Coburn 2000a: 137). Part of the negative effect of neo-liberalism, it is held, is through its undermining of particular types of welfare state (the latter itself having both direct effects as well as being one of the underlying structural causes of social cohesion). The rise of neo-liberalism and the decline of the welfare state, moreover, are themselves tied to globalization (global competition and the mobility of capital) and the changing class structure of advanced (disorganized) capitalist societies (Coburn 2000a: 135). More attention, therefore, Coburn concludes, should be paid to understanding the '*causes* of income inequalities' rather than just their 'effects'. The 'rise' and 'fall' of the Welfare State, together with the presumed class causes and consequences of these relations, themselves located in the globalizing dynamics of late capitalism, are thereby drawn (back) into the analysis, itself carrying important implications for notions of the causal pathways involved in inequality–health status relationships, and vice versa (Coburn 2000a: 137; see also Muntaner and Lynch 1999 for a similar class-based line of argument).

Scambler too finds much to commend in the 'reinvigorating contributions' of Coburn, Muntaner and Lynch, amongst others, complementing their own agendas through his own (realist) rethinking of the linkages between *real class relations* and health inequalities (2002: 97; see also Higgs and Scambler 1998; Scambler and Higgs 1999) Many would be sympathetic, Scambler states, to the general notion that class affects health. His own 'Greedy Bastards Hypothesis' (GBH), however – which states that Britain's persisting, even widening, health inequalities are the '(largely unintended) consequences of the ever-adaptive behaviours of members of its (weakly globalized) power elite, informed by its (strongly globalized) capital-executive' – pinpoints one, maybe even '*the*, prepotent *sociological* mechanism' (Scambler 2002: 103). The *de-standardization* of work and the new inequality, in other words, including derivative processes like the new *individualism*, and hence the widening of health inequalities, 'have their genesis in, although they cannot be reduced to, the adaptive behaviours of the GBs, above all others' (Scambler 2002: 103). To this, Scambler adds the concept of *capital flows*, itself highly apposite in tracing these relations and their mobilizing/globalizing dynamics, including not simply material capital, but also biological capital, psychological capital, cultural capital, spatial capital, perhaps even 'emotional capital' (Williams 1998a). What this amounts to, then, succinctly stated, is the following:

> . . . relations of class (allowing for the hugely disproportionate sway of GBs) systematically affect the flows (typically *variable*, and arguably of special salience for particular conditions at *critical periods* of the lifecourse . . .) to individuals of different types of capital with potential to impact on health and longevity. The point of intersection between these capital flows and the individual is the class habitus. It is important to acknowledge, of course, that class relations are not the only relations to affect capital flows; and that uninterrupted flows do not in any case guarantee health and longevity, nor (even heavily) interrupted flows rule them out. (Scambler 2002: 104)

These, to be sure, are promising avenues of inquiry, rearticulating critical realist agendas on *real, intransitive* (existing independently of their identification), *transfactual* (relatively enduring and continuous, despite variability of outcomes in 'open' systems), class relations along the way (Scambler 2002: 106; see also Archer et al. 1998).

As for Wilkinson's response, a number of points are again worth noting here in the context of these debates. Coburn's call to bring 'the social back in', Wilkinson retorts, sounds very much like a 'voice from the past' (2000c: 997). Writers on the social determinants of health, he argues, have long since made clear the economic and political roots of these relations. Tying the problem too closely to neo-liberalism rather than *relative* deprivation, however, 'limits the theory to a historically specific instance: widening income differences seem likely to be damaging, almost whatever their source' (2000c: 998). The Welfare State, moreover, Wilkinson claims, is not necessarily the only underpinning of income inequality. The 'real political analysis', therefore, has to go 'much deeper into the fundamentals of market society, wage labour and individualism'. A proper understanding of the relationship between income distribution and population mortality rates, he concludes, 'takes us close to the heart of it' (2000c: 998). Muntaner and Lynch's (1999) class-based critique of Wilkinson's neo-Durkheimian research programme receives a broadly similar rebuff. In practice, Wilkinson states,

> it may make rather little difference whether a change in income distribution comes from an exogenous change in class relations or from some other possible influence on income distribution. The result will feed back to the social environment, affecting levels of prejudice, social distinction, tendencies to exclusion, the exercise of power, and the creation of insecurity, and finally, to the insidious tendency of some people to be made to appear as inadequate failures in contrast to the successful and wealthy. (1999: 539–40)

Why, moreover, he continues,

> pay attention to the rate of exploitation and define it in terms of income flows and the division of the social product unless income distribution is important? . . . Why ignore factors other than class relations that contribute to income differentials? Why insist that class relations are more determining of income distribution than determined by it? To suggest that income distribution is wholly determined by

antecedent class relations and that these relations are more powerful influences on health than their consequences, either for income distribution or for the psychosocial processes related to it which I have discussed, is a tortuous path to choose. Rather than clinging to this misconceived 'materialism', why not address the structural determinants of the psychosocial welfare of modern populations and, instead of worrying about its subjectivity, realize that it is precisely because these things so dominate our subjectivity that they are so important? (1999: 540)

The debate rolls on, in short, as indeed it *should*.

Turning now to gender, a similarly complex picture emerges here, in keeping with the above debates. Wilkinson's work again is suggestive here, albeit in ways which require further development. Psychosocial factors, for instance, may affect health in a variety of respects, including: (i) the stresses and strains of gendered social roles, relations, power and status hierarchies; (ii) the indirect effects of psychosocial factors on gendered forms of risk-taking and health-related lifestyles; and (iii) differential interpretations and responses to bodily signs and symptoms, themselves reflected and reinforced through gendered forms of emotion management (which in turn are embodied, experienced and expressed through the gendered habitus).[7] Kawachi and colleagues (1999), for example, in their study of gender inequalities at the geographical level in the United States, found not simply that women's experiences of mortality and morbidity were higher in those states with low levels of political participation and economic autonomy, but that living in such states also had adverse effects for men too. There is, Wilkinson argues, a 'culture of inequality, in which social relations are more violent, more aggressive, and less supportive, in which male behaviour is more macho – or laddish – and in which there is a tendency to scapegoat weaker or more vulnerable sections of society, including women, ethnic or religious minorities' (1999: 540).

A number of other points, however, are also worth flagging up in this context, themselves part and parcel of promising new agendas and debates on gender and health in a rapidly unfolding field. The first, of course, itself alluded to above, concerns the fact that gender and health includes a focus on *men* as well as women: a realization, whilst seemingly obvious, which is only now occurring in academic, professional and policy-making circles alike (see Sabo and Gordon 1995, for instance). There are, indeed, a number of signs that men's health is now on the agenda. The *British Medical Journal*, for example, recently devoted a special issue to this very topic, including articles by Doyal (2001) on 'Sex, gender and health: the need for a new approach' and Banks (2001) on 'No man's land: men, illness and the NHS'. Key points raised here include the following: (i) men do care about health issues but find it difficult to express their fears; (ii) socially constructed gender characteristics (in addition to biological risk factors) are important in shaping the capacity of both men and women to realize their full health potential; (iii) men face particular problems because of the relation between masculine identity and risk taking; and (iv) greater sensitivity to sex and gender is needed in medical research, service delivery and wider social policies, including medical school training and consultations between male doctors and patients (Banks 2001; Doyal 2001). International links, moreover, are now being forged. The First World Congress on Men's Health, for instance, was held in Vienna in November 2001, which in turn established the International Society for Men's Health. The European Men's Health Initiative was also launched at the Congress. These steps were further consolidated, at the same time, by the publication of the US-based *International Journal of Men's Health* (Baker 2001: 1014).

Again, however, the need for more adequate theorization of such issues is clearly apparent – theorizations which connect work in health with broader debates on gender and embodiment in feminisms, men's studies and related fields of inquiry. A complex set of questions arise here, for example, to do with *similarities* as well as *differences within* and *between* genders, and the need to go beyond existing dichotomous frameworks. The all too easy claim, for instance, that 'women get sick and men die' – itself a characteristic finding in research on gender inequalities in health – may still hold true. This, nonetheless, as various commentators point out, 'belies the complexity of the relationship between gender and health status', itself variable according to which measures are being used (see Box 3.2), amongst other things (Annandale 1998: 123; see also Macintyre et al. 1996). An over-generalized sociological wisdom is at work here, in other words, premised on the search for male/female difference, which (unthinkingly) underpins much of the research in this area to date (Annandale 1998: 123). We need, in short, as with class, to 'remove the theoretical blinkers' around gender and health, including a need to move beyond existing dichotomous frameworks, to get 'behind' the *scripts* and *roles* of gender to their *meanings* and *performances*, and to display a greater openness to the possibility that, in some areas of health and health behaviour, 'there may be important *similarities* as well as *differences* between men and women' (Annandale 1998: 158–9, my emphasis). In doing so, moreover, echoing previous arguments, the line between the biological and the social must itself be rethought in less either/or terms.[8]

Further light is shed on some of these issues by Annandale and Hunt's (1990) study of sex, gender role orientation and health, which was undertaken in the West of Scotland amongst a sample of 35 year olds in which high/low 'masculinity' and 'femininity' were measured using the BEM sex role inventory. A key finding, in this respect, was the association between 'feminine' gender role orientation and poor subjective health status, and 'masculine' gender role orientation and relatively good subjective health status: one which held in *both men and women*. This, of course, Annandale and Hunt stress, is not to suggest that those with a more masculine gender role orientation, male or female, are necessarily 'healthier' by some 'objective' standard; it is simply that they *define* themselves this way. It could, moreover, be the case, Annandale later comments, that the 'more socially valued "masculine" self-concept of these individuals itself incorporates a more positive self-evaluation of health'. This indeed may be 'particularly important for the reporting of mental health and milder symptomatology' (1998: 155).

BOX 3.2: GENDER AND HEALTH

- Current trends suggests that the marked female *mortality* advantage, evident for most of the twentieth-century, is declining. The *all*-age sex mortality ratio in England and Wales, for example, achieved virtual parity by the early 1990s, a finding which may in part be attributable to very low death rates amongst younger adults and by declining advantage amongst women in middle to late middle age (Annandale 1998: 128–33).

- In 1971 *life expectancy at birth* was 69 years for males and 75 years for females. By 2000 this had reached 75 years and 80 years, respectively (ONS 2002: 119). In 1998, there were over twice as many women as men aged 85–9, rising to four times as many by the age of 90 and over (Drever et al. 2000: 8).

- *Morbidity* data reveal a similar picture of closing gaps, depending on which dimensions of health are being assessed across the lifecourse. The General Household Survey (2000–1), for instance, revealed little difference between males and females in terms of the following measures of self-reported sickness: general health, (limiting) long-standing illness, restricted activity (ONS 2002: 120).

- *Mental health*, in contrast, shows marked gender variations. Disorders of *thought* (schizophrenia and various types of dementia, for example) display a more or less even gender balance; disorders of *emotion* (such as depression, anxiety, phobias) show a marked female excess; disorders of *behaviour* (such as violence, suicide, drug and alcohol abuse) show a marked male excess (Busfield 2002; Meltzer et al. 1995).

As alluded to above, however, it is a question not of masculinity, but of plural masculini*ties*, hegemonic, marginalized or otherwise (Connell 1995). The merit of this shifting analytical focus is that it highlights not simply male dominance in relation to women – which itself is increasingly questioned, if not in 'crisis' (Faludi 1999) – but also inter-male dominance, and the complex interplay of practices and privileges within and between these respective dimensions of gender relations (Connell 1995; Morgan 1993; Seidler 1994). The claim, in this respect, that masculinity is 'dangerous' to health, and that aspects of it must be challenged, countered or resisted, itself becomes problematic, not least due to its 'presumption that all men benefit equally from being male' and that 'masculinity is a unitary construct' (Watson 2000: 141).

Within all this, it is clear, issues of embodiment again loom large: the lived body, that is to say, in the context of everyday life. Health, as Saltonstall puts it, is a 'lived experience of being bodied which involves action (practical activity) in the world' (1993: 13). Gender, as such, is an 'integral part of the process'. Watson (2000), for example, in his recent research on male bodies, notes an important *tension* in this respect between the promotion of personal responsibility for health, and personal responsibility derived from the gendered and rather functional demands of *pragmatic* embodiment, which ultimately constrain 'healthy choices'. Embodiment, he suggests, is thus an *integrating* concept that engages with the multi-layered discourse and agendas around public health and health promotion (Watson 2000: 143).

A similar set of points may be raised in relation to 'race' and the ethnic patterning of health, itself giving rise, as Smaje (1995) puts it in his review of current evidence, to a diverse and intriguing body of findings (see Box 3.3).

Again it is a question here not so much of either/or explanations, but of working with more complex multi-dimensional explanations which acknowledge the role of *both* psychosocial and material factors associated with discrimination and disadvantage. This includes, for example, the psychosocial distress associated with experiences of racism and racial harassment (Kai and Hedges 1999), together with feelings of identity and difference, inclusion and exclusion, which carry important implications for health. This, it seems, is particularly important at the present time, given a paradoxical 'hardening of racisms' in the context of an emerging 'ethnic diversity' (Annandale 1998: 192). What we have here, in other words, is a situation in which the shifting nature of bodies, identities, communities and nations, in the so-called 'global era', fuels new risks and opportunities, tensions and anxieties, both bloody and harmonious (Eisenstein 1994). Wilkinson's (2000b) point that reducing income differentials reduces the likelihood of discrimination or victimization of vulnerable groups – which is backed up by recent research evidence – should also be borne in mind, underlining the complexity of contemporary determinants of health.

Like class and gender, however, much of the work to date on ethnicity and health has suffered from inadequate theoretical engagement and lack of a broader understanding of debates on 'race' and ethnicity, particularly with respect to structure and identity (see, for example, Anthias 2001). Assumptions, as a consequence, all too often creep in, intentionally or not, with racist or essentialist overtones (Annandale 1998). Smaje (1996, 2000), for example, in a recent attempt to address if not resolve these difficulties (including the defence of a more complex notion of 'culture'), returns us to Bourdieu's theory of practice, the application of which, he argues, concerns the *interplay* of ethnicity as 'structure' and ethnicity as 'identity'. A pragmatic test for a 'useful' theory, Smaje claims, in keeping with the everyday sense of ethnicity, would be its ability to 'explain the concept both as a mode of identity (an affective claim by which we identify a human collectivity to which we feel a belonging, thus distinguishing "us" from "them") and as a principle of social structuring (by which ethnic collectivities enjoy differentiated access to a variety of social

BOX 3.3: ETHNICITY AND HEALTH

- In 2000–1 approximately one person in fourteen was from a minority ethnic group in Great Britain, with a younger age structure than the white population (ONS 2002: 30).

- There is evidence of excess *mortality* amongst men and women born in Africa, men born in the Indian sub-continent, and men and women born in Scotland. Stroke-related mortality too is strikingly high for men and women born in West Africa and the Caribbean. Those from the Caribbean and Pakistan also have *infant mortality rates* about double the national average (Acheson 1998: 23).

- Findings from the Fourth National Survey of Ethnic Minorities (Nazroo 1997a, 2001) – a representative survey of ethnic minority and White people living in England and Wales undertaken in 1993–4 – provide further evidence of *disadvantage* and *diversity* across many measures of *self-assessed health status*. Indian, African, Asian and Chinese respondents, for example, reported the best health across all dimensions assessed (itself broadly comparable with the white population, only being worse for diabetes). Both Pakistani/Bangladeshi and Caribbeans, in contrast, reported worse general health and had higher rates of diabetes than whites. Pakistani/Bangladeshis were also more likely than the white population to report heart disease, and Caribbean (women) were more likely to report hypertension. Within particular ethnic groups, moreover, there was a strong association between health outcomes and socio-economic position (Nazroo 1997a: 135).

- The ethnic patterning of *mental illness* is highly contentious, particularly regarding the apparently high rates of schizophrenia and other forms of psychosis amongst the African Caribbean population. Evidence also suggests low rates of mental illness amongst South Asians, but high rates of attempted suicide among young South Asian women, which is itself the source of further controversy (see Nazroo 1997b, however, for findings which only partially support this picture).

resources)' (1996: 140). In addition, of course, sociologists of health and illness must themselves pose questions concerning the possible relationship between concepts of 'ethnicity emergent from this identity–structure duality and a systematic patterning of health' (1996: 140).

Bourdieu's theory of practice, for Smaje, provides one more or less promising way forward in this respect. This is a theory, as already noted, which treats identity and structure as *dynamic* and *mutually constitutive* via associated notions of habitus, capital and field (see Chapter 2): a relationship, that is to say, involving a 'dialectic of objectification and embodiment'. In doing so, it is held, Bourdieu avoids both the 'reification of structure (objectivism) and its complete abolition (postmodernism)' (Smaje 1996: 163).[9] Instead of closing down inquiry by way of simplistic divisions such as material/cultural, or ethnicity/socio-economic status, the way is paved therefore for analysts to consider the social contexts within which ethnicity and health are framed and practised, constructed and maintained, experienced and expressed, enacted and embodied. This, Smaje stresses, is an approach which does justice to the complexities of social life. It is also one, he maintains, whilst defending culture and identity, which in no way denies the daily realities of socio-economic discrimination and racism faced by many ethnic minority groups (see also Anthias 2001).

Further important light on these structure–identity issues is provided by Nazroo (2001) in his recent work on ethnicity, class and health. One of the most consistent findings, he notes, using data from the Fourth National Survey of Ethnic Minorities (see Box 3.3), is the strong relationship between socio-economic status and health across outcomes and for each ethnic group: 'the data strongly suggest that class effects are similar for ethnic minority and white people' (2001: 156). Socio-economic differences, in other words, play a large and important role in the ethnic patterning of health. Taking account of socio-economic factors when explaining these relations, however, is far from straightforward. It is also important, Nazroo notes, to focus on other forms of disadvantage that might play some role in ethnic inequalities in health. 'The structural context of ethnicity', that is to say, 'needs to cover a number of additional issues' (2001: 160). These include a focus on: (i) the lifetime accumulation of disadvantage; (ii) living in a 'racist society'; and (iii) the 'ecological effects' of concentration in particular geographical locales which themselves are distinctive vis-à-vis those populated by the white majority (2001: 160–1). Again the *sense* of disadvantage, in *addition* to *direct* experiences of racism, is raised here, with growing evidence of its effects on health across a wide variety of outcomes for ethnic minorities (Karlsen and Nazroo 2001). This, however, Nazroo comments, may not be straightforward either: challenging racial harassment and discrimination, for example, may have more positive outcomes, on certain measures of health status at least, than internalizing anger (Nazroo 2001: 161; cf. Freund 1990, discussed earlier).

Ethnicity nonetheless, to repeat, cannot (unproblematically) be reduced to class or socio-economic position, involving much more than this, including, of course, important identity issues. Racist categorizations imposed on ethnic minorities, for example, themselves Nazroo suggests best viewed perhaps as negative 'external' definitions, are only part of the story here. Ethnicity also includes other, more *positive* elements, whereby groups establish their own (collective) identities: 'internal' definitions, in Nazroo's terms, based on notions of inclusion and belonging which provide a sense of identity and access to social (and political) resources (2001: 162). Ethnic identity, from this viewpoint, is not fixed but fluid, contextual and changeable over time. It is, moreover, Nazroo stresses, simply *one* element of identity, the significance of which is itself historically, situationally and contextually contingent. The concept of ethnic identity, then, from this standpoint, promises

> exciting new avenues to follow in the exploration of the relationship between ethnicity and health. *Ethnic identity as a source of pride and political power* provides an interesting contrast to ethnicity as a sense of discrimination and relative disadvantage, a contrast which could be of great relevance to Wilkinson's (1996) arguments on the relationship between relative deprivation and health. Indeed, there is evidence to suggest that the concentration of ethnic minority groups in particular locations is *protective to health* . . . perhaps because this allows for the development of a community with a strong ethnic identity that enhances social support and reduces the sense of alienation. Such a conception of ethnic identity also allows a contextualised culture to be brought into view. Identification with cultural traditions that may be both *harmful* and, now we can separate ethnicity from the outsiders' negative definition, *beneficial* to health, are of obvious importance to health promotion. (Nazroo 2001: 163, my emphasis)

All in all, what this amounts to, in summary, as these brief excursions into current debates on the cross-cutting axes of inequality and their 'deeper' relations suggest, is a vibrant agenda: one which takes us far beyond the limits of neo-positivist approaches, forging important new linkages (themselves albeit in need of further development) with mainstream theory along the way.

Conclusions

The conclusions to be drawn from this chapter are, I hope, easy to discern. First and foremost, contemporary (health) inequalities are complex and multi-dimensional, with increasing attention paid to their cross-cutting axes. A widening gap is indeed evident here, with Britain located around the middle of contemporary Western countries. Clearly, then, there is plenty of scope for improvement, with or without the spin of New Labour.

These complex patterns, in turn, require increasingly sophisticated forms of explanation, particularly with respect to the so-called 'challenge of the gradient'. Wilkinson's work, it has been suggested, provides *one* more or less promising *contribution* to these debates, alerting us to the role of psychosocial factors in the 'afflictions of inequality'. Emotions, as we have seen, are an important part of the equation here, shedding some promising new light on the (black box) processes linking social structure to health. This, indeed, echoing other recent work in this domain, opens the door to a more fully embodied perspective on the experience and expression of (health) inequalities across the lifecourse: one located in both time (clock/calendar, social, biographical), and space/place, itself actively taken up and embodied, which moves us far beyond micro-oriented horizons, challenging former divisions such as mind/body, nature/culture, biology/society along the way. Emotions, from this viewpoint, *qua* existentially embodied modes of being-in-the-world, provide a key index of prevailing social arrangements, equitable or otherwise, through experiences and expressions of pride and shame, anger and anxiety, fear and resentment, empowerment and disempowerment, inclusion and exclusion. Relations between ongoing health inequalities (and life-events) research, and sociological work on biography, emotions and embodiment, as this suggests, are reciprocal and mutually informing.

However, to repeat, it is a question not of *either* (neo-materialist) *or* (psychosocial) explanations here, but of working instead toward new *enhanced* and enriched approaches to the *social causation* of contemporary health inequalities, which combine elements of both – the relative play of which is itself likely to vary according to differing types of disease and disorder across the lifecourse. This, in other words, whatever Wilkinson's take on these issues, is not so much an endorsement of the *'extreme'* or *'strong'* position, as Elstad (1998) puts it, that psychosocial pathways are *decisively* important in contemporary Western societies. Instead it involves the somewhat *'weaker'* view, which allows for the *relevance* of psychosocial pathways, themselves structually caused, it should be remembered, without ruling out the direct consequences of material deprivation (Elstad 1998). Both material and psychosocial approaches, we should add, acknowledge the role of income inequality (albeit with differential weight placed upon it), thereby supporting policies which work toward greater equity (Elstad 1998).

The search for 'deeper' relations, nonetheless, continues apace, whether expressed in terms of reinvigorated (realist) class agendas, or more adequately theorized and understood approaches to gender and the ethnic patterning of health, or both for that matter, including their interrelations and intersections. This, indeed, is to be welcomed: part and parcel of an ongoing series of debates, themselves far from settled, which reconnect with mainstream agendas, not least those surrounding globalization and (disorganized) capitalism. One particularly promising future direction of research, only touched on here, concerns the tracing of various forms of *capital*, from biological to social, material to emotional, through which these very processes flow, both globally and in the (habitus-mediated) lives of each and every one of us across the biographically embodied lifecourse. This, of course, includes growing up and growing old, themselves key phases of the lifecourse, yet neglected sociological topics until quite recently. It is to these embodied matters of childhood, health and ageing, therefore, that we turn in the next chapter.

Notes

1   The Acheson Report (1998) made thirty-nine recommendations on a broad front, including both 'upstream' and 'downstream' measures designed to tackle poverty and income inequality, meet material needs, prioritize the health of families with children, and provide equitable access to effective health care. In particular, it was recommended that: (i) all policies likely to have a direct or indirect effect on health should be evaluated in terms of their impact on health inequalities; and (ii) a high priority be given to improving health and reducing health inequalities in women of childbearing age, expectant mothers and young children; and (iii) further steps should be taken to reduce income inequalities and improve the living standards of poor households.

2   See also Graham (2000b) on this point, and Wadsworth (1991, 1997) on health across the lifecourse.

3   To the extent, moreover, that the 'psychosocial' has a ring of the disembodied about it, appeals to emotion notwithstanding, it remains problematic. Hence the emphasis, if not corrective, throughout the chapter on *embodiment*.

4   For other interesting studies on these links, see Craig (1989) on goal-frustration and the onset of gastrointestinal disorders, and Andrews and House (1989) on the intriguing relationship between 'conflict over speaking out' (CSO) events and functional dysphonia (a difficulty in vocal production) in women. See also Gerhardt (1979a) for a theoretical reconstruction of the life-events paradigm.

5   See also Freund's (2001) recent analysis of bodies, disability and space, discussed in Chapter 5.

6   Debates on social capital, for example, were notably high on the agenda of the British Sociological Association Medical Sociology Group Conference in September 2001. See also Baum (2000) and Lynch et al. (2000b) discussed later in this chapter.

7   To emphasize these psychosocial factors is not of course, in keeping with the general line taken in this chapter, to deny the role of other factors or explanations. A variety of hypotheses and explanations for gender and health, in fact, are available to draw on here. Verbrugge (1985), for example, lists the following: (i) biological risks; (ii) acquired risks; (iii) psychosocial aspects of symptoms and care; (iv) health reporting behaviour; and (v) prior health care and caretaker (physician sex-role bias) as causes.

8   For a further discussion of these and related issues, see Annandale and Hunt's (2000) edited volume *Gender Inequalities in Health*, particularly the chapter by Carpenter (2000), who advances the following eight key propositions on gender and health: (i) there is a need to start from gender – rather than women – and health; (ii) the biological, social and cultural influences on male and female health are more similar than different; (iii) there is much 'structured diversity' in health experiences among women and men, as well as between them; (iv) gendered patterns of mortality and morbidity are not just a statistical artefact; (v) 'natural' and social selection play a part in gendered patterns of health; (vi) gendered patterns of health and illness are the historical product of 'social structuration'; (vii) social relations can have positive or negative health effects; and (viii) women's advantage in life expectancy is a 'mixed blessing'.

9   Bourdieu's position, nonetheless, as Smaje himself concedes, is not unproblematic. See, for example, Crossley (2001), Jenkins (1992) and Williams (1995) for various commentaries on the merits of Bourdieu's work. See also Chapter 2.

4

Children, Ageing and Health: Bodies across the Lifecourse

An adequate sociological engagement with embodiment must inevitably, at some point, confront the twin issues of growing up and growing old. Like bodies in general, however, it is only recently that a sustained sociological focus on childhood and ageing, themselves distinct bodies of literature and sub-branches of sociology, has emerged.

Studying these issues has a number of payoffs, within and beyond the sociology of health and illness. Firstly, it draws attention to the limits and (adult-centric) blind spots of past sociological scholarship and debate, helping redress and re-embody these agendas along the way. Secondly, it again throws into critical relief the need to rethink relations between the biological and the social, nature and culture, particularly in an era where technological developments render these boundaries increasingly uncertain. Thirdly, it forces us to confront, in new and challenging ways, notions of identity and agency, risk and choice, experience and expression, across the biographically embodied lifecourse. Finally, a focus on children and the vicissitudes of ageing in a changing social world underlines the sociological importance of *lifecourse* issues and their links to ongoing debates surrounding (health) inequalities.

This chapter picks up on some of these issues therefore, and the opportunity they provide for a broader series of critical reflections on current sociological scholarship and contemporary forms of embodiment in late/postmodernity. Taking the theme of childhood bodies first, a path is traced from a preliminary balance sheet of the social construction of childhood, to other more fully embodied approaches to children, health and risk across the public/private divide, including 'translation' of childhood bodies in a 'hybrid' world.[1] The remainder of the chapter, in contrast, moves us towards the other end of the lifecourse, focusing more squarely on issues of ageing, from mid-life onwards towards 'deep old age'. In doing so, both negative and positive scenarios are sketched. The very question of 'limits' again arises here: one succinctly captured in that well-worn cry 'Who wants to live for ever?'. Answers to this age-old question, as we shall see, are many and varied in these ambivalent times.

Constructing childhood: a corporeal balance sheet

Social constructionism, without doubt, has provided a powerful perspective and dominant approach within the newly emerging sociology of childhood, challenging notions of childhood as somehow 'natural' and 'unvarying'. From Ariès's (1962) pioneering historical insights into the emergence of childhood as a distinctly modern phenomenon – the mid-eighteenth century in particular, Ariès shows, was something of a watershed in the European 'birth' of childhood – through Hockey and James's (1993) insightful analysis of images and metaphors of 'growing up' and 'growing old', to other sociological attempts to construct and reconstruct childhood, children and identities (James 1993; James and Prout 1993), these various strands of constructionism can be traced.

Childhoods, from this perspective, are themselves 'relative', 'variable' and 'intentional', thereby abandoning any notion of the 'universal' child with which to engage (James et al. 1998: 28). Staged models of the 'naturally developing child' – cast within the Piagetian mould of developmental psychology – are likewise abandoned. Far from being 'passive', 'dependent' and 'vulnerable' (mere objects rather than subjects of socialization), the emphasis instead is on children's own meanings, identities and constructions, both amongst themselves and in their dealings with the adult world (James 1993). In these and other ways, constructionism has indeed advanced the sociology of childhood as a culturally and historically contingent matter.

Problems remain, nonetheless, as various commentators within the sociology of childhood have themselves come to recognize (Prout 2000a, 2000b). The bodily and material dimensions of childhood, in particular, have tended to be neglected or downplayed (lest hard-won ground be lost) in favour of the social dimensions of childhood. The result is a somewhat one-sided, disembodied or dematerialized picture of childhood, given a more or less wholesale shift from the biological to the social. Either the body is notable by its absence in such accounts, or it makes its appearance in discursive garb but little more. Here again we return to issues raised in Chapter 1 concerning the limits of social constructionism, particularly its strong variants.

Armstrong's (1983) Foucauldian rendering of children's bodies, for example, illustrates these issues well: one in which the child is constituted, nay 'invented', via the historical manoeuvrings of paediatric discourse (together with moral and educational concerns), *qua* 'object' and 'problem'. Paediatrics, he shows, which started life as a speciality concerned with diseases of children (problems located *within* the child), subsequently concerned itself with child health and development in general (problems located *around* the child). As such, it constituted a particular branch of medical power/knowledge which classified and codified, mapped and measured, fabricated and invented children's bodies, 'normal' and 'pathological' alike. As these surveillance mechanisms increased in scope and coverage in the twentieth-century, so too did the apparent 'dangers' from 'inadequately supervised' children: 'Nervous children, delicate children, neuro-pathic children, maladjusted children, over-sensitive children and unstable children were all essentially *inventions* of a new way of seeing childhood' (Armstrong 1983: 14, my emphasis). The 'battered child', the 'deprived child', the 'neglected child', the 'abused child', also appeared at this point: all again products of these latter day developments and discourses (Armstrong 1983: 59).

This, indeed, is an insightful and valuable account of the construction of childhood bodies within paediatric discourse. It does nonetheless, returning to the points raised above, relegate the body to discourse, productive or otherwise. A largely passive view of the disciplined, docile body, moreover, is again evident here: one from which the sociology of childhood is itself trying to escape. The social construction of (childhood) bodies, to repeat, has its limits therefore.

Other perspectives, in contrast, provide somewhat more promising ways forward. Prout (2000a), for example, takes up Shilling's (1993) notion of the 'unfinished' body, which itself builds on the insights of Elias (1978/1939, 1982/1934), amongst others, yet goes beyond them.[2] The emphasis here, in moving beyond a purely constructionist framework, is very much upon the socially and biologically unfinished nature of bodies at birth: bodies which change across the lifecourse through processes that are *simultaneously* biological and social, conceived in *relational* rather than additive terms. It is not, moreover, simply a question of one-way traffic here. The relationship between body and society instead is *reciprocal*, with society shaping bodies and bodies shaping society. This, Prout (2000a) suggests, despite Shilling's own adult-centric concerns, holds great potential for sociological studies of childhood, bringing the body back in, but doing so in ways which go beyond either/or frameworks. We need, in short, as this suggests, to re-embody childhood, quite literally incorporating the biological, whilst retaining the notion of children as active negotiators and constructors of their worlds. It is to various attempts to do just that, through an *embodied* focus on children, health and risk, that we now turn.

Embodied matters: children, health and risk

Our starting point here (echoing Chapter 3) is the *lived* body, a body which is mindful, active and emotional through and through, providing the very basis of our being-in-the-world and our relations with other similarly embodied actors and agents. Part and parcel of broader debates on the body and society, these embodied insights have steadily filtered through to the sociology of childhood in recent years, extending and developing them in a variety of promising ways.

An early example of these embodied concerns can be found in Allison James's (1993) work on childhood identities and the enactment of bodily difference, both at home and at school. Experience of the body, she shows, particularly bodily differences such as height, weight, gender and performance, serve as important markers of social identity, providing children with a changing series of *resources* in their relations amongst themselves and with adults. This, James stresses, involves an *active* apprehension and use of the body in the social world, forging meanings which themselves are contextually contingent. A 'big' child at nursery school, for instance, may suddenly become 'small' again on entry to primary school, thereby highlighting the shifting nature of bodily meanings and the institutional contexts within which they arise and are enacted. Revisiting these themes in her more recent work, James (2000) brings to the fore the *temporal* dimensions of these embodied matters and their skilful presentation through an emphasis on children's labour *with* and *as* their bodies. Childhood, she writes,

> is the embodiment of time . . . For particular moments in time, through combining close and careful observation with considered action, some children can make their bodies appear other than they are as a conscious strategy of action to re-represent the self . . . For other children their body work may take place at a more implicit, even unconscious level, as they learn to 'fit in' and to accommodate their bodies to different stylistic demands of the home, the school and the playground . . . in the daily, successful negotiation of the ever-changing nature of their bodies and of the self which it presents, children are exploring not only their present social relationships but also laying the groundwork for those future, more adult ones. (2000: 36, my emphasis)

Mayall (1998a, 1998b, 1996) too, in criticizing (medical) sociology for its traditional neglect of childhood, advances a number of important linkages and embodied insights. Three key issues, in this respect, emerge. Firstly, attention to issues of health and illness aids understanding of children's social positioning as a 'minority group'. Secondly, in keeping with the general thrust of this chapter, children present a clear-cut case for considering people as *embodied* health care actors. Thirdly, taking account of children within the sociology of health requires a rethinking of the division of labour and the inter-generational relationships within it (Mayall 1998a).

Let us take each of these issues in turn. The key to understanding children as a minority group, Mayall suggests, relates to the concept of *generation* and its intersections with gender. This is a concept, she suggests, which allows us to study the 'extent to which, and the ways in which childrens' lives are structured through their relationships with adults and through adult's understandings of what children are, and how their childhoods should be lived' (1998a: 274). Children's own contributions, within inter-generational relationships, to the construction of their own childhoods should, however, equally be studied. The fact that children, at one and the same time, are set 'apart' as belonging to a different generation than adults, but still must 'work towards establishing their own identities and social lives through intergenerational relationships', is therefore 'key to the development of a sociology of childhood' (1998a: 274). These generational issues, moreover, located in the 'triangle' of children, parents and the state, and inflected through gender, are further underlined by the fact that children themselves hold 'dual status' in time, as people 'now' and people 'in the future' (1998a: 275; see also Jenks's [1996] discussion of the 'futurity' of the child and Box 4.1).

The second notion, of children as embodied health care actors, takes us to the heart of the matter. Childhood, Mayall argues, provides a 'dramatic case for the study of embodied experience, for children's bodies are the critical site of their own experience and of adult interpretation and behaviour' (1998a: 276). Childhood too, of course, provides a key site for the role of emotions as 'mediators between bodies and minds' (1998a: 277; see also Mayall 1998b). A key issue here concerns the differential value placed on bodies and emotions at home and at school. It is at home, Mayall suggests, that children learn to take charge of their bodies as health care actors. At school, in contrast, adult views of children and childhood prevail, which constitute a more restrictive, less enabling context for children's own embodied competence and agency to show forth. Children, in effect, become 'socialization projects'. School routines and social policies, moreover, in conjunction with the physical condition and spatial layout of buildings, may inhibit children's enactment of health care responsibilities if not encourage 'unhealthy' choices and exposure to risks (Mayall et al. 1996). In these and in other ways, Mayall suggests, drawing upon children's own accounts in support of her case, children experience

> tensions between their bodies and minds and how each is valued; time and site are both implicated. Adults at both home and school require that children learn to juggle their own evaluations of mind and body. At home, their bodily achievements are valued only some of the time . . . children's urge to learn through physical activity meets some encouragement but sometimes rebuff from tired parents. At school children are required to subdue their bodies during class time in the interest of the academic curriculum, but they are also asked at specific times to develop their bodily skills in formal sports and are allowed to exercise their bodies out in the playground, also at pre-determined times. (1998a: 278–9)

The school and home, from this embodied vantage point, constitute contrasting social arenas for children, based on the nature and type of adult–child relations which prevail. Emotions, in turn, provide a bridge or link between the body and social order: 'children's wellbeing rests at least in part on their bodily wellbeing; and they shape their bodily activity to meet the demands of circumstances' (1998a: 280).

Here we arrive at Mayall's third key point about the division of labour. It will no longer do, she rightly argues, simply to 'sideline' children as 'socialization projects'. The study of inter-generational relationships, the reconceptualization of children as embodied social agents, together with the rhetoric and reality of children's rights, all require 'rethinking the contributions of children, women and men to the social order, and the inter-relations of their contributions' – insights which extend far beyond the sociology of health, to mainstream sociology in general (1998a: 283). Children, in short, at home and at school, are key contributors to the social order, including crucial health care, health maintenance and health promotion work, hitherto little recognized within the sociology of health and beyond.

BOX 4.1: PROFILING CHILDREN

- In 2000 there were 12.1 million children aged under 16 in the UK (with more boys than girls): a 3 per cent increase on the 11.7 million children in 1991, but fewer than the 12.5 million children in the UK in 1981.

- The majority of children grow up in a family with two parents, although this proportion had fallen from 92 per cent in 1971 to 74 per cent in 2000–1 in Great Britain.

- In 2000, 10 per cent of the population of children were from a minority ethnic group, with different patterns of family structure in different groups: 'couple families', for example, were particularly high for those of Indian and Pakistani/Bangladeshi origin (92 per cent and 81 per cent, respectively, compared to 79 per cent of dependent white children).

- Norway was the first European country to appoint an advocate for children in 1981. The Children Act (designed to promote and protect children's welfare) was passed in England and Wales in 1989. The UK also ratified the United Nations Convention on the Rights of the Child in 1991 (Botting 2002: 17; see also Alderson 2000 and Lee 2001).

(Source: ONS 2002: 17–18)

These insights find further support in a variety of other recent studies concerning children's health-related knowledge and practical activities. Backett-Milburn's (2000) study of middle class children and parents, for example, found official health promotions messages and behaviours rhetorically endorsed and practically contested, resisted and reworked, through a series of negotiations and factors within families. Children, in this context, were themselves active agents in negotiating, modifying or resisting these official health-related norms, 'carving out areas of corporeal independence for themselves which reflected the nature and demands of their own worlds' (Backett-Milburn 2000: 100). For these middle class parents and children, the 'lived experience of the body, corporeal and social, often sat uneasily alongside currently approved tenets of healthy life-styles and body maintenance', thereby revealing many 'tensions and contradictions between respondents' expressed ideals of health and bodily maintenance and their practical accomplishment' (2000: 99).

Children, as these and other studies show, are certainly knowledgeable about health-related matters, however 'partial' this may be from an official adult-centric health promotion viewpoint. Oakley and colleagues (1995), for example, in their study of health and cancer prevention, found that children (9–10 year olds) and young people (15–16 year olds) had considerable knowledge about factors contributing to 'good' and 'bad' health and about the causes and prevention of cancer. Children's perceptions of factors affecting good and bad health, moreover, were often found to integrate personal and environmental factors, thereby suggesting a 'lack of distinction between those under individual control and those stemming from living conditions' (Oakley et al. 1995). Williams and Bendelow (1998b: 2000), building on this work, conducted a detailed analysis of children's writing and drawing of the 'malignant body'. A broad range of corporeal depictions and portrayals of cancer were evident here. These included: (i) 'monstrous/ demonic' bodies, conjuring up images of dark mysterious forces of a nightmarish, Kafka-like quality; (ii) 'dys-figured/absent' bodies, including hair loss, amputations and bodily disfigurements of various kinds; (iii) 'combustible' bodies, associated with smoking and depicted through smoke and fires within the lungs and thoracic cavity; (iv) 'pathological' bodies, depicted in terms of rogue, mutating cells inside the body and/or carried in the bloodstream; and, finally, (v) 'mortal' bodies, in which coffins, tombstones, angels of death, provided the guiding scheme of imagery. Children, as this suggests, were actively involved in symbolically reordering this 'matter out of place', rehearsing and rearticulating a series of age-old images and metaphors, fears and anxieties, of fatality, contagion and blame in the process of doing so (cf. Douglas 1966, 1970; Sontag 1978).

Studies of sick children themselves provide further important insights into these matters. Bluebond-Langer (1978; Bluebond-Langer et al. 1991), for example, in a variety of (collaborative) work on children with cystic fibrosis and cancer, draws attention both to the *knowledgeability* of these children and their siblings about the stage and progression of the disease, and to the *meanings* which crystallize and coalesce around the body of the sick child across the illness trajectory (see also Burton's [1975] study of the family life of children with cystic fibrosis). Children, in such circumstances, may themselves become 'experts' of a sort, given their status as observers and commentators both on their conditions and on those of fellow sufferers: processes themselves augmented through learning the meaning of particular hospital routines, rituals and medications. There is also, as Bluebond-Langer's (1991) collaborative work on an oncology Summer Camp experience in North America shows, a considerable degree of acceptance of one another amongst those taking part in such activities and events. What for healthy children may seem stigmatizing attributes, such as hair loss and other negative effects of therapy, were translated by these participants into bodily signs and symbols of inclusion and identity, thereby reaffirming a common sense of membership and underlining the active negotiation of bodily meaning and experience. Despite concerns about developing and maintaining relationships with healthy peers, and a desire to do so, the camp experience, in other words, provided these children with 'support, understanding, encouragement, and acceptance', and an opportunity to 'learn more about their disease and its treatment' (Bluebond-Langer et al. 1991: 79).

These issues, in turn, raise related questions to do with bodily vulnerability and the 'cultural performance of sickness' in childhood (James 1998): a process, that is to say, of learning and recognition, scripting and enactment of various 'signs' and 'symptoms', through the cultural idiom of sickness, which itself provides an index of prevailing child–adult relations and forms of power, hierarchy and status (cf. Prout 1986, 1989). Christensen (1993, 2000), for example, in her ethnography of Danish primary school children, compares and contrasts adult's attribution of vulnerability to children with children's own embodied meanings, concerns and performances when everyday accidents and illnesses occur. Drawing upon Frankenberg's (1990) distinction between the *'somatic'* body (the objectified, clinical body, restricted in time and space) and the body *'incarnate'* (the permeable, subjective body as experienced), Christensen shows how adults, faced with minor childhood illnesses or everyday accidents, transform children's experiences of the body incarnate into those of the somatic body, thereby objectifying the body, fragmenting and classifying its parts, and constituting the exterior body as a shield or boundary between the body and the world (2000: 45). Plasters and bandages, for instance, act as 'substitute skin', protecting the broken surface of the child, re-establishing, toughening and hardening the surface of the body (2000: 51). Children's concerns, in contrast, lay much more with interruption of their bodily connections and relations to the social and material world, rather than the adult-centric focus on the penetration of bodily surfaces or the naming of the bodily part that hurt. Children, then, 'spoke from the perspective of the body incarnate, the body as experience, in action, involved with the environment as well as in interactions with others' (2000: 47). Calls from an injured child to 'look' in such contexts, often quite dramatically enacted, seldom met with judgement or correction from other children. Instead they were viewed as an invitation to observe and share their experience of the body, rather than a request for help of a medical or non-medical kind. Adults, on the other hand, commonly read this as a call for help, telling the 'over-dramatizing' child to make 'less fuss' if the event, on closer (somatic) inspection, turned out to be 'innocent' (2000: 51).

It is at this point that a broader series of issues arise to do with risk and identity construction amongst children and young people. Green's (1997a, 1997b) work on children's talk about accidents, for example, albeit in a less directly embodied vein,

is a case in point. Talk about accidents, she shows, is a key resource for the construction of children's social identities. Children, in their stories, claimed
responsibility for managing their own accident roles, thereby constructing both
themselves and their peers as 'mature risk assessors and managers'. The stories themselves, moreover, were used to construct gendered identities, to explore the rules and
rituals of 'appropriate' risk behaviour, and to delineate the boundaries of peer
groups. Whilst girls, for instance, were more likely to talk about their responsibilities
for others as an appropriate part of their risk assessment role and claims to competence, boys' accident stories were typically vehicles for the creation of 'courageous
risk taking' and 'physically competent' identities: accidents taken and bravely borne
(Green 1997a: 468). Rather than diminishing subjectivity, therefore, discourses of
risk can be used to construct and mobilize particular (gendered) social identities
(Green 1997a), including the pleasures of risk taking itself (Bendelow et al. 1998;
Hart and Carter 2000) and the notion of 'leisure as resistance' (Wearing et al. 1994).[3]
Compared to girls, as Prendergast and Forrest (1998) put it, boys speak 'hard', act
'hard' and ultimately, to their detriment perhaps, learn to be 'hard': a paradigm of
'proper' masculine selfhood (cf. Connell 1995) that sharply pre/proscribes forms of
behaviour, risk taking and emotional expression.

Physical education too, of course, provides another key site where bodies and
identities are constructed and displayed, if not exposed and put 'at risk'. Many girls
and boys in fact, as Kirk and Tinnings's (1994) work with Australian secondary
school children reveals, experience degrees of *disembodiment* or *estrangement* from
their bodies in physical education lessons: a site where physical culture is instanti-
ated in a most immediate, visible, visceral fashion. The problem with physical
education as a site of health promotion, from this perspective, lies in a 'failure to
understand how engagement in physical activities exposes the body and thus places
self-identity at risk' (Kirk and Tinning 1994: 621). Girls may be particularly at risk
here, as Young's insightful work *Throwing Like a Girl* (1990) suggests.[4] They are also,
Prendergast shows, forced to conceal and to be ashamed of other key bodily events
and symbolic transitions, such as menstruation, through the formal and informal
agendas of the school, including its material organization and spatial patterning
(inadequate blocked or dirty toilets), forms of discourse (teasing, name calling, and
the like), and, social interaction with boys (the raiding of school bags, for example,
and the public display of their 'stuff' to the rest of the class) – the net effect being to
'burden girls with a weighty legacy of "mindfullness"' (2000: 117). Again we confront here the fact the schools themselves, even with the best of intentions, may be
far from 'health-promoting' environments.

The argument here, to summarize, is clear. Gendered modes of embodiment, and
the forms of identity and risk taking they involve, 'healthy' or otherwise, are crucial
to the construction and negotiation of children's worlds, across the public/private
divide. Childhood, in short, may well be constructed, but this itself is both lived and
embodied through and through: an abiding theme in a world of change.

Translating childhood bodies: a 'hybrid' world?

We have covered a heterogeneous array of material on children's bodies, moving from social constructionist approaches to other, more recent attempts to fully *embody* childhood in a mindful, corporeal fashion. This, in many respects, is the current state of play in the sociology of childhood. Mention should also be made, however, of another more or less promising attempt to integrate these insights on childhood bodies, through the sociology of *translation* in general and the 'hybrid' writings of Bruno Latour (1987, 1993) in particular.[5] Prout (2000a, 2000b), for example, is a key exponent of this viewpoint, given his previously articulated concern with the limits of a purely constructionist approach to childhood. Picking up on the earlier suggestion that the 'unfinished' body holds much promise for the sociology of childhood, what we have here, Prout argues, is the appearance of childhood bodies in a variety of roles, including the 'construction of social relations, meanings and experiences' in child–child, adult–child relations, as 'products *of* and resources *for* agency, action and interaction', and as 'sites for socialization through embodiment' (2000b: 11). By emphasizing body/society relationships in this way, Prout claims, the very notion that it is possible to understand social relations without due attention to body matters and the matter of bodies is thereby undermined. What emerges, instead, is an account of children as

> *hybrids of culture and nature,* a vision that accords well with Latour's notion that social life can only be properly understood as inescapably impure, constituted in and through 'heterogeneous networks' . . . Once social life is recognized as heterogeneous, no *a priori* parcelling out of entities (people, bodies, minds, artefacts, animals, plants etc.) into culture or nature is thinkable. Amongst these both the body and childhood can be comprehended as *complex entities* in which a medley of culture and nature is given as the condition of possibility . . . The implications of this move, however, exceed either the body or childhood. It takes us towards an appreciation of all those other entities which issue from the *imbrications of culture and nature.* The social becomes a construction not only of and by humans (whether adults or children), not only of and by bodies (not to mention minds), but also of and by technologies. (Prout 2000b: 11–13, my emphasis)

An illuminating account of such hybrid worlds and Latourian issues is provided by Place (2000) in his detailed ethnography of children's bodies in intensive care. In the paediatric intensive care unit (PICU), he notes, children lie immobilized in that liminal space between life and death, thereby dramatically challenging and transforming notions of children as 'full of life'. The sociology of 'translation' or 'actor-network theory' (Callon 1986a, 1986b; Latour 1987, 1993), in this respect, provides a useful theoretical framework for the *transformations* which ensue and are sustained by staff caring for these critically ill children and their hybrid bodies. In settings such as this, Place shows, the definition of what precisely the corporeal elements of a child's body are is very much open to negotiation, given the manifold attachments of non-corporeal, technological elements, including processes of 'technodressing', which involves cannulation, intubation, catheterization and the placing of artefacts both inside and on the surface of the corporeal body (Place 2000: 175; see also Chapter 8). The contesting of such bodily boundaries, therefore, raises important questions as to the 'natural' status of children's bodies, redirecting attention instead to the notion that *heterogeneity* is the rule, including the *corporeal*, the *technological* and the *figurative*.

The skilled work that the PICU staff perform in *holding together* and *disentangling* (as required) two types of body is also highlighted here. On the one hand, we have the physical, corporeal body of the child. On the other hand, we have its conceptual analogues, which represent the corporeal body through digitalization, codes and mathematical symbols. In this liminal 'no man's land', Place shows, staff are skilled in both *combining* and *separating* these elements into human and non-human elements, as necessary: failure in either respect undermining their claims to expertise (2000: 193). What is natural and what is social, therefore,

> become blurred. It [the child's body] is neither social or natural, whilst at the same time it is *both*. The critically ill body would not exist without instruments of visualization (it would die if not visualized). It is not possible to conceptualise such a phenomenon without the attachments of artefacts in a *socio-technological imbroglio*. And yet, they *are* also separated, made to be separate social/human and technical/non-human elements. (2000: 193, my emphasis)

The sociology of 'translation', then, as the foregoing discussion suggests, helps knit the diverse elements of childhood bodies together, in ways which, at one and the same time, point to the complex relations and translations of a heterogeneous, hybrid world. Examining childhood bodies, from this latter stance, becomes a matter of 'tracing through the means, the varied array of materials and practices involved in their construction and maintenance – and in some circumstances their unravelling and disintegration' (Prout 2000b: 15).

Lee (2001) too provides another recent 'extension' of these debates through his own hybrid 'assemblage' of Deleuzo-Guattarian and Latourian borrowings. What this amounts to, he asserts, is a strategy of 'emptying "being" and multiplying "becoming"' (2001: 141): an incomplete, provisional, changeable, dynamic process, that is to say, which itself calls into question the division between nature and culture, the mature and the immature, and hence the difference between adults and children.[6] Childhood ambiguities proliferate, therefore, at one and the same time as notions of standard adulthood are problematized. Thinking of all humans, even adults, as 'incomplete becomings', Lee states,

> is certainly compatible with today's concern with flexibility, with the increasingly mediated character of society and with the tendency for the state's central control of populations to diminish. As we multiply the term 'becoming' we prepare ourselves to understand our own futures as they unfold. But if these terms are to be truly useful in analysing and, perhaps, helping to change childhoods . . . we must

not be tempted to use them as an excuse for ignoring existing realities . . . To find
that becomings are multiple or that all humans are fundamentally dependent on
extensions, is not the end of analysis, but the beginning. (2001: 117)[7]

Considering childhoods in this way, in short, raises a broader series of questions
about the lifecourse in general and adulthood in particular: issues, as we shall now
see, which have echoes and resonances with certain strands of current thinking on
the 'undoing' or 'undiscipling', if not destabilization, of ageing itself.

Ageing bodies: dilemmas and debates

The meanings of aging and old age are scattered, plural, contradictory, enigmatic.
They are confirmation that the mysteries of age have furnished the human imagination with limitless opportunities to express itself. Age is everywhere, but the
world's cultures have taught us that age has no fixed locus. (Katz 1996: 1)

We all age, of course, from birth (if not conception) to death, cradle to grave.
Currently, however, the term is most commonly applied to that part of the lifecourse
from 'midlife' (itself a fluid term) onwards into so-called 'deep old age'. As with
childhood, sociologists have been slow to engage with issues of ageing. This, however, as the following pages attest, is now being redressed by an upsurge of interest
in ageing (bodies) and the lifecourse in late/postmodernity.

Set against the backdrop of the so-called 'greying' of Western populations (see Box
4.2) and the evolution of the modern state – one in which parity in the number of
people over 60 and the number of children under 15 has now been achieved for the
very first time in Europe (Gilleard and Higgs 2000: 7–8; Phillipson 1998) – a variety of
factors account for this literal and metaphorical 'coming of age': age itself providing a
key marker of social and civic identity, conceived in more heterogeneous terms. Gilleard
and Higgs, for example, in their tellingly entitled book *Cultures of Ageing* (2000), highlight the following reasons for the 'centrality of ageing' in contemporary Western
society. Firstly, as mentioned above, more people than ever before are both reaching
retirement age and experiencing an even larger proportion of their lives as retired. The
arena of ageing, on this numerical count, is 'simply a lot larger than ever before, with
all the variety that large numbers bring' (2000: 9). Secondly, the majority of people
reaching this stage of the lifecourse, it is claimed, have 'more disposable income than
before', thus enabling a greater engagement with contemporary 'lifestyle culture'
(2000: 9; see also Kohli 1988). Thirdly, of course, the body has become a key issue
across the lifecourse, an emblem of self and the site of 'discipline' and 'release', in
health as elsewhere. Fourthly, the 'baby-boomer' generation (themselves former
shapers of post-war 'youth culture'), are now nearing retirement, thereby contesting
and/or reshaping notions of what it is to be 'old'. Finally, Gilleard and Higgs venture,
we have the 'changing nature of the contract between citizen and the state', particularly

evident in recent decades, which includes a less determinative role between the financial possibilities of retirement and the state's pension and welfare provision. This, in turn, suggests diverse patterns which point to non-state sources of income and wealth, together with the changing nature of working life (2000: 9). Changing *demographic* profiles, in short, together with a diversity of *resources*, an upsurge of interest in *body* matters in consumer culture, the *retirement* of the baby-boomer generation, and shifting *state policies*, all point to the complex and contradictory, if not contested, terrain of ageing in late/postmodernity (Gilleard and Higgs 2000).

BOX 4.2: THE 'GREYING' POPULATION

- There were 48 million people aged over 15 in the UK in 2000, of whom 23 per cent were over state pension age (currently 60 for women and 65 for men). This represented an increase in the number of people over state pension age of 18 per cent by 2000, compared to 1971, with over three times as many aged 90 in 2000 compared to 1971 (women accounting for 78 per cent of this age group) (ONS 2002: 28–9).

- The prospect of people reporting (limiting) long-standing illness rises with age. Almost half of men and women aged 75 and over in Great Britain, for example, according to current estimates, report limiting long-standing illness compared with around a tenth up to the age of 44 (ONS 2002: 120–1; see also Chapter 5, Box 5.1).

- These 'greying' trends are characteristic of other countries in the European Union (EU). In 2000, for example, 15.6 per cent of the total UK population was aged 65 and over, compared to the EU average of 16.2 per cent. The percentage of the EU population aged 65 and over has increased by more than half in fact since the 1960s, with the largest increase evident in countries such as Finland and Spain (ONS 2002: 29).

- Life expectancy at birth in the 1990–5 period was: 79.1 in Japan; 77.9 in Sweden; 77.8 in Canada; 77.4 in Greece; 75.2 in Ireland; and 67.3 in Turkey. Projected figures for 2025–30 are: 82.8 (Japan); 82.3 (Sweden); 82.2 (Canada); 81.7 (Greece); 80.6 (Ireland); and 74.8 (Turkey) (OECD 1995: Table A4, 104).

- Globally, the number of people aged 60 years or over is expected to triple by 2050, increasing from 606 million currently to 2 billion, the most marked increase being in people aged 80 and over, with an expected five-fold rise (ONS 2002: 29–30).

A burgeoning literature in sociology, social gerontology and related fields of inquiry is now in fact evident, making any adequate discussion of these perspectives and debates a book-length rather than a chapter-bound project. It is possible nonetheless, in keeping with other commentators (Bury 2000; Featherstone and Hepworth 1998), to divide this work somewhat arbitrarily into those who, broadly speaking, point to issues of *structured dependency* and *disadvantage* in old age (what may be termed '*negative ageing*'), and those who point to other, more positive *possibilities* and *prospects*, some of whom take a more *postmodern* line (hence '*positive ageing*'). These divisions, needless to say, are far from watertight, with some inevitable injustices done to particular authors and viewpoints en route. As a heuristic device, nonetheless, this has its merits. It is with these caveats and disclaimers in mind, therefore, that we proceed.

Dependency and disadvantage: 'negative ageing'

As far as old people are concerned this society is not only guilty but downright criminal. Sheltering behind myths of expansion and affluence, it treats the old as outcasts. (de Beauvoir 1972: 2)

The traditional Western view of ageing has been associated with loss, dependency and decline: a second kind of 'childishness', in Shakespeare's terms, 'sans teeth, sans eyes, sans taste, sans everything' (*As You Like It* II, vii). This, however, Hockey and James (1993) comment in their analysis of metaphors and images of 'growing up' and 'growing old', is just *one* version or vision of old age. There are indeed alternative ways of seeing and understanding these issues, with some encouraging signs that such transformations are taking place, both politically and economically (Hockey and James 1993: 5).

One particular challenge in this respect, echoing de Beauvoir's (1972) comments above, comes in the shape of what may broadly be termed political economy critiques. These critiques, as the term implies, stress the *structuring* of dependency through state and welfare policies, thereby contesting the notion of 'biology as destiny' or the inevitability of 'dependency' in old age. Key exponents of this viewpoint include scholars such as Phillipson (1982), Townsend (1981) and Walker (1980) in the UK, and Estes (1979, 1991), Estes and Minkler (1984), Myles (1984) and Olson (1982) in the US. The situation with regard to ageing, it should be stressed, is somewhat different in the UK and in the US. In the latter case, for instance, Gilleard and Higgs comment, ageing is more often associated with a period of 'relative affluence' rather than poverty, the net effect being to focus on the inequalities which exist *within* the older population and the 'intergenerational crisis' regarding the resources allocated to the retired (2000: 20; see also Katz 1996 for a critical discussion of the 'intergenerational crisis/generational equity' debate in the US).[8] Located in the context of increasing challenges to post-war visions of services/welfare to the elderly as a key element of citizenship, including the current 'pensions crisis',[9] and the limits of a biomedical view of ageing, old age for these theorists is very much a socially and politically created or constructed status. What we have here, in other words, these UK/US differences notwithstanding, is a view of ageing in which social structure, shifting economic and political relations, and the changing division of labour (including gender) are all key factors which in turn carry important implications for health and disability in later life (Phillipson 1998: 18).

Research in this vein sets out to demonstrate the extent of the health problems in later life, even when heterogeneity is recognized. Arber and Ginn (1991, 1995, 1998), for example, have done much to document these issues in the UK, in their work on gender and later life. It is essential, they argue, when studying older people, to analyse material resources such as income, assets, car ownership, housing and the quality of the home environment, and how they interrelate with the 'bodily resources of physical health and functional abilities, as well as access to personal, social and healthcare' (Arber and Ginn 1998: 144). 'Ageism', moreover, broadly defined as the socially created disadvantage or negative attitudes associated with age (Bytheway 1995), may impact on bio-ageing in at least three ways: firstly, through socio-economic disadvantages, which enhance the risks of illness, disability and death; secondly, through the internalization of negative attitudes about ageing and old age, which undermine self-confidence and expectation in dealing with the physical and social world; and, thirdly, through institutionalized ageism, which limits access to key facilities and resources which promote health and well-being, prevent disease and facilitate recovery (Gilleard and Higgs 2000: 135). Although most older people can live independently, older women are more likely to suffer from disabling conditions, which means they require help from others in the community or from state sources (Arber and Ginn 1998: 144). We need, then, to be sensitive to the relationship between 'structural inequalities and health among older people, in particular how material and social resources in later life are shaped by gender and class, and how these have been fashioned by earlier phases of their personal biography' (1998: 151).

There is, to be sure, much merit in these arguments of structured dependency and the empirical studies to back them up, challenging in the process many misplaced assumptions about ageing, and pointing to areas in which the health and quality of life of people in the later phase of the lifecourse can be improved. A number of criticisms, nonetheless, have been made of these political economy approaches, in their traditional form at least. Townsend's (1981) notion of 'structured dependency', for example, may appear somewhat 'over-deterministic'. These perspectives have also, it is argued, tended to be somewhat gender-blind: a charge, Phillipson (1998: 20) comments, which carries more weight in the UK than the US perhaps, Arber and Ginn being notable exceptions. As for the broader meanings and purposes of older people's lives, these too, it is claimed, have been neglected (Phillipson 1998: 20).

We can trace, in this respect, a shift in these writers' own concerns in recent years: one characterized more or less accurately as a transition from political economy to 'moral economy' or 'critical gerontology'. Phillipson, for example, in *Reconstructing Old Age* (1998), discusses these shifts in his and other's thinking since the publication of his previous book, *Capitalism and the Construction of Old Age* (1982). These include not simply the continuation of political economy perspectives, but also work from within the humanities (Cole et al. 1993; Moody 1992) together with the emergence of biographical and narrative perspectives in gerontology (Biggs 1999; Gubruim 1993). Taken together, these diverse intellectual trends may be seen as

> illustrating the emergence of a *critical* as opposed to traditional gerontology . . . The critical elements in this gerontology centre around three main areas: first, from political economy, there is awareness of the structural pressures and constraints affecting older people, with divisions associated with class, gender and ethnicity being emphasized . . . Second, from both a humanistic as well as a biographically orientated gerontology, there is a concern over the absences of meaning in the lives of older people, and a sense of doubt and uncertainty which is seen to pervade their daily routines and relationships. Third, from all three perspectives, comes a focus on the issues of empowerment, whether through the transformation of society (for example, through the redistribution of income and wealth) or the development of new rituals and symbols to facilitate changes through the lifecourse. (Phillipson 1998: 13–14)

Katz's (1996) work too is worthy of mention here: a Foucauldian-inspired analysis of 'disciplining old age' through gerontological knowledge which, in his own terms, contributes to and extends 'critical gerontology'. Critical gerontologists, Katz claims, echoing the above points, 'admonish gerontology for its narrow specificity, advocate stronger ties to the humanities, endorse reflexive methodologies, historicize ideological attributes of old age, promote radical engagement, and re-signify the ageing process in heterogeneous and indeterminate terms' (1996: 4). Studying the disciplinarity of gerontology, moreover, strengthens the 'critical connections between gerontology and contemporary theories of disciplinarity, subjectivity and discourse' (1996: 4). On the one hand,

> we need to critique the epistemological grounds, theoretical methods, and academic hierarchies in gerontology; on the other, we must investigate the conditions, subjects, limitations, and social technologies that make the production of gerontological knowledge possible. The aim is to go beyond an understanding of what gerontology says and grasp what gerontology does in the world. (1996: 7)

Herein lies a paradox, however, which any such analysis throws into critical relief. The realities and subjects of old age, Katz notes, 'continually confound and outpace' the experts, scientists and policy makers who seek to know them (1996: 134). An 'uncertain and unpredictable history' emerges, therefore, which takes us from the 'disciplining' to the 'undisciplining' of old age, including the disciplinary marginality and intellectual fragmentation of gerontological knowledge itself. Above all, Katz states, borrowing from Deleuze and Guattari, 'it is as "intellectual nomads", disregarding boundaries and well-worn paths, that those of us who study ageing can imaginatively reformulate our project and our epistemology' (1996: 141).

Critical gerontology, in short, drawing on these diverse strands of thought, provides the basis for exploring the changes in the social construction of ageing and the tools for illuminating the contradictions and conflicts experienced by old people in the negotiation of their day to day lives (Phillipson 1998).

(Postmodern) prospects and possibilities: 'positive ageing'

It is here at this very point, set against the backdrop of rapid social transformation and change, that the outlines of a somewhat more positive view of ageing and its possibilities can be discerned. Historical sociologists such as Laslett (1996/1989), for example, drawing on demographic patterns and forecasts, have suggested 'a fresh map of life' based on the emergence of the so-called 'Third Age' and the extension of longevity to an ever-greater proportion of the population. The key issue here, for Laslett, is the period in middle and early old age which is freed from the demands and constraints of the labour market, where 'valued goals' and 'personal fulfilment' may realistically be pursued. Laslett's 'map of life', in this respect, proceeds from the First Age of childhood dependency – itself open to criticism in the light of our preceding discussion – to the Second Age of independence (of 'earning and saving'), to a distinctive Third Age which extends to the majority of the population. The latter, Laslett stresses, may itself be experienced in many different ways within and across the lifecourse, depending on one's circumstances and attitudes – including early entry through choice or early retirement, for example, extending potentially far beyond this point. The Fourth Age, in contrast, is characterized by Laslett as 'dependence, decrepitude and death' (the equivalent perhaps of Shakespeare's 'mere oblivion'). Whilst at some point 'inevitable', entry to the Fourth Age is not, Laslett stresses, fixed. Some time around 80–5 years of age, nonetheless, is what he has in mind as a working supposition.

This view, in turn, derives, though not uncritically, from Fries's (1980, 1989) notion of the 'compression of morbidity', in which old age is likely to be accompanied by shorter periods of ill health. An optimistic stance or positive image of ageing is, therefore, clearly evident in Laslett's work. Despite reservations about Fries's predictions – particularly his claim that the number of very old persons will not increase – Laslett indeed betrays a vibrant view of body and mind, with the Third Age seen as a means of *postponing* the Fourth Age as long as possible. This precept, in short,

> lays down that the whole course of our experience, and especially the Third Age, must be so conducted by each person, in the continued activity of body and mind, *that the Fourth Age will come as late and be as brief as possible.* Evidence is certainly accumulating to support the view that some progress towards this end, both physiological and psychological, is beginning to occur. It is not indicated

unfortunately that, if final illness comes late, it is likely to be short. But much is made by experts of being energetic and staying engaged, of systematic exercise and often of a controlled diet, in preventing the condition giving rise to disabling symptoms and in extending expectation of healthy active life . . . Personal effort can and does postpone decrepitude, and makes older people better company. (1996/1989: 82, my emphasis)

Such is Laslett's viewpoint: one very much in keeping with Young and Schuller's own stance on these issues in their appropriately entitled book *Life After Work* (1991). In both cases, as Gilleard and Higgs comment, a vision can be found of a 'third age that emphasises the citizenship that pensioner status was meant to provide British older people' (2000: 38). Problems, however, are clearly evident here. The very notion of the Fourth Age as the repository of serious morbidity and disability, for example, as Laslett himself acknowledges, is hard to sustain: indeed it runs the risk of simply transferring negative views of ageing onto the 'oldest old' (Bury 2000: 94). The heterogeneity of the oldest old themselves, moreover, may mean that some aspects of the 'compression of morbidity' argument are themselves applicable to very old age (Bury and Holme 1991). This, in turn, calls into question the *inevitable* equation of age with illness or disability at some point or other in the lifecourse (Bury 2000: 94). To this, of course, we may add the arguments of the previous section on structured inequalities and social disadvantage, particularly amongst women, which deflate (if not wholly puncture) the optimistic bubble of this viewpoint.

This optimistic stance, nevertheless, extends far beyond the work of Laslett, Young and Schuller to other late or postmodern perspectives on ageing and the lifecourse, themselves, as noted earlier, finding parallels in some of the more recent (hybrid/heterogenous) approaches to children and childhoods. Gilleard and Higgs, for example, argue that ageing has become more 'complex, differentiated and ill defined, experienced from a variety of perspectives and expressed in a variety of ways at different moments in peoples' lives' (2000: 1). Ageing, they stress, is the subject of intense personal reflection and widespread public and policy debate, serving only to increase the 'contradictions it embodies'. It is indeed, we are told, this very fragmentation of a 'highly socialized biological process' which makes ageing such a key feature of our times (2000: 1). The emphasis here is very much on the role of culture in shaping the experience and expression of ageing, set in the context of broader late and postmodern concerns over identity, the body and citizenship, thereby providing a critique of those *functional* and *structural* models which continue to dominate the field of ageing studies. 'Ageing', moreover, echoing the above debates, should be distinguished from 'older age'. Old age, it seems, does not figure much in the 'plastic' or 'flexible' lifecourse of men and women in contemporary society. Instead, it acts as a kind of 'reference point around which various cultures of ageing revolve' (Gilleard and Higgs 2000: 3). In practice, of course, these cultures of ageing have their own representations of old age, thereby making any complete separation of the two unnecessary. For Gilleard and Higgs, nonetheless, it is principally by their *resistances to old age* that these cultures are shaped and defined. Whether or not they offer ways to ward off old age, shrink it to a bitter but palatable pill or prepare for it as an eventual resting place, no organizations or institutions seek to portray old age to the individual as either an aspirational commodity to choose or a socially valued process to join. Old age lies sullen and unchanging – represented as the end of the social; a point in life after which further choices are irrelevant. (2000: 4)

Further insights into these and related issues may be gleaned from the work of Featherstone and Hepworth, both singly and in combination, who have done most perhaps to move these cultural agendas of ageing forward in a postmodern vein (see also Featherstone and Wernick 1995 on 'images of ageing'). In an early, far-sighted analysis of the 'mask of ageing' and the 'postmodern lifecourse', these authors highlight the *emerging cultural tendencies* toward *de-institutionalization* and *de-differentiation* of the lifecourse, whereby less and less emphasis is placed on age-specific role transitions and scheduled identity development. As a trend for the future, it is argued, postmodern change will lead to some 'blurring of what appeared previously to be relatively clearly marked stages and the experiences and characteristic behaviour which were associated with those stages' (Featherstone and Hepworth 1991: 372). In taking this stance, Featherstone and Hepworth are nonetheless careful to avoid a view of the lifecourse in which culture is free to mould nature at will. To be an embodied person and to become a fully fledged member of society, they acknowledge, necessarily involves developmental sequences of biological growth. The point at which it is 'assumed that development is complete', however, will show 'considerable cultural variation' (Featherstone and Hepworth 1991: 375–6). This is a viewpoint, in other words – expressed more fully in Featherstone and Hepworth's (1998) most recent work – which points to new postmodern forms of 'bio-cultural destabilization'. Gilleard and Higgs too, as noted above, question any straightforwardly foundationalist notion of the biological body as the unquestionable basis or 'bottom line' in discussions of ageing, pointing instead (whilst giving biology its due) to the manifold ways in which the ageing body is culturally differentiated (2000: 131).

Located in the context of the postmodern lifecourse, the mask of ageing, for Featherstone and Hepworth, is a further sign of attempts to 'undermine traditional age-related categories' (1991: 382). In particular it draws attention to the possibility that a certain tension or distance exists between the 'external appearance of the face and body and their functional capacities, and the internal or subjective sense or experience of personal identity which are likely to become more prominent in our consciousness as we grow older' (1991: 382). Fairhurst (1998), for instance, has drawn attention to the importance of altering one's dress, behaviour and presentation of self in line with chronological age and age-related stereotypes, even if one does not *feel* one's age: a dilemma succinctly captured, for those who disregard such conventions, by the term 'mutton dressed as lamb'. This, in turn, raises some pertinent questions. To what extent, for example, are emotions 'age-specific'? Are there indeed any emotions which can *unambiguously* be identified with old age? Thomas Hardy's poignant poem 'I look into my glass', Hepworth (1998) comments, is particularly apposite in this respect: a poem, written in middle age, which perfectly conveys the disjuction felt between his ageing body and the 'still youthful "throbbings" of his heart'. This, Hepworth states, highlights both the social unacceptability of certain deeply felt emotions in later life, and the limitations of age-related stereotypes themselves. It also implies that the 'concealment of the subjective emotions behind a mask of physical ageing may itself become the focus of considerable emotional labour' (1998: 175).

Whilst the mask of ageing seems to remain the most appropriate image as far as the present generation of the elderly are concerned, however, there are signs that

> for certain sections of the population in entering *middle age* (in particular the middle classes), images and expectations are gradually beginning to change; a new language of ageing with a much greater expressive range has been gradually emerging. And the quest for a new public language to challenge and destabilise traditional cultural images of middle age for both women and men is a significant feature of the culture of mid-life as it has emerged in the West since the Second World War. (Featherstone and Hepworth 1991: 383)

It is on this basis, in short, given the cultivation of lifestyles, the salience of 'body projects', a playful, youthful 'exploratory' approach to culture, and the multi-media (hyper-real) environments and 'post-scarcity' values of postmodern society, that opportunities for 'positive ageing' and the social reconstruction of middle age are to be found. What more could one ask for?

Is this, however, we may legitimately ask, too optimistic a stance? It would certainly seem so, compared with the largely 'negative' images and 'pessimistic' scenarios of ageing presented earlier. Is it, though, a question of choosing between these accounts? Perhaps not. Bury (2000), for example, takes what appears to be an eminently sensible middle way here, arguing for a greater rapprochement between these two seemingly competing or contrasting viewpoints. Integrating these perspectives, he suggests, which to date have tended to operate in isolation from one another, requires a closer and more realistic understanding of problem-orientated research by the 'optimists' and a greater recognition of social discontinuity and change amongst the 'pessimists'. Sociological concepts of biographical continuity and disruption across the lifecourse, for instance,

> which combine attention to the influence of social and economic hardship, with a recognition of the possibilities of significant positive changes in social relations, hold out the prospect of a fruitful sociological focus. The relays between biography and history, modernity and postmodernity, and continuity and change, constitute a major vantage point for future medical sociological research on health, ageing and the lifecourse. (Bury 2000: 102–3)

Not so much 'either/or', then, as 'both/and'.

A (technological) question of 'limits': 'Who wants to live forever?'

A key issue underpinning much of this debate on ageing bodies again concerns the question of 'limits': from the (biological) limits of the human lifespan, to the (social) limits of positive and negative views of ageing, and what should be 'done' or 'undone' about ageing and death.

Debates surrounding the menopause, for instance, male and female alike, are a case in point. On the one hand, we have those advocates of 'anti-ageing' remedies such as hormone replacement therapy (HRT). This, it seems, has less to do with cessation of the menses or loss of fertility as such, than with the desire to stay 'young', to enhance sexuality, to promote a 'positive' mental attitude or outlook and to reduce the risk of disease in old age associated with post-menopausal status, such as cardiovascular problems and osteoporosis (Gilleard and Higgs 2000). For some indeed, HRT is nothing short of 'a biological revolution for women' – the very subtitle of Cooper's book *No Change* (1987). As for the male menopause, or 'andropause', as it is now known (itself the subject of much debate), there has, Gilleard and Higgs (2000) observe, been a steady increase in the number of 'anti-ageing' clinics in America offering various treatment plans for sufferers of this condition.[10] Viagra too, in Britain, has 'rapidly bypassed its role as a treatment for specific pathologies to become the means for older men to "reverse" their ageing and restore a synthetic youthful sexual performance that is widely seen as crucial to their self-esteem' (2000: 77; see also Chapter 1).

Feminist writers such as Greer (1991), on the other hand, take issue with this gung-ho, hi-tech embrace of anti-ageing remedies. Far from being a sign of inevitable decline, Greer argues, the menopause is in fact women's best chance of 'liberation', an opportunity to emerge 'chrysalis'-like from the chains of oppressive patriarchal ideologies of the ideal feminine body in which women become tools of sexual and reproductive destiny. What emerges here is an alternative vision of post-sexualized ageing, embodied and celebrated through the menopause: one, as Featherstone and Hepworth (1998: 158) note, which harks back to pre Judaeo-Christian notions of menopausal 'crone'-like women in harmony with cyclical nature (see Walker 1985, for example). Accepting the 'natural' limits of the ageing body, from this latter viewpoint, is at one and the same time to embrace and embody 'gains' rather than (simply) 'losses'.

Another clear illustration of these issues is to be found in the work of (postmodern) thinkers and writers such as Callahan (1987), Longino and Murphy (1995) and Moody (1995). All, in their different ways, have sought to place material and moral limits around society's responsibilities and obligations to the 'old'. Again what this amounts to, as Gilleard and Higgs comment, is a 'common agenda towards a greater acceptance of age and decline . . . a reduction in the level of techno-economic investment in the last year(s) of life and the need to be more mindful of the limited return from such efforts' (1998: 4.1).

The deliberate placing of limits around the delivery of health care to the very old

(Callahan 1987), replacing hi-tech treatment with the meaningful contemplation and indeed the voluntary acceptance of human finitude, is therefore a key theme in these accounts: a conferral of 'limits', that is to say, through conscious collective action and deliberate choice. For Moody, indeed, we need to recover (however difficult this might be) what, in Habermasian terms, may be seen as a 'communicative ethics' of shared discourse through free and open communication: a juxtaposition of 'freedom', that is to say, with the 'colonization of the lifeworld' in old age, the last stage of which, Moody claims, is currently 'emptied of any meaning beyond sheer biological survival' (1992: 417; see also Chapter 7). The 'biomedicalization of old age', on this count, is well and truly rejected in favour of a kind of 'late modern communicative rationality or de-radicalised postmodernity', whereby meaning is restored both to 'old age' and to 'dying' itself, *qua* human finitude (Gilleard and Higgs 1998: 4.7).

These (postmodern) viewpoints on human finitude meet their own limits, however, at one and the same time as they vindicate such concerns, in the face of those for whom various techno-futures/future technologies present themselves as more or less attractive options. Again many different strands and arguments arise here, some of which have already been touched on above. These range from various medical 'magical bullet' scenarios, *qua*, 'aspirational medicine', through the benefits of fitness, body maintenance and preventive medicine/gerontology, to other, more 'virtual' prospects and 'post-human' futures: a 'radical or ultra-modern strategy', as Gilleard and Higgs put it, which seeks to *eliminate all possible limits* to the human lifespan, redirecting the biologism of gerontology in the process towards an intimately 'plastic ageing' (1998: 5.1; see also Chapter 8).

Work proceeds apace, for example, on various drugs and medications, such as synthetic catalytic scavengers (or SCS compounds), thought capable of extending the (human) lifespan. These compounds have already been shown to work in worms, with mice too now responding to such treatments. Other research suggests that modifying a single gene in a worm can double its lifespan (Meek 2001).[11] The net effect of these and other developments, particularly in the era of the new genetics, where tinkering with our DNA is a tantalizing prospect for the anti-ageing lobby, is an erosion of the conventional belief that the maximum human lifespan is fixed at about 120 years. This, in turn, raises complex issues and debates over *quality of life* rather than *length of life*. An enhanced life-span, Meek (2001) comments, would indeed have strange consequences. *Anti-ageing drugs*, for example, could be administered from, say, age 20 onwards (once growing up was safely out of the way). This could make a '35-year-old the equivalent of a 28-year-old; at 50, you'd seem around 36; at 100, as spry as a present 63-year old' (2001: 28). It might also put heavy demands on *love*, where a fifty-year marriage these days is something of a record. What, for instance, of a '100 year *marriage*, or 150. What if one partner took anti-ageing medication and another didn't? What if friends, as well as lovers, siblings, children, aged at different rates?' What of '*multi-generational*' relations? (2001: 28).

All this, moreover, without any mention of the profound impact this would have on 'working life' as we know it today.

Other virtual scenarios and sci-fi futures equally suggest themselves. Returning to Featherstone and Hepworth, for example, models of ageing into old age, they contend, must anticipate *ever more advanced* forms of 'bio-cultural destabilization' (1998: 161). Mindful of both positive and negative views of technology, they nonetheless take issue with writers such as Greer (1991) for whom a particular cultural image of the natural body is 'reified' through a negative attitude towards technology. The potential for women to *integrate technology into their bodies* as a source of *positive* empowerment is thereby denied or dismissed. Perhaps, Featherstone and Hepworth suggest, this is because too rigid a distinction or too powerful a dichotomy between nature and culture, and too deeply suspicious an attitude towards technology, is at work here (1998: 163–4). Such a separation, it is claimed, is no longer valid. All culture is now, in effect, *technoculture,* which in turns points to the 'flexibility' and 'mutability' of the boundaries and limits of the body (1998: 164). Technology, in other words,

> should not be regarded simply as a set of tools or techniques for the efficient domination of nature, rather, technology unlocks the potential of human beings to *create new forms of constructed natures.* To make nature anew is one of the dreams of technology in the western tradition. Technology ceases to be merely tools which can be picked up and abandoned when obsolete, *technology enables human beings to reconstitute and refabricate new environments, or worlds, which they can inhabit.* (Featherstone and Hepworth 1998: 164, my emphasis)

The effects of technoculture on our perceptions of the body and the ageing process, from this viewpoint, include the potential for greater 'reflexivity' about our bodies via information technology – itself hailed as a de-professionalizing, democratizing force. Expressed more strongly, this itself harbours the potential to 'escape' from the limits of the human, fleshy, mortal body, via the anonymity of the Internet, where playful disguise or masquerade through 'computer cross-dressing' and the capacity to 'morph' are real, or, perhaps more accurately, hyper-real, possibilities (Featherstone and Hepworth 1998: 167–8; see also Featherstone and Burrows 1995). Nanotechnology too – miniaturized medicine in the making which restores/refreshes parts no other technology can reach – suggests a further breaching of the boundaries between the organic, the machine and the human, pointing yet again in this post-human direction of techno-bodies turned inside out or outside in (Featherstone and Hepworth 1998: 168; see also Featherstone, 1999; Featherstone and Burrows, 1995; and chapter 8). It is only a short step here, Featherstone and Hepworth intimate, to various other spheres of artificial life or 'post-anthropogenetic' domains in which the genetic structures of lifeforms are de-coded, replicated, manipulated and engineered to spawn new life forms (1998: 165). The prospect stretches before us, moreover, in true cyberspeak or sci-fi fashion, of a future where 'cyberminds are endlessly downloaded from outdated machines into new expectant motherboards' of 'cryofresh freaks' seeking to 'freeze time' and 'reverse history', and of 'ironic scientists' who penetrate flesh and bones to 're-order the very molecules of DNA' (Gilleard and Higgs 1998: 5.1).

The body, culture and technology, as this suggests, interpenetrate in complex ways in the late/postmodern era. The digital prospects and glittering horizons of cyberspace, moreover, compress or collapse physical space anew, transporting us beyond the confines of our current lived and embodied spaces into new 'virtual' arenas and forms of sociality and sociability – itself of no small importance for those whose mobility is currently curtailed by the physical limitations of their ageing bodies. All in all, what this amounts to, Featherstone and Hepworth argue, in keeping with their *positive*, if not unlimited, image of ageing, is a situation in which the 'singular bounded spaces of culture and the lifecourse are becoming undone' (1998: 172).

Here we return full circle to the limits of these more positive scenarios themselves, particularly some of the over-inflated claims as to the promises of cyberspace, age-related or not (see, for example, Slouka 1995; Williams 1998c). Suffice it to say, for present purposes, that debates over the very limits of ageing and the (de)merits of human finitude are likely to become increasingly heated in the technoculture of our times, particularly when the very 'book of life' has now been read, doubtless with various 'editorial' suggestions to follow. Watch this space . . .

Conclusions

We have come, in this chapter, on a rather long, if not tiring, journey through certain key aspects of the lifecourse, taking on board the cultural phasing and phrasing of both 'growing up' and 'growing old'. The literature, as we have seen, in either domain, is diverse, if not contradictory, particularly with respect to ageing. It does, nonetheless, throw into critical relief a number of important issues to do with embodiment, culture and technology, in sickness and in health: issues addressed both here and elsewhere in the book.

Whilst differences clearly exist between the situations and experiences of childhood and ageing, not to mention the literatures and debates bearing upon them, a number of commonalties are evident. First, the former 'marginalized' status of childhood and ageing is itself, quite rightly, being critically challenged on a number of fronts, connecting to key transformations in society and an upsurge of discussion and debate on these very matters within and beyond the academy. This, in turn, goes hand in hand with an emphasis, theoretical and methodological alike, on the *active* construction of childhood and ageing: a giving of 'voice', that is to say, to the hitherto 'silenced' as a counterweight to the all too easy equation of these phases of the lifecourse with vulnerability, if not dependency.

A second commonality concerns the various attempts, themselves gathering momentum, to rethink relations between mind and body, biology and society, nature and culture, reason and emotion, in ways which go beyond these former dualities. The 'unfinished' or 'translated' bodies of childhood and the 'bio-cultural destabilization' of ageing are just two examples of these trends, themselves located in new technological or 'hybrid' worlds.

The final issue, of course, already noted above, concerns an emphasis on the *life-course* itself: one which connects 'growing up' to 'growing old'. This, in turn, opens up the possibility of connecting patterns of accumulating (dis)advantage, from childhood onwards, to issues of health and illness in later life. Again, this underlines the need for greater *dialogue* between the positive and negative viewpoints on ageing identified above. It also alerts us to the importance of child health inequalities themselves, both now and for later phases of the lifecourse. Childhood, nonetheless, is a process of *being* as well as *becoming*. We should not therefore lose sight of the significant worlds they embody and inhabit in the *here and now*, passing them over in favour of a *future*-orientated, adult-centric outlook.

It is time, in short, to re-embody children as active constructors and negotiators of health, and to grapple with the contradictory cultures and prospects of ageing bodies in the twenty-first century: an era, it seems, in which the 'certainties' of growing up and growing old have themselves become ever more 'uncertain', if not 'undone'.

Notes

1   I do not therefore address in any depth or detail (except through the studies discussed) the growing body of *methodological* literature on 'researching children' (see, for example, Harden et al. 2000; Lewis and Lindsay 2000; Pole et al. 1999). Nor do I dwell on the important, yet rather more specific, empirical research on child health inequalities and their implications for health in later phases of the lifecourse. (See, for example, Wadsworth [1991, 1997] on this latter count. See also Chapter 3 for a more general discussion of inequalities in health, including time and biography.)

2   Elias's work, whilst commended for weaving biological and social processes together in a meaningful way through the *'civilizing process'* – one involving the *rationalization, socialization* and *individualization* of bodies (Shilling 1993) via the 'mannered' habitus and its 'cultivated' dispositions – is likewise critiqued for its largely *passive* portrayal of its recipients, who are very much *made* by rather than *makers* of society. What is missing, in short, is any sense of childhood as *'staged* and children as *active, creative performers'* (Prout 2000a: 116, my emphasis).

3   Smoking, for example, as Wearing et al.'s study of adolescent women suggests, may provide a pleasurable escape and a symbol of resistance to authority and the 'good girl image' both at home and at school: 'a space for females to construct one aspect of their public identity which resists passivity and compliance' (1994: 639).

4   Gendered use of the body, Young (1990) observes, manifests itself amongst girls in at least three particular ways: firstly, in a hesitance and caution that precedes action; secondly, in a *reactive* rather than *proactive* engagement with objects; and, thirdly, in a tendency to use only certain 'parts' of the body rather than putting the whole of the body behind an

action. These issues, she suggests, are perfectly illustrated through throwing and catching, which in turn she puts down to *training* and *objectification* in a 'sexist society' (1990: 153).

5   Whilst the *purifying* practice – what Latour terms the modern critical stance – creates distinct ontological zones (of the human/non-human kind), a second set of practices, by '*translation*' – which correspond to 'networks' – creates mixtures (imbroglios) between entirely new types of beings or 'quasi-objects': 'hybrids of nature and culture' (Latour 1993: 10).

6   Approaches, harking back to Chapter 1, which capture the dynamic interplay of specificity and plasticity, being and becoming, are perhaps the best way forward here (cf. Rose 1997).

7   This, in turn, leads to Lee's own formulation and defence, fruitfully or otherwise, of an 'immature sociology': one, he tells us, which has less to do with seeing the world the way children see it, and more to do with the confidence to work creatively and imaginatively in this newly developing field of inquiry, thereby avoiding the need or temptation to model work on the problem space defined by 'mainstream' sociology (2001: 3).

8   Critics of such alarmist rhetoric, Katz notes, highlight its 'neo-conservatism, pessimism and demographic determinism'. Their talk of 'economic crisis, intergenerational conflict and unaffordability of public spending', moreover, 'is unsubstantiated and implausible'. It also, Katz adds, 'victimizes' the elderly, blaming them for rising levels of poverty and taxation in the US whilst stereotyping them in the most abstract and ahistorical terms (1996: 130–4)

9   The 'pensions crisis' is due to a complex array of factors, from people living longer and saving less, to company schemes running into trouble and reductions in the value of funds through a falling stock market. Taken together, what this amounts to, according to some in the pensions industry, is a 'pensions meltdown'. The Association of British Insurers, for example, has calculated that working people are £27 billion short of the savings they need to finance their retirement (Grice 2002). This, in turn, has prompted talk within New Labour, at the time of writing, of a move, however unpopular, toward compulsory pension contributions by people not in company or personal schemes – a move, it is reported, which some ministers see as highly likely given that the Government's decision to 'top up' the basic state pension for the poorest pensioners will prove 'impossibly expensive' in the long run if today's workers do not make adequate provision for their old age (Grice 2002).

10 See also Hepworth and Featherstone (1998) for a detailed discussion of the 'male menopause', Wei Leng (1996) for a 'feminist cyborg politics of menopause', and Goldstein (2000) on women's experiences of the menopause.

11 It is not, however, clear that such results will be consistent across species. Thanks to Sharon Boden for this point.

5

Bodily *Dys*-order: Chronic Illness as Biographical Disruption?

Much has been written over the years on the sociological theme of chronic illness as 'biographical disruption'. Bury, in particular, has been a key figure here, his classic formulation of these issues in the early eighties, in conjunction with the work of American writers such as Strauss and Zola, marking a decisive step forward, not simply for the sociology of chronic illness, but for the sociology of health and illness in general. It is useful, however, from time to time, to take stock of such tried and trusted concepts, lest they fall into unreflexive usage with little or no prospect of further theoretical elaboration or empirical development. Just how useful a concept is biographical disruption, for instance, given the diversity of experience which characterizes chronic illness and disability in contemporary Western society? Are we talking here of chronic illness as biographical disruption, biographical disruption as chronic illness, or both? Might biographical disruption itself, moreover, on a more speculative note, be a more or less pervasive feature of life and living in conditions of late modernity, where reflexivity and risk mean few (if any) of us can take our bodies/selves for granted? These are some of the questions this chapter seeks to address, if not answer.

A few caveats and disclaimers, nonetheless, are in order at the outset, lest the purpose and intent of this chapter be misconstrued. Firstly, a distinction clearly needs to be drawn, in raising such questions, between the role of biographical disruption as an *explanatory concept*, on the one hand, and its status as an *empirical datum*, on the other. The usefulness of the concept, from this viewpoint, lies in what it can illuminate, theoretically speaking, about chronic illness, something which is not necessarily undermined by evidence as to the *limiting conditions* of its application. Limiting conditions, nonetheless, are important to flag up. So too are some of the theoretical assumptions upon which the very concept rests. Secondly, far from simply *augmenting* a (modernist) concern with biographical disruption, recent interest in embodiment – alongside broader postmodern and post-structuralist critiques – also entails a critical questioning of *what* the concept itself explains (the very *conditions*, that is to say, for any such reassessment, radical or otherwise).[1] The chapter, in this sense, forms part of this broader critique, albeit one, from the latter postmodern viewpoint, which does not go 'far enough'.

What, then, does the notion of chronic illness as biographical disruption entail, and what of its fortunes within the sociology of health and illness to date?

Mapping a 'biographically uncertain' terrain

In contrast to early sociological approaches to chronic illness which drew upon Parsonian (1951) sick role theory and labelling perspectives on deviance (see Gerhardt 1989, for example), more recent approaches – stemming from the pioneering work of Strauss and Glaser (1975) in the grounded theory tradition (Glaser and Strauss 1967) – have sought to understand the *meaning* and *experience* of chronic disabling illness for both sufferers and their families. Central to these developments, particularly in the British context, has been the notion of chronic illness as a 'disruptive event' or 'critical situation' (Bury 1982).

Illness, particularly chronic illness, Bury suggests, is an experience in which the structures of everyday life, its taken-for-granted features, and the tacit stocks of knowledge upon which they rest are profoundly disrupted. Chronic illness, in this respect, 'involves a recognition of pain and suffering, possibly even death, which are normally only seen as distant possibilities or the plight of others' (1982: 169). It is in this sense a 'major kind of disruptive experience', or, in Giddens's (1979) terms, a 'critical situation'. Three aspects of this disruption, in particular, are singled out for discussion here. First, there is disruption of *taken-for-granted assumptions and behaviours*, and the breaching of commonsense boundaries. This, 'what is going on here?' stage, Bury comments, involves attention to bodily states not usually brought into consciousness and decisions about seeking help. Chronic illness, pain and suffering, in this respect, effect a transition from our normal phenomenological modes of bodily 'dis-appearance' – a body, that is to say, which 'passes us by in silence', in Sartre's (1969) terms – to a state of corporeal 'dys-appearance' (a *dys*functional appearance) (Leder 1990). 'How I suffered last night', Daudet writes in his intimate notebook *In the Land of Pain*, 'in my heel and in my ribs. Sheer torture . . . There are no words to express it, only howls of pain' (2002/1930: 15). Pain, as this suggests, becomes a form of 'bodily alienation' or 'betrayal' (Bendelow and Williams 1995; Williams 1996) which, whilst embodied through and through, may still nonetheless be depicted as the experience of 'psychophysical dualism' (Jackson 1994; Vrancken 1989), given the desire to rid ourselves of 'it', *qua* thing-like presence.

A second dimension of disruption occurs at the level of the *explanatory frameworks* normally used by people, necessitating a fundamental rethinking of the person's biography. Key questions here include those of a 'why me?', 'why now?' nature: questions which, given the 'clinical reductions' of modern medicine and the absence of any overarching metaphysical frames of reference, prove hard to answer. It is here, as we shall see below, that work concerning the narrative reconstruction of illness, and the symbolic attempt to repair ruptures between body, self and society, has provided invaluable insights into the meaning and experience of chronic illness (Hyden 1997; Williams 1984). Pain, of course, may shatter all meaning, its very meaning the absence of all meaning (Morris 1991). 'Are words', moreover, Daudet continues, 'actually of any use to describe what pain (or passion, for that matter) really feels like? Words only come when everything is over, when things have calmed down. They refer only to memory, and are either powerless or untruthful' (2002/1930: 15). The shape and weight of lived experience, nonetheless, as Daudet's own reflections amply testify, is created out of the 'dialectic between cultural category and personal signification on the one side, and the brute materiality of disordered processes on the other' (Kleinman 1988: 55).[2]

Thirdly, we have the *practical* response to this disruption, which involves the *mobilization of resources* in the face of an altered situation. The notion of biographical disruption, at this level, brings into sharp focus the meaning as well as the *setting* within which it occurs, including the resources – physical as well as social, temporal as well as financial, medical as well as cultural – available to individuals and their families in the face of their adversity. A truly sociological focus on biography, in this respect, 'suggests that meaning and context cannot be easily separated' (Bury 1991: 543).

Two types of meaning, building on these insights, coalesce around chronic illness. Firstly, the meaning of chronic illness can be viewed in terms of its practical *consequences* for individuals and their families. Here, Bury (1988) suggests, the effects of the onset of disruptive (disabling) symptoms on everyday life, both at home and at work, are brought to the fore, including the giving of time to the management of symptoms or medical regimens and the socio-economic costs associated with long-term illness (see Blaxter 1976 and Locker 1983 for example). Secondly, the meaning of chronic illness may be seen to reside in its symbolic *significance*. Different conditions, for example, carry different symbolic connotations and imagery, which vary markedly within different segments of the cultural order. This, in turn, has a profound impact upon how individuals regard themselves and how (they think) others see them. Work on the stigmatizing consequences of conditions such as epilepsy (Scambler 1989), for instance, and the identity consequences of radical surgery (Kelly 1992a, 1992b) fit well within this latter framework of symbolic meanings.

Work over the past fifteen years or so has drawn heavily on this conceptual framework, including the associated problems of *uncertainty* (such as *diagnostic* uncertainty, *symptomatic* uncertainty and *trajectory* uncertainty) which chronic illness engenders and the 'medical merry-go-round' it entails (Robinson 1988), with many elaborate rituals regarding medical regimes followed, to little or no avail (Jobling 1988). The sociology of chronic illness, however, has done more than simply document the *problems* people face. It has also paid careful attention, through its interpretative lens, to the variety of *responses* (successful or otherwise) it calls forth, and the importance of change over time. Again some useful distinctions have been drawn here by Bury (1991, 1997) in his commentary on research and prospects in the field. '*Coping*', for example is perhaps best seen, Bury argues, as a cognitive process whereby the individual learns *how* to tolerate or *put up with* the effects of chronic illness. The term, in this sense, refers to feelings of personal worth and a 'sense of coherence' or 'potency' given the biographically disruptive experience of illness. 'Normalization', as a form of coping, for instance, involves a process of 'bracketing off' the impact of illness, so that its effects on the person's self-identity remain relatively slight, or treating the illness or treatment regimen as 'normal' in order to incorporate it more fully into the person's identity and public self (Kelleher 1988). Kelly (1991, 1992a, 1992b), very much in this vein, reports on a variety of differing ways of coping with ulcerative colitis (for example, technical, *intra*- and *inter*-personal) and the effects of an ileostomy. Schneider and Conrad (1983) in the US, and Scambler (1989) in Britain, have also discussed a range of coping methods which people with epilepsy use to manage their condition. Coping, then, involves 'maintaining a sense of value and meaning in life, in spite of symptoms and their effects' (Bury 1991: 461).

'*Strategy*', in contrast, Bury suggests, directs attention to the actions people take, or *what people do* in the face of illness, rather than the meanings and attitudes they develop. The concern here is with the *strategic mobilization of resources* (the third dimension of biographical disruption mentioned above), in order to maximize favourable outcomes and to maintain a sense of hope for the future. Studies such as Weiner's (1975) on the skilful management of rheumatoid arthritis and Locker's (1983) work on the mobilization of resources to advantage, are indicative of this type of research (see also Blaxter 1976). In an earlier work (Williams 1993), building on Fagerhaugh's previous study (1975), I too highlighted the strategic dilemmas, both at home and at work, involved in 'getting about' and 'keeping up' with chronic respiratory illness. Together with the wider class distribution of these conditions and the considerable social disadvantage they may bring in their wake, what this amounts to is an implicit, if not explicit, endorsement of the World Health Organization's (1980) view of disability as an 'emergent' phenomena: one constituted at the intersection of physiological 'impairment' and the wider 'handicapping' structures of society.[3]

Finally, *style*, for Bury, refers to the way in which people respond to and present important features of their illness and treatment regimens: 'cultural repertoires' which bring into focus 'variations in the symbolic meanings, and social practices within different segments of the cultural order' (Bury 1991: 462). Radley (1989), for example, has paid particular attention to these features of illness in his work on chronic heart disease. Drawing on the earlier work of Herzlich (1973), together with his previous research into illness adjustment (Radley and Green 1987), Radley suggests that the 'bodily constraints which are resolved in the course of chronic illness need to be located in the practices and in the discourse of the people concerned' (1989: 233). This, echoing Bourdieu's (1984) insights into the class-related habitus and the struggle for distinction (see Chapter 2), is illustrated through the two contrasting adjustment modalities of '*accommodation*' and '*active-denial*'. Accommodation tends to occur when roles are more 'flexible' and where choices about how symptoms are to be presented can be developed through more 'elaborate' (middle class) forms of communication and discourse with others. 'Active-denial', in contrast, involves the adoption of a style whereby the illness is opposed through increasing engagement in everyday activities and where communication is more 'restricted' in nature (Radley 1989).

Bury's concept of biographical disruption, therefore, as the foregoing discussion suggests, has proved an abiding (foreground/background) theme within the sociology of chronic illness since the early 1980s – from the *meaning* to the *consequences* of chronic illness, and from specific styles of adjustment to the practical strategies and forms of coping it entails. It has also, through the championing of lay perspectives and experiences, served to articulate the voices and concerns of those who might not otherwise have been heard. Much of chronic illness, as Anderson and Bury's (1988) edited collection amply shows, is suffered in 'silence' behind 'closed doors' out of public view. To the extent that the sociology of chronic illness and disability has been instrumental in bringing this reality to light, it has indeed contributed much to the 'mapping' of these conditions: issues which extend far beyond the traditional biomedical remit. These 'biographically informed' perspectives, however, have come under increasing attack in recent years from a variety of quarters.

On the one hand, disability theorists and activists, in keeping with the increasing 'politicization' of disabled people since the 1960s, have advanced a range of critiques of this particular line of sociological inquiry, and/or the assumptions which underpin it. Whilst the World Health Organization's (1980) model of impairments, disabilities and handicaps, mentioned above, has implicitly, if not explicitly, underpinned much (sociological) work to date, including official surveys (see Box 5.1), writers such as Oliver (1990) reject this model in favour of an approach in which disability is seen instead as a form of 'social oppression' and a loss of 'social rights', including the prejudices and barriers which mitigate against full participation in society on equal terms (Swain et al. 1993). In endorsing notions of the *impaired* body, and associated themes such as biographical disruption, medical sociology, it is claimed, is complicit (wittingly or otherwise) in a 'medicalized' approach to disability – one which is closer to a 'personal tragedy' model than an endorsement of 'social oppression'. Disability, in short, from this viewpoint, contra the WHO and its 'allies' in medical sociology, is an outcome not of bodily pathology, but of social disadvantage and oppression, one which demands and necessitates collective action/mobilization.[4]

BOX 5.1: THE PREVALENCE OF DISABILITY AMONG ADULTS

- The Office of Population Censuses and Surveys conducted four studies of disability in Great Britain between 1985 and 1988, based on the International Classification of Impairments, Disabilities and Handicaps (ICIDH). It was estimated that there were over 6 million people with one or more disabilities – over 1 million assigned to the lowest (1) severity category and 200,000 to the highest (10) category – of whom 400,000 (or 7 per cent) were living in some kind of communal establishment. Almost 14 per cent of adults living in private households had at least one disability.

- Amongst those living in private households, the most commonly cited cause of disability was musculo-skeletal complaints, particularly arthritis. Ear and eye complaints and diseases of the circulatory system were also commonly reported. For those living in communal establishments, mental complaints, notably senile dementia, were most frequently mentioned, followed by musculo-skeletal (arthritis) and nervous system (stroke) complaints.

- The majority of adults, particularly the more severely disabled and those living in communal establishments, had more than one type of disability.

- Rates of disability, unsurprisingly, rose with age; slowly at first, then accelerating after 50, and rising very steeply after 70. Almost 70 per cent of disabled adults were aged 60 or over, and nearly half were aged 70 or over. These patterns, in turn, were gendered, with more disabled women than men.

(Source: Martin et al. 1988: xi–xii, 16–36).

On the other hand, postmodern writers such as Nicholas Fox (1993), whose views we encountered in Chapters 1 and 2, have challenged modernist readings embedded in this biographically based model of the 'suffering self'. Pain, for instance, although allegedly a 'private' or 'inner' sensation, has been problematically transformed, according to Fox, through a modernist model of the 'fabricated' human subject within the sociology of health and illness. The anatomical body is not in fact, he suggests, the 'carapace of the self'. If the self does inhabit such an 'interior' location, then this is best seen as a *consequence* of discourse. On this reading, it is 'not the self which experiences pain or attributes meaning to it, the self *is* the pain, *the self is an effect of meaning*' (Fox 1993: 145, my emphasis). Discourses on health and illness within the medical and human sciences, in other words, contribute to a particular territorialization of the 'pained' Body without Organs – a 'political locus, stratified by discourse, desire and physical sensation (including pain)' – organized in terms of the 'organism': a biomedical or biopsychosocial body with organs. The modernist focus on issues of biographical disruption, in similar fashion, serves to 'fabricate' a subject who is effectively 'trapped' within her/his 'pained' body and is required to 'adjust' or 'adapt' to the limitation this engenders. As a consequence, the effects of the disciplines of the body (including sociology) in constituting this kind of subject remain 'obscured' (Fox 1993: 146).

These critiques do indeed raise important issues for discussion and debate, including a problematization of the very assumptions underpinning much sociological research to date, biographically informed or otherwise. Problems remain, nonetheless, with both positions, not least in their treatment of the body. Whilst certain strands of postmodernism, for instance, take embodiment seriously, all too often what we are presented or left with (as noted in Chapters 1 and 2) is a peculiarly 'disembodied' form of embodiment. As for disability theorists, the main issue perhaps concerns an inadequate recognition of the *impaired* body: one bypassed in large part in favour of the social model of disability as oppression. Hughes and Paterson (1997), for instance, in their article on the social model of disability and the 'disappearing' body, highlight a number of problems and paradoxes here (see also Paterson 2001). The sociology of the body and the social model of disability, they state, appear to be moving in differing directions: the former towards and the latter away from the problem of embodiment.

> In harbouring an essentialist, natural standpoint relative to the body the social model of disability creates a conceptual barrier to the development of a sociology of impairment and creates a disembodied notion of disability . . . The distinction between disability and impairment de-medicalizes disability, but simultaneously leaves the impaired body in the exclusive jurisdiction of medical hermeneutics. While the sociology of the body seeks to challenge biomedical monopoly over knowledge about the body, the social model of disability concedes it. (Hughes and Paterson 1997: 330)

This, to be sure, is hotly contested terrain. Suffice it to say that signs of rapprochement are now beginning to appear, including an opening up of questions surrounding impairment itself. Crow (1996), for example, herself a disabled feminist who has been active in the disability movement for over a decade, has cogently argued that impairment must be brought 'back in' to the disability debate. Bury (1996) too argues for what he terms a 'relational' view of disability which focuses on the *interactions* between the individual and his or her social location. This, he stresses, addressing the disability movement's concerns, helps move policy makers away from a narrowly defined medical viewpoint (see also Kelly 1996, Pinder 1996, Williams 1996 and Williams and Busby 2000 for further variants on this theme). What is needed, in short, as Shakespeare and Erickson comment, is another model which, in going beyond either/or frameworks, takes proper account of both the *personal* and *physical* experience of disability and the *social* dimensions. It needs, too, to recognise the *psychological* processes and the cultural patterns and representations which influence the way we think about disabled people and as disabled people. These four dimensions of analysis, inextricably entwined, produce the disability phenomenon which millions of people experience every day. (2000: 195, my emphasis)[5]

A key issue here, returning to the biographically embodied themes of this chapter, concerns the connection between the *bodily* aspects of self and identity in *chronic illness*: the latter, to re-emphasize, a major cause of disability given changing demographic patterns. Social identity and self-concept, Kelly and Field (1996) note, are intimately related to the body: a physical body which, in turn, requires us to acknowledge both biological and social facts. Bodies 'change in chronic illness'. Chronic illness, *qua* biographical disruption, also involves 'changes in self-conceptions which are reciprocal to bodily experiences, feelings and actions' (Kelly and Field 1996: 247). Self, needless to say, is not 'the same as the body', nor does self exists in some 'reductionist psychologistic sense'. On the contrary, it is continually being (re)constructed, including various narratives and autobiographical experiences and self-presentations. Self, then, is linked to the body in so far as 'common-sensically self and body are experienced as one and the same thing' (Kelly and Field 1996: 245; see also Crossley 2001 on issues of *reflexive embodiment*). When bodily demands conflict with desired self-presentations, however, 'the individual becomes acutely aware of the discrepancy between body and self' (Kelly and Field 1996: 249). The interplay between self and identity, therefore, from this viewpoint, provides a 'theoretical bridge', or point of sociological purchase, on relations between biological and social facts. Biological and physical facts, in other words, are sociologically significant because: 'a) they impinge directly on self, b) they provide the signals for identity construction, and c) they act as limiting factors on social action for the sufferer' (Kelly and Field 1996: 251–2).

What, then, remains to be said about the merits of biographical disruption, both conceptually and empirically? How best might the sociology of chronic illness develop in this light? And what broader debate does this flag up at the beginning of the century? These are some of the questions and issues that we now turn to in the remainder of the chapter.

Contextualizing illness: paradoxes, pleasures and pains

Biographical disruption, as the foregoing discussion suggests, is indeed, contra its critics, a useful concept, shedding important sociological light on the nature of chronic disabling illness and the coping processes, practical strategies and symbolic styles of adjustment it calls forth. A further set of observations, nonetheless, can be made which advance the critique of biographical disruption in other, more fruitful directions, mapping new terrain and new alliances along the way.

The first of these concerns the fact that, as a concept, biographical disruption is predicated, in large part, on an *adult-centred* or *adult-centric* model of illness. The bulk of chronic illness, to be sure, strikes in the middle to later years of life, most socio-logical studies themselves tending faithfully to reproduce this picture. Biographical disruption, then, on this count, is indeed an apposite term, denoting the shift (how-ever gradual or imperceptible) from a 'normal' state of health to one of illness. In doing so, however, the whole question of conditions from birth or early childhood, including congenital abnormalities and deformities, is neglected or downplayed: conditions which, from the very start of life, are integral to an individual's bio-graphically embodied sense of self. Struggles doubtless occur *whenever* the condition emerges. Compared to socially set standards and cultural prescriptions of 'normal-ity', moreover, the lives of such individuals may appear (profoundly) disrupted. Yet it remains the case that these biographies have not, in any real or significant sense, *shifted*. Continuity rather than change remains the guiding principle, including important elements of *biographical confirmation or reinforcement* (see below). The (adult-centric) transition from health to illness, from this viewpoint, remains a prob-lematic assumption upon which much biographically oriented research to date has unquestioningly rested.

A second, more contextual issue arises here concerning a variety of so-called 'normal' crises, adult-centred or otherwise, in conditions of general adversity and material deprivation. Cornwell's *Hard-Earned Lives*, for example, documents the cheerful stoicism and pragmatism with which much illness was greeted by many East-Enders in her study, including notions of 'normal illnesses' and 'health prob-lems which are not illnesses' (1984: 130–1). Health, she shows, may indeed be a 'matter of luck', but illness, like hard work itself, is only to be *expected* (a normal part of life one might say) and not therefore to be moaned about. The 'moral prescription for a healthy life', in other words, is in fact 'a kind of cheerful stoicism, evident in the *refusal to worry, or to complain, or to be morbid*' (1984: 129, emphasis added). Biographical disruption, as this suggests, carries particular class- and age-related con-notations, as well as gender and ethnic dimensions, which remain at present under-played/under-researched.

More recent studies confirm these contentions. Pound and colleagues (1998), for example, building on Cornwell's earlier work, provide some valuable insights into the nature and experience of stroke amongst predominantly elderly working class people in the East End of London. The theme of stroke as something which was 'not that bad', they show, contrasted markedly with the commonsensical view, in lay and medical circles, that the condition 'shatters lives'. Stroke, in this respect, became a 'normal crisis', which itself made sense in the context of patterns of co-morbidity and the 'hard-earned lives' which many of these elderly East-Enders had experi-enced. Age again is a key factor here, *mediating* between the experience and response to chronic illness. By the time people have survived into their 70s, 80s and 90s, these authors suggest, their experiences may have equipped them with 'considerable skills which enable them to deal with crises and successfully adapt to new situations such as chronic illness' (Pound et al. 1998: 502). Alternatively, it may simply be that older people, particularly those from working class backgrounds, have 'lower expectations of health and may anticipate illness as *inevitable* in old age, or meet it with a greater sense of acceptance' (1998: 502; see Chapter 4 for debates on ageing and health).[6] Seen in this light, chronic illness, particularly in the context of a life-time's general hardship and adversity, may be a biographically *anticipated* or planned-for event: not so much the 'slings and arrows of outrageous fortune', but the 'normal chaos' of (everyday) life and living, including the realms of love and intimacy (Beck and Beck-Gernsheim 1995).

Bury himself, indeed, as Pound et al. acknowledge, takes up these issues of *timing* and *context* in his later work on the 'oldest old' in England today (Bury and Holme 1991; see also Bury 1997: 133–40). Most of us, it seems, Bury and Holme note, oper-ate with a definite 'social clock' which 'guides our expectations of events within the biographical context' (1991: 94; see Chapter 3). This, in turn, explains the finding, pertinent to any consideration of biographical 'disruption', of a divergence between

> subjective evaluations and objective circumstances . . . the former usually present-ing a more favourable picture than the latter would seem to warrant. People regularly suffer from pain, for example, yet look forward to the day; they are severely restricted physically, yet are never bored; their housing is deficient in amenities such as plumbing, yet it does not, it seems, worry them as they 'have been used to it all [their lives]'; even those few who, by any standards, might be considered poor are reluctant to admit to having to 'go without'. (Bury and Holme 1991: 159)

Prejudging the issue of illness as biographical disruption cannot, on these grounds, be justified (if, that is, we are to take *biography* seriously). Instead, *timing* and *context*, *norms* and *expectations*, alongside our *commitment* to events, anticipated or otherwise, are crucial to the experience of our lives, healthy or sick, and the meanings with which we endow them.

If Pound et al.'s study forces us to confront issues of biographical *continuity* in the lives of these East-Enders, and Bury and Holme's work on the oldest old drives home the point about 'social clocks' and the discrepancy between subjective evaluations and objective circumstances, then Carricaburu and Pierret's (1995) research brings into sharp focus important elements of *biographical reinforcement* as well as disrup-tion, both *individual* and *collective*, in the lives of HIV-positive haemophiliac and homosexual men. The meanings given to infection, they show, arose as these men reinterpreted their individual and collective pasts: reinterpretations which rein-forced components of identity that, prior to HIV infection, had been built around haemophilia and homosexuality, respectively. For haemophiliacs, for example, the transition to HIV-positive status simply *confirmed* a lifetime's illness experience. For homosexuals, in contrast, it served to reaffirm their struggle, both individually and collectively, personally and politically, as gay men. Biographical reinforcement rather than disruption, therefore, appeared the more apposite concept in the lives of these men. Although not identical, Carricaburu and Pierret's research builds in this respect upon the earlier work of writers such as Corbin and Strauss (1987) regarding the 'three steps' in identity work – defining and redefining the self, refocusing of direction, and integration – Charmaz's (1987) concept of the 'restored self', and Yoshida's (1993) notion of the 'pendular self' in chronic illness (particularly its 'supranormal' modality).

We must also, at this point, confront the counter-intuitive possibility that illness harbours its own promises, if not pleasures. Parsons (1951), for example, was clearly alive to these issues in his classic sociological formulation of the sick role, which highlights the *motivational* aspects of illness *qua* deviance, and the potential for *secondary gain* (see Chapter 9). Illness itself, moreover, needs locating in the context of a broader series of corporeal transgressions of which it is part. The desire to break or befuddle (corporeal) boundaries, it is clear, is not some dim and distant relic of the Rabelasian carnivalesque past (Bakhtin 1968). Nor is it solely the province of the sexually adventurous or perverse. We all indeed, in some shape, sense or form, take pleasure in the breaching of corporeal boundaries, if not the horrors of the grotesque or the lure of the excessive. These transgressions may be quite mundane, from the humble burp, fart or picking of one's nose (Goffman's 'creature comforts'), to the teenage obsession with the squeezing of spots, and the perverse pleasures of scratching/scab removal following, say, a nasty bout of chicken pox (with all the connotations of cleansing and purification this implies). The equation of pain with displeasure, likewise, is far from clear-cut; sado-masochism is merely one of many cases of these complex relations/reworkings. 'No pain, no gain', as noted in Chapter 2, is a common refrain in contemporary culture, refracted and reflected through myriad activities and events. Even when pain is distress or displeasure, moreover, the possibility remains that *expressions* of distress may themselves be more or less pleasing or pleasurable, even though the distress itself is not. (Trigg 1970). The agonies and the ecstasies of that heroic, if not erotic, depiction of Saint Sebastian provide yet another illustration of these themes: his pierced flesh a symbol of both suffering and transcendence, virtue and faith.

These observations, in turn, are buttressed, within and beyond the illness narratives literature, through testimonies of the 'heightened' or 'accentuated' state of being which illness may engender (Rose 1995), the transformations, revelations and *aesthetic* projects it entails – a 'rising to the occasion' or a form of '*exemplification*', expressing the *sublime* horrors of illness (Radley 1999) – not to mention the moral dimensions of telling and bearing witness to illness, and of being cared for by others (Frank 1995, 1997). Bodies, illness and ethics, in these and other ways, are intimately related and inextricably intertwined, opening up a variety of possibilities (see Chapter 9). Illness, from this perspective, is indeed a 'moral occasion', transforming its 'badness' into something potentially 'good', thereby attempting to rescue a valued life, distilling vital lessons en route through a process of *becoming* (Frank

1995, 1997).[7] Caution is needed here, of course, given these moral qualities and aesthetic dimensions of illness do not so much deny suffering or negate themes of biographical disruption, as actively *work with* and *transform* them. Illness, nonetheless, as this attests, is a complex affair, harbouring may possibilities, paradoxes and potential reworkings, including perhaps elements of pleasure as well as pain, gains as well as losses: part and parcel, that is, of the unfolding drama of illness and the vicissitudes of embodiment to which it speaks.

Chronic illness as biographical disruption or biographical disruption as chronic illness?

Discussion of the above issues leads to another key point. Whilst sociological accounts of illness as biographical disruption abound, biographical disruption as a *cause* of chronic illness has been less well documented, despite its implicit presence within the illness narratives literature. G.H. Williams's (1984) classic study of the genesis of illness as narrative reconstruction, for example, may be read in precisely these terms. A significant part of Bill's working life, for example, the first of Williams's three case studies, had been 'disrupted'. It was indeed shortly after assuming his 'expanded responsibilities' as a 'working gaffer' that things began to 'go wrong' (1984: 180). Bill's attachment to *workplace toxicity* as a causal factor in the genesis of his illness, in this respect, was closely related to his image of society as a place of '*exploitative relations* and power inequality' (1984: 198, my emphasis).

Gill, in contrast, Williams's second case study, located her illness in a '*web of stressful events and processes*: a genesis arising out of particular features of a woman's relationships in the modern world' (1984: 189). Accounting for her illness, in this respect, involved a 'socio-psychological' interpretation of the relationship between 'personal identity and social roles in modern society' including the contradictory demands of social being and womanhood itself (1984: 198). If *biographical disruption triggered* the illnesses of Bill and Gill, then for Betty, Williams's last respondent, these secular notions of causality were altogether irrelevant. Illness, instead, was 'necessitated and justified by reference to her intrinsic relationship to a suffering God' (1984: 198). The biographically troubling question 'why me?', from this latter stance, became a more religiously founded *theodicy* of pain centred on the question 'why not me?' For Betty, in other words, '"there is an end in it" [a *telos*] and all analytic puzzlement and personal doubt evaporate in the glare of God's purpose' (1984: 195–6).

Again we confront here the different cultural and existential meanings of illness, some of which confer a *less than disruptive gloss* on what, for others, may seem a fairly miserable, if not abject, existence. We also glimpse, as suggested earlier, the manner in which the very genesis of chronic illness may itself be narratively 'read back', legitimately or otherwise, into a set of former life crises and biographical events: factors which, not infrequently, provide a radical critique of existing social arrangements and biographical circumstances. 'Once you begin to look at causal models as narrative reconstructions of the genesis of illness experience in the historical agent,' Williams ventures, 'moral or religious, and indeed political and sociological factors become central to elucidating illness experience' (1984: 197).[8]

These issues find further support in Skultans's (1999) recent analysis of illness narratives in Soviet-occupied Latvia. Such narratives, she shows, provide a powerful testimony of how life in such adverse circumstances – including the dispossession of private land, enforced (military) labour, and severe material and financial hardship – all too frequently result in illness, from neurasthenia to alcoholism. Latvian illness narratives, in this sense, as Skultans herself comments, do not simply reverse Bury's preoccupation with the biographically disruptive consequences of chronic illness. They provide a story in which the values elucidated therein stand in stark contrast, as an act of political resistance, to the dominant ideologies foisted upon Latvian people throughout the period of Soviet occupation.

The relevance of biographical disruption, as these examples indicate, extends far beyond the traditional remit and concern with the personal *consequences* or *significance* of chronic illness, providing suggestive *aetiological* links, via the emotionally expressive body, to ongoing research within the life-events (Brown and Harris 1978, 1989b) and inequalities literature (Wilkinson 1996, 2000a; see also Chapter 3). It also, moreover, resonates with certain key features of life and living in reflexive modernity: something, as we shall see below, which consolidates and complicates the picture still further.

Reflexive possibilities and problems: 'doing' chronic illness and the 'ailments' of late modernity

How, precisely, do these biographical themes mesh with the broader social transformations currently sweeping through the contemporary Western world in its late or postmodern guise? This, indeed, is an important question, with many possible answers. For Kelly and Field, for example, these very trends are seen to have had a 'potentially profound effect' on the experience of chronic illness, involving both *continuities* and *discontinuities* with the past (1998: 9). In a world of 'less determinative social structures', it is argued (including more 'flexible' patterns of work and a wide range of 'explanatory discourses'), there is the potential for the experience of chronic illness to be 'less disruptive' and 'non-normal' than in the past. The 'narrow' definition of what is and what is not 'normal', in other words, has been replaced by a recognition (if not always acceptance) of

> a range of appearances and lifestyles. That is, 'normality' itself is seen as more differentiated and relativistic, encompassing an increasingly wider range of 'differences in normality'. Thus, the assumption that chronic illness will inevitably disrupt normal patterns in a pathological manner is no longer valid, or at least its validity is a theoretical problem. (1998: 18–19)

Key advances in (medical) treatment and management, the commonplace nature of chronic conditions in everyday life, and the potential contained therein for an increasing 'tolerance' (if not celebration) of diversity and difference: these and many other factors, Kelly and Field suggest, point to a number of different options for 'doing' chronic illness in contemporary society (1998: 18). Whilst the body/self, from this perspective, is a continuing presence in this and other eras, the very nature of this 'presence' has profoundly altered in the current context. The bodily limitations and activity restrictions of chronic illness, nonetheless, Kelly and Field rightly maintain, cannot be ignored. For many people, indeed, chronic illness is still 'greatly life limiting'. Any new paradigms therefore must be able to embrace both the 'change and diversity' of contemporary society and the 'continuing physical and material bases of chronic illness' (1998: 19). At the very least, it is argued, some 'reconsideration' of the standard sociological concepts used to describe and analyse chronic illness may be required (1998: 19).

This, to be sure, is a persuasive line of argument. Let me, however, add a further (albeit speculative) dimension to these debates, one which takes us far beyond the realm of chronic illness as conventionally understood in the sociology of health and illness. What this amounts to, in effect, is the following question: is biographical disruption itself a more or less pervasive feature of life and living in late modernity, where reflexivity and risk abound? Reflexivity, Giddens (1990, 1991) suggests, becomes a *chronic*, defining feature of late modernity, something – in keeping with the 'manufactured risks' and 'uncertainties' of contemporary life and living (Beck 1992; Giddens 1994) – which involves a never-ending cycle of biographical appraisals and reappraisals, assessments and reassessments across all aspects of modern social life, including health. Bodies and selves, in this context, are continually 'problematized'. Few, if any, of us, it seems, can (wholly) take our bodies or selves for granted these days. Whether through advice books or psychotherapy, emotion work or body maintenance, health promotion or predictive medicine, television or telemedicine, our bodies and selves are continually called into question: developments which spawn their own particular ailments/pathologies ('pathologies of reflexive self-control', as Giddens [1991] puts it), from 'panic' bodies (Crawford 1994; Kroker and Kroker 1988; Lupton et al. 1995) to anorexia/bulimia nervosa (Bordo 1993; Crawford 1984; MacSween 1993; see also Chapter 2).

This, at first glance, may appear to contradict the earlier line of argument concerning the limitations of biographical disruption, particularly in the latter stages of the lifecourse where expectations surrounding health and illness may be somewhat lower and 'normal crises' loom large. This seeming paradox, however, is simply explained. Reflexivity is indeed a more or less pervasive feature of life in late modernity, implicating both body and self in its internally referential grasp. The key words here, nonetheless, are 'more or less pervasive'. Whilst these processes, as noted in Chapter 4, may well extend into the far reaches of the lifecourse, they are perhaps most readily apparent amongst certain segments of the (new) middle class, including the 'worried well', where the cult of health has reached 'unhealthy', if not obsessive, proportions. For the East-Enders in Cornwell's (1984) study, in contrast, like the 'oldest old' in Bury and Holme's (1991) research, things may indeed appear quite different.

Here we confront the limits of these 'overly reflexive' approaches themselves, ones which paint these transformations in broad brushstrokes with little attention to empirical detail. We also return to the earlier point, concerning the importance of meaning, timing and context: issues which any truly satisfactory sociological discussion of biographical disruption, reflexively grounded or not, must of necessity confront. Our bodies/selves may be more likely to *dys*-appear in conditions of late modernity – their taken-for-granted features thrown into critical relief – but this, to repeat, appears more *troublesome* and *intrusive* for some rather than others: a social patterning, in effect, of these reflexive themes in more or less predictable ways. Where, then, does this leave us as to the nature and status of biographical disruption as a 'core' concept, and what future directions of study does it signal, within and beyond the sociology of health and illness? It is to these final questions that we now turn in closing.

Conclusions

Taking Bury's notion of chronic illness as biographical disruption as our point of departure, the stance in this chapter is perhaps best described as a series of late modern *revisions* of this 'core' concept, rather than its (postmodern) deconstruction or abandonment altogether. Whilst a distinction has been drawn between the *analytical* utility of biographical disruption as a concept, and its explanatory potential as an *empirical* datum, both issues have been explored here to profitable effect. It is also important to distinguish, as noted earlier, between the continuing presence of the body/self in this and other eras, and the nature of this presence in contemporary Western society.

Biographical disruption, it has been argued, whilst containing many promising insights, neglects a range of other possibilities in which illness may already be a central part of one's biography, either from birth, early childhood or in later life, including the notion of so-called 'normal crises' (cf. Pound et al. 1998). Other important elements of *biographical continuity*, if not *reinforcement*, also suggest themselves, both individual and collective alike (cf. Carricaburu and Pierret 1995). Reference to chronic illness in blanket terms as biographical disruption, therefore, is somewhat problematic: a stereotype perhaps, which individuals may well try to distance themselves from in various ways (cf. Barbour 2001), creating further forms of social distance in the process (cf. Bury 2001). Corporeal themes of *dys*-appearance (cf. Leder 1990), to put it slightly differently, may or may not occur. To the extent, moreover, that this does arise at some primordial phenomenological level (the body appearing in a *dys*-functional way, that is to say), it may quickly be reworked in other less *dys*-orienting terms. Attention to *meaning* and *context* (themselves core features of biography according to Bury), *timing* and *purpose*, *commitment* and *expectation*, suggests that what for some may be a disruptive experience may, for others, be part and parcel of normal everyday life, particularly in circumstances of general hardship and adversity, illness-related or otherwise. The positive as well as negative dimensions of illness, perhaps even the counter-intuitive possibility of some semblance of pleasure in the face of pain, reinforce these points: part and parcel of a more complex multi-dimensional picture of illness experience.

Bury's emphasis on chronic illness *resulting in* biographical disruption may also be complemented with a focus – highlighted most clearly within the illness narratives genre – on biographical disruption as a *precipitating or engendering* (chronic) illness. This, in turn, provides a promising new bridge between the sociology of chronic illness, the sociology of emotions and ongoing research concerning the social patterning of illness and disease within the life-events and inequalities literature (see Chapter 3). Finally, in a more speculative vein, the very notion of biographical disruption has been placed in the context of the reflexive dimensions of life and living in late modernity. Whilst writers such as Kelly and Field (1998) provide a largely 'positive' reading of these trends and opportunities (in relation to the 'doing' of chronic illness), they may also, as we have seen, spawn their own particular ailments, panics and pathologies: especially amongst those body-conscious, health-obsessed segments of the socio-cultural order (see also Chapter 2).

As to future agendas, these are very much informed by the points raised above. Greater attention to the *timing, context and circumstances* within which illnesses are 'normalized' or 'problematized', for example, and the placing of these issues in a life-course perspective, provide promising avenues of future work in this area. The role of biographical disruption as an aetiological factor in the onset of chronic illness may also be profitably pursued, not simply through further narrative-based work of the kind identified above, but also through the forging of new alliances with ongoing research in the sociology of emotions, the life-events paradigm and the inequalities in health literature. Finally, at the broadest level, further empirical work is needed on the extent and impact of reflexivity itself on the 'doing' of chronic illness, and the pursuit of health in general *within* and *between* differing segments of the socio-cultural order. The future of biographically informed research, to conclude, looks promising, in health and beyond.

Notes

1   I am grateful to the anonymous reviewers of an earlier paper on these issues for drawing these points to my attention.
2   Whilst Kleinman is cited here in this connection, his work, strictly speaking, stems from anthropological rather than sociological concerns regarding 'suffering, healing and the

human condition'. Bury's work, in this respect, is one amongst many strands and influences on the recent upsurge of interest in illness narratives. See also Frank (1995) and David Morris (1998), both of whom are discussed more fully in Chapter 9.

3   The World Health Organization's (1980) International Classification of Impairments, Disabilities and Handicaps (ICIDH) defines these terms as follows: (i) *impairment*, 'any loss or abnormality of psychological, physiological or anatomical structure or function' (functional limitation); (ii) *disability*, 'any restriction or lack of ability to perform an activity in a manner or within the range considered normal for a human being' (activity restriction); and (iii) *handicap*, 'the disadvantage that limits or prevents fulfilment of a role that is normal (depending on age, sex and social and cultural factors) for that individual' (social disadvantage). As the ICIDH makes clear, the relationship between these different dimensions of *disablement* is not necessarily linear in nature. Relations between impairment, disability and handicap are indeed *mediated* at many different levels by many different factors, some better understood than others (Locker 1983).

4   There has, Barnes and Mercer comment, been an 'extraordinary expansion of self-help groups and organizations controlled and run by disabled people on a world-wide basis', including the emergence in 1981 of the British Council of Disabled People, which 'now represents 113 national and local organizations and has a membership of over 400,000 disabled individuals' (1996: 2). See also Williams and Busby (2000) for a discussion of the diverse roots and strands of the disability movement, including Zola's important influence in the US (Zola 1982, 1991).

5   See also Freund (2001), who, in keeping with these extensions and developments, attempts to show how a 'socio-materialist' approach, which locates mind-bodies in space, can contribute to the social model advanced by disability theorists. The social model he ventures, in these reworked terms, offers insights into relationships between bodies, embodied agency and the social organization of space-time (Freund 2001: 689).

6   This viewpoint, readers may note, sides more with a pessimistic than an optimistic view of ageing, as discussed in Chapter 4.

7   See, however, Bury (2001) for a critique of these 'romantic' if not 'sentimental' readings of illness.

8   Various attempts have been made to develop frameworks or typologies for analysing illness narratives. Hyden (1997), for example, usefully distinguishes between the following: (i) illness *as* narrative, in which the illness is expressed and articulated in and through narrative (illness, in a sense, is the narrative here); (ii) narrative *about* illness, in which the narrative conveys knowledge and ideas about illness (in medicine, for example); and (iii) narrative *as* illness, whereby a narrative, or insufficient narrative, generates illness (when brain injury, for instance, impairs one's ability *qua* narrator). Bury (2001) too elucidates/elaborates what he takes to be three types of narrative form: (i) *contingent narratives*, which address beliefs about the origins of disease, the proximate causes of an illness and its immediate effects on everyday life (themselves, he notes, containing 'hints' of a 'life-events' approach to illness occurrence, as suggested above); (ii) *moral narratives*, which provide accounts and help to constitute changes between the person, illness and identity, and which help to (re-)establish moral status or maintain social distance; (iii) *core narratives*, which reveal connections between lay persons' experience and deeper cultural levels of meaning attached to suffering and illness, including sub-forms such as *tragic, heroic, ironic/comic* and *regressive/progressive* narratives (Bury 2001: 268–80; see also Chapter 9 on narrative [bio]ethics).

6

Dormant/Mortal Bodies: Sleep, Death and Dying in Late/Postmodernity

How wonderful is Death
Death and his brother Sleep!
One pale as yonder wan and horned moon
With lips of lurid blue
The other glowing like the vital morn,
When throned on ocean's wave
It breathes over the world:
Yet both so passing strange and wonderful!
(Percy Bysshe Shelly,
The Daemon of the World, Part I)

This chapter takes a closer look at two further key aspects of embodiment which both, in their different ways, serve to delimit our conscious involvement in social life, at one and the same time as they confirm or, perhaps more appositely, affirm it. The first of these, the dormant corporeal matter of sleep, has surprisingly received scant attention within sociology to date. The field instead is dominated by scientific studies of sleep, including sleep disorders and their sequelae, alongside philosophical musings on sleep and dreams and psychoanalytic interpretations of the latter as the 'royal road to the unconscious', in Freud's famous phrase. Literature too abounds with references to sleep, from Shakespeare to de la Mare, Shelly to Cervantes. Yet sociology, by and large, with some notable exceptions (Aubert and White 1959a, 1959b; Schwartz 1970; Taylor 1993), has failed to (fully) grasp the significance of sleep. Reasons for this neglect include the predominant waking concerns of sociology, past and present, and the tendency to see sleep, to the degree it is considered at all, as a primarily biological, psychological or (in the case of dreams) psychoanalytic matter with little or no sociological interest. A moment's reflection, however, reveals the rich sociological significance of sleep for the functioning of society and the well-being of its members, including a considerable degree of socio-cultural training and management, learning and organization within the timespan of individuals and societies alike. Sleep is fundamental to any given society, permeating its institutions and the capacities of its embodied agents, its spatio-temporal arrangements and discursively constructed boundaries, its rituals and its mythologies. The fact that sleep is 'lived through', moreover, underlines its sociological relevance as an event we continually prepare for and rehearse, schedule and organize, as part and parcel of our normal everyday (waking) lives. It is time, in short, to wake up to the sociological significance of sleep, in health as elswhere.

The second key issue, which, in contrast to sleep, is now firmly established on the sociological agenda, concerns the related corporeal matter of death and dying in the Western world, both past and present. I use the term 'related' advisedly. Clearly sleep, death and dying are distinct bodily states which cannot (unproblematically) be conflated or equated with one another. I would not wish to imply otherwise. Bringing them together in the scope of a single chapter does, nonetheless, have its merits, providing, I hope, an instructive point of comparison and contrast. This, moreover, is no mere flight of fancy on my part. Relations between sleep and death, as we shall see, can be traced throughout the course of Western culture and history (as Shelly's poem amply testifies). Both indeed, in their different ways, point to or intimate that mysterious, 'dark', 'liminal' (cf. Van Genep 1960/1909) side of life to which we are all, *qua* embodied human beings, inescapably bound as we slip away, happily or otherwise, from the conscious (waking) demands of society. The key words to stress here, then, in this respect, are *comparison* and *contrast*, themselves suggestive if not pushed too far. Herein lies the warrant for this particular chapter and the lines of analysis which follow.

In the first part of the chapter, some basic biological issues concerning sleep are briefly considered. This, in turn, paves the way for a similarly brief discussion of the sociological significance of sleep, painted in broad brushstrokes. Debates surrounding the medicalization and/or healthicization of sleep are then taken up and addressed more fully in the third section, before moving, in the final two sections, to issues surrounding the mortal body in late/postmodernity, including the embodied dilemmas of dying in the (sequestered) space of the hospice.

What, then, of the dormant corporeal matter of sleep? It is to this very issue, without further ado, that we now turn.

What is sleep (for)? Some biological considerations

Debates as to the nature and purpose of sleep date back to the Ancient Greeks. Aristole, for example, in *Parva Naturalia* (1957), stressed the conservatory or preservative role of sleep in giving rest to the senses, its activation said to be caused through the vapours of digestion and withdrawal of blood from the brain during sleep (section III, summary 345). Despite important developments in sleep science since this time, particularly over the past forty-five years or so, sleep continues, in many ways, to be one of those great mysteries of life: something we all do, yet tricky nonetheless, for all that, to fathom or pin down precisely, let alone define. As a liminal state, somewhere between wakefulness and death, sleep involves a suspension of normal everyday consciousness which seemingly 'descends upon' or 'comes over' us, the exact moment of which is difficult, if not impossible, to consciously recall/recover in waking life. There is, Merleau-Ponty comments, a 'moment when sleep "comes"', the body itself transforming 'ideas into things, my mimicry of sleep into real sleep' (1962: 164). We may, furthermore, wake many times from sleep without knowing it, feeling strangely unrefreshed when we finally emerge from our slumber.

Sleep, to complicate things further, cannot easily or unproblematically be equated with going to bed, the taking of rest, the closing of our eyes, or even, for that matter, the dreaming of dreams. We should not forget, moreover, that a considerable amount of energy is expended in sleep, including mind shifts, transformations in brain activity, and the continuing performance of a variety of other vital functions such as heartbeat and respiration: factors which underline the complexity of sleep's hidden story. Two key factors nonetheless, Dement argues, emerge as defining criteria: first, the 'perceptual barrier' sleep erects between the conscious mind and the outside world; secondly, its more or less immediate reversibility (as opposed to the irreversibility of death) (Dement with Vaughan 2000: 7).

Underpinning these issues lies a rich pattern of movements – monitored through the scientific recording of electrical brain waves (EEGs) and landmark discoveries such as the detection of REM (rapid eye movement) in 1952[1] – from beta to alpha waves, then to theta waves, sleep spindles and K complexes, delta waves, and from there on to REM sleep, the very point at which dreaming occurs[2] and all voluntary muscles (of necessity) become paralysed given heightened brain activity. This, in turn, suggests that to view sleep in totally undifferentiated terms masks as much as it reveals about its nature, rhythms and cycles (Dement with Vaughan 2000; Hobson 1989). The total sleep cycle in fact, technically speaking, comprises four stages of non-REM (NREM), followed by a period of REM lasting approximately 20–30 minutes, with the whole cycle taking between 90 and 100 minutes to complete (Flanagan 2000: 75). An eight-hour sleep will therefore 'typically divide into six hours of repeated descent into NREM, in which a total of one to two hours will be spent in deep (delta) sleep and approximately one and one-half hours in REM sleep' (Flanagan 2000: 75).

So much then for definitions or types of sleep. How precisely does sleep occur and what is it for? The occurrence of sleep, Dement explains, involves a delicate balancing act between the wakefulness centre and signals of our brains and accumulating sleep debt. The biological sleep drive, on the one hand, operates continuously, accumulating as debt throughout our periods of wakefulness (however short or long these may be). This drive, on the other hand, is offset or opposed by a non-continuous so-called 'biological clock dependent alerting function' which maintains our wakefulness (during the 'day'): a process, taken as a whole, which occurs within a circadian rhythm (that is, daily cycle) of approximately twenty-four hours. As sleep debt accumulates during periods of wakefulness, and our biological clock dependent alerting signal becomes weaker, the more likely we are to fall asleep (Dement with Vaughan 2000).

These biological processes, in our dim and distant ancestral past, may have been more or less attuned to the natural rhythms of day and night – a process, that is to say, of light-sensitive, clock-dependent alerting during the day, and the cancelling of accumulating sleep debt during the night. Development such as the harnessing of fire and the advent of Edison's electric light bulb, however, have fundamentally altered these 'natural harmonies', for better or worse, extending our 'days' and changing, if not transcending, the limits of our 'biological clocks' and the complex 'biorhythms they regulate' (Dement with Vaughan 2000: 98–9, 131–2; see also Coren 1996; Melbin 1987).[3]

As for the effects of sleep deprivation – the longest recorded period of which amounts to some 264 hours of continuous wakefulness (Dement with Vaughan 2000) – these include varying degrees of impairment in analytical abilities, memory, perceptual and motor control. Sleep more generally, echoing Aristotle's early insights: (i) plays a variety of restorative, conservatory and building roles (Flanagan 2000); (ii) is crucial to our moods and sense of well-being; and (iii) displays a complex relation to immune function (Dement with Vaughan 2000). It also has a complex relationship with health status, including the impact of pain on sleep and the influence of sleep on pain (tolerance) (Hakki Onen et al. 2001). The higher percentage of REMing in development (which declines with age) also suggests an important role in helping build and/or strengthen brain connections – especially the visual system – that remain 'unfinished' or 'incomplete' *in utero* (Flanagan 2000: 89). These and other scientific hypotheses and insights, including the role of REM in 'stockpiling' neurotransmitters that the brain will need for the day ahead, suggest a 'credible basis for thinking that sleep serves a proper biological function' (Flanagan 2000: 91; see also Hobson 1989). We cannot it seems, currently at least, do without sleep. Nor perhaps, would we wish to do so.

These issues nonetheless, at one and the same time, highlight the fact that actual patterns of sleep cannot simply or unproblematically be *reduced* to this biological base, displaying instead considerable socio-cultural pliability or variability, scheduling and management. It is to these latter sociological themes and issues therefore that we now turn, without of course leaving the biological out altogether in doing so.

The sociological significance of sleep

The key point of departure for the sociological study of sleep, expressed succinctly, runs as follows: *when, where* and *how* we sleep are all, to a considerable degree, socio-cultural matters, including processes of social scheduling and management in our waking lives. This, in turn, is dependent on history and culture, time and place. Sleep is no mere biological given. Nor can it solely or simply be reduced to this biological base. To do so is to rule out a host of other important social, cultural and historical factors which themselves play an equally crucial role in the shaping and patterning of sleep. We have, that is to say, considerable socio-cultural discretion, for better or worse, over our sleeping patterns and arrangements. A 'doing' of sleep, in Taylor's (1993) terms, emerges here, whether this serves our biological need well or poorly; reducing, cancelling or increasing our 'sleep debt' accordingly.

Sleep, to put it more formally, is irreducible to any one domain or discourse, *arising* or *emerging* through the interplay of biological and psychological processes, environmental and structural circumstances (that is, facilitators and constraints), and socio-cultural *elaboration*, conceived in temporal/spatially bounded and embodied terms. Within this formulation, principles of *irreducibility* and *emergence* are maintained, without in any way ruling out discursive, structural or physiological factors in the process. Sleep, in short, is a complex, multi-faceted, multi-dimensional phenomena, which is irreducible to any one domain or discourse.

At stake here are a number of more specific, interrelated, sociological concerns, which themselves provide an instructive background to the health-related themes which follow. Let us take each of these issues in turn.

The 'doing' of sleep and rest – body techniques and beyond

There is, Mauss (1973/1934) reminds us in his classic essay on body techniques, no 'natural' way for the body. Instead, the very ways we *use* our bodies, including their movement and gestures, deportment and gait, tastes and values, are themselves the product of elaborate socio-cultural learning processes, revealing, at one and the same time, the deepest dispositions of the habitus at work. If this is true of body techniques in general, then it is particularly true of sleep and rest. Mauss himself, for example, recounts how war taught him to sleep 'anywhere' – on horseback, standing up in the mountains, on heaps of stones. Never, however, was he able to 'change bed without a moment's insomnia' – only on the second night, we are told, could he quickly get off to sleep (Mauss 1973/1934: 80). All sorts of different ways of sleeping, in fact, are practised around the world. Members of some societies, for instance, have nothing to sleep on except the floor, whilst others have 'instrumental assistance' of various sorts, including beds, pillows or mats. The Masai are quite accustomed to sleeping on their feet, whilst those in other parts of Africa take their rest in what, through Western eyes, may seem very peculiar positions indeed: resting in fields 'like storks', some 'on one foot', with or without a pole or stick to lean on (Mauss 1973/1934: 81).[4]

These and other observations, as we shall see below, suggest that sleep, like rest, is a socio-culturally shaped form of corporeal inactivity, particularly its *preparatory* phases and the rituals surrounding it (Schwartz 1970), which very much bears the imprint of society and the marks of culture – a process, that is to say, which, whilst actively learnt, becomes 'naturalized' in various unthinking ways.

Night-time/daytime: the temporality of sleep

An encounter with sleep, Aubert and White (1959a) observe, represents a qualitative break in time-concepts, placing a formidable social barrier between two successive 'days' and the social activities contained therein. Not only does sleep provide the opportunity for a 'fresh start', it also serves as a convenient 'temporal resource' enabling us to get more or less out of the day, depending on our particular circumstances (Aubert and White 1959a: 53). We may, for example, decide to 'burn the midnight oil' to get an important task done. Alternatively, faced with boredom and/or (in)voluntary detention of various sorts, one may choose – albeit with varying degrees of success – to 'sleep time away'. Plenty of sleep before an important event such as an exam, job interview or competitive sporting fixture may also be a wise investment of our time, as is taking to our beds when we are ill (sleep as 'nature's cure'). Practising the art of the 'catnap' may likewise prove crucial, particularly in cases such as Ellen MacArthur's solo sailing feat during the Vendée Globe event. Sleep has also, Taylor (1993) comments, become something of a 'leisure pursuit' in recent times. Asked what they intend to do with their weekends, vacations or retirement, many people apparently cite sleeping as both an 'acceptable' and 'desirable' pastime. The *meaning, purpose* and *legitimacy* of sleep time, as this suggests, vary according to the context and circumstances within which sleep occurs, as well as the characteristics and intentions of sleepers themselves (Taylor 1993: 468).

These observations on sleep and time, in turn, are buttressed in relation to the current 'assault' on darkness. Whilst night-time may still be our best time to sleep, biologically and environmentally speaking, our actual sleeping patterns, as already noted, display considerable variability given our flick-of-the-switch lighting arrangements, our heat-controlled environments, and the twenty-four-hour society we live in: developments Edison himself would no doubt approve of. Large numbers of people, to be sure, still sleep at night-time, but staying up late or working through the night is increasingly common, extending well beyond the province of the night-watchman or the shiftworker. Night, in Melbin's (1978, 1989) memorable phrase, is a 'frontier', the new frontier in fact, which society has increasingly colonized like land before it. An era is now underway, he states, in which we are replacing our cyclic community with activities that never stop. Though night-time affairs are a modest portion of contemporary life, they are increasing more than most of us imagine. Society has broken from the boundaries of daytime. Organizations no longer sleep and instead pay attention to events that happen everywhere. News networks, embassies, field units of international corporations, brokerage houses, and military bases stay in touch with their headquarters night and day. Various shifts monitor the weather, crime, political developments, trends in commodity markets . . . There is widespread factory shift work, transportation, police coverage, and use of telephones all hours. Airports, gasoline stations, hotels, restaurants, and broadcasters operate incessantly. Emergency services . . . are constantly available. Meanwhile, isolated individuals bend over books and papers on desks in their homes, watch television after midnight, or walk in the streets and listen to the night breathe. (1989: 3)[5]

Alvarez (1995) adds a further important point here. The physical conquest of 'outer darkness', he proclaims, has now given way to the gradual illumination of 'inner darkness' (the 'darkness inside the head') through disciplines such as psychoanalysis, not to mention the (electrical) impulses of sleep science. In these and other ways, the temporal dimensions of sleep, in our incandescent age, are thrown into critical relief.

The public and the private – the 'civilizing' of sleep?

Discussion of these learnt and temporal dimensions of sleep, in turn, pave the way to a consideration of the historical shaping and transformation of sleep across the public/private divide. In the Middle Ages, for example, Elias (1978/1939, 1982/1939) shows, sleep was a relatively 'public', undifferentiated, unrestrained matter (anywhere at any time).[6] The physical space within which sleep occurred, moreover, was frequently shared with (many) others. People, we are told, slept naked, whilst the sight of the fleshy human body was a common occurrence, especially in bathhouses. Erasmus, for example, in *De Civilitate Morum Puerilium* (1530), instructed his readers thus (should they happen to share a bed with a stranger at an inn on their travels): 'If you share a bed with a comrade, lie quietly, do not toss your body, for this can lay yourself bare or inconvenience your companion by pulling away the blankets' (cited in Elias 1978/1939: 161). La Selle's *Les règles de la bienséance et de la civilité chrétienne* (1729), in contrast, almost two centuries later, clearly states: 'You ought neither to undress nor go to bed in the presence of another person' – the tone becoming appreciably stronger in the later 1774 edition (Elias 1978/1939: 162). Gradually, therefore, along with other 'natural' bodily functions, sleep became increasingly privatized – garments worn in bed, for instance, were slowly introduced from the Renaissance onwards, whilst the sharing of a bed, by the eighteenth century, was quite exceptional (for the upper classes at least) – part and parcel of the long-term development of the 'civilizing process' for Elias and the rising thresholds of shame and embarrassment.

The upshot of these developments, Elias (1978/1939: 163–8) makes clear, is that the bedroom has become one of the most 'private' and 'intimate' areas of human life, and sleeping, like most other bodily functions, has increasingly shifted 'behind the scenes' of social life – issues which resonate with Giddens's (1991) notion of the 'sequestration of experience' in late modernity (see also Schwartz 1970).

It is also worth mentioning, in this connection, the manner in which sleep, or the discourse of dormancy, is used to 'civilize' or 'tame' other bodily acts and activities. It is now commonplace, for example, to describe (illicit) sexual liaisons through the 'discourse of dormancy' – 'She's sleeping with him', 'He's sleeping with her', 'They're sleeping together' (Taylor 1993). Carnal activity, in this respect, is now dressed up as corporeal inactivity, naked desire as bodily slumber. Schwartz adds a further important point here. Such terminology, he suggests, 'lifts the relationship beyond a purely physical basis and stamps it with an intimacy that cannot be claimed when the termination of the social relation coincides with the termination of its sexual component' (1970: 494). Sleeping with someone, from this viewpoint, connotes an intimacy far beyond sexual intercourse.

Death too is commonly expressed in and through the language of sleep – the 'Big Sleep', to 'rest in peace' (Taylor 1993) – in a way which transforms its finality into something altogether more liminal and less threatening. The connections between sleep and death in fact can be traced back to Greek mythology. Nyx (the goddess of Night) had many offspring, including the twin gods Hypnos and Thanatos: the gods of sleep and death, respectively, born of mother night (see also Gadamer 1996 on these relations). A discursive twist emerges here, one, it seems, which resonates with and reinforces the notion that the dead are merely slumbering passengers on the way to 'another' place, the status of which remains uncertain to us earthly mortals. Death, in other words, is 'tamed', in part, at least, through the idiom of sleep and the discourse of dormancy. We also, of course, put animals 'to sleep' when they become too old, too ill or too troublesome for their owners. This, in turn, perversely perhaps, provides a further extension to the notion of the 'doing' of sleep, highlighting both the 'active', widespread (acceptable to some) nature of this very practice, and its translation into an altogether more 'passive' register, thereby softening, humanizing or civilizing its moral and ethical dimensions in the process.[7]

The 'social patterning' of slumber – power, surveillance and the 'sleep role'

The socially prescribed and culturally patterned role of the sleeper, as these preceding points suggest, is a central one in any given society. Without these 'institutional arrangements' – given an ever more complex division of labour and specialization of functions such as ours – society would, quite simply, be impossible. Sleep and its social organization, from this sociological viewpoint, is a *functional prerequisite* of society, institutionalized in a variety of ways. We all, of course, have a basic human need and right to sleep. Today, however, in the Western world, the institutionalized role of sleeper translates a cluster of rights, duties and obligations which themselves resonate, more or less closely, with certain core features of the Parsonian 'sick role' (Parsons 1951).[8] These are as follows:

Rights

1 Freedom from noise and interference from others, except in times of emergency.

2 Exemption from normal role obligations/relinquishing of conscious (waking) involvement in society.

3 No loss of waking role status whilst asleep.

Duties/obligations

4 To sleep at night and therefore to conform to the general pattern of sleep time, unless legitimate social circumstances, such as work arrangements, dictate otherwise.

5 To sleep in a bed, or similar device, in a private place, away from public view, in proper attire (that is, pyjamas, nightdress, and so on) – the latter, however, is not an absolute requirement and is indeed increasingly flouted today.

Similar points may be ventured in relation to the institutionalized role of dreamer. Some cultures, for example, have elaborate collective rituals and symbolic practices surrounding the significance of dreams and the portents they provide (dream life, that is to say, as heavily 'socialized'). In contemporary Western times, however, dreams have become relatively 'unsocialized' events, save for the attentive probing of the psychoanalyst (Aubert and White 1959b: 4).[9]

Talk of a prototypic (Western) sleep role, in turn, raises associated questions concerning not simply the rationalization of the sleeping/waking cycle over time, but also the social patterning of sleep in relation to a broad range of socio-structural and socio-demographic factors. Amounts and patterns of sleep, for example, are known to vary across the lifecourse, from infancy to old age: itself a complex product of biological, social and cultural factors, not to mention deteriorating health status in old age (see, for instance, Blaxter 1990). Studies have also found an excess of tiredness amongst women in comparison to their male counterparts (Popay 1992; Ridsdale 1989). The same applies to class. Not only is the patterning of sleep, energy and rest likely to vary in more or less predictable ways here, mirroring inequalities in health more generally, but so too is its very definition, conceived through differences in habitus and modes of bodily hexis (see Bourdieu 1984 and Chapter 2).

Results from the 2001 'Sleep in America' poll, conducted under the auspices of the National Sleep Foundation (NSF), shed further light on these social patternings. The amount of sleep obtained during the working week, for example, was strongly related (in inverse fashion) to the number of hours worked each week: an average sleep time of 7.00 hours, with an average increase of about 45–50 minutes reported per weekend night. Sleepiness interfering with one's daily activities at least a few days a month was also found to be more common amongst females (45 per cent vs 34 per cent), those with children (50 per cent vs 32 per cent), shiftworkers (52 per cent vs 36 per cent), those with lower levels of marital satisfaction (52 per cent vs 35 per cent) and/or care-givers of a child or person who is unable to live independently (50 per cent vs 34 per cent), than amongst their counterparts (NSF 2001). Insomnia, likewise, was more common amongst females (55 per cent vs 47 per cent), shiftworkers (61 per cent vs 47 per cent), those with household incomes of $35,000 or less (57 per cent vs 46 per cent), those with children (58 per cent vs 46 per cent) and caregivers (58 per cent vs 47 per cent) (NSF 2001).

Underpinning these institutional issues and role prescriptions lie broader questions of power, surveillance and control. None of us, of course, are immune from the need to sleep. Sleep, in this regard, is no respecter of status – an 'indifferent judge between high and low', as Sir Philip Sydney put it. We do, nonetheless, have varying degrees of *discretion* over our sleep patterns and sleeping arrangements according to status, rank and authority, which in turn relates to the earlier point about the *legitimacy* of sleep time according to its context and circumstances, including the characteristics of sleepers themselves. Vulnerability and safeguards surrounding the privacy of sleep similarly vary according to these and other dimensions of social hierarchy. The Queen, for example, *may* have considerable discretion over her sleeping patterns and arrangements, enjoying a high degree of privacy with soldiers on guard to ensure a silent night. The homeless, in contrast, are not so fortunate. Certain groups of people, such as children, prisoners, hospital patients, moreover, have their sleeping as well as waking lives far more closely monitored and managed than others, for better or worse, at times and in circumstances far from their own choosing (see Schwartz 1970 for a range of insightful observations on sleep, social rank and power). From the night-watchman to the hospital nurse, the monitoring of sleep and the protection or policing of its boundaries is indeed a core feature of society: a fact succinctly captured in the title of Dement's book, taken from Shakespeare's *Hamlet* (Act II, Scene II: 289), *Some Must Watch, While Some Must Sleep* (1972). Sleep, in keeping with these observations, may also be *prescribed* or *proscribed* as a form of punishment: the sending of naughty children to bed early (even if they don't sleep), an example of the former; the withholding of sleep for purposes of interrogation or torture, an instance of the latter (one likely to wear down the most recalcitrant of individuals). These and other insights, in short, suggest that sleep itself can profitably be analysed in terms of power and status, privacy and privilege, including the observer/observed relationships within which it is located, across the social spectrum (Schwartz 1970; Taylor 1993).

The sleep industry

Meanwhile, a whole sleep and rest 'industry' has grown up, supplying us with every-thing from (sexy) nightwear and pharmacological aides, to the ultimate bed where a 'silent night' is more or less guaranteed. What we have here, it seems, is yet another prime example of the capitalist desire to 'cash in' on our lives, whether asleep or awake, including a range of sleep-related products now available on the Internet (for example, sleepnet.com's 'sleep mall' for the tired shopper). Mention should also be made of the notion of 'beauty sleep' and its commercial marketabil-ity, particularly targeted at women, in this lucrative cosmetic climate. The benefits of sleep, as this suggests, are marketed in gendered ways. Professional 'salon' cosmetic houses such as Decleor, Gatineau and Elemis, for example, heavily promote their night-time skin-care ranges through appeals to the biological functions of sleep and its effects on skin tone and condition – which include increased cellular renewal, relaxation of pores to absorb richer, more potent, more expensive, active ingredients, and so forth.[10]

The symbolic associations between sleep, sexuality and death (mentioned above) have likewise been seized upon, marketed and sold by the leisure and entertainment industries. From Walt Disney's production of *Sleeping Beauty* to Oliver Sacks' *Awakenings*, and from *Sleepless in Seattle* to *Sleeping with the Enemy* and *Nightmare on Elm Street*, dormancy itself has become a media spectacle, if not a box office hit. Jonathon Coe's recent bestseller *The House of Sleep* (1997) is another case in point. Sleep, in short, in these and other ways, is now big business within this expanding 'industry': one which spans, as we shall see below, not simply commercial interests but also therapeutic concerns through a variety of dormant expertise.

What, then, of relations between sleep, health and medicine? Has sleep, for instance, fallen prey to a creeping process of medicalization? And if so, at what cost?

Are we a 'sleep–sick' society? The latest chapter in the medicalization story?

Debates concerning the medicalization of society, as noted in Chapter 1, have raged over the years on a variety of fronts. A number of critical points, returning briefly to these debates, are important to bear in mind in this context, not least that processes of medicalization are complex, if not contradictory, occurring at differing levels, and that sociologists should therefore proceed with due caution in making any such claims. This, it was argued, includes the need for a balanced assessment of gains as well as losses, and a facing up to the limits of our own explanatory frames of refer-ence, whether or not the charge of an imperialist motive or intent cuts any ice on either side of the great dividing line. Medicalization, moreover, it will be recalled, may itself be distinguished from healthicization: the former turning the moral into the medical, the latter transforming health into the moral (Conrad 1992: 223). What, however, of sleep? To what extent is sleep the latest chapter in the medicalization and/or healthicization story? Certainly it is possible, with all due caution, to point towards a variety of evidence in support of these contentions, or, at least, to the *prospect* of their materialization in the (not too distant) future.

Sleep 'problems', according to leading sleep experts – such as William Dement (Dement with Vaughan 2000) and Stanley Coren (1996) – and the latest research findings, are an all too common occurrence in contemporary Western society: a neglected matter made all the worse for this very fact, with potentially life-threatening consequences. These 'malfunctioning sleep processes', it is claimed, can arise from 'problems in any component of the body machinery – from the biological clock; from injury, toxicity, physical illness; from work and schedule problems. Sleep disorders can last one night, a few weeks, or be lifelong . . . some are completely invisible until they become catastrophic, some could not be more visible' (Dement with Vaughan 2000: 128). Figures from the previously mentioned (NSF) 2001 'Sleep in America' Poll, for example, reveal that some 69 per cent of adults report having 'sleep problems a few nights a week or more' (a slight increase on the 1999 and 2000 figure of 62 per cent) (NSF 2001). Sleep problems, of course, come in many different shapes and sizes, defined, for NSF survey purposes, as any of the following: 'difficulty falling asleep, waking up a lot during the night, waking up too early, waking up feeling unrefreshed, snoring, restless leg syndrome or sleep apnea'.[11] Whilst many adults report such problems, however, almost one in seven according to the 2001 NSF survey, few it seems (for better or worse) have actually been diagnosed or treated. Approximately one half of adults (51 per cent), for instance, reported experiencing one or more symptoms of insomnia at least a few nights a week in the past year, yet only 6 per cent were diagnosed and far fewer were treated. Similar findings emerge for reports of sleep apnea (38 per cent) and restless leg syndrome (13 per cent), the corresponding figures being 5 per cent and 3 per cent, respectively, for diagnosis, with treatment in the 1–3 per cent range. Poor sleep, in short, 'has a price', including the 'struggle of many millions of individuals to stay alert at home, in school, on the job'. Fatigue, moreover, contributes to more than '100,000 highway crashes, causing 71,000 injuries and 1,500 deaths each year in the United States' (NSF 2001).

Further support for these contentions, and the figures to back them up, can be found elsewhere on the other side of the Atlantic. Current estimates, for example, suggest that some 10 million Britons are not getting enough sleep – around one in four adults, in fact, are thought to suffer from *chronic* lack of sleep – the consequences of which include reduced concentration, damage to the immune system and increased risks of stroke, obesity, depression and even cancer (Browne 2000). Not only this, but some 45,000 Britons die or are seriously injured through tiredness on the roads: a figure which parallels that of accidents due to too much alcohol. To this we may add the fact that 13 million prescriptions for benzodiazepine sleeping pills were issued in 1999 alone. This is on top of 'booming sales of over the counter remedies, such as Nytol, and sales of orthopaedic beds and soporific CDs' (Browne 2000: 12).

We are, Dement proclaims, in keeping with Coren (1996) and other sleep experts, a 'sleep-sick society', including the fact that half of us 'mismanage our sleep to the point where it severely affects our health and safety', and that on average 'each of us sleeps one and a half fewer hours each night than our grandparents did a century ago', thereby falling short of the 'recommended' eight hours (Dement with Vaughan 2000: 2).[12] 'Ignorance' moreover, it is argued, is the 'worst sleep disorder of them all' (Dement with Vaughan 2000: 9). Whilst developments in sleep science proceed apace – sleep medicine itself having grown into a 'mature clinical discipline with . . . skilled practitioners able to diagnose and treat a huge array of disorders' – this vast reservoir of knowledge and practice, we are told, has yet to filter through to the wider population of doctors and the public at large (Dement with Vaughan 2000: 10). Not only do doctors simply 'miss' or 'ignore' a 'veritable flood of sleep disorders', as the NSF figures attest, but people all around us, it is claimed, are 'fatigued and exhausted every day because they don't understand how to manage their sleep, betrayed by their ignorance about the mechanisms of sleep debt and the intricate biological clock that ticks away inside us' (Dement with Vaughan 2000: 3). People, from this view-point, lack the most basic information about how to manage their sleep, leading to a 'huge amount of unnecessary suffering' (Dement with Vaughan 2000: 9). The fast pace of life in our round-the-clock society, it appears, has much to answer for, with or without Edison's help. The events of 11 September 2001 likewise took their toll, in this respect, with nearly half of respondents in the 2002 NSF sleep poll reporting symptoms of insomnia in the nights immediately following the attacks – women more so than men (NSF 2002). There is, in short, a 'hidden epidemic of sleep disorders in our midst', resulting in many accidents and fatalities which could in fact be prevented: issues complicated by the lack of medical training in and attention to these matters (Dement with Vaughan 2000: 5–6).

This very condemnation, however, at one and the same time, provides a potent wake-up call or rallying cry to take sleep matters seriously across the lay/professional divide. Sleepiness, as Coren states,

is a health hazard to individuals. It may also be a danger to the general public, because of the probability that a sleepy individual might trigger a catastrophic accident such as those associated with Chernobyl, the *Exxon Valdez*, and the space shuttle *Challenger* . . . Perhaps some day society will act to do something about sleepiness. It may even come to pass that some day the person who drives or goes to work while sleepy will be viewed as being as reprehensible, dangerous or even criminally negligent as the person who drives or goes to work while drunk. If so, perhaps the rest of us can all sleep a little bit more soundly. (1996: 286–7)[13]

Terms such as sleep *problems*, sleep *disorder*, sleep *debt* and sleep *deprivation*, the reader will notice, are often used interchangeably/indiscriminately in this claims-making process. It may be useful, however, for our purposes, to distinguish between sleep *disorders*, on the one hand, and sleep *debt* or *deprivation*, on the other. Sleep disorders, to be sure, result in sleep debt or deprivation. They do nonetheless imply some recognized underlying medical condition or complaint. Sleep debt or deprivation, in contrast, has more to do with factors such as competing work and leisure commitments which interfere with or reduce/squeeze our sleep time. This enables us, as we shall see later, to link the former up, sociologically speaking, with processes of medicalization and the latter with more general processes of healthicization.[14]

Prescriptions for our so-called 'sleep-sick society', like the disorders and deprivation they claim to alleviate, come in many shapes and sizes. These range from: (i) the 'judicious usage' of sleep medications (that is, *prescription hypnotics*) for conditions such as insomnia – justified by leading authorities such as Dement, not to mention the market interests of pharmaceutical manufacturers, on the grounds that past problems of barbiturates and benzodiazepines have now, in large part, been dispensed with through a new class of safer, more effective hypnotics known as imidazopyridines (for example, Ambien) which induce sleep with 'the fewest side-effects' in most people (Dement with Vaughan 2000: 163)[15] – through (ii) *relaxation techniques, stimulus control, cognitive techniques* and *sleep state restriction*; to (iii) *alternative therapies* of various sorts (for example, hypnosis, biofeedback, acupuncture, herb and flower remedies) and *over-the-counter remedies/self-medications*. Alternative therapies, however, Dement cautions (in typical biomedical fashion), have not been 'truly tested'. Over-the-counter remedies and self-medications, likewise, get short shrift here: these, he claims, have 'no proven efficacy' and their purchase is an 'eloquent testimony' to the 'underuse of prescription hypnotics' which have 'improved a great deal over the years' (Dement with Vaughan 2000: 163).

Equally interesting, given the charge of 'ignorance' and the points about healthicization raised above, are the latest calls, cast within an educational, self-empowering mould, for basic principles of so-called '*sleep hygiene*'. People, Dement argues – in his tellingly entitled book *The Promise of Sleep: The Scientific Connection between Health, Happiness and a Good Night's Sleep* 2000) – should 'take responsibility for educating themselves about sleep', including principles and practices of sleep hygiene which need 'scheduling into' their lives in the name of health and well-being. The simple goal of 'good sleep hygiene', from this point of view,

> is to do everything possible to foster good sleep at night. Sleep hygiene includes non-psychological elements, such as avoiding caffeine before bedtime, but *many of the elements are behavioural. Keeping a regular schedule is one of the most important behaviours for healthy sleep*. A regular schedule *helps train your sleep cycle* in the same way that running at the same time every morning conditions you to prepare for exercise at that time. Sticking to a regular sleep schedule seven days a week is a sacrifice worth making if it helps you maintain peak condition throughout the week. *Consider it 'doctor's orders'*. (1999/2000: 15, emphases added)

These calls go hand in hand with the work of a range of sleep societies and organizations, including the British Sleep Society, the American Sleep Disorders Association, and various sleep websites on the Internet. Sleepnet.com, for example – established in 1995 and bearing the motto 'Everything you wanted to know about sleep but were too tired to ask' – is a website designed to link all sleep information located on the Internet so as to 'empower the public'. Currently sleepnet.com contains over 80,000 pages with more than 2 million page views per month, including information on 'sleep disorders', 'sleep links', 'forums' of various sorts, not to mention the 'sleepmall' facility with its many sleep-related products for purchase. The US National Sleep Foundation (NSF) website (www.sleepfoundation.org) – which is dedicated to improving public health and safety around sleep and sleep disorders – also provides a range of materials, activities and events, including publications, information on sleep disorders, a 'press room' facility, sleep links, together with guidelines on both sleep services and 'getting involved'.[16]

What we have here, it seems, is indeed the prospective encroachment, if not colonization, of sleep by various forms of expertise, whether cast in terms of medicalization or more general processes of healthicization. On the one hand, the charge, by experts such as Dement at least, is of 'neglect' or 'ignorance' on the part of (medical) professionals and the public alike. On the other hand, this very criticism, as mentioned above, provides a potent rallying call to take sleep matters seriously, including the tackling of sleep *disorders* and sleep *deprivation* alike, whether through the medical regimen (the medicalization of sleep *disorders*) or the more general links forged between sleep, health and happiness (the healthicization of sleep), which in turn encompasses the cancelling of sleep *debt/deprivation* through basic lifestyle principles of 'sleep hygiene'/the promotion of 'healthy sleep habits'. Within this process, as we have seen, more and more sleep 'problems' are revealed/uncovered: 'problems' framed (if not diagnosed) in and through a variety of dormant expertise, including various 'prescriptions' for our so-called 'sleep-sick society'. Sleep, in these and other ways, becomes caught up in a tangled web of health and illness, morality and risk, safety and danger, across the lay/professional divide.

This, of course, is not to deny the very real problems which sleep deprivation or disorder may bring, both to the lives of individuals concerned and to society as a whole – the (hidden) costs of which are only now being counted. Nor is it to deny that sleep science in general, and medicine in particular, aided and abetted by broader public awareness/education campaigns, may make a valuable contribution to the alleviation or prevention of these 'problems', and the unnecessary suffering they entail. It is, however, to suggest that the unfolding sociological issues at stake here provide a fascinating example of a hitherto unexamined area, within and beyond these medicalization/healthicization debates.

Already, it seems, these transformations in public/professional consciousness are under way, in the American context at least: changes which suggest the taking of sleep matters seriously, and the increasing trend towards the healthicization of sleep in lay and popular culture. From here, indeed, it may only be a short step to the fetishization of sleep amongst certain segments of the (American) populace, which itself may be quite 'unhealthy' in a performance-obsessed culture (see also Chapter 2). One example of these trends was recently reported in an article with the eye-catching header: 'Snooze control: The latest Hollywood fad is free. Regular shut-eye is the best way to stay healthy and stress-free' (Kirwan-Taylor 2001). When celebrities talk numbers these days, the article proclaims 'they're not talking million-dollar fees. They're talking hours of sleep.' When people in New York look at their watch these days, moreover, it is reported, 'it's because they are trying to schedule their eight hours'. (Kirwan-Taylor 2001). This creeping obsession, the article claims, is now beginning to take hold in the UK too. Not only does sleep carry a range of health benefits, it is concluded – thereby enticing readers to convert to the cause if they haven't done so already – it is also the 'cheapest form of "stress relief" around' (Kirwan-Taylor 2001). The healthization, if not fetishization, of sleep, in short, could indeed be all the rage, healthy or otherwise.

Let me, however, add a further dimension or twist to these debates, albeit a more speculative one. The argument until now has been that current deployments of expertise, legitimate or otherwise, concern the *promotion/defence* of sleep, and/or the realization of sleep's potential for human health and happiness. It may, nonetheless, not be too wild or fanciful to paint an alternative, Brave New World, scenario in which future developments, in the era of new technologies/the new genetics, push in precisely the opposite direction, reducing if not eliminating our biological need to sleep, for a variety of reasons. The body, Giddens (1991) stresses, is increasingly incorporated or bound up with the internally referential systems of late modernity, including the reflexive project of self this entails and the technological means now available to mould or transform the body and its boundaries at will. From plastic surgery to the new genetics, the possibilities (welcome or otherwise) are endless (see Chapter 8). Will sleep, then, we may legitimately ask, be next in line? Melbin, very much in this vein, flirts with just such a possibility. Sleep, he notes,

> is a complex array rather than a single entity. Eventually we will unbundle its parts and do away with some of them. Already people keep irregular waking hours . . . Researchers try to isolate some of sleep's elements and discover what might substitute for each physical recovery for dreams and so on. They are already investigating the use of specific drugs that may regulate the timetables of certain physiological functions. People want to have the choice of when to sleep and whether to sleep at all. The prospect of dispensing with it is not so far in the future. The feat is within the capability of a culture that learned how to improve fertility in humans, how to prolong their length of life, and how to transplant organs from one body to another, and that now creates new organisms by genetic transfer. A society that can accomplish those things, in which people's attitudes and organizational needs unite to encourage science in the goal, will undo sleep if it wishes. (1989: 133–4)

The social, scientific and biological challenges, to be sure, weigh heavily in the balance, as do the ethical dilemmas and debates this raises. Whose interests, precisely, would be served here? Edison perhaps would approve, but who else? And what of medicine's own role: continuing defender or promoter of sleep, or (un)willing agent in its demise? Our hunch may well be the former (protector of sleep in the name of health), but who knows, particularly when the faction-riven nature of medicine is taken into account, and various other allied interests both now and in the future who might profit from any such developments are factored into the equation. To the degree, moreover, that these new technologies were 'safe', without any adverse effects, then the very problem of sleep disorders and deprivation might, rightly or wrongly, be reduced, if not resolved, 'overnight' – an attractive option for some maybe, given the current so-called 'epidemic' in our midst, but, again, at what cost? Whatever one's qualms, dispensing with sleep, like the mastering of light before it, will become an *option*, Melbin predicts, including various forms of 'artificial' slumber.

What we have here, to summarize, are a variety of criss-crossing trends and potential future scenarios, from medicalization to healthicization, fetishization to the (optional) elimination of sleep. Some no doubt, whatever technological developments come our way, will continue to hold to the promise of sleep, both lay and professional alike, appealing to its 'natural' properties and potential in an 'artificial'/'inauthentic' era such as ours. Sleep, moreover, is an important if not pleasurable pastime for many people, a vital escape route from the conscious demands of society. For Schwartz (1970: 486), indeed, some other functional equivalent would need to be found (or invented?) if nature no longer decreed our need to sleep. Others, in contrast, may be more or less ready converts to the 'attractions' of technologies which promise to do away with sleep, particularly perhaps those whose sleep quality, for whatever reason, is poor, and those who wish to extend their 'days' still further. Not an option then for all of us, or, perhaps more correctly, for us all the time? Our usage instead, with or without medicine's blessing, may be more selective than that: designer, streamlined or 'micro' sleep maybe, to widen our degrees of freedom in an era where a premium is placed upon flexibility in all walks of life. Either way, it does indeed provide an intriguing, if not troubling, prospect to ponder (or sleep on).

Death and dying in late/postmodernity

If sleep constitutes one key dimension of embodiment in which the conscious demands of society, and our waking roles within it, are (temporarily) relinquished, then death constitutes the other, this time albeit an irreversible one. It is perhaps a myth to suppose that death, or knowledge of death, has ever been greeted with total equanimity. Human beings, Bauman notes, are the only ones who not only know they are going to die, but also know that they know and cannot 'unknow' their knowledge (1992a: 3). As the possibility of impossibility and the impossibility of possibility, death cannot be 'believed', 'magicked' or 'scienced' away (Lofland 1978). Every society, in fact, is ultimately a collection of 'men [*sic*] banded together in the face of death' (Berger 1967). The fact of mortality and knowledge of it, in this respect, is socially 'dealt' with and culturally 'processed', thereby transforming the 'condition of impossibility of a meaningful life into the major source of life's meaning' (Bauman 1992a: 9).

The growth of social reflexivity, the relationship between the body and self-identity, and the shrinkage in scope of the 'sacred' mean that these mortal dilemmas become particularly acute in the current era (Mellor and Shilling 1993). As the 'scandal of reason', death throws into critical relief the human inability to reconcile the transcending power of 'time-binding mind' with the 'time-bound' transcience of our 'fleshy casing' (Bauman 1992b: 1). In the absence of overarching metaphysical systems of 'containment', individuals in late modernity increasingly find themselves 'alone' or 'exposed' in the face of death. The more people prioritize issues relating to the self, and the more they invest in their bodies, the more difficult it becomes for them to face up to and to cope with their own mortal demise. Death, so the argument goes, becomes increasingly *individualized* and *privatized* in reflexive modernity.

The gradual privatization and shrinkage of public space accorded death has been carefully mapped by Ariès (1976, 1981). According to him, a major change in the social response to death and dying occurred in the middle of the nineteenth-century: one involving a 'complete reversal of customs' and a loss of collective rituals. Death at this time was 'driven into secrecy', made 'invisible' and shrouded in a 'veil of silence'. As a consequence, death has grown fearful again, imbued with its 'old savagery': 'we ignore the existence of a scandal that we have been unable to prevent; we act as if it did not exist, and thus mercilessly force the bereaved to say nothing' (Ariès 1981: 562). Not only did this mark the 'beginning of the lie' for Ariès, one in which dying patients were not told the prognosis, it also involved the 'medicalization of death' as the dying were removed from their homes and the community and placed in the 'sanitized space' of the hospital in order to conceal its new 'indecency'.

Gradually, the nineteenth-century fight against plagues of consumption and pestilence, coupled with the twentieth-century image of medicine battling specific diseases, suggested a war against mortality itself: a denial, in Illich's (1975) terms, of the 'good death'. In a 'good death', Illich argues, (wo)man's fear and image of death was 'tamed' by a series of preparations and rituals designed to give the dying control over their death. The individual, in other words, presided over his or her own death. Today, in contrast, this 'good death' has been supplanted by the concept of the 'natural death', a death which 'comes under medical care and finds us in good health and old age' (Illich 1975: 180). In the 'natural death', the individual power of decision making and control are ceded to the medical and hospital staff, who, in effect, have become the 'new masters of death'. Health, from this viewpoint, has been 'expropriated down to the last breath. Technological death has won its victory over dying' (Illich 1975: 207–8).

Elias (1985) echoes these sentiments in his book *The Loneliness of Dying*, noting how the modern individual, in intensive care, can be cared for according to the latest biomedical knowledge and techniques, but often neutrally as regards feeling. 'Never before', Elias remarks, 'have people died so noiselessly and hygienically as today . . . in social conditions fostering so much solitude' (1985: 85). It is perhaps, he concludes, given the taboos surrounding death and dying and the isolation of such events from 'normal' social life (itself intimately bound up with the 'civilizing process' [Elias 1978/1939]), 'not yet quite superfluous to say that care for people sometimes lags behind the care for their organs' (1985: 91).

These issues, in turn, connect up with broader trends towards the 'sequestration of experience' in late modernity (Giddens 1991): a process involving the separation from routine day to day life of potentially disturbing existential crises and moral dilemmas including sickness, madness, criminality and death. The organization of life in late modernity, in this way, serves to strengthen the physical and symbolic boundaries between life and death, thereby accentuating the above-mentioned individualization of selves and bodies. Little by little the dead cease to exist: a situation which Baudrillard (1993/1976) has appositely termed the 'extradition' of the dead in Western society.

The very exclusion of death from everyday life and 'normality', however, means that it haunts us all the more powerfully. Death, returning to Bauman (1992a, 1992b), spurs life efforts, 'saturating' the struggle for 'survival'. A new 'survival strategy' has come to the fore in late modernity, he suggests, focused on the 'deconstruction of mortality' itself through a variety of self-care measures. Individuals, in keeping with this strategy, are exhorted to do something about death in the here and now. No one dies a 'general' death anymore, Bauman proclaims. Mortality instead is split into a 'multitude of individual occurrences', each possessing its own principally defeatable and hence 'preventable' cause. Body regimes and individual lifestyle choices are therefore proposed in order to reduce our chances of dying from coronary heart disease, stroke, cancer, and so on, thus diverting attention away from these mortal dilemmas through the sheer investment of time, effort and money this entails (see Chapter 2). Within this policy, immortality can be 'deferred' or 'forgotten' through the endless battle for health and fitness. The paradox of this strategy, however, as Bauman himself notes, is that

> the ultimate meaning of staving off the danger of dying of cause A is the increase in probability that my death, when it comes, will be described by cause B,C . . . Z. 'I do not want to die' always translates, in its pragmatic conclusions, into 'I would rather die of that rather than this'. As the 'that' cannot be exhausted, the truth of this translation must not be admitted into consciousness, and this requires that survival effort scores ever new successes. Survival needs constant reassurance; and the only convincing reassurance is the death of others: *not me*. (1992b: 10)

The battle over death, in short, can never be won. The price for exchanging immortality for the constant vigil of health, therefore, is 'life lived in the shadows of death' (Bauman 1992b: 20).

Against this dominant sociological view of death 'hidden' if not 'denied', 'displaced' if not 'sequestered' from public view, is an alternative stance in which death is seen as very much 'alive and kicking', so to speak. Armstrong (1987), for example, challenges Ariès's interpretation that a 'veil of silence' descended over the subject of death between 1850 and 1950. A change certainly occurred in the way death was spoken about, Armstrong argues, but Ariès is mistaken in his assumption that this involved the replacement of speech by silence. Silence itself, from a Foucauldian perspective, functions as an element alongside the things that are said. Between the mid-nineteenth century and its close, there was in fact an increasingly 'vocal discourse' on the certification, management and disposal of the dead. Medicine, in particular, ushered in a new regime of investigation and analysis concerning the body, one which no longer examined the 'familial bonds of the dead for the mirror to the truth of life', but instead sought to scrutinize the internal organs of the physical body itself, where the core of life and death were now thought to reside (Armstrong 1987). Rules at this time were also laid down regarding the maximum time the body could be kept in the home, the location of cemeteries, the height of their walls, the distance between plots, and the length of time before a plot could be disturbed (Armstrong 1987).

In contrast to this nineteenth-century medical interrogation of the corpse, Armstrong (1987) suggests, a 'new regime of truth' began to emerge in the late 1950s and early 1960s – one which Ariès himself correctly identifies as a 'complete reversal of attitudes'. Within this new 'psycho-social' paradigm, the former 'conspiracy of silence' regarding death was condemned, which in turn resulted in a shift from the 'interrogation of the corpse' to that of the 'dying patient'. From this point on, the truth of death ceased to be located in dark recesses of the silent corpse, and instead became embodied in the words and deeds of the dying patient (see, for example, Kübler-Ross 1969). As a consequence, the 'secret became broken', silence was allowed a new place in discourse, and the 'confession' was enacted. The dying, *qua* subjects, were therefore encouraged to speak (Armstrong 1987: 656). Gradually, as the focus of interest shifted to the analysis of bereavement, meaning and 'awareness of death' (Glaser and Strauss 1965, 1968), a new series of practices and organizations arose in order to accommodate and express this 're-assessment of human sensibility', including the founding (by Dame Cicely Saunders) in 1967 of the modern day hospice directed towards 'managing the anguish of the dying patient' (Prior 1989: 12).

Contrary to prevailing sociological views, therefore, it is possible to argue that death, as in the past, continues to be a very public affair (see also Kellehear 1984). Critics may nonetheless object that actuarial, demographic and medical discourses are not exactly 'public', and that death is still largely hidden behind the walls of the hospital or, more recently, the hospice. There is, however, one very public arena in which death makes a more than daily appearance, namely the mass media. It is indeed, Walter and colleagues (1995) argue, the mass media which really challenge the 'public absence of death' thesis. From *westerns* and *thrillers*, to other more recent fads and fashions for *ghost* movies (such as *Truly, Madly, Deeply* and *Ghost*); *cyborgs* programmed to kill (the *Terminator* movies); *near-death experiences* (*Flatliners*); and the problems of *corpse 'disposal'* (for example, *The Cement Garden* and *Shallow Grave*), death makes a regular appearance on our cinema screens and home videos. Similarly, in TV dramas such as *Casualty*, death or its imminent possibilities is a central feature of the storyline. Part of the popular appeal of TV series such as *Prime Suspect* and *Cracker*, no doubt, has been their vivid portrayal of dead, assaulted and violated bodies: corpses which are probed and poked, photographed and dissected for 'clues' to their assailants.

Death is also, of course, well covered in media reportage of personal tragedies involving private citizens, such as motorway disasters, aeroplane crashes, the abduction and murder of children. Indeed, far from being averse to portraying the humanity of those killed and the emotions of those who grieve – as Gorer (1955, 1965) claimed in his classic 'pornography of death' thesis – reporters actually home in on these issues like 'flies to a glowing light' (Walter et al. 1995: 584). A 'public invigilation of private emotion' is at work here, involving the simultaneous arousal and regulatory 'keeping watch over' the affective dispositions and responses associated with death (Walter et al. 1995: 584).

Events surrounding the tragic death of Princess Diana on 31 August 1997 throw many of these issues into critical relief. Both those involved in 'mourning for Diana' and those who sought, in various ways, to distance themselves from it found the waves of emotion which followed hard to comprehend. The mourning, indeed, extended far beyond London (where Diana's corpse lay), with media around the globe dominated by her death and record-breaking television audiences on the day of the funeral – not to mention the millions of floral tributes, messages of condolence and mementos left in the wake of her death (a popular shrine to the dead princess). Early September that year, Walter comments,

> was one of those rare occasions when lay people and social scientists pondered the same questions: had the British suddenly changed their character? why such grief for someone relatively few had ever met? was it crowd hysteria, or media manipulation? what on earth was going on? The everyday world had been rendered strange, not only for social scientists . . . but for every man and woman. People we thought we knew were acting strangely, and everyone – including those who were acting strangely – wanted to know why? (1999: 19)

Answers to such questions, themselves the subject of much debate, are beyond the scope of this chapter.[17] It does nonetheless serve to illustrate the thrusting of death into public view, spectacularly or otherwise (see also Kear and Steinberg 1999).

To these illustrations of death in the news, updating still further, we may of course add the terrifying events of 11 September 2001, in which many thousands died through the (suicide) bombings, including attacks both on New York's World Trade Center and the Pentagon. Again the manifold issues this raises, and the analyses it demands, are beyond the scope of this chapter or book.[18] Suffice it to say that death and its aftermath once more were on full public view here, engendering a variety of emotional responses and shock waves throughout the world.

These issues, in turn, feed into a more general set of arguments concerning the 'presence' of death in contemporary Western societies. With more people than ever before having to live for an extended period of time with life-threatening conditions (for example, cancer, heart disease, stroke, HIV) – what Lofland (1978) refers to as the transition from 'quick' to 'slow' dying – the modern pretence that death does not exist becomes less and less viable. Instead, a variety of strategies for (more openly) dealing with death now exist in the complex 'death culture' of our times. Far from living in a 'death-denying' society, Seale (1998) asserts, dying and bereaved people in contemporary culture are often able to assert membership of 'imagined communities' of anonymous others through the narrative construction of personal biographies, drawing upon a variety of cultural scripts stemming from medicine, psychiatry, the media and many other lay, professional and popular sources. The maintenance of the human social bond in the face of our mortal demise, from this vantage point, is continually reaffirmed through a variety of ('resurrective') practices, both routine and extraordinary in kind. As such, the 'threat to security about being in the world posed by knowledge of mortality, is transformed in human social activity into an orientation towards continuing, meaningful existence' (Seale 1998: 1).[19]

A 'revival' of death, as Walter (1995) puts it, is currently underway here, itself comprised of two distinct strands: one late modern, the other more postmodern in character. The late modern revival, he argues, is more *expert-led* or -driven, asserting not simply the *right* of individuals to know they are dying and to express how they feel, but their *need* to do so, thereby creating a more 'open awareness' (cf. Glaser and Strauss 1965). The more radical postmodern revival, in contrast, points to the 'wide diversity in how human beings encounter death; some individuals for example do not want to know they are dying or choose not to express their fear or grief – this may work for them and must be respected' (Walter 1995: 186). The postmodern revival, in this sense, which takes individualism to its logical conclusion (asserting the authority of the individual not only over religion, but also over medicine), may be summed up, to quote the refrain of the famous Frank Sinatra song, as 'I did it my way'. To the extent that this occurs in the company of others, however, then 'Come fly with me', Walter argues, may be the more apposite song title (1995: 188–9).

Bauman (1992a, 1992b) adds a further twist here through his own insightful deliberations on the 'postmodern' deconstruction of 'immortality' itself. In keeping with his general aim – to expose death-related practices where we least expect to find them – life within consumer culture, he asserts, becomes transformed into an endless circulation of commodities which itself can be read as a constant series of rehearsals of 'reversible death'. Here, within this latter day postmodern life strategy, the irrevocable termination of life is instead substituted for 'temporary disappearance' as consumer bliss reaches its final stage of secularization. The impact of such daily rehearsal, moreover, is that death loses it sting, something Bauman likens to preventive inoculation: 'if taken in daily, in partly detoxicated and thus non-deadly doses, the awesome poison seems to lose its venom. Instead it prompts immunity and indifference to the toxin in the inoculated organism' (1992a: 188). In this way, transcience and ephemerality are forged into daily practice, glorified and ritualistically celebrated through 'reversible' death. Deconstructed in this way, immortality reveals mortality as its 'only secret'. Mortality, in short, need not be deconstructed but lived (1992a: 191–2): rehearsed, consciously or otherwise, on a daily basis, thereby laying the ghost to rest.

'Public' or 'private', 'absent' or 'present': what, then, are we to make of these differing views of death and dying in Western society? Is it possible to 'reconcile' them or are they inherently contradictory? One way out of this (im)mortal dilemma is to suggest that, at an *institutional* level, all societies, past, present and future, have to organize for death. Death indeed, as we have seen, is the mainspring of life's meaning and opportunities, the foundation upon which the whole (precarious) edifice of Western culture is built. Whilst the social organization of death and dying has undoubtedly changed across the centuries – from a communal event surrounded by local rituals, to one of increasing secularization, rationalization and medicalization – a number of 'revivalist' trends have nonetheless emerged in recent years which are beginning to 'challenge' these dominant modernist approaches: responses which have never really been about 'denial' as much as 'deferral' and sequestration. These span a diverse array of issues, from the 'public invigilation of private grief' via the media, to the so-called 'postmodern' deconstruction of immortality itself in consumer culture and the 'celebration' of '(reversible) death' this supposedly entails. Here, the 'vanguards of change' appear not only to be the so-called 'experts' in the field – medicine, psychiatry, the social sciences, the hospice movement and bereavement counsellors – but also the dying and bereaved themselves: people who are increasingly joining together in a common call for 'open awareness contexts' and a 'dignified', if not 'heroic' (Seale 1995), end to life (see the following, however). Modernist 'life' strategies therefore increasingly rub shoulders with postmodern ones in the complex death culture of our times. Life, in these and other ways, is continually reaffirmed in the face of death: a *'turning away'* (Seale 1998) from death, perhaps, in favour of the bustle of daily life and the forging of life's meaning.

Matter out of place? (Un)containable bodies/(un)dignified dying in the hospice

The foregoing discussion, at best, is a preliminary, if not premature, conclusion to these mortal matters in late/postmodernity. Further insights, in this respect, can be gleaned through Lawton's (1998, 2000) illuminating ethnography of dying in palliative care. Drawing on patients' own experiences of the dying process, Lawton pays close attention to the ways in which notions of the body and self, time and space, shift from the initial diagnosis of terminal disease to eventual death. Three issues in particular, for our purposes, merit further discussion here. The first concerns Lawton's well-made point regarding the problems evident in much of the literature discussed above, which uses homogeneous categories such as the 'dying patient' and the 'dying process'. Different *types* of death and dying are glossed therefore, which themselves carry different implications not simply for self and others, but also for wider academic discussions and debates on these very matters. In contrast to such general categories, Lawton's findings indicate the importance of focusing on the body of the patient and the disease processes taking place both *within* it and on its outer corporeal *surfaces*. Doing so, it is argued, helps explain why some patients are now sequestered within hospices whilst others are not: issues linked, in conjunction with broader pressures to cut beds (which itself impacts on hospice admission policies), to the manner in which disease spread destroys both the ability to act and the physical boundaries of the body (Lawton 2000: 37).

The case of Annie, for example, graphically illustrates these issues: a 67-year-old woman with cancer of the cervix, which, despite surgery and post-operative radiotherapy, subsequently spread to the pelvic wall. One of the main problems precipitating Annie's admission to the hospice for symptom control was the development of a fistula which resulted in faecal leakage. As the fistula enlarged, Annie ceased to have any control over her bowel or bladder function. Because the management of the effects of this breakdown of bodily control ceased to be effective, all plans for discharge, Lawton explains, were abandoned (1998: 127). As one nurse tellingly put, Annie literally 'rotted away below', causing her and other patients much distress, including the 'terrible smell', prior to her passing away some six weeks after first admission (Lawton 2000: 126–8).

Here, in this and similar accounts of the ravages of diseases within the hospice, we encounter the second main point stemming from Lawton's study – one which sociologists of the body, particularly those of a strongly constructionist persuasion, would do well to heed. What this amounts to is a simple yet fundamental corporeal point concerning the intimate connection between the integrity of the self and the integrity of the fleshy, material, organic body. In order for selfhood to be realized and maintained in contexts such as contemporary England, Lawton argues,

certain specific bodily capacities and attributes *must* be possessed: the most important being a bounded, physically sealed, enclosed body (what I term the corporeal
capacity for 'self-containment') and also the bodily ability to act as the agent of one's
own embodied actions and intentions. Patients who lose either, or both of these
bodily attributes . . . fall out of the category of personhood. In both their own and
other people's evaluations; they experience a diminishment of self. (2000: 7)[20]

What we have here, in effect, is the transition from 'subject' to 'object' and the
constriction of space and time consequent upon this loss of bodily attributes and
abilities: a process of 'social' death prior to 'biological' death.

The third key point returns us to debates on the sequestration of death and dying
in late/postmodernity. The nature and types of dying considered here, Lawton
argues, when viewed in the context of cultural beliefs about pollution and taboo (cf.
Douglas 1966, 1970) and the broader pressures on hospice admission policies, mean
that the hospice is not simply a liminal space (cf. Van Gennep 1960/1909), but a
'non-place' within which the 'taboo processes of bodily disintegration and decay are
sequestered'. Understanding the hospice as a 'no place', in other words, 'allows it to
be understood as a central part of contemporary English culture. Setting these phenomena apart from mainstream society, it could be argued, enables certain ideas
about living, personhood and the hygienic, sanitised, bounded body . . . to be symbolically enforced and maintained' (Lawton 2000: 144).

Death, in short, has many faces, some of which appear more difficult to face than
others, given the corporeal dilemmas and fleshy predicaments posed: threats not
simply to the dying but to those around them in managing this 'matter out of
place'.

Conclusions

Taking as its starting point the neglected sociological matter of sleep, a number of
dormant issues and embodied dilemmas have been traced in this chapter. Prime
among them, as we have seen, is the prototypic sleep role and the (prospective) medicalization and/or healthicization of sleep in contemporary Western society. Sleep, it
has been argued, is no mere biological or psychological entity. It is indeed crucial to
the social organization and workings of society as whole, including the 'doing' of
sleep, its social patterning, and the issues of power and status this raises. In these and
other respects, the sociological issues surrounding the dormant body in the dormant
society suggest some promising new research agendas. Sociological studies of the following, for example, would yield rich dividends, in health and beyond: (i) lay
perspectives on sleep and health; (ii) the social *patterning* of sleep; (iii) *practices* of sleep
scheduling and sleep management; (iv) *problems* of sleep and health; (v) the *propensity* to help-seeking and the types of help sought across the lay/professional divide;
(vi) issues of *power* and *status* surrounding sleep; (vii) the commercial exploitation of

sleep-related *products* (including pharmaceuticals) in the dormant marketplace; and, finally, (viii) the future *prospects* of sleep (the *promotion* or *prevention* of sleep, that is to say, in the new millennium). Many of these issues, moreover, key into ongoing debates on inequalities in health, the 'colonization' of the lifeworld, and the recent upsurge of interest in body matters in general.

In contrast to sociological neglect of the dormant body, debates surrounding the mortal body in late/postmodernity are now firmly on the sociological agenda. Both sleep and death in their different ways, as we have seen, are legitimate corporeal releases from the *conscious* demands of waking life, one reversible, the other not. Sleep and *dying*, moreover, throw the 'liminal' dimensions of embodiment into critical relief. The limits, sociologically speaking, of the much debated 'death-denial' thesis have also been aired in the context of 'revivalist' debates. Sleep itself perhaps, extending Bauman's insights further, may be construed as a 'mini-rehearsal' of death, albeit a 'welcome' one, enacted on a daily basis in more or less ritualistic fashion. Perhaps the main issue to emerge, however, concerns the need to distinguish between different *types* of dying, and the dilemmas of embodied selfhood they raise. Here we return to the corporeal limits of strongly constructionist perspectives, postmodern or otherwise, whilst simultaneously confronting the complexities of death and dying in these ambivalent times.

Notes

1   Technologies surrounding the measurement and monitoring of sleep abound. These, for example, include electroencephalographs (EEGs) to monitor brain activity, electrooculograms (EOGs) to measure eye movements, and electromyograms (EMGs) that record muscle tone and bodily movement (Flanagan 2000: 76). To this we may add other measures of daytime sleepiness such as the Multiple Sleep Latency Test and the Epworth Sleepiness Scale (see, for example, Dement with Vaughan 2000).

2   The widely held view that dreaming occurs only in REM sleep is, however, according to critics such as Flanagan (2000), erroneous. Most 'ordinary folk and scholars', he argues, 'are surprised to find out that mentation goes on during non-rapid-eye-movement (NREM) sleep as well as during rapid-eye-movement (REM) sleep'. Almost everyone is surprised, moreover, to discover that 'sleep-walking, sleep-talking, nocturnal emissions, and night-terrors are NREM phenomena – as is most snoring' (2000: 5). See also Hobson (1989), from which Flanagan draws much of his evidence.

3   Not only was Thomas Alva Edison (1847–1931) a prodigious American inventor – the man behind over 1,300 inventions in fact, from the light bulb to automatic telegraph systems, the phonogram to the electronic typewriter – he was, by all accounts, imbued with a strong work ethic (as his manifold inventions attest) and a personal desire to eliminate 'unproductive' sleep, which he likened to overeating and condemned as an inefficient waste of productive time (see, for example, Coren 1996).

4   See also Johnson (1930) and Johnson et al. (1931) for early work on bodily positioning in restful sleep.

5   Gleik (2000), more recently, makes a number of related observations on our time-compressed, accelerated (techno)culture and the fast-paced lifestyles we lead.

6   For other historical studies of sleep, see Dannenfeldt (1986) and Ekirch (2001). Thanks to Jonathan Reinarz for the steady flow of historical sources.

7   I am grateful to Sharon Boden for drawing this point to my attention.

8   For an earlier discussion of the 'sleep role' and the notion of sleep as an effective 'period remission' from the demands of conscious waking life – an article drawn to my attention following my own initial formulation of these issues – see Schwartz (1970).

9   See also Woods (1947) on the 'world of dreams' and Flanagan's *Dreaming Souls* (2000).

10 Thanks again to Sharon Boden for highlighting these issues.

11 The American Sleep Disorders Association – a professional medical association of sleep medicine practitioners and sleep researchers – lists seventy-eight recognized sleep disorders in its *International Classification of Sleep Disorders, Diagnostic and Coding Manual* (cited in Dement with Vaughan 1999/2000). These include *dyssomnias* of various kinds, (which cause difficulty either initiating or maintaining sleep, or result in excessive sleepiness), *parasomnias* (those disorders of partial arousal or disorders that interfere with sleep stage transitions), *medical and psychiatric sleep disorders* (which, as the name suggests, concern sleep disorders associated with medical, neurological and psychiatric conditions) and *proposed sleep disorders* (sleep problems, that is to say, for which there is not enough information, to date, to firmly establish them as sleep disorders) (Dement with Vaughan 1999/2000: 450–64; see also Shapiro 1994).

12 The issue, of course, as to where precisely this 'recommended eight hours' sleep, cited here and elsewhere, comes from – beyond, that is, general reference to medical wisdom or 'sleep experts' – and the nature and status of the evidence upon which these claims are based, remain intriguing questions for further (sociological) investigation. One potential source, pointed out to me by Peter Conrad, concerns the epidemiological research (the Alameda county study) of Belloc, Breslow and Berkman – which received a lot of attention in the US – on the relationship between health status and health practices, including the effect of seven to eight hours sleep on health and longevity (see, for example, Belloc and Breslow 1972; Berkman and Breslow 1983).

13 One such case has recently occurred in Britain: the case of a 'dozing driver' who caused ten deaths when his vehicle slid from the road onto a railway line resulting in a subsequent train crash (the Selby rail disaster). The judge said that driving whilst sleepy was as bad as drink-driving, and sentenced the defendant (whom he dismissed as 'arrogant' in believing he could make a 150-mile journey after staying up all night on the telephone to a woman friend) to five years imprisonment (Wainwright 2002).

14 Dement adds a further important caveat here, however. Problems such as insomnia, he states, are not in fact sleep disorders at all. Insomnia, that is to say, is 'not a disease – it is a *symptom* . . . simply some sort of difficulty with sleep . . . [which] . . . has many different causes' (Dement with Vaughan 2000: 130, my emphasis).

15 Various methods, techniques or medications to *stay awake* should also be mentioned at this point, including the (not so) humble shot of caffeine.

16 Mention should also be made here to a range of other off-the-shelf books and self-help guides designed to educate the public about sleep and to ensure we all sleep soundly. These include, in addition to Dement's *The Promise of Sleep* (2000), books such as Idzikowski's *Learn to Sleep Well* (2001) and Van Straten's *The Good Sleep Guide* (1996).

17 Walter (1999), for instance, concludes that very little in fact, on closer inspection, is new here.

18 For a rapid series of responses to these events, see Fuller (2001, 2002) and Ray (2001). See also the conclusion to the book.

19 Seale (1998) in fact appears to operate with the dual notion that denial, at the sociological level, may be erroneous, whilst simultaneously capturing something important (if only a 'turning away') at the individual/psychological level. See also Seale (1995) on 'heroic' scripts of death and dying in late modernity.

20 Whilst (feminist) critiques of bodily containment/the body as container have appeared in recent years, in favour of more 'fluid' (Battersby 1993, 1998) or 'leaky' positions (Shildrick 1997), Lawton's underlying point is clearly important in any such debates.

Reason, Emotion and 'Mental' Health: Where Do We Draw the Line?

Are we 'unhappier' now in the Western world than in past decades? To what extent is the 'doing better, feeling worse' syndrome a characteristic feature of life and living in the twenty-first century? What factors are at play here? And how should we interpret this alleged upward trend in mental health 'problems' (and the expertise designed to 'treat' them): a disclosing of the hitherto undisclosed, a real increase, or the product of shifting professional boundaries and/or lay constructions of these very matters? These are some of the questions I wish to pick up on in this chapter, with particular reference to emotion and mental health. What light, in other words, do emotions shed on these debates, within and beyond the sociology of mental health? This, in turn, as we shall see, involves a critical rethinking of current terms of reference and an opening up of some new research agendas along the way. Central to this enterprise, building on past chapters, is the need to return to and rethink age-old divisions such as reason and emotion, biology and society: issues taken up and addressed in the first two sections of this chapter. The chapter then proceeds to sketch out more fully the dilemmas and vicissitudes of emotions in social life today, especially their 'colonization' through various forms of therapeutic expertise. The strengths and weaknesses of prevailing notions such as mental health and illness are likewise reappraised, the embodied implications of which are drawn together in concluding. What, then, of those two 'age-old adversaries', reason and emotion?

Reason versus emotion?

An encounter with madness, whatever its form, begs questions for which the 'higher court' of reason, in the Western world at least, stands judge and jury. It is Foucault perhaps, more than any other theorist of his time, who has done most to 'open up' the historically shifting dialogue between 'reason' and 'unreason' *qua* 'madness'. We no longer understand unreason today, Foucault declares, except in its 'epithetic form: the *Unreasonable,* a sign attached to conduct or speech, and betraying to the layman's eyes the presence of madness and all its pathological train' (1971: 83). As with 'madness', so with 'mental disorder' more generally in modern times. The theorization of mental disorder in terms of the 'regulation' of 'reason' and 'rationality', Busfield argues, provides the most 'useful conceptualisation for analysing the boundaries of mental disorder, its regulation and its relation to gender' (1996: 69) – the 'identification', that is to say, of '"unreason" and "irrationality"' through constructs of mental disorder, as an "affirmation of reason"' (1996: 71).[1]

This, without doubt, echoing Busfield, is a fruitful way forward, extending to current debates over the '(in)appropriateness', if not '(un)reasonableness' or '(ir)rationality', of a wide array of contemporary mental disorders such as anxiety, phobias, anorexia nervosa and drug addiction (1996: 72) – themselves, of course, gendered (see Box 3.2, Chapter 3).[2] What it neglects, however, without denying it, is a sustained set of reflections on the *contribution* of emotions to 'mental' *health* and well-being as opposed to illness, and, through this, to the 'rationality' of the individual (Edwards 1981) and the 'rational functioning' of society as a whole. Emotions may at times sabotage processes of rational thought and decision making, however defined. They may also get 'out of hand' in ways for which professional help seems appropriate. Their 'absence' nonetheless, as a variety of recent research has shown, is no less devastating (Damasio 1994).

Without emotion, society would indeed be an empty, dull, disenchanted affair, with little or nothing to commend it. Emotions, from this viewpoint, are 'enchanted' ways of being-in-the-world, rendering our own and others' embodied conduct both meaningful and intelligible. Sartre (1971/1939), Heidegger (1962) and Merleau-Ponty (1962), in their different ways,[3] all point (directly or indirectly) to the existential importance of emotions to our mooded being or dwelling in the world, thereby paving the way for a fully fledged *intersubjective* approach to emotions in social life which, at one and the same time, is thoroughly *intercorporeal* in nature (Crossley 1998, 2001; see also Davidson 1999). This, in turn, avoids the tendency, so common in the history of Western thought and practice, to view emotions negatively as failures in instrumental reasoning: 'a view which would consign everything, from Platonic love to the passion of a football crowd to the category of "pathological" or "dysfunctional"' (Crossley 1998: 29).

It is at this very point that the question of so-called '(in)appropriate' emotion looms large, itself related to the historically and culturally shifting nature and types of 'rationality' alluded to above, and the *contextual* circumstances within which they are embedded. At least four possible models of reason–emotion relations, ana-lytically speaking, suggest themselves in this respect: models which provide an important point of reference on the trail to a more 'reasonable' notion of 'mental' or emotional health as a fully embodied phenomenon.

Domination/sequestration

Within this traditional or orthodox Western viewpoint, emotions – *qua* chaos, the irrational or the 'miasma of the indeterminate' (Bauman 1991) – are banished/driven out, displaced/replaced, by the steady (male) hand of reason. Unqualified support for this strongly oppositional viewpoint is in fact, on closer inspection, quite difficult to find. Aristotle and Spinoza, for example, both accorded emotion more than a peripheral role in their respective rationalist philosophies.[4] Weber himself, the sociological heir to the Kantian tradition, may also be read in a somewhat more favourable light than many of his critics give him credit for, regarding his treatment of emotion and his (incapacitating) fear of the irrational (Albrow 1990).[5] The domination/sequestration theme, nonetheless, serves to capture in spirit, if not content, an important point of reference in the history of Western thought, or, perhaps more correctly, the advent of rational modernity, and the quest for 'dispassionate rationality' to which it has given rise. Emotion, then, from this viewpoint, is indeed the 'scandal of reason', conceived in instrumentally rational terms (Bauman 1991).

Liberation/liquidation

If the traditional, orthodox viewpoint is premised on the formal opposition between reason and emotion (the latter denounced in favour of the former), then the same may be said, in reverse, of those alternative traditions of Western thought and prac-tice in which emotion is championed over rationality. What we have here, in other words, is a situation in which the opposition between reason and emotion is more or less radically *reversed* rather than overturned. Romanticism, for example, with its own (one-sided) appeal to emotion vis-à-vis the excessive rationalism of the Enlightenment (Barbalet 1998), fits more or less readily within this latter viewpoint, as do current critiques of the more postmodern or post-structuralist variety: a liqui-dation, in effect, of the Cartesian rationalist subject. Emotions, it follows, stand in need of liberation from the calculative hold of rational modernity, and the stifling emotional legacies to which it gives rise.

Calculation/cultivation – 'managed' hearts and McDonaldized emotions

The limits of the two approaches above, in turn, pave the way for a somewhat more complex, subtle and sophisticated understanding of reason–emotion relations – a calculation/cultivation viewpoint, traceable across the course of Western history, but perhaps most fully manifest in the current era. It is not so much a question here, as these very terms of reference suggest, of emotion *dominated* by or *liberated* from reason, as the management of the former by the latter, for better or worse. A channelling of affect, in effect, emerges here through the calculative deployment of emotion *in the service* or under the guidance of rationality.

A variety of work may be drawn on in support of these contentions – from Elias's (1978/1939) 'civilizing process' to Hochschild's (1983) 'managed heart', and from Giddens' (1991, 1992) reflexive self to the 'postemotional' claims of Meštrović (1997). There are, to be sure, important differences between these authors, not least in the degree to which the emotional body is adequately theorized. All nonetheless converge, through advocacy or critique, with respect to the *cognitive penetrability* or rational (de)control of emotions: an 'arranged' marriage which is not without its tensions or costs. Emotions, moreover, become 'things' to be managed or monitored, manipulated or manufactured, in this way or that – labourers put to work according to the latest rational imperatives or market dictates of late/postmodernity. In Hochschild's (1983) work, for instance, the individual, *qua* emotion manager, dances to the tune or market dictates of late capitalist imperatives, via feeling rules and the commodified forms of deep and surface acting they engender (see Chapter 9).[6]

What this amounts to, in summary, is a 'hybrid' situation in which the rational, calculative attitude is deployed in the *management* of emotions: the rational (de)control of affect, positively or negatively construed. This is a viewpoint which takes us so far, but not perhaps quite far enough, in revealing or recovering the full story of relations between reason and emotion within Western thought and practice, both past and present.

Consummation/unification – an intimate/passionate marriage

Here we arrive at a fourth and final viewpoint on this relationship, one in which the 'marriage' between reason and emotion is well and truly 'consummated'. It is not, as this suggests, a question of rationality dominating or managing emotions, or, for that matter, one of emotions freeing themselves from the suffocating hold of rationality, but one of their more or less happy/harmonious convergence. If emotions, as Crossley (2000) argues, are not the sorts of things we can 'step out of'; if the view of mind and body (upon which the reason–emotion division is transposed) is rendered suspect and begins to crumble; if other forms of rationality are taken into consideration beyond the narrowly instrumental sphere, then a place may indeed be found for the notion of *rational emotion*.

A number of examples of recent work may be drawn upon in support of these contentions. Reflective thought, Damasio (1994) shows, requires the 'tagging of cognition with emotions'. Without this capacity, decision making itself becomes difficult, if not impossible, as there is no criterion with which to 'drive cognition' in a given direction. Emotions, it follows, are central to the 'effective deployment' of reason, providing it with *salience, direction* and *purpose (goal formation)* (see also de Sousa 1990). The case of Phineas Gage, Damasio notes, provides a classic illustration of these reason–emotion relations. A nineteenth-century railway worker, Gage suffered damage to his frontal lobes when an iron bar shot through them by an accidental explosion. Along with the 'emotional deficits' which followed this damage, Gage had great difficulty in planning his ordinary life, making disastrous social decisions whilst dithering endlessly over inconsequential issues. A number of patients with similar damage have now been studied, the general conclusion being that it is this 'socio-emotional guidance system' which is affected, both in the brain of Phineas Gage and in those of his modern day counterparts. Emotions, as this suggests, guide reason, furnishing us with priorities amongst multiple goals and options (Damasio 1994; see also Oatley and Jenkins 1996).

What makes this a less than optimal position, Barbalet comments, is that it remains somewhat 'apprehensive' about the possibility of emotion *undermining reason*, particularly its technical or instrumental forms (1998: 44). Emotion, it seems, can only contribute *so much*: a more balanced assessment, to be sure, but one in which emotion continues to play a largely supportive, if not subservient, role.

A more 'radical' suggestion, for which there is now plenty of support, is that instrumental reason, like any other form of reasoning, is itself founded on particular emotions (a passionately held belief and cherished ideal). Barbalet (1998), for example, approvingly cites James's (1956/1897) essay 'The sentiment of rationality' in this context. Within both this and other essays by James, the human passion for 'clarity' and 'order' is emphasized: a passion, that is, for 'generalizing, simplifying and subordinating' (James 1932/1909, quoted in Barbalet 1998: 54).[7] To divorce reason from emotion, in this respect, is like trying to separate two sides of the same coin. From this it follows that rationality itself is fundamentally embodied. We human beings, Johnson states, 'have bodies. We are "*rational* animals", but also "rational *animals*", which means that our rationality is embodied' (1987: xix).

Emotion, from this viewpoint, is no mere '*adjunct*' to cognitive processes or the '*means*' to practical knowledge.[8] Instead it is woven into the *very fabric* of our 'reasoning', from scientific observation and the generation of hypotheses, to 'moral understanding' and the 'communicative rationality' of the Habermasian lifeworld (Habermas 1984, 1987): emotions, that is to say, as 'accountable', 'contestable' and 'defeasible' (Crossley 1998, 2000). We can, for example, in the main, be 'reasoned' both 'in' and 'out' of certain emotional states according to the communicatively rational criteria and 'validity claims' they raise. Even so-called 'emotional outbursts', Crossley notes, do not preclude the notion of 'communicative reasoning', or the 'intersubjective reality' upon which it rests. Emotion, from this latter, more Habermasian viewpoint, is integrated within the order of communicative rationality . . . emotional responses raise validity claims which can be challenged or confirmed and . . . like any cognitive belief, an emotional response is something that we believe we can talk people out of when they are wrong . . . Thus *there is no reason why our social worlds cannot be simultaneously constituted through emotion and communicative rationality.* Indeed, we can say that *emotion forms part of the sphere of communicative rationality.* (Crossley 1998: 30, my emphasis)

Just as ('appropriate') emotions, however defined, may contribute to the development of knowledge, so too the growth of knowledge may contribute to the development of ('appropriate') emotions (Jaggar 1989). Rather than repressing emotion in Western epistemology, therefore, it is necessary to fundamentally 'rethink the relation between knowledge and emotion and construct conceptual models that demonstrate the *mutually constitutive* rather than oppositional relation between reason and emotion. Far from precluding the possibility of reliable knowledge, emotion as well as value must be shown as necessary to such knowledge' (Jaggar 1989: 157).

Underpinning these issues, Barbalet (1998) comments, is the attempt to bring emotions of a 'foreground' and 'background' nature into fuller focus, and to highlight the manner in which conventional understandings of reason and emotion serve to mask as much as they reveal (see also Heller 1990). The conventional opposition between reason and emotion, in this sense, may in large part be due to the 'cultural discounting of certain "background emotions": emotions which underpin instrumental rationality but are seldom acknowledged or seen as belonging to some other category (e.g. attitudes, customs) which fundamentally obscure their emotional nature' (Barbalet 1998: 29–30). Context, moreover, as noted above, is crucial here. Differing emotions, and the same emotions in different contexts, have different relations with reason itself, however defined (Barbalet 1998: 32). There is, in short, 'no one single rationality, but rather a set of traditions of rationality that are normatively governed and whose influence varies across time and place' (Busfield 1996: 73) – traditions, we may add, which may be more or less 'reasonable' as far as emotion is concerned.

Enough I hope has been said to cast a 'long shadow' not simply over the first domination viewpoint – in which emotions are 'driven out' or 'pathologized' by the steady hand of (male) disembodied reason (Lloyd 1993; Rose 1994, Seidler 1994, 1998) – but also with respect to oppositional thinking in general. The argument here, returning more fully to issues of mental health and illness, is that debates over the problematization, if not pathologization, of emotion through the shifting boundaries of rationality, important as they are, themselves need setting in the context of broader debates about the *contribution* of emotion to rationality and to social order in general. The latter, indeed, is crucial to issues of mental health. Taking this line, moreover, provides a more fully rounded or balanced picture of emotions in social life, health-related or otherwise. This, however, is merely one 'preparatory step' in bringing the emotional body 'back in' to debates on 'mental' health and illness.

Biology versus society?

The next issue to tackle, head on, returns us to associated divisions of the biology/society, mind/body variety: issues raised, if not resolved, in past chapters, of particular relevance here given developments in biopsychiatry and the dominance of biochemical explanations. The consequences of modern life for individuals, Lyon comments, are increasingly defined and treated through illness constructions grounded in the 'neurochemical features of individuals': developments reinforced through the marketing of new so-called 'wonder drugs' such as Prozac for an infinite array of 'problems' associated with supposed 'defects' in our serotonin levels (1996: 64). Rates of prescription for anti-depressant drugs, such as Prozac, have mushroomed in recent years, as have prescriptions of Ritalin for the various 'attention deficit' and 'hyperactivity' disorders diagnosed in (ever earlier phases of) childhood (Crossley 2003). The Prozac debate, indeed, is particularly revealing on this count. For writers such as Kramer (1993), for instance, it provides a biochemical route to a person's 'true self'. For writers such as Breggin and Breggin (1994), in contrast, it is nothing short of a 'pharmaceutical conspiracy', which masks the underlying problem, confusing real depression with being slightly unhappy (see also Breggin 1993 on 'toxic psychiatry' and the 'psycho-pharmaceutical complex'). Huge profits, indeed, are at stake here, with Prozac earning Eli Lilly an estimated $2.6 billion a year, catering worldwide to approximately 40 million people across 100 countries (Hoe 2001).

To this increasingly narrow/reductionist neurochemical search for explanation, and hence treatment options, we may add sociology's own reluctance, harking back to Chapter 1, to reopen the biology–society debate in health or elsewhere. The tendency, as Lyon puts it, to

> flip-flop between these two distinct types of explanation (biological or social) depending on the 'dimension' in question, or simply to grant primacy to one form of explanation and ignore the other, does little to encourage the exploration of new models which may bridge or obviate this division and lead to new forms of analysis. (1996: 56; see also Chapter 3)

It is no longer therefore a question of biological *versus* social, (or social construction versus social causation, for that matter) accounts of 'mental' health and illness. Mental disorder, Busfield comments, may indeed be a ' "label" in the sense that, like all words, it is a social construct, but it is not "merely" a label. It has a referent that has an *ontological reality . . . beyond the multiplicity of "voices"* to which we must attend' (1996: 60, my emphasis). This, in turn, requires us to abandon traditional mind/body divisions,[9] of which medicine and psychiatry, not to mention sociology, have contributed much, and to 'confront the question of how the social realm itself is *embodied*: a notion which can give form to the relationship between the social structural milieu in which humans live, their subjective experience, and the *flesh* through which that existence is lived' (Lyon 1996: 69, my emphasis).

Emotion, it is clear, provides just such a 'bridge' between the social and biological domains, 'resituating' the body in the world whilst avoiding reductionist pitfalls en route. Through emotion, 'bodily, psychological and social phenomena can *simultaneously* be represented and explored' (Lyon 1996: 57, my emphasis). No mere 'interior', individual or psychological matter, emotion equips us for and arises in the social world. A sociological commitment to emotion, therefore, provides an 'alternative analytical framework that both challenges assumptions regarding the division between biology and being, and provides a new perspective on the interrelationship of these different orders of phenomena' (Lyon 1996: 69). This, indeed, as mentioned above, is particularly important given the 'second biological psychiatry' and associated trends 'from Freud to Prozac' (Shorter 1997). It also, as we saw in Chapter 3, carries us far beyond micro-orientated concerns towards more macro-orientated horizons: a relationship in which the emotional body plays both a *structured* and *structuring* role.

Having critically discussed the need to go beyond the reason–emotion, biology–society divides, and to bring mind and body together in doing so, what, then, remains to be said on the matter of emotions and mental health?

Colonizing emotions? The deployment of therapeutic expertise

A crucial issue underpinning much of the discussion so far, like sleep in the previous chapter, concerns the potential/prospective colonization of emotion through various forms of expertise, in the name of mental health and illness. One must, of course, as previous chapters attest, proceed with due caution here given the complexity of these relations, and the potential 'gains' as well as 'losses' involved.[10] Emotional 'disorder', nonetheless, is said to be on the 'increase' across the developed world, varying in magnitude from nation to nation, but almost all showing significant rises.[11] Oliver James (1998), for example, in reviewing current evidence, reaches what he takes to be the inescapable conclusion that depression, violence and compulsive behaviour have all increased considerably since the 1950s. For once, he states, 'it is no exaggeration to use the word "epidemic" in describing a social trend' (1998: 31).[12] Things, of course, returning to the questions posed at the beginning of this chapter, may not be quite so simple, particularly when issues such as 'diagnostic bracket creep' are taken into account. The boundaries of the category of depression, for example, continue to expand, as does the 'list of other types of "disorders" for which Prozac is prescribed. According to some commentators, Prozac is commonly prescribed for persons who do not at all fit the criteria of depression, but who are labelled as "dysthymic" or even "sub- or borderline dysthymic" (i.e. emotion "inappropriate" to the circumstances)' (Lyon 1996: 61).[13]

Prozac, then, from this viewpoint, is indeed part of the problem. Psychopharmacology, that is to say, has succeeded in *reducing* our tolerance to the ups and downs of our emotional lives, moving the goal-posts so to speak, by offering opportunities for a 'quick fix' solution to our 'problems' (Shorter 1997: 232). Is this, then, we may rhetorically ask, the dawn of Huxley's *Brave New World* (1982/1932): *Soma* for the masses – a 'holiday from the facts', one cubic centimetre said to cure 'ten gloomy sentiments' – or, perhaps more correctly in these McDonaldized times (Ritzer 1995), a 'happy meal' dished out in handy bite/pill-sized chunks (Meštrović 1997)? Take your pick. The greatest care, says Mustapha Mond in Huxley's prophetic novel, is taken

> to prevent you from loving anyone too much. There's no such thing as divided allegiance; you're so conditioned that you can't help doing what you ought to do . . . And if ever, by some unlucky chance, anything unpleasant should somehow happen, why there's always *Soma* to give you a holiday from the fact. And there's always *Soma* to calm your anger, to reconcile you to your enemies, to make you patient and long-suffering . . . Anybody can be virtuous now. You can carry at least half your morality about in a bottle. Christianity without tears – that's what *Soma* is. (Huxley 1982/1932: 217)

A Brave New World indeed (see also Chapter 8).

To these 'cosmetic' forms of 'psychopharmacology' (Kramer 1993), and the 'chemically assisted' selves they promote – trends, Lyon (1996) claims, which suggest a continuing process of 'medicalization' of social-structural problems today (see also Crossley 2003) – we may add the broader array of so-called 'psy therapies' currently on offer. From self-help books to agony aunts, counsellors and psychotherapists to 'celebrity status' doctors and 'holistic healers', we are increasingly advised and instructed, encouraged and cajoled, on how best to manage ourselves and ride the emotional waves of everyday life, at home and in the workplace. As Hochschild observes: 'While the counsel of parents, grandparents, aunts and uncles, ministers, priests and rabbis holds relatively less weight than it would have a century ago, that of professional therapists, television talk show hosts, radio commentators, video producers, magazine and advice book authors assumes relatively more weight' (1994: 2).

Not only have the number of so-called 'experts' in the field mushroomed in recent years, but lay people themselves are increasingly coming to 'frame' their problems in '(proto-)professional' terms (de Swaan 1990). Authors of advice books, for example, like other commercially based advice givers, act as 'emotional investment counsellors', recommending 'how much, and in whom, to "invest" emotional attention' (Hochschild 1994: 2). Others pitch their message much wider, extending far beyond the realm of personal relationships to success in all walks of life through the boosting of one's 'emotional intelligence' (Goleman 1996): something, it is claimed, which can be nurtured and strengthened in us all.

An upsurge of interest in 'philosophical counselling' has also occurred in recent years as a guide to life and living. This emerging trend can be traced from Alain de Botton's best seller *How Proust can change your Life* (1997), to Lou Marinoff's popular book *Plato Not Prozac: Applying Philosophy to Everyday Problems (2000)*. De Botton's more recent offering, *The Consolations of Philosophy* (2000), ventures further, advocating Socrates on unpopularity, Seneca on frustration, Epicurus on not having enough money, Montaigne on inadequacy, Schopenhauer on the perils of a broken heart, and Nietzsche on difficulties. Companies too, it seems, may profit from such wisdom, as attested by books such as Tom Morris's *If Aristotle Ran General Motors: The New Soul of Business* (1998). Philosophers, in short, are now being put to work in ways they may or may not approve of: a 'phi' *revival*, if not *rival* perhaps, to the 'psy' therapies?[14]

In this and countless other ways, the individual, Rose (1990) observes, is not some 'isolated automaton' to be dominated and controlled by others. Rather s/he is a 'free citizen', endowed with personal desires and enmeshed, for better or worse, in a dynamic network of relations with others. A 'therapeutic culture of self' has emerged, in other words, involving expert-led techniques of 'self-inspection and self-rectification' which 'measure the psyche' with ever increasing precision. It is in the space opened up *between* the imposition of controls upon conduct by public powers, and the forms of life adopted by each individual, that the

> vocabularies and techniques of these psycho-sciences operate . . . These technologies for the *government of the soul* operate not through the crushing of subjectivity in the interests of control and profit, but by seeking to align political, social and institutional goals with individual pleasures and desires, and with the happiness and fulfilment of the self. Their power lies in the capacity to offer means by which *regulation of selves* – by others and by ourselves – can be made consonant with contemporary political principles, moral ideals and constitutional exigencies. They are, precisely, *therapies of freedom*. (Rose 1990: 257, my emphasis)

Within these therapies, as the above quotation suggests, a strong emphasis is placed on the achievement (if not maximization) of personal 'happiness' and 'fulfilment' through 'self-discovery', 'self-assessment' and 'self-actualization' (Craib 1994). The public face of psychotherapy and counselling, Craib comments, is a comforting, understanding one, enabling people to 'find themselves, take responsibility for themselves and satisfy their needs' (1994: 6). In doing so, however, psychotherapy itself has become caught up in the very ideology of late (reflexive) modernity (Giddens 1990, 1991) which, from client to client, it is called upon to disentangle: one based on powerful illusions of 'personal growth' and 'fulfilment' which are never quite 'achievable' (Craib 1994: 158). The cultural pressures to help people, Craib states (with his psychotherapist's hat on), often normal pressures to ease suffering, to be effective, to be good at our jobs, make us vulnerable to the denial of the necessity and inevitability of certain forms of human suffering. We set out to cure and we construct blueprints of what people ought to be feeling, ought to be like, and we can too easily set about trying to manipulate or even force people into these blueprints. (1994: 8)

It is important, therefore, Craib stresses, to emphasize the 'negative' message(s) of psychoanalytic theory. Predicated as it is on the fatal 'flaws' of the human condition, psychoanalysis cannot, it follows, be offered as a guide to 'the good life', or as a 'cure' that is bound to work. There are no guarantees or miracle cures, it takes a long time, and, if it is to 'work', it invariably involves some painful, anxiety-provoking moments: a process in which notions of happiness and personal fulfilment may indeed seem little more than ideological ideals, late modern or otherwise (Craib 1994: 190). A central paradox emerges from this viewpoint. In order to protect the values threatened by the changes we are currently living through, Craib contends, psychoanalysis may have to reject its 'popularity' (itself a moot point), 'holding on' to the very 'principles for which it is so often criticised' (1994: 192).[15]

To summarize, whether through a 'designer chemical self' or a lengthy dose of talking therapy, ours is an age in which we are seduced, via myths of (unfulfilled) 'happiness' and the 'good life', into thinking that our emotional lives are somehow faulty, deficient or lacking if we feel disappointed or dissatisfied with our lot. In certain cases, of course, this may well be unwarranted, if not unreasonable or pathological. In many other instances, however, it is not: an authentic existential marker and a realistic assessment of life in a 'runaway world' of 'manufactured risks' (if not emotions) and uncertainties (Giddens 1994, 1999).

Crossley (2000) casts a more Habermasian light on these issues, one (touched on earlier) which draws together many of these themes and emotional dynamics in a similarly critical/'colonizing' vein. The strength of the Habermasian approach, Crossley asserts, is that it enables us to examine the emotion–psychiatry–order nexus from both a 'systems' and a 'lifeworld' perspective. The former pertains to economic and political systems (the imperatives, that is, of system integration). The latter, in contrast, relates to the socially and normatively integrated sphere of communicative action (*qua* social integration) (Crossley 2000: 277): action, that is to say, based on mutual understanding and communicatively rational forms of interaction (does what we say make sense? is it sincere? do we have to right to say it?) within the lifeworld (see the *consummation/unification* view of reason and emotion relations discussed above). This enables Crossley to put into a critical perspective the *technical control* of emotion promised by the 'emotion industry' (which includes psychiatric and GP services, psychotherapy and counselling, self-help manuals and pharmaceutical products), contrasting it with the rational regulation of emotion in the lifeworld *qua* communicative action (2000: 278). Emotional life, from this viewpoint, whilst communicatively rational and normatively integrated within the lifeworld, is becoming increasingly 'colonized' by various forms of expertise: a process by which the instrumental rationality of system mechanisms and imperatives comes to dominate or eclipse the communicative rationality of lifeworld members, thereby resulting in demoralization (see also Cornwell 1984; Scambler 1987, 2001).

In some respects, of course, this echoes the views of Rose (1990) and others discussed, albeit from a Habermasian rather than a Foucauldian perspective. It adds to them, however, Crossley (2000) notes, in important new ways. Firstly, the growth of the emotion industry is itself linked with a *shift* from the *communicative rationality* and *social integration* of the *lifeworld* towards politically and economically driven regulation by *expert powers* (*system integration*), highlighting that something important and valuable is being lost in the process. Secondly, the dynamics which fuel these shifts, rather than simply their effects, are also emphasized – the dynamics, that is to say, of economic and administrative expansion. Thirdly, in contrast to Rose, the Habermasian perspective incorporates not simply the psychological and psycho-therapeutic wings, but also the medical and pharmacological wings of the emotion industry, suggesting that the growth of both related to one and the same process: *the colonization of the lifeworld*. Finally, in considering both *supply*- and *demand*-related factors pertaining to this burgeoning emotion industry, it enables us to consider the 'rather peculiar possibility that the growth of the emotion industry may be part of exactly the same problems it claims to alleviate: that is, the growth of the emotion industry is a response to the psychological problems generated by the colonization of the lifeworld and cultural impoverishment' (Crossley 2000: 292). The industry, moreover, may itself create 'dependency' (2000: 292).

The Habermasian perspective, as this suggests, allows us to link the vicissitudes of our emotional lives with the logic of advanced capitalism and the conflict contained therein between *social integration* (lifeworld) and *system integration*. The colonization of emotions, in summary, involves

> an erosion of the mechanisms for socially integrating emotion, through the advance of system mechanisms and imperatives. Integral to this, moreover, the Habermasian approach has allowed us to consider that emotions are not just technical objects of intervention, that *they have a rational character too, but a colonization of emotional life increasingly eclipses this rational dimension in the name of technical intervention.* Our 'inner nature' is ever more subject to a process of instrumental rational domination, at the cost of a *loss to its communicatively rational accountability.* The costs of this, at a social level, are a loss of autonomy at the level of everyday life: *the capacity for regulation of emotion within the lifeworld is being lost to the system.* Furthermore, this involves a *demoralization of the lifeworld,* as emotion passes from the normatively regulated sphere of the lifeworld into the rather more *anomic and instrumentally rational functioning of the system.* (Crossley 2000: 293 my emphasis)[16]

Here we return full circle to debates over reason and emotion, including the very notion and viability of *rational emotion* identified earlier. As to questions of whether 'pathological emotion' is really on the increase, or whether professionals/experts are themselves simply moving the goal-posts or boundaries of the rational and the irrational, the implications of this latter Habermasian approach suggest that both, in fact, may be true: 'twin aspects of the same processes' (Crossley 2000: 285). A troubling prospect indeed.

Conclusions

Emotions, I have argued, are central to mental health as well as illness and to reason itself in its manifold guises. Janus-faced to be sure, emotions are the *sine qua non* of social life. Taking this line has enabled us to tackle a number of associated conceptual issues along the way, including the division between reason and emotion, the biological and the social, in the context of current debates over the colonization of emotion in late/postmodernity.

To (continue to) co-opt emotions solely or simply within the framework of mental illness and/or the irrational, therefore, is to neglect their key role in the *health* and well-being of individuals and society more generally, including issues of social cohesion, integration and solidarity. It is also, to repeat, to downplay the crucial role of emotions in reason and rationality, however defined, confusing a part (their 'subversive' potential) for the whole, thereby perpetuating dominant Western views (themselves 'unreasonable'). What this amounts to is a call to: (i) rethink and *re-embody* reason in other, less 'unreasonable' terms; (ii) reinsert emotions more positively into current sociological debates on (mental) health and social life; and (iii) critically examine the role and function of various forms of expertise, *qua* emotion industry or psy complex, in the creation or alleviation (or both) of emotional 'problems', and the promotion of emotional health and well-being. In these and other respects, the aim has been to bring emotions 'back in', so to speak, to any such debates, freeing them along the way from the one-sided focus or strait-jacket of irrationality and pathology, whilst simultaneously questioning prevailing notions of happiness and well-being in late/postmodernity.

Let me conclude, however, on a somewhat more speculative note. If, as I have argued, we need a *full-bodied*, if not sensual or passionate, approach to emotions in social life – one which no longer falls (solely or simply) into irrational traps, pathological ruses or dualistic divides – then the very notion of a sociology *of* 'mental' health becomes something of a misnomer or contradiction in terms. Adherence to such terms of reference, that is to say, may perpetuate rather than slip the divisions which, throughout this chapter, we have been trying to escape; particularly the mind/body divide. Like the sociology *of* the body, moreover, this creates yet further subject–object divides in which we (disembodied, objective?) sociologists reflect on the minds, bodies and feelings of those we seek to study. It may in this respect, to the extent that 'health' is an issue, be better to think in terms of *emotional health* (as a fully *embodied* phenomenon), than a sociology *of* 'mental' health. Appeals to emotional health, echoing the above points, help to: (i) avoid the medico-centric and/or dualist ring of mental health; (ii) put embodiment centre-stage; and (iii) bring emotions to the fore in *all* discussions of health, including the 'afflictions' of inequality (see Chapter 3). Seen in this light, former references to mental health throughout this chapter must themselves be put in quotes given their problematic (Cartesian) status: one which notions such as the lived (Williams and Bendelow 1998a), mindful (Scheper-Hughes and Lock 1987) and expressive (Freund 1990) body overcome. A critical rethinking of 'mental' health along these lines, to conclude, is both timely and topical. The danger in not doing so is that the sociology of 'mental' health becomes yet another dualistic snare or 'strait-jacket', wittingly or otherwise, in keeping with two centuries of 'unreasonable' Western thought and practice. Let us hope not.

Notes

1 For other interesting discussions of these and related matters, see Radden (1985) and Edwards (1981): the latter focusing more specifically on issues of 'mental health *as* rational autonomy'. See also Elster (1999).

2 Whilst it is tempting here to talk of a 'feminization' of mental health work (or the female 'psy' complex) over the course of the twentieth-century – first, through a growing proportion of psychiatric disorder amongst women; second, through a growing proportion of women in the mental health labour force – such a conclusion, Busfield (2002) notes, is clearly over simple. There is, indeed, in keeping with the general upsurge of interest in men's health (see Chapter 3) and the disturbing rise in (young) male suicide (DoH 1998, 1999), a growing emphasis on men in mental health practice in recent years, including the 1998 campaign by the Royal College of Psychiatrists entitled 'Men Behaving Sadly'. The gendered landscape of psychiatric disorder, in this respect, clearly changes over time according to a diverse array of factors (Busfield 2002).

3 Sartre, nonetheless, is open to criticism here, given his view that emotion effects a quasi-magical transformation of the world which is somehow regressive or irrational. It is us rather than the world, moreover, from this Sartrean viewpoint, that we change in and through emotion (Crossley 1998).

4 Plato too, whilst likening reason to a 'charioteer' and emotions to galloping horses, nonetheless recognized that without the galloping horses, the skill of the charioteer would be 'worthless' (Jaggar 1989).

5 For Weber, the rational and the irrational were maintained through 'creative activity': something, he believed, which could result in one 'intensifying the other' (Albrow 1990). See also Turner (1993).

6 Hochschild's critique, in this respect, rests on a Rosseauesque championing of the 'unmanaged' heart, however difficult this may be to recover, which returns us to the Romantic liberation viewpoint discussed previously.

7 Hume (1969/1739–40) too takes an interesting line here, raising the possibility that emotion, *qua* passion, does not simply 'drive' or 'direct' but, in an important sense, constitutes Reason ('properly understood') as a 'calm' and 'reflective' form of passion – an 'enlightened self-interest', albeit with gendered (read 'masculine') connotations (Lloyd 1993: 55).

8   The role of cognition in emotion can be traced back to Aristotle. Cognition, for example, may 'trigger' an emotion. Emotion, in contrast, may 'influence' a cognition. A cognition may also have emotion as its intentional or propositional 'object'. See, for example, Elster (1999), and the Lazarus (1984; Lazarus and Lazurus 1994) – Zajonc (1984) debate.

9   The notion of 'mental disorder', Busfield states, 'embodies [*sic*] a clear dualism of mind and body', one which, *whilst widely contested*, remains a 'fundamental feature of medicine and lay discourse' (1996: 54; see also Lupton's [1998a] recent study on this latter point concerning lay discourses of the 'emotional self').

10 In some cases, Busfield comments,

> problems widely recognised, but not viewed as mental or health matters, come to be viewed as *'medicalised'* – that is, they come to be subject to the medical gaze. In other cases, such as neurasthenia and hysteria, conditions virtually *disappear* from the psychiatric lexicon and are *declassified*; in yet others one medical problem is *transformed* into another, both being seen as suitable for professional attention. (1996: 59, my emphasis)

11 Psychiatric disorders, as conventionally understood/officially classified, fall into three main categories: (i) disorders of *thought*, such as schizophrenia and various types of dementia; (ii) disorders of *emotion*, such as depression, anxiety states and phobias; and (iii) disorders of *behaviour and personality*, such as substance use, disorders of alcohol and drug dependence. These, as shown in Chapter 3, are themselves socially patterned in various ways according to factors such as class and gender. See, for example, the OPCS *Surveys of Psychiatric Morbidity in Great Britain* (Meltzer et al. 1995) and current UK Government targets for mental health (by 2010) (Department of Health 1999).

12 James (1998) reviews evidence from a variety of countries, including large-scale community studies in America, Sweden and Britain (Appendix I). He also reviews evidence on the links between low serotonin and depression, aggression, substance abuse, compulsive disorders and other problems such as chronic fatigue (Appendix II).

13 Only certain emotions, such as sadness, fear, anxiety, however, Busfield (2002) notes, are incorporated into the psychiatric lexicon in this fashion via disorders of depression, phobia and anxiety states. Other candidates, in contrast, such as jealousy, anger and hate, whilst now receiving some attention in treatment programmes, are not framed as distinct disorders in quite the same way.

14 Thanks to Anita Noguera for bringing this to my attention.

15 For other feminist critiques of psychotherapy and associated forms of psychological and psychiatric intervention, see Showalter (1987) and Ussher (1991), both of whom champion women's own voices and experiences in patriarchal society and in misogynist culture, past and present. See also Horgan (1999) for a more general critique of the 'ineffectiveness' of these and other treatments to date.

16 In taking this line, Crossley is not, in keeping with my own viewpoint, denying the importance of these technical interventions in certain cases or circumstances. Emotions, he notes, can and do get 'out of hand', causing 'disruption' of various sorts in the lifeworld. To the degree, therefore, that the boundary between rational and irrational emotion is 'correctly drawn' within psychiatric practice, there is 'no problem': technical interventions themselves are 'justified because they would only be applied to those individuals whose emotions defy communicative understanding and reason' (2000: 283). A danger lurks here, however, as before, due to the fact that there can be 'no hard and fast criteria for *differentiating the rational and the irrational*' (Crossley 2000: 283, my emphasis).

8

Hi-Tech Bodies: From Corporeality to Hyperreality?

Medicine is making the news for a variety of reasons these days, some better than others. A prime headline maker, in this respect, concerns the seemingly endless series of medical 'breakthroughs' which are now occurring, itself part and parcel of both the media's hunger for stories and broader trends and developments in biotechnologies at the dawn of the new millennium. Open a paper, turn on the television, listen to the radio or surf the Internet, and there, ready and waiting for you, are an array of amazing, bewildering, dazzling or terrifying tales of these 'cutting-edge' technologies – from the latest fads and fashions in cosmetic surgery, to debates on xenotransplantation, and from advances in the new genetics, to telepresence surgery and a host of other treatments for 'virtual' patients in 'virtual' clinics.

Herein lies the starting point of this chapter, which examines these trends and developments at three interrelated levels: firstly, the extent to which medical technology renders our bodies increasingly 'uncertain' at the beginning of the twenty-first century – the alleged 'crisis of meaning', that is to say, as to what bodies are and what they might become (Shilling 1993); secondly, the analytical purchase which the 'cyborg' (Haraway 1991) provides on these contemporary forms and cultures of technological embodiment; and, finally, the issues this raises, at the broadest level, with regard to late or postmodern interpretations of contemporary medical practice. In doing so, the opportunities and risks of these new technologies, and the (bio)ethical dilemmas they raise, will be implicit if not explicit themes running throughout the chapter, themselves linked both to previous chapters on issues such as ageing and the following chapter on caring and ethics.

The body in high-technology medicine: uncertain times?

> We may be about to enter into a posthuman future . . . Many assume that the posthuman world will look pretty much like our own . . . only with better health care, longer lives, and perhaps more intelligence than today . . . But the posthuman world could become one that is far more hierarchical and competitive . . . and full of social conflict as a result . . . It could be one in which any notion of 'shared humanity' is lost, because . . . we no longer have a clear idea of what human being is. (Fukuyama 2002: 218)

A paradox, as suggested above, lies at the heart of current (bio)technological developments. On the one hand, our ability to control or transform bodies, for better or worse, has dramatically increased in recent years. This itself, on the other hand, engenders increasing uncertainty as to the very nature and boundaries of bodies. It is here that the 'leaky' (postmodern) figure of the cyborg can be found, rendering previous forms of embodiment problematic. Hypothetically and materially, Haraway (1991) states, the cyborg is a 'hybrid' cybernetic device and organism: a 'scientific chimera', but also a social and scientific reality in the contemporary era; a 'myth and a tool', 'representation and an instrument'.

Cyborgs exist when two types of boundaries are simultaneously breached: that between animals (or other organisms) and humans, and that between self-governing machines (automatons) and organisms, especially humans as models of autonomy (Haraway 1991). The 'cyborg', then, is a 'leaky' figure born of the 'interface' between 'automaton' and 'autonomy', nature and culture, masculinity and femininity, Self and Other, rendering these divisions indeterminate and thus, in Haraway's vision, offering the potential to escape from their oppressive confines. Today, Haraway proclaims, 'we are all chimeras, theorized and fabricated hybrids of machine and organism; in short we are cyborgs. The cyborg is our ontology, it gives us our politics.' Foucault's biopolitics, from this viewpoint, is but a 'flaccid premonition of cyborg politics, a very open field' (Haraway 1991: 150). These issues, in turn, map on to a broader series of changes and transformation for Haraway: from representation to simulation; the bourgeois novel (realism) to science fiction (postmodernism); depth and integrity to surface and boundary; biology as clinical practice to biology as inscription; hygiene to stress management; sex to genetics; labour to robotics; mind to artificial intelligence; Second World War to star wars; white capitalist patriarchy to the informatics of domination (1991: 161–2). We are, she claims, living through a movement from an 'organic, industrial society' to a 'polymorphous information system' tied to science and technology, which is premised on the 'informatics of domination' (see also Chapter 2).

Whilst this may sound wild and fanciful, the 'cyborg', 'posthuman' or 'transhuman' is not, it is clear, just a creature of science fiction, television or film. There are already, Gray and colleagues argue, many 'cyborgs' among us in society, from fighter-bomber pilots in state-of-the-art cockpits to our grandmother with a pace-maker (1995: 2–3; see also Gray 2002; Rawdon Wilson 1995; Tomas 1995). Haraway, in similar fashion, notes that medicine, like science fiction, is 'full of cyborgs, of cou-plings between organism and machine' (1991: 150). Even the 'quickest tour' of the human body, from head to toes, reveals the great variety of ways in which medicine can turn humans into 'cyborgs' – from *restorative* or *normalizing*, to *reconfiguring* or *enhancing* technologies (Gray et al. 1995: 3). It is time, therefore, to examine these issues more closely at a number of different levels and in a variety of corporeal ways within the technological clinic or 'transhuman bodyshop' of twenty-first-century medicine: a 'posthuman' era, according to some commentators (cf. Fukuyama 2002, quoted above), in which the next generation may well be the last of 'pure' humans (Deitch 1992).

Plastic bodies

First, advances in medical science and technology have rendered bodies increasingly *plastic* (able, that is, to be moulded at will). Technologies of cosmetic or aesthetic sur-gery, for example, in addition to reconstructive surgery, have greatly expanded the limits of how the body may be restyled, reshaped and rebuilt (Davis 1994). *Aesthetic* surgery, following Gilman (1999), is a label for those procedures which society, at any given time, deems 'unnecessary', 'non-medical' or a sign of 'vanity'. *Reconstructive* surgery, in contrast, is understood as 'restoring function': distinctions which first emerged in the Renaissance, reappearing in the course of the nineteenth-century (Gilman 1999: 10). Most modern procedures employed in aesthetic surgery date from around the 1880s and 1890s (Gilman 1999: 3). Today, however, the line between reconstructive and aesthetic procedures, as Gilman himself notes, is 'blurry' (1999: 8–9; see also Davis 1994).

Amongst the rapidly growing array of technologies now on offer are face-lifts, arm lifts (brachioplasty), rhinoplasties (nose contouring), otoplasty (ear surgery), eyelid corrections, lip enlargements, hair transplants, chemical peeling and dermabrasion, breast correction (mastoplexy, reduction, augmentation), the stripping of varicose veins, fat removal, body contouring (liposuction or suction lipectomy) and penile enlargement/implants, not to mention transgender surgery. In these 'body sculpting clinics' flesh is either 'added or taken away', wrinkles disappear, breasts become inflated or deflated (cf Conrad and Jacobson 2003), and body shapes are trans-formed (Davis 1994). As a consequence, notwithstanding frequent complications – from scarring, bleeding, secondary infections and skin discoloration, to nerve damage, loss of sensation and impaired motor ability (Glassner 1995: 170) – the con-stant (re)makeability of the human body and the power of medical technology are visually sustained in each 'exhibit' (Balsamo 1992, 1995a, 1995b).[1]

Within consumer culture, Glassner (1995) observes, 'professional body remakers' function like 'surrogate psychiatrists': we literally expect them to make us into 'some body new' (1995: 161). The extension of plastic surgery into the realm of body improvement has led to a 'veritable boom' in cosmetic surgery as a kind of aesthetic technological 'fix' (Clarke 1995: 147). Within the US, for example, some 296,000 aesthetic surgical procedures were undertaken in 1981, a figure which had risen to 477,700 operations by 1984 (Gilman 1999: 3). By 1996, however, results from the American Academy of Facial Plastic and Reconstructive Surgery pointed to a staggering 825,000 plastic and reconstructive procedures on the face alone (an increase of 9 per cent since 1993) (Gilman 1999: 4). One out of every thirty-five surgical procedures performed in the US in 1993, in fact, was 'aesthetic', with surgery of the eyelids and hair transplants both enjoying big increases between 1993 and 1995 (increases of 37 per cent and 61 per cent, respectively) (Gilman 1999: 4).

Whilst women make up the vast majority of this elective market – the most frequently performed surgery in the US in 1995 being eyelid surgery (blepharoplasty) – a growing male market is now evident, with nose jobs (rhinoplasty) being the most common procedure in the US in 1995 (Gilman 1999: 4). As for Britain, its smaller cosmetic surgery market is projected to be worth more than £250 million by 2004 (Meek 2001: 22). The growth in aesthetic surgery has also been matched by an increasing professionalization of aesthetic surgery – itself the fastest growing medical specialism in the US – a profession, Davis remarks, which 'expresses and reproduces gender symbolism', with men 'doing the operating while women are the recipients of surgery, the objects to be operated on' (1998: 23–4)

Given our tendency to 'confuse beauty with health', cosmetic surgery stands a good chance of winning ever wider public acceptance over the coming decades (Glassner 1995: 170). All over the world, in fact, Gilman notes, people are having aesthetic surgery in ever increasing numbers, becoming something of a 'world-wide phenomenon in the past few decades': a globalization of aesthetic surgery, in effect, which has spawned numerous centres linking surgery and tourism (1999: 8).

Not only does plastic surgery throw into critical relief the commodified nature of the body in consumer culture, it also indicates the extreme lengths to which individuals will go in order to mould and shape their bodies in line with prevailing cultural mandates of beauty. As Glassner states:

> Bodies themselves have become objects to be sold in American society. Surgeons sell not just corrections to the body . . . but something far more transitory, *fashions*. They alter the size and shape of our buttocks, breasts, noses, or eyes to fit current styles . . . No longer can we merely dress up the body we happen to have, or improve it by losing weight or having a beauty makeover or straightening out the curve in our nose. We actually purchase a 'new body'. (1995: 175)

In these and other ways, we stride (or stagger?) into the new millennium knowing that we must become better, we shall become better. We can change our bodies and our lives. We will fit ourselves into society by restricting our bodies to make our souls happy. We imagine the world outside ourselves as a happier place than our inner world. For the acquisition (not merely the pursuit) of happiness – or at least the absence of sadness – is the greatest promise of our post-Prozac world. Aesthetic surgery is one of the means by which we believe we can accomplish this goal. (Gilman 1999: 330)

Viewed in this context, aesthetic or cosmetic surgery is at once both *symptom* and *solution*, oppression and liberation all at once: something, paradoxically, which enables women to feel 'embodied subjects' rather than 'objectified bodies' (Davis 1994: 161). It also, as the two quotations suggest, adds another dimension to the debates on (un)happy bodies considered in the previous chapter.

The story of 'plastic' bodies does not, however, end here. Recent advances in medical technology, for example, are also now busy spinning plastic into tissue. Using biodegradable plastic seeded with cells, computer-aided 'scaffolding' has been constructed to provide a template for the formation of new tissue. As the cells divide, this plastic structure is covered and eventually degrades, leaving only tissue ready for implantation in the patient (Langer and Vacanti 1995). This approach has already been demonstrated on animals, and during the past few years, human skin grown on polymer substrates has been grafted onto burn patients and the foot ulcers of diabetics, with some success. What we have here, in other words, is a form of 'artificial engineering', plastic or otherwise, albeit with one important proviso: this time the 'engineers' are the 'body's own cells' themselves (Langer and Vacanti 1995: 100; see also '[genetically] engineered bodies' following). This, however, is merely the tip of the biotech iceberg, as the following pages attest.

Communal/interchangeable bodies

Moving from its surface to its interior, the body has also become increasingly *bionic*, with cardiac pacemakers, valves, titanium hips, polymer blood vessels, electronic eye and ear implants and even polyurethane hearts (Synnott 1993). Developments in nanotechnology and micro-engineering, moreover, as we shall see later, add a further miniaturized dimension to the these debates, opening up new corporeal possibilities for biotechnologies to repair or replace, control or transform us from *within*, so to speak (see 'digitalized/miniaturized bodies' following).

Communal/interchangeable or *spare part* bodies are likewise very much in evidence now through developments such as organ donation and transplantation surgery (Fox and Swazey 1992; Synnott 1993). An important historical precursor to these donor/recipient relations, Hirst and Metcalfe (2001: 288) remind us, concerns the transfusion of blood: a taken-for-granted, if not 'natural', procedure nowadays perhaps, but something which caused much controversy when experiments first began in the seventeenth-century. As for organ transplants, the landmark here was

December 1967, when Christian Barnard, a South African surgeon, transplanted the heart of a recently dead person into a man with a chronic heart disease, who died eighteen days later. Advances in organ transplantation in the 1980s – including advances in surgical techniques, intensive post-operative care and new immuno-suppressive drugs to combat rejection, together with techniques of tissue typing and matching of donor-recipients – have resulted in relatively high success rates, with programmes now established in most industrialized countries (Hirst and Metcalfe 2001: 288).

Single organ transplants are routine practice nowadays, ranging from kidney grafts (the most common and successful procedure), through heart and/or lung transplants, to cornea transplants to restore sight. Body parts, Hogle (1995) notes, have become increasingly 'widget'-like in this respect (standardized items, that is to say, to be replaced as needed on demand). In particular, the organization, procurement and delivery of human organs has been transformed from an altruist patient-centred enterprise to an increasingly international 'for-profit' market-based industry. As the production of human organs and tissues becomes ever more routinized, parallel processes have developed to create '"product-specific" handling, marketing and even accounting systems' (Hogle 1995: 209). Technical developments, therefore, are increasingly centred on 'presentation' of the materials for transplant (fast-acting liquids for freezing the contents of the entire peritoneal cavity, for example). Whilst previously the term 'presentation' referred to the storage of materials *after* explanation and during transplant to the end-user, now presentation begins much earlier,

> within the body itself. Recognizing the considerable market potential of the human materials industry, pharmaceutical and medical supply companies have developed new products and entire new industries designed specifically for use in donor cadavers. These include free-oxygen scavengers, 'hibernation hormones', new perfusion and preservation fluids, and other chemicals to preserve tissue integrity before being removed, and to make the materials more 'immunologically silent' to prevent problems later when they are replaced inside another body. In essence, the human materials are being structurally, chemically and functionally transformed to make them more universal. In this way, they become not only substitutable mechanical parts, but more like off-the-shelf reagents, available for use in a variety of end-users. (Hogle 1995: 208)

Through these 'core technologies', cadavers are being transformed into what Hogle (harking back to our earlier discussion) terms 'donor-cyborgs' as the physical body is 'reprogrammed' and 'retooled' for new uses. When the donor-cyborg reaches its 'almost-total-technology state', its parts are dispersed and distributed throughout the 'communal body' to innumerable others. In this way, transplanted human body parts become the 'seeds' that reproduce and replicate new 'cyborgs' (Hogle 1995: 207; see also Hogle 1999).

Problems remain nonetheless due to the limited number of donors available: a classic situation of demand outstripping supply, itself exacerbated by events such as the Alder Hey scandal.[2] Faced with such difficulties, organ trafficking has indeed become big business in the global marketplace, the ultimate form of human sacrifice perhaps, expressed in and through the dilemmas of the cash-nexus. What this amounts to, Scheper-Hughes states, is a 'politics of the belly' involving an 'object of desire' for one population, and a 'commodity of last resort' for 'the other', both contributing to new forms of 'late modern cannibalism' (2001a: 1–2). Commercialized transplant medicine, in this respect, in association with advanced biotechnologies and global capitalism – whose 'tastes and desires' extend far beyond organs to 'skin, blood, tissues, reproductive and genetic materials of "the other"' (Scheper-Hughes 2001a: 5) – has allowed global society to be unequally divided into 'organ givers and organ receivers': the former an 'invisible and discredited collection of anonymous suppliers of spare parts'; the latter viewed as 'cherished patients, treated as moral subjects and as suffering individuals' (Scheper-Hughes 2001a: 4–5). *Their* names, biographies and medical histories are 'known and their proprietary rights over the bodies and body parts of the poor, living and dead, are virtually unquestioned' (2001a: 4).

A graphic illustration of these processes as, explored both by Cohen (2001) and by Scheper-Hughes (2001b), concerns the emergence of the fetishized kidney for organ sellers and organ buyers alike (see also Finkel 2001). Human sacrifices, of course, of whatever sort, have gone on for millennia. What is different today, however, Scheper-Hughes stresses, is that the sacrifice is disguised as '"donation", rendered invisible by its anonymity and hidden under the medical rhetoric of life saving and gifting. In all the ultimate fetish is the idea of life itself as an object of endless manipulation' (2001a: 5). The development of the powerful immuno-suppresive drug Cyclosporine, Cohen (2001) highlights, has greatly expanded the population of potential organ donors – a drug, that is to say, based on the *recognition* of what needs to be *suppressed* – and hence of quiet 'invisible' sales, even in the United States (where it is wrapped in layers of 'prestational and Christian rhetoric' [Cohen 2001: 11]). This in turn serves to 'corrupt cadaver-based waiting lists', including blatant 'auto-cannibalism and kidney sales by subaltern and generally stigmatized populations' through the use of this expensive 'miracle' drug (Scheper-Hughes 2001a: 4). Cyclosporine, in other words, '*globalizes*, creating myriad biopolitical fields where donor populations are differentially and flexibly materialized' (Cohen 2001: 11–12). 'Difference', in doing so, is 'selectively suppressed, allowing specific populations to become "same enough" for their members to be surgically disaggregated and their parts reincorporated': a 'multiple biopolitics of suppression', in effect (Cohen 2001: 12).

Faced with these and other dilemmas, Scheper-Hughes and Cohen established the 'Berkeley Organs Watch' in November 1999, at the University of California, Berkeley, from which they now co-ordinate research on transplant practices worldwide – a map, to all intents and purposes, of the 'routes by which organs, doctors, medicine, capitalism and donors circulate' (Scheper-Hughes 2001b: 34) – with findings broadly available online. Working in various sites in Argentina, Brazil, Cuba, Ecuador, India, Israel, the Netherlands, South Africa, Turkey and the US, they have so far identified the following disturbing issues:

> (1) race, class, gender inequalities and injustices in the acquisition, harvesting and distribution of organs; (2) widespread violation of national laws and international regulations against the sale of organs; (3) the collapse of cultural and religious sanctions against body dismemberment and commercial use in the face of the enormous market pressures in the transplant industry; (4) the emergence of new forms of debt peonage in which the commodified kidney occupies a critical role; (5) the coexistence of 'compensated gifting' of kidneys within extended families and 'coerced gifting' of kidneys by domestic workers and by hopeless prisoners in exchange for secure work and reduction in prison sentences; (6) popular resistance to newly mandated laws of presumed consent for organ donation; (7) violations of cadavers in hospital morgues and police mortuaries in which organs and tissues are removed without consent for barter or sale; (8) wasting of viable organs in the context of intense competition between public and private transplant units; (9) medically substantiated allegations of 'kidney theft' from vulnerable patients, mostly poor and female, during routine surgeries. (Scheper-Hughes 2001b: 35–6)

Mention should also be made, at this point, of other types of implants from body to body at the cellular level, including various cell therapies such as adult bone marrow stem cell transplants to replace a person's bone marrow, foetal cell implants (taken from organ-aborted foetuses) to compensate for cellular deficiencies, and foetal stem cells for use not simply in diseases such as Parkinson's, but also for the development of replacement tissues grown in laboratories. By 2001 indeed, Hirst and Metcalfe report, private companies were offering parents a new service. For 'a fee, they could have a "named" sample of their newborn baby's foetal stem cells deep-frozen and stored, so that – if the need ever arose – the cells could be reintroduced into the donor in adult life, for example, to repopulate his or her bone marrow after treatment for cancer' (2001: 292–3). Is such 'storage', we may ask, morally acceptable, or will a new 'gift relationship' emerge: one in which new parents are willing to donate some of their baby's foetal stems cells for the 'common good' (Hirst and Metcalfe 2001: 293)?

Not only are bodily organs interchangeable at the human to human level, they also now (threaten to) cross species boundaries, as xenotransplantation attests – the use, that is to say, of animal organs or cells for human transplant surgery. This, to be sure, raises a number of ethical dilemmas, issues made all the more pressing with the announcement in late 1995 of a new development enabling scientists to produce customized pigs whose organs would be less likely to induce fatal rejection in the human recipient. The company involved, Imutran, reported the creation of 'Astrid', the first of these pigs, which was duly given much media attention. Such developments, along with the creation of other 'transgenic' animals (animals carrying genes from another species), and the use of animals in tissue engineering such as the infamous mouse with the human ear – another issue which received considerable media coverage in early 1996 – pose many moral, social and cultural questions about individual and species bodies, boundaries and the constitution of the 'natural'.

This again raises, in acute form, thorny questions about the meaning(s) of corporeality, self-identity and the nature of death. If the pig, for example, is seen as a ritually 'unclean' animal, one involving 'matter out of place' and the 'transgression' of cultural boundaries (cf. Douglas 1966), then how would we see ourselves with an animal heart inside us, and how does this square with, say, orthodox Jewish beliefs, or those of a vegetarian/vegan or anti-vivisectionist? Does the body become degraded, defiled or debased in some way as a consequence, and if so, what implications does this have for our sense of who or what we are? Organ transplantation in general, Joralemon (1995) notes, challenges traditional body/self integrity by distinguishing between the brain and other, 'more replaceable' parts of the body, thereby reinforcing a traditional Cartesian mind/body split. Sharp (1995) raises similar issues, stressing the disjunction between the need to *personalize* and the need to *objectify* bodies and organs. Whilst medical personnel put great emphasis on objectification (the heart is only a 'pump'), transplant recipients experience conflict between this mechanistic/reductionist view of bodies and their wider cultural beliefs about embodied selfhood – the sacred heart, for instance, as the very 'core' of the person (see, for example, Birke 1999; Williams and Calnan 1996b).[3]

These cultural risks and dilemmas of embodied selfhood are further complicated, at the clinical or biological level, by risks associated with the transmission to humans of animal viruses such as porcine endogenous retrovirus (PERVs). Regulatory medical and scientific watchdogs such as the UK Xenotransplantation Interim Regulatory Authority which came into being in 1997, are therefore faced with a complex array of factors regarding the risk and opportunities of research into xenotransplantion: issues which must be 'resolved' before any human studies can get underway. Opinion, as one might expect, is divided here, ranging from advocates of such procedures, who stress the reduction in transplant waiting lists and the enhancements to quality of life for those whose organs are failing (an end to the black market perhaps?), to those who object to the use of animals on moral grounds, and/or those who feel such techniques are just plain 'wrong' and 'unnatural' (Bryan and Clare 2001: 145). In an important sense, nonetheless, as Bryan and Clare stress, xenotransplantation is 'already here':

> Around the world a few hundred people have pig cells in their bodies. In operating theatres in the USA and Europe, surgeons have had their dress rehearsals for putting whole pig organs into humans. All they need is the go-ahead from the regulators. One of those surgeons . . . predicts that within ten or twenty years xenotransplants will be a routine procedure. (2001: 207)

Itself a hybrid creature of the new millennium, xenotransplantation, in turn, intersects with a range of other key developments in genetic engineering and cloning technologies. Developments on these latter fronts, in fact, point to a range of other, more 'acceptable' alternatives to the use of trangenic pig organs, or to transplantation surgery in general as we know it today. The ultimate goal, Langer and Vacanti (1995) state, is to *manufacture* organs and tissues rather than simply *move* them, including the prospect of organs grown from stem cells taken from embryos cloned specifically for the purpose. In time, moreover, scientists hope to be able to 'trick stem cells in adult bodies to regress to an earlier stage of development, so that they can be reprogrammed to make any cells at any time', thereby doing away with the need to grow embryos for their stem cells (Bryan and Clare 2001: 206). Here we anticipate the next key issue of genetically engineered bodies and the prospect (or spectre) of 'designer' babies.

(Genetically) engineered bodies/designer babies

If *plastic*, *bionic* or *interchangeable* bodies suggest one cluster of possibilities in this Brave New World of twenty-first-century medicine, then developments in human reproduction, and the 'birth' of the new genetics (including so-called 'reproductive genetics' [Ettorre 1999]) suggest another: the dawn of an age in which bodies may become increasingly *engineered* or (re)programmed, if not *chosen* or *selected* (Synnott 1993: 34–5), thereby rendering many of these former 'breakthroughs' potentially redundant or moribund.

Clarke (1995), for example, echoing Haraway (1991, 1997), highlights what she takes to be a shift from 'modern' approaches to reproduction – techniques centred on achieving and/or enhancing *control* over bodies and reproductive processes via monitoring, planning, limiting, bounding and the setting up of boundaries – to postmodern strategies based on new reproductive technologies which emphasize the 're/de/sign' and *transformation* of reproductive bodies and processes in order to achieve a variety of goals (see also Clarke et al. 2000).

On the one hand, Stanworth (1987: 1) notes, these new reproductive technologies – which include (modifications of) *in virtro* fertilization techniques and a host of other hormonal and infertility treatments – appear to offer a range of possibilities for extending the pleasures of (assisted) parenthood to those who, for whatever reasons, have hitherto been unable to have a child.[4] Future developments on the male front, moreover, include the transplantation of donated precursors of sperm cells into the seminiferous tubules of the testes of infertile men. Vaccines (immunocontraceptives) able to disrupt sperm function are also now currently being developed for men and women whose desire is not to conceive (Alexander 1995).

On the other hand, however, these new technologies extend the boundaries and possibilities of medical and scientific practice in ways which threaten to outstrip human understanding, public morality and control (Stanworth 1987). Key issues here include: the ethical and practical problems surrounding the manipulation of eggs, sperm and embryos outside the human body; the problems of 'parenthood', especially 'motherhood'; and the 'threats' to identity which these technologies pose for the 'products' they create (Stanworth 1987). What is potentially being transformed here, critics argue, is our conceptualization of what it is to be human, male, female, reproductive, parent, child, foetus, family, 'race' and even population (Clarke 1995: 149). All must now be questioned and renegotiated as a consequence of these technological developments.

These issues, to be sure, have been hotly debated in feminist circles. For some, the creation of these new reproductive technologies is seen as the end-stage of men's desire to control women and appropriate reproductive power (Corea 1985; Rowland 1985, 1992). The danger lurks, from this standpoint, that biological mothers will eventually be reduced to 'mother machines' (Corea 1985) or 'living laboratories' (Rowland 1985, 1992), eroding still further women's bodily and metaphysical privacy. Physiologically, women's bodies are 'opened, scrutinized, manipulated, parts extracted and then reintroduced' (Steinberg 1990: 86). This enables practitioners to unselfconsciously '*speak* of disembodied parts of women – "the ovaries", "ripe eggs", and of "recovering" these parts even as they *materially* scrutinize, alter or remove these parts of women's bodies' (Steinberg 1990: 86).

Casper (1995) goes further. What this amounts to, she asserts, echoing earlier themes, is the emergence of 'foetal cyborgs' and 'techno' mothers. This, for example, includes: foetal visualization technologies; foetal diagnostic technologies; technologies which enable a foetus to live inside a brain-dead woman's body; technologies which transform aborted foetuses into 'materials' for scientific research and new forms of biomedical therapy; technologies which produce physiological knowledge about foetuses; and, finally, an array of foetal treatment technologies, including 'foetal surgery' (Casper 1995: 186–7). Women, as a consequence, become erased, alienated and depersonalized in the process of reproduction.

Others, however, have argued that it is not so much the technologies themselves which are problematic, but the context in which they are developed and applied, particularly the thorny issue of access ('*who*' exactly is allowed to conceive). The call for a return to so-called 'natural motherhood' – itself a much debated term (Arney and Neill 1982) – is therefore resisted. Instead, it is argued, women must themselves participate in both the development and (re-)evaluation of these technologies, rather than leaving them in the hands of 'malestream' (biomedical) science (McNeil et al. 1990; Stanworth 1987). Many women undergoing these forms of treatment, moreover, as Denny's (1996) study convincingly shows, view them positively as a 'resource' rather than a mechanism of (patriarchal) 'control' or 'oppression' as radical feminists claim: something, she argues, which cannot simply be explained away as false consciousness through pro-natalist ideologies.

Post-structuralist feminists too have rejected the notion that the 'real female body' is passively 'acted upon', preferring instead to view it as being both inscribed and constituted through (re)productive discursive practices and processes. From this perspective, these new reproductive technologies are themselves viewed as producing subjectivity rather than 'false consciousness' (Lupton 1994). Consequently, there is a focus on the *struggles* and *resistances* between men and women and the shifting configurations of knowledge/power this involves (Sawicki 1991). The ultimate goal here is to produce a feminist body/politics which allows women to speak about their bodies in their own chosen ways and thereby to resist dominant scientific and technological discourses (Jacobus et al. 1990).

These issues and struggles themselves key into broader developments and debates in recent years surrounding the new genetics, including the previously mentioned notion of 'reproductive genetics' (Ettorre 1999). Developments in molecular biology in the late 1960s and the 1970s – themselves underpinned by Watson and Crick's discovery, in 1953, of the double helix and the cracking of the four-letter DNA base code – are generally seen to have laid the foundations for the emergence of the new genetics in the 1980s (Petersen and Bunton 2002: 41). This, in turn, set the stage for the subsequent international collaborative effort – if not competition between two rival camps of publicly and privately funded scientists – to systematically read the complete DNA sequence: the mapping (note the cartographic metaphor) of the human genome or book of life, that is to say. The 'completion' of this project was officially announced on 12 February 2001,[5] providing us with the correct order or sequence of the 3 billion 'letters' or base pairs of the DNA code which make up the 30,000–40,000 genes in the human genome (about a third of that initially expected when the project first began).[6]

Whilst often left undefined, the new genetics, Petersen and Bunton (2002: 30) note, is characterized by (neo-liberal) *ideals* of 'empowerment', thereby serving to distance itself from the eugenics of old, which is duly dismissed as coercive and 'pseudo-science'. The historical diversity of eugenic discourses and programmes, however, these authors stress, serves to problematize any such neat and tidy divisions, pointing instead to important lines of convergence with respect to the 'broad goals and the similar contexts giving rise to both' (2002: 30). Perhaps the key defining characteristic to date, nonetheless, concerns the hype surrounding the very advent of the new genetics itself, including many (at best) premature promises. The mapping of the human genome, according to many writers and commentators, promises to radically transform both medicine (Anderson 1995) and our lives in general over the coming decades, particularly when the merging of *genetic* and *digital* technologies is taken into account (Rifkin 1998). As Bill Clinton (2001) remarked in his Dimbleby lecture, the sequencing of the human genome, in his time of office, was 'thrilling . . . We've already identified the major genetic variances that predict breast cancer, we're very close on Alzeheimer's and AIDS and Parkinson's.' 'There's no question', he proceeded to state, that 'pretty soon . . . women . . . in their childbearing years will be able to bring children home from hospital with little gene cards and life expectancies in excess of ninety years'.

Media reports, in similar fashion, abound of scientific claims regarding genetic associations with disease, behaviours and personality traits. Scarcely a day goes by, in fact, without some new(s) claim breaking: something akin to a 'gene-of-the-week' genre it seems (Conrad and Gabe 1999: 505). In doing so, moreover, the complexity of genetic associations and causal relations is all too frequently lost or glossed, privileging genetic factors when in fact they may simply be *contributory* (Holtzman and Marteau 2000; Petersen and Bunton 2002). It is as if, Conrad and Gabe remark, there were an 'oversimplified Mendelian assumption, termed O-GOD (one gene, one disease), which involves a direct and virtual one-to-one relationship between genetics and behaviour' (1999: 507).

This, of course, is not to belittle such efforts or their potential future payoffs. Important discoveries (as the Clinton quote suggests) have indeed already been made, including the identification of genes responsible for conditions such as cystic fibrosis, Huntingdon's disease and certain types of breast cancer. The implications of finding genes for behaviours or personality traits, however, are far from clear-cut, raising particular controversy and debate. Genetics, to repeat, is likely to play *a part* in many human diseases and behaviours, of which doubtless we will hear much more in the future. Many early claims, nonetheless, have been somewhat exaggerated, whilst the much-hyped promises of gene therapy have yet to materialize (Conrad and Gabe 1999: 507).

Debates surrounding the prospects of genetic testing and screening programmes throw many of these issues into critical relief. Again a mixed bag of possibilities suggest themselves here, not simply for those with a family history of hereditary disease (Parsons and Atkinson 1992, 1993), but for all of us in future modes of risk assessment. On the one hand, for example, genetic screening could provide us (all) with a more or less useful print-out of our likelihood of this or that disease, or our prospects of living to a ripe old age, thereby enabling us to take 'appropriate' (lifestyle) steps to lower our risks. On the other hand, however, it could also provide the basis for various discriminatory practices and violations of our civil liberties, in the workplace and elsewhere, including our potential insurability. This, coupled with the potential for anxiety inflation, and the tendency to individualize collective problems, makes any such developments far from unproblematic.

A particularly controversial issue here, in the sphere of 'reproductive genetics' (Ettorre 1999),[7] concerns pre-natal screening for genetic diseases and disabilities – including pre-implantation diagnosis of embryos – alongside other potential *enhancements* of humans through embryo genetic manipulation of various sorts. These technologies raise serious concerns not simply (as mentioned previously) about new forms of genetic stigmatization or discrimination (Shakespeare 1995, 1999), but also about 'backdoor eugenics' (Duster 1990): eugenics, that is to say, by *outcome* rather than policy intent (Conrad and Gabe 1999; Kerr and Shakespeare 2002; Petersen and Bunton 2002). Genetics, moreover, as Shakespeare (2003) notes, has the power, through such tests and procedures, both to *avoid* the birth of disabled people, and to *expand* the disability category itself by *destabilizing* the non-disabled identity through the diagnosis of future illness or risk of illness in the currently a-symptomatic. The era of 'designer babies' also now beckons, through developments such as genetic pre-selection for donor compatibility in relation to sick siblings: something which recently received official sanction in Britain from the Human Fertilization and Embryology Authority (Meek 2002). Already we glimpse here the fact that whilst genetics is 'fundamental for understanding human heredity, physiology and development', its social and cultural uses extend 'far beyond scientific knowledge' (Conrad and Gabe 1999: 507). The rising genetic paradigm, in other words, is 'influencing how we think about life, including disease and disability, human capacities and failings, social problems, kinship and quality of life' (Conrad and Gabe 1999: 507). It also, of course, extends from the 'local level to the global level', shaping our social relations within and 'across national borders', redirecting the relationship between 'citizens and the state' in the very process of doing so (Petersen and Bunton 2002: 1).

As for gene therapies, existing (somatic) approaches comprise several different techniques, including *ex vivo* ('outside the living body') therapy and *in situ* ('in position') therapy, currently used for the treatment of cystic fibrosis (Anderson 1995). A third form of treatment, although still at the experimental stage, is *in vivo* ('in the living body') therapy, whereby physicians, it is claimed, will simply inject corrective gene carriers into the bloodstream of the patient in much the same way as many drugs are administered now (Anderson 1995: 98–b). To date, however, as noted above, the promises of gene therapy remain just that: gains to be had in the future perhaps, the complex multi-factorial nature of many diseases notwithstanding, but with little significant impact upon treatment so far. Initial optimism then, on this count, has been tempered somewhat, though not of course extinguished (Hirst and Metcalfe 2001: 318–21).

These very issues, however, receive a further twist in the light of (therapeutic) cloning. The reproductive cloning of animals, as we know, has already occurred: Dolly the sheep, born on 5 July 1996, is now a household name, if not a celebrity.[8] The sole survivor of more than 277 embryos constituted this way, Dolly was a miracle in the making. The Dolly story, Franklin comments, points to our capacity to 'rewrite genealogy with unprecedented molecular precision' (2001a: 6). Dolly herself indeed is something of a paradox, a 'singleton despite signifying the threat of multiplicity' (2001a: 6). These cloning techniques, moreover, open up new prospects and markets, not simply in the (re)production of identical genetically engineered animal organs for xenotransplants,[9] but in the control or reprogramming of human cell lines themselves (see also Franklin 2001b). We are entering, as this suggests, through these and countless other biotech 'breakthroughs', a new era of biocapitalism or bioprospecting (Fuller 2000; Lock 2001), if not biocolonialism or biopiracy, expressed through 'immortalized' patent cell lines and the like; a 'cashing-in', quite literally, on our biological heritage with huge profits to be made in the global marketplace (Lock

2001).[10] Geron, for example, the American pharmaceutical corporation for whom the patented technique used to make Dolly the sheep was re-licensed, hope to make

> smarter cell lines that can produce tissue replacement therapies for a wide range of human medical applications. A heady vista of new market opportunities beckons in the space opened up by the new scale of biological control available through cellular and genetic recapacitation. The idea is that a person's own cells might be recapacitated to provide bespoke replacement tissue that is potentially life-saving in the event of major illnesses such as kidney failure, cardiac conditions, cancer and a host of other disorders. The techniques are known as human therapeutic cloning and they effect an expansion in the use of cloning techniques to include human applications. (Franklin 2001a: 8)

This may (depending on your viewpoint) sound promising, particularly when allied to public reassurances about the distinction, itself much debated, between the *therapeutic* and *reproductive* cloning of humans. Cloning, however, is a hit-and-miss affair which is still very much in its infancy. Warnings have emerged, moreover, that reproductive cloning is fundamentally unsafe, with random 'slips' occurring in the genetic make-up of cloned animals, and reports of premature ageing (Chapman 2001: 37). Dolly, indeed, has just painfully stepped back into the spotlight, at the tender age of five-and-a-half, with reported arthritis (an extremely rare condition in normal sheep of that age, whose lifespan is somewhere between 10 and 15 years). This, of course, could be pure coincidence. It does, nonetheless, cast fresh doubts on this controversial field, thereby adding grist to the mill of the anti-cloning lobby. News of Dolly's arthritis indeed, Professor Ian Wilmut (head of the original cloning team) commented, was only one minor new doubt to add the pile. 'It is a technology of enormous promise', he stated, 'but we do need to be a little cautious in the way in which we use the technique' (quoted in Meek and Scott 2002: 3).

The world's first cloned human embryo (a six-cell cluster) was publicly announced on 25 November 2001. Produced in America by a privately funded biotech company – Advanced Cell Technology (ACT) of Worcester, Massachusetts, which hopes to develop embryonic stem cells to cure diseases – the achievement, to say the least, is controversial, raising hopes and fears. 'Our intention', the company's vice-president of medical and scientific development stated, 'is not to create cloned human beings, but rather to make lifesaving therapies for a wide range of human disease conditions, including diabetes, stroke, cancer, Aids and neurodegenerative disorders such as Parkinson's and Alzheimer's disease'. The entities created, moreover, the company's chief executive added, are 'not individuals. They're only cellular life. They're not human life' (quoted in Boseley and Campbell 2001). The fear, nonetheless, given the publicly stated intention and evident activities of (maverick) scientists such as Severino Antinori, is that human cloning (*reproductive* as opposed to *therapeutic* cloning, that is to say) is just around the corner: a development which ACT, in keeping with most scientists in the field (including Dolly's creator, Ian Wilmut), strongly condemns, adding that it will probably be about ten years before treatments from therapeutic cloning are publically available (Boseley and Campbell 2001).

The cracking of the DNA code also, of course, has important implications for the cracking of crime through the introduction of genetic fingerprinting and the prospect of DNA-based identity cards. DNA is a powerful new forensic tool which, according to various commentators, promises to 'clear up' a range of crimes, both past and present, serving perhaps as the 'ultimate deterrent', with 'justice' for victims and the wrongly accused/convicted alike (Cook 2001). DNA testing is now so advanced, in fact, that a sample can be obtained from a chewed pen top. Impressed by these developments, the UK Government is reported to have allocated an extra £202 million to increase the number of scene-of-crime officers trained in DNA gathering techniques, and to expand the natural DNA database from its present size to more than 3 million – the estimated total of the criminally active population (Cook 2001: 24). These developments, as with medicine, have raised serious concerns about the erosion of civil liberties. Fears have been expressed, for example, that there will be a new class of people kept permanently under suspicion (even though nothing has been proved against them), through the retention of their profiles on the active DNA database: a continuous process of computer-generated cross-checking, in effect, in relation to all manner of crimes. Corroborating evidence is still of course required. DNA testing, nonetheless, promises to be a 'powerful weapon' in the 'fight against crime' (Cook 2001: 25).

These debates, in turn, resonate with health promotion and public health agendas, not least the *surveillance* issues they raise and the tensions between *individual* and *collective* uses of these new genetic technologies in the name of health and illness. Petersen and Bunton (2002: 3), for example, echoing many of the above points and issues, pose a number of pertinent questions. 'To what extent, and in what ways', they ask, 'does the focus on molecular biology challenge established understandings of "the environment" and of population health?' What are the 'political and practical implications of the efforts to incorporate new genetic ideas into the strategies and practices of public health?'[11] And 'are the promises of the new genetic-based public health (e.g. increased choice, improved health) likely to be fulfilled?' An assessment of how genetics is shaping the public domain/domain of public health, they continue, should also involve consideration of the impact of genetic knowledge and practice on people's everyday lives and relationships. 'What', for instance, 'do such developments mean for people's view of their own bodies, concept of self, and how they conduct themselves, interact with others and plan their lives?' 'Who', moreover, 'has access to the new genetic technologies, and is there any potential for inequalities to arise as a result of the widespread uptake of genetic knowledge in public health?' 'What scope', finally, is there for 'people to contest the imperatives surrounding genetic-based public health?' (Petersen and Bunton 2002: 4).

What this amounts to, in general terms, is how to ensure that the benefits of these 'advances' outweigh the risks, itself no simple task. Providing people with genetic information on their risks for this or that condition, for example, as mentioned earlier, may have a series of deleterious consequences, raising the anxiety levels of individuals and populations alike. Far from promoting change, indeed, receipt of genetic information on risk may in some cases actually *discourage* it (Marteau and Lerman 2001).[12] The wider structural determinant of health and illness should also, of course, not be forgotten or allowed to recede from view here. Sociological critiques of health promotion and the 'new' public health, in these and other respects, are revisited anew in the light of the new genetics – including *structural, surveillance* and *consumption* critiques alike (Bunton et al. 1995). The implications of genetics for sport are another huge area for discussion and debate. Answers to these and many other questions – from issues of citizenship to the global dimensions of the new genetics, which includes, of course, such contested developments as GM foods and GMOs (genetically modified organisms) (see, for example, Petersen and Bunton 2002) – remain far from clear-cut at present: part and parcel of an open, rapidly changing field and an ongoing/unravelling debate.

What is clear, nonetheless, within all this is that themes both old and new alike are very much in evidence here: a point articulated earlier when trying to define what exactly is 'new' about the new genetics. The new genetics, in this respect, as Kerr and Cunningham-Burley (2000) appositely put it, involves a complex mixture of *modern* (certainty, progress), *counter-modern* (anti-progress, de-demoncratization) and *reflexive* (choice/risk) values and rhetoric (cf. Beck 1992; Giddens 1990, 1991). Reflexive modernization itself, on this reading, *sustains* rather than radically breaks free of modernity/counter-modernity (see also Wynne 2002 on reflexivity 'inside out'). Public and professional 'doubts', in other words, have not so far

> disrupted human genetic research or its clinical application . . . *Much of what is claimed to be new and different from practices and knowledge of the past turns out to be remarkably similar.* Reductionism and determinism continue to infuse contemporary methods and theories. Scientific and social progress are collapsed anew. Certitude and surveillance remain powerful guiding principles. Even the special focus on physical and mental impairments and behavioural traits is not new; nor is the emphasis on compassion and suffering, both key aspects of the medical model of disability. The contemporary emphasis on individual choice and personal responsibility, and practices like expert counselling and risk estimation may have replaced some of the more extreme practices of old, but within this wider context they can be seen to be *subtle reconfigurations, rather than entirely new modes of practice.* (Kerr and Cunningham-Burley 2000: 290, my emphasis)

Here we encounter a final irony, if irony it is. Sociological critiques of the new genetics, Kerr and Cunningham-Burley (2000: 298) point out, are themselves part and parcel of these very processes of reflexive modernity which writers such as Giddens (1990, 1991) and Beck (1992, 1995, 1997) point to. When expressed within the public domain, however, this, it is argued, harbours its own radical potential, exposing doubts and uncertainties, debunking professional rhetoric, and thereby opening up new possibilities for broader processes of participatory democracy (Kerr and Cunningham-Burley 2000; see also Kerr and Shakespeare 2002; Petersen and Bunton 2002 on the pros and cons of 'active citizenship' in this context, and Scambler 2001, 2002, for a broader series of reflections in a more Habermasian vein). Sociology, in short, has a vital role to play in these debates, both now and in the future: whatever it may hold.

Digitalized/miniaturized bodies: virtual medicine and e-health

No discussion of medical technology would be complete without consideration of other recent departures and developments such as minimally invasive surgery and 'virtual' medicine. Whilst many of these technologies are still in their infancy/at the prototype stage, they do, nonetheless, in keeping with the other developments discussed previously, promise a more or less radical transformation of the relationship between medicine and the body in years to come. Medical technologies and techniques, for example, are getting not simply smarter but also smaller: miniaturized or micro-modelled versions of former interventions in the technoscientific transitions of our times. 'Big science' and 'big technology', Clarke and colleagues remark, 'now sits on your desk or in a pillbox' (2000: 4).

Keyhole surgery, for instance, despite recent concerns over the standardization of training and competence, is already well established. Reduced trauma from minimally invasive surgery, it is claimed, will result in fewer operations requiring lengthy hospital stays. As a consequence, Wickham (1994) speculates, traditional surgical wards will become largely redundant, hospitals will need to cope with increased patient through-put, operating theatres will have to be re-equipped with these new technologies, and hospital staff will need to be retrained in order to manage them. Many traditional specialities, moreover, from this perspective, will merge, and much conventional nursing care will shift to the community rather than the hospital (Wickham 1994). Other developments in microengineering or *nanotechnology* (super-microtechnology) take us one or more (micro)steps down the line, to devices such as 'smart pills' which will be capable of transmitting information on nerve function or blood flow to distant monitoring facilities (Featherstone 1999: 11). Nanontechnology, Clinton (2001) boldly proclaims, 'will enable us to identify tumours when they are just a few cells in size, raising the prospect that we will be able to cure all cancers'. Researchers too, he notes, are working on 'digital chips to replicate sophisticated nerve movements in spines, raising the prospect that they will work for damaged spinal cords the way pacemakers do for hearts'. Whether or not this turns out to be more or less 'invasive', however, is a moot point. The era of 'miniaturized medicine', nevertheless, is on its way.

Medicine is also, of course, as these very technologies imply, becoming increasingly computerized and digitalized, including the advent of so-called 'e-health' and 'telemedicine': developments which themselves connect to the new 'global' health economy, providing new ways to 'organize, compare and rank bodies' (Cartwright 2000: 349).[13] A panoply of 'screens' for example, Frank (1992) observes, now pervade the high-technology hospital (and medicine in general, we might add). Firstly, there are those screens which *exteriorize direct images* of the body's interior (such as ultrasound screens/foetal visualization and diagnostic technologies, MRI, PET and CT scans). Secondly, there are screens which display *online digital images*, coded into graphs and pictorial display, of bodily processes and functioning (ECG monitors, for example). Thirdly, there are screens which display *symbolic images* such as patient charts, schedules and other secondary data. Finally, there are *commercial television screens* found in ever-increasing numbers in hospital waiting rooms, lounges, wards and patient rooms. In this respect, Frank comments, the Foucauldian clinical gaze gives way to the Baudrillardian 'hyperreality of images without grounding'. Instead of the patient's body being at the centre of contemporary medical practice and discourse, we now find 'multiple images and codings' whereby the body is endlessly 'doubled and redoubled' through a self-referential chain of simulacra (Frank 1992: 83). Modernist concerns with *corporeality*, from this (Baudrillardian) viewpoint, are slowly but surely giving way to postmodern concerns with *hyperreality*.

Graphic workstation computers and specialist tracking devices, in keeping with these digitalized developments, have now made it possible to build an advanced prototype simulator for minimally invasive surgery called the 'virtual clinic'' (McGovern 1994; McGovern and McGovern 1994). The system, McGovern explains, uses tracking devices attached to actual surgical instruments which are inserted into a fibreglass body mould. Graphic representations of the body change as the instruments are moved, whilst interaction is visibly displayed on a high-resolution computer monitor located at the head of the 'virtual' patient. Data produced by computer tomography (CT) and magnetic resonance imaging (MRI) are used to supply a visual *re*-presentation of the actual patient's anatomy. Computer manipulation allows the 'virtual surgical instruments' to interact with the 'virtual tissues' in a way that resembles what happens in 'real life', with new images automatically created as these 'virtual' tissues are dissected (McGovern 1994: 1054).

The benefits of such computerized training systems include the ability to reproduce surgical anomalies, work out the best operative procedures, improve surgical techniques and thereby minimize errors on actual patients. In neurosurgery, for example, researchers are trying to combine live video information with three-dimensional computer images of the brain in order to help in planning operations. These methods enable surgeons to locate the best site for a skin incision, craniotomy and a brain incision, thus minimizing the risk of damage to normal brain tissue (McGovern 1994).

A related set of developments concern 'tele-presence' surgery, performed on a patient in an operating theatre containing a stereoscopic camera and a robot. At a *separate location* the surgical control workstation has a three-dimensional monitor with surgical input–output devices which closely resemble actual instruments that would be used in an operation (McGovern 1994). The notion of robots 'trying their hand' at surgery may strike us as bizarre, if not downright scary. Surgeon-controlled automation of this kind, nonetheless, as noted above, promises to make operations safer, thereby allowing patients to recover more quickly. Operations 'at a distance', moreover, have many potential applications, including military use in battlefield situations and scenarios.[14] Such developments, indeed, are already underway. A robot called Zeus, for instance, was unveiled in February 1998, allowing surgeons – subject to successful completion of adequate trials – to perform heart bypasses through incisions the width of a pencil. Using specifically designed instruments that are thin enough to be fitted into an endoscope, Zeus, in the words of its designers, will do for the 'surgeon's hands what the microscope did for his [*sic*] eyes' (quoted in Prigg 1998: 7). Another version of this technology is also being planned, allowing surgeons hundreds of miles away to perform operations on a high-speed telephone line (Prigg 1998: 7) – developments which return us to issues of telepresence surgery discussed above, including battlefield applications (McGovern 1994).

Two further illustrations, themselves highly visible, if not spectacular, underline these digital departures in medicine and beyond. The first concerns the advent of RealVideo Surgery: live surgery, that is to say, transmitted over the Web via digital video (Thacker 1999). This, Thacker reports, was first performed on a 57-year-old woman undergoing heart surgery at Providence Hospital in Seattle, preceded a few months earlier by the first live webcast of birth on the Internet (1999: 318). Reasons for doing so, according to a statement issued by the Providence hospital staff, include the utilization of networking technologies for: (i) 'educational' purposes (both public and professional); (ii) remote advising and pedagogy (enabling medical students to pose questions to surgeons in future webcast operations); and (iii) the future of 'virtual surgery', whereby trial operations can be performed on a virtual patient (Thacker 1999: 319). RealVideo in this respect, given its fusion of computer/networking media and contemporary biomedicine, is an instance where

> the anatomical-medical body is productively articulated as a *complex visceral-digital hybrid*, enframed by medical discourse. As with the anatomy theatre, such a performative instance, in renegotiating what will come to constitute the (scientific) body, must form a coherent political economy so that (medical) body, (surgical) event and (distributed) media may converge in communicating transparency and the truth of bodies. (Thacker 1999: 333, my emphasis)

Performance artists such as Orlan and Stelarc add a further dimension to these virtual dramas and theatrical displays. Orlan, for example, was filmed by CNN having the seventh in a series of plastic surgery operations, the cumulative effects of which are designed to challenge conventional Western notions of beauty and the status of the female body. Stelarc's forte, in contrast, is to perform in a variety of settings with technological devices *attached* (the Third Hand), *inserted* (the stomach sculpture) and

Net-connected (accessed and remotely activated by people in other places) (Stelarc 1999). The Internet, Stelarc claims, does not facilitate the demise or disappearance of the body. It generates instead new 'physical couplings' involving 'multiplicity', 'connectivity' and powerful new possibilities and strategies for 'projecting body presence' through the 'interface' (Stelarc 1999; see also Ayers 1999; Farnell 1999; Goodall 1999).

If surgical operations broadcast live on the Web provide one spectacular image or theatrical display of the body in the era of computerized medicine, with or without the likes of Orlan or Stelarc to embellish them, then the Visible Human Project (VHP), and the 'digital slices of life' it sustains, provides another (see also Moore and Clarke 2001 on 'cyberanatomies'). This, Waldby (1997, 2000) comments, is a further innovation in 'computerized medical vision' which takes actual human bodies and renders them 'visual digital data': the 'most recent and thorough attempt', in fact, 'to enframe the body within the logic of the computer' (Waldby 1997: 232). Developed by researchers at the National Library of Medicine in Baltimore, what we have here in effect is a digitalized 'atlas' of the actual human body, observable as a three dimensional image from any angle, in the greatest depth and detail, and accessible through the Internet. But whose body, one may ask? The answer, echoing past medical history, is a 39-year-old male convicted murderer who pledged his body, upon execution, to science: a body quite literally frozen and dissected in 1 mm slices, prior to its digitalization and virtual reconstruction. The images produced in this way, Waldby comments,

> seem unmediated. They have the documentary realism of photographic aesthetics at their disposal, the realistic colours of anatomical photography as opposed to the purely conventional colour-coding found, for example, in CT scans, colour which is all too clearly an aid to the eye and nothing else. Unlike tomography images these images are inclusive, no feature of tissue or bone is selectively foregrounded. They look like the 'real thing', the way the body would look if sliced across its breadth. Once restacked the slices can be reformulated into the simulacrum of a whole body, *a body which looks opaque and self-enclosed but which can be opened out at will in any way desired, to any depth, and then be re-enclosed, completely at the disposal of vision.* (1997: 236, my emphasis)

The VHP, in this respect, is a dramatic example of the ways in which

> bodies are worked over in the interests of technical frames of reference and treated as objects within a technical optics. We can see that the VHP is a visual text produced by the *literal reworking of the body's materiality according to the logics of computer storage and computer vision.* (1997: 236, my emphasis)

Waldby's point is indeed an important one. No mere digitalized display, what we have here in fact are *material* forms of discipline or effacement, transgression or violence – the slicing up and restacking of a criminal body – achieved through a *spectacular* act of medical mastery which itself has *(bio)political* as well as *epistemological* functions (Waldby 1997, 2000).[15] A chilling prospect indeed.

This is not the end of the matter, however. Bodies, in fact, are now on public display for all to look at and to learn from, through an extraordinary new technique known as 'plastination'. The process, invented by Günter von Hagen in 1978 at the Heidelberg University Institute of Anatomy, has led to a much hyped public exhibition, 'Body World', of more than 200 authentic 'plastinates', including whole bodies, individual organs and transparent body slices, providing 'unparalleled insights' into the human body: a 'completely new vision' of the human body, in fact, it is claimed. All visitors, we are told, leave body world 'changed'. 'Fascination', in this respect, yields to 'reflection' and in many cases the 'determination to take better care of one's health and body'. Anatomy lessons for the masses, with or without health education/promotion in mind. Whatever next!

Here, perhaps, is a fitting place to stop as art and science are collapsed anew. Where, however, we may justifiably ask, does this leave us in this topsy-turvy world of corporeal if not hyperreal possibilities? It is to this we now turn in closing.

Conclusions

At the beginning of this chapter, three main questions or issues were raised. First and foremost, to what extent have (bio)technological trends and transformations, in medicine and beyond, led to increasing uncertainty if not a 'crisis' of meaning about bodies and their boundaries – what bodies are, that is to say, and what they might become? Such an interpretation, it seems, in the light of the preceding discussion, is indeed possible, throwing into critical relief a series of moral, ethical and existential dilemmas, alongside broader sociological debates on the (post)human body in the new millennium. From plastic surgery to virtual medicine, these corporeal dilemmas can be traced. These and other medical 'advances', we might say, are both *instrumental* in and *symptomatic* of this corporeal uncertainty in twenty-first-century Western society, developing and extending the rationalization of the body in important new ways, yet rendering it ever more elusive, if not problematic, in doing so. Rationalizing currents and technologizing processes, from this viewpoint, create their own (corporeal) doubts and uncertainties.

A 'crisis' for whom, however: academics and/or the public at large? We must clearly be careful here in making any such sweeping claims and generalizations. Views on these very matters, for instance, are likely to vary *within* as well as *between* different segments of the socio-cultural order, and *across* the lay/professional divide. This, in turn, includes potentially important differences between those with and without first-hand experience of such technologies (see, for example, Robinson 1994; Williams and Calnan 1996b). Claims to a corporeal crisis of meaning then, on this count, may themselves be more or less qualified depending on who, precisely, we have in mind, and the evidence for or against any such interpretation.

Second, following directly on from this first point, what purchase (both analytically and empirically) does the cyborg give us on the contemporary forms of 'technological embodiment' or 'biocultural destabilization'? The thrust of the arguments presented here would seem to suggest that, in an era where human–machine couplings are almost infinite, medical technology has at its disposal a variety of means to transform us into cyborgs, from cardiac pacemakers to genetic engineering, and from the nebulized asthmatic to the accident victim in the intensive care unit (with or without a digital chip implant for a spinal cord injury). In making this claim, however, the analytical power and discriminatory potential of the concept is surely reduced. It is perhaps more fruitful, therefore, to conceptualize cyborgs along a continuum ranging from the all-too-human pole at one end, to artificial intelligence devices at the other, with a broad range of human–machine couplings or fusions in between (Featherstone and Burrows 1995). In contrast to (overly) optimistic visions of the cyborg as a 'leaky' figure in a 'post-gender' world, moreover, it is possible to argue that these technological developments, to date at least, uphold rather than transcend the gendered forms of embodiment they seek to unravel (Cherniavsky 1993; Foster 1993; Springer 1991). This, in turn, reinforces the more general point that, rather than challenging traditional mind/body divisions, the possibility lurks (in much of this) of a hi-tech form of neo-Platonism: a desire, that is, Stelarc's reassurances notwithstanding, to slip the body *qua* meat, as evident in the cyberpunk genre (Gibson 1984) and the digital dreams of cyberspace (see Williams 1998c, for example, for a critique).

Here we arrive at the third main issue concerning late or postmodern interpretations of these technological transformations in contemporary medical practice. A postmodern reading of these trends (in keeping with cyborg/post-human visions) is certainly possible, particularly when their 'transformatory' possibilities are taken into account, extending far beyond modernist concerns with the mere 'control' of bodies, with globalizing pretensions to boot (cf. Clarke et al. 2000). A casting of these issues in a more 'late modern' mould, however, is perhaps preferable, alerting us to important themes of *continuity* and *change*, the full implications and unfolding (global) dynamics of which are only now becoming apparent. The new genetics, as we have seen, is a prime example, expressing *reflexive*, *modern* and *counter-modern* themes – a tension, in other words, between reflexivity and objectivity, doubt and certainty, choice and coercion, change and continuity (Kerr and Cunningham-Burley 2000). Either way, the global dynamics of these issues should not be underplayed or underestimated. We live in an era, that is to say, in which 'big science', miniaturized or otherwise, is itself 'big business': part and parcel, as Clarke et al. (2000) appositely put it, of the 'bigger picture' with 'Western roots' and 'global rhizomes'. It is also well to remember, in the context of these debates, that these very technologies, whilst coding, enframing and digitalizing bodies in various ways, are, nonetheless, material in design and effect, involving various forms of corporeal transgression (if not violence) and the reproduction of bodily hierarchies in the name of science, technology and the 'visions' they embody (Waldby 1997, 2000).[16]

Ultimately, of course, whether we choose to view these developments through a late modern or postmodern lens is immaterial or academic, for the lay populace at least, for whom medicine continues (in large part) to serve as a critical resource (albeit one where the critical is becoming increasingly critical). Hi-tech medicine, to repeat a well-rehearsed theme of this book, is a fountain of hope and a font of despair, including both gains and losses, themselves the subject of much controversy and debate in lay, popular and professional cultures alike, overseen by various regulatory bodies, advisory committees and (non-)governmental watchdogs. We have, in short, been put on the 'conveyor belt' of (bio)technology. The question we must continually ask ourselves, nevertheless, is whether or not our 'humanity' (itself of course a contested notion) is being 'compromised' in the process (O'Neill 1985; Scheper-Hughes and Lock 1987 – see also Chapter 9). It is not, in other words, so much a question of *what* we can do, but *how far we should go*. 'True freedom', Fukuyama remarks, means 'freedom of political communities to protect the values they hold dear, and it is that freedom we need to exercise with regard to the biotechnology revolution today' (2002: 218).[17] To the extent that sociological critiques highlight such issues, facilitating new forms of public engagement and participatory democracy in the process, we can indeed 'make a difference' (Kerr and Cunningham-Burley 2000; Scambler 2001, 2002).

The body, to conclude, both literally and metaphorically, incorporates and expresses the tensions and dilemmas of hi-tech medicine/biotechnology and the broader social relations of which it is a part: a heady brew of certainty and doubt, rights and responsibilities, hope and despair, stirred through the dynamics of reflexive modernity and its (in)flexible logic, with cell lines tied to stock markets in the corporeal, if not hyperreal, world of global (bio)capitalism and bioprospecting. A 'runaway world' (Giddens 1999) indeed, 'post-human' or otherwise.

Notes

1 See also Chapter 4 on interventions into the ageing process and various attempts to extend the human lifespan.
2 The Alder Hey scandal concerned the revelation and subsequent public outcry over the unauthorized removal and storage of organs and tissues from hundreds of dead children at a hospital in Merseyside in the UK. This, it transpired, was part of a broader picture, with huge numbers of organs retained across the country, without relatives ever being told.
3 There have also been a number of reports of recipients taking on donor characteristics, *without* prior knowledge of who the donor was.
4 See also Tober (2001) on donor insemination and relations between the sperm banking industry, sperm donors and women who purchase donor sperm, including its *transmutation* from *commodity* to *gift* at the point of collection and sale.
5 More or less completed, that is to say, over 90 per cent in fact at the time of this announcement, with the final 10 per cent promised within the next two years.

6   The associated Human Genome Diversity Project (HGDP), in contrast, came to an abrupt end, due to its 'colonizing' connotations, which met with 'grass roots' opposition. The 'colonisation of an individual's, a family's or an ethnic group's DNA', nonetheless, as Kerr and Cunningham-Burley state, 'remains essential to this scientific and corporate endeavour' (2000: 288). See also Lock (2001) on the HGDP and Steinberg's (2000) analysis of 'industrial', 'colonial' and 'liberal' utopian discourses on the new genetics: discourses, at one and the same time, which locate science within/desegregate it from social hierarchy and practice.

7   Although this concept may appear to be biomedical, it is not. It is instead, Ettorre explains, a 'sociological concept employed to demonstrate that powerful social and cultural processes are involved in the organization of genetic tests for pre-natal diagnosis, already identified as an intricate sociotechnological system' (1999: 539–40).

8   So far, mice, cattle, sheep and now pigs have been cloned.

9   For example, scientists at PPL therapeutics (which is next door to the Roslin Institute) have cloned a group of genetically engineered pigs, a litter of five born on Christmas Day 2001, each having had a gene inactivated or 'knocked-out' – the gene for 1,3 galactosyl transferase, a natural enzyme which adds sugar to the surface of pig cells, thereby triggering tissue rejection (Connor 2002). PPL's share prices, needless to say, were boosted no end by this news, rising from 24.5 p to 77.5 p in a day (Foley 2002). This, by all accounts, is a 'critical milestone' in the production of animal organs and tissues for human operations. The hurdle of convincing safety authorities, nonetheless, remains, including the previously mentioned risk of virus transmission (such as PERVs) from pigs to humans (Connor 2002; see also Bryan and Clare 2001, discussed earlier). If these techniques prove to work safely, however, which is a big if, and if current fears are allayed, the financial rewards are vast. Connor, for instance, quotes an American analyst who predicts the 'global "market" in solid organs to be worth about $5bn (£3.5) and $6bn for "soft" tissue transplants' (2002).

10   See also Clarke et al. (2000), Haraway (1997), Kerr and Cunningham-Burley (2000) and Petersen and Bunton (2002) on *transnationalization, globalization* and *commodification* process in relation to the new genetics and associated biotechnologies.

11   Petersen and Bunton draw attention here to the rapid development of so-called 'genetic epidemiology' since the 1980s: a discipline structured by 'advances in molecular biology, techniques of statistical modelling, and computer technology', which seeks to 'describe and explain the distribution of genetic traits and diseases in populations or families' (2002: 25).

12   Marteau and Lerman's (2001) article is in fact part of a recent special issue of the *British Medical Journal* devoted to 'putting genetics in perspective' (Zimmern et al. 2001), including papers on: the integration of genetic medicine in primary care (Emery and Hayflick 2001); the complexities of predictive testing (Evans et al. 2001); and the implications of genetics for developing countries (Bloom and Trach 2001).

13   A conference was held, for example, at City University in London (4–6 April 2001) entitled 'e-Health: a Futurescope'. IBM are also developing an online Health Village™, composed of patients, clinicians, health management personnel and health organizations.

14   Many of these technologies, in fact, have military origins or applications.

15   Featherstone (1999) makes a different, yet equally crucial, point about the material matter of bodies in our 'virtual' age, and the limits as well as the opportunities this entails. Whilst 'virtual mobility' and 'spatial escape' via communication techniques with distant others is now a possibility, he notes, temporal escape is a much more difficult proposition. Technology, in other words, 'has no prospect of mastering time: if we can't escape time, we can't escape the body . . . The finitude of the human life course and lived body in time still impose limits on our capacity for technological mastery' (1999: 12).

16   These and related themes are very much to the fore in a special issue of *Current Sociology* on the 'ambivalent legacies and rising challenges of technologies', including, *inter alia*: (i) the embedded nature of these new technologies; (ii) their material relations and variable

outcomes in different social orders; (iii) their capacity to 'reproduce' old conditions as well as to create new social dynamics; and (iv) the mediating cultures between these technologies and their users. See, for example, Sassen (2002), Wajcman (2002), Webster (2002), Wynne (2002).

17 Fukuyama's take on these post-human issues is not, it should be stressed, without its critics. Rose (2002), for example, takes Fukuyama to task on two main counts: first, his problematic notion of human nature (indebted as it is to the likes of E.O. Wilson and the claims of evolutionary psychology); and, second, the abstraction of his conclusions, particularly those concerning the potential *regulation* of these biotechnologies, from practical politics or economy.

9

Caring Bodies/Embodied Ethics

One of the key dimensions of embodiment, as we have seen, concerns our emotional relations with the world and with other similarly embodied human beings, with all the contingencies this implies. Issues of sickness and health, disability and death, as the foregoing chapters attest, throw many of these issues into critical relief. It is time, however, to address more fully and directly the embodied dimensions and ethical dilemmas of caring as such, itself a prime expression of the gendered division of labour across the public/private divide. Frank's (1991a) notion of the 'communicative' body as a mode of praxis, based on the medium of recognition, provides a useful starting point here: a body (more an ideal than a reality) which is really about expression, sharing and mutual recognition through a diverse array of human experience from dance to illness. It is against this backdrop or 'shadow presence' of the communicative body and its caring modalities, therefore, that this chapter proceeds, approaching these very matters (of necessity perhaps) from different angles, perspectives and viewpoints.

In the first section I return to Parsons's (1951) sick role, for the psychodynamic insights concerning illness and therapy contained therein. The second section, following directly on from this discussion, takes up the issue of consumerism in health care, assessing its applicability (or otherwise) to the contemporary medical encounter in the light of the foregoing discussion. The remainder of the chapter, in contrast, takes us well beyond the confines of the formal medical encounter, addressing, respectively, broader issues concerning gender and the emotional division of labour in health care, the politics and ethics of care, and the future of health care at the dawn of the twenty-first century. What, then, of Parsons? Are his early insights worth revisiting at this late stage of the day, given subsequent developments both in medical sociology and in contemporary medical practice? Let us see.

The psychodynamics of the sick role: the return of the repressed?

Issues of professional power and dominance (Freidson 1970), relations between the voice of medicine and the voice of the lifeworld (Mishler 1990), problems of uncertainty (R.C. Fox 2000), the 'ceremonial order of the clinic' (Strong 1979b), these and many other matters pertaining to the doctor/patient relationship have been high on the research agenda of medical sociologists over the years, whether cast in *consensual*, *conflictual* or *negotiative* terms. Recent Foucauldian perspectives shed further light on these issues, particularly the fabrication of new subjectivities and forms of (self-)surveillance, within and beyond the consultation.

It is Parsons (1951), however, who is credited with the first systematic sociological statement of these matters in his classic formulation of the 'sick role'.[1] These issues, of course, have been well debated in medical sociological circles, so much so in fact that we may well be entitled to feel sick or fed up with the sick role: an exemplar of Parsons's structural-functionalist slant on things, the problems of which are now fully apparent.[2] There are good reasons, nonetheless, for revisiting these Parsonian insights, not simply because a close rereading of this extraordinarily rich work on medicine and illness reveals the many misplaced criticisms levelled against him, but also for the psychodynamic issues it raises surrounding illness and the sick role – issues all too frequently lost in standard textbook accounts of the Parsonian legacy for medical sociology.

It is these latter *emotional* and *psychodynamic* issues, therefore, that I wish to pick up on here, at the level of both *aetiology* and *therapy*. Doing so, as we shall see, provides insights into the *positive* as well as the *negative* aspects of illness with which the therapeutic process must contend: issues which hark back to points raised in Chapter 5. Parsons's analysis of these matters, moreover, as he himself acknowledges, was heavily influenced by a detailed reading of Freud – prompted by Elton Mayo – and his own subsequent training in psychoanalysis. This, coupled with a long-standing interest in biology and a preliminary training in medicine, meant that Chapter X of *The Social System* (1951), in which Parsons lays out his sociological views on medicine, was to some extent inevitable.

Taking up the question of *aetiology* first, health and illness for Parsons are clearly caught up in the motivational balances and functioning of the social system, such that 'too low a general level of health, too high an incidence of illness, is dysfunctional' (1951: 430). Illness, in this sense, is a form of 'deviant behaviour' which society, functionally speaking, has a vested interest in minimizing given its interference with effective role performance. Illness is not, however, Parsons stresses, something which just 'happens' to people. Rather, motivational factors, conceived in action terms, are involved in the aetiology of many illnesses, thereby opening themselves to 'therapeutic influence through motivational channels' (1951: 430). Motivational factors and unconscious desires and wishes, for instance, may well be implicated in people's 'differential exposure to injuries or to infections' (1951: 431). There may also be important 'secondary gains' to be had from illness (a point we shall return to shortly). Illness indeed, consciously or otherwise, is one mode of response to 'social pressures', one way of 'evading social responsibilities'. Participation in the social system, therefore, is 'always potentially relevant to the state of illness, to its etiology and to the conditions of successful therapy' (1951: 431). This, of course, is not to deny that 'somatic states' which are not motivationally determined may play a greater or lesser role in many illnesses. A 'continuum', in fact, is evident here, ranging from the most 'completely "mental" of mental illnesses and the corresponding processes of psychotherapy, through the various ranges of psychosomatic phenomena to the category of the completely "somatic" . . . where illness is simply a "condition" with which human techniques have to cope' (Parsons 1964: 331). Overall, however, a 'component of motivatedness', Parsons insists, is evident in 'almost all illness': one which the social structuring of the doctor/patient relationship controls therapeutically, albeit in latent ways (1964: 331–2).

The full emotional import and psychodynamic of these issues become clear in the *therapeutic* context of medical practice, conceived in terms of the reciprocal cluster of rights and obligations of the sick role and physician role, expressed through Parsons's (in)famous *pattern-variable* schema. The formal characteristics of this role structure again have been extensively discussed elsewhere (see Gerhardt 1989, for example). I shall not therefore dwell on them at any length. Suffice it to say that the four core aspects of the sick role – namely *exemption from normal role obligations, lack of responsibility* for illness, *desire to get well*, and the seeking of *technically competent help* – are related to the technical expertise of the doctor, who, by virtue of special institutionally validated training and experience, is qualified to 'help' the patient via this 'co-operative' relationship based on trust and a 'common task' orientation. Expressed in Parsons's pattern-variable terms, both roles are *universalistic, functionally specific, affectively neutral* and *collectivity orientated*. The sick role, however, may be viewed as a *negatively* achieved status, through failure to keep well, whilst that of the physician is cast in a *positively* achieved light. The issue of 'secondary gain' again arises here. The privileges and exemptions of the sick role, Parsons notes, may themselves become objects of secondary gain which the patient is 'positively motivated', usually unconsciously, to secure or retain. The problem of the 'balance of motivations to recover', therefore, 'becomes of first importance' (1951: 437).

Three salient features of *patients'* situation are discussed by Parsons: their need for help, their 'technical incompetence' in medical matters, and their emotional involvement. The urgency of the need for help, the first of these factors, will, of course, vary with the nature and severity of the condition. Feelings of helplessness and the need for help, Parsons stresses, are nonetheless 'very real' in a sufficient proportion of cases, particularly as sick people are not regarded as 'responsible' for their condition. They are also likely to be anxious about their condition and the future (1951: 440). The nature of the help received, furthermore, places patients in another dilemma, given their lack of technical knowledge about what needs to be done and how to do it. The 'burdens' that physicians may ask patients and their families to endure, moreover, are often quite severe, including (post-operative) pain and suffering (the 'getting worse before you feel better' scenario), and the risks of death or permanent disablement (1951: 441–2).

Here we arrive at the third complex issue of emotional investment and 'adjustment'. This, quite simply, Parsons observes, is a situation of 'strain': itself complicated further by 'free-floating anxieties' about death. Two types of reaction are prominent here for Parsons – a kind of emotional 'shock' at the *beginning* of illness, and anxiety about its *future*. In both cases, he suggests, taking American values as his point of reference, there is reason to believe that most 'normal persons have an unrealistic bias in the direction of confidence that "everything will be alright"' (1951: 443). One response, for example, may be to 'deny' illness or aspects of it, to refuse to 'give in'. Another may be exaggerated self-pity, a complaining demand for more help than necessary as an attention-seeking mode of behaviour. Either way, the physician's response (or 'emotional toning') inevitably influences the emotional state of the patient in a *reciprocal* fashion: the encounter itself having a certain 'sacred' quality given the mortal issues which surround and suffuse it. The net effect of these factors, for Parsons, is that sick people find themselves in a situation in which they are a 'peculiarly vulnerable object for exploitation'. They are also, he comments, in a situation which makes a 'high level of rationality peculiarly difficult'. The individual, in other words, is liable to a whole series of 'irr- and non-rational beliefs and practices', including elements of superstition (1951: 446).

Turning now to the *physician*, the prime responsibility here, of course, is with the patient's welfare through the facilitation of recovery to the best of the doctor's ability. Again, however, this is far from straightforward. The general effect of the existence of large factors of known impossibility and *uncertainty* in current medical knowledge and practice is to impose strains upon the physician too, making it more difficult to have a '"purely rational" orientation to his [*sic*] job than if his orientation were such as to guarantee success with competent work' (Parsons 1951: 450). The functional equivalents of *magic*, indeed, may arise at precisely this juncture – what Parsons terms 'pseudo-science' characterized by an 'optimistic bias' and its associated rituals – given the uncertainties and role strains involved in medical practice. Physicians, moreover, work in situations of considerable 'intimacy' which are highly charged with emotional and expressive symbolic significance. Issues of bodily exposure, bodily contact and bodily intervention are obvious examples, as are fears of bodily 'injury', raising strong sentiments and requiring careful management by physician and patient alike. The physician's need of access to private or confidential

information about the patient's life, and the seeking of consent to surgical procedures, raise similar issues (1951: 452).

Perhaps the key issue for our purposes, however, concerns the fact that the physician tends to acquire, through processes of a largely *unconscious* nature, various
types of 'projective significance which may not be directly relevant to his specifically
technical functions' (Parsons 1951: 453). These issues, in psychoanalytic parlance,
are related to the 'transference' phenomenon, which derives from the psychological
needs of the patient, who invests the physician with an 'inappropriate' and unrealistic significance, not infrequently related to a reactivation of parental roles in
childhood. *Transference*, Parsons states, is most conspicuously encountered in 'psychiatric cases', but there is 'every reason to believe that it is always a factor in the
doctor/patient relationship, the more so the longer their duration and the greater
the emotional importance of the health problem and hence the relation to the
physician' (1951: 453). Taken together, these issues, in conjunction with the physician's own handling of the *counter-transference* phenomenon, present a 'very
considerable set of complications' to the functioning of medical practice on the level
of human adjustment: issues which the specific duties and obligation of these reciprocal role structures are designed to meet and overcome, both *latently* and *manifestly*.

The professional constellation of *achievement, universalism, functional specificity,
affective neutrality* and *collectivity orientation*, in particular, functions to ensure that a
specific series of mechanisms are in place to meet these strains and overcome the
obstacles to the 'effective practice of scientific medicine'. Not only does this enable
the physician to 'penetrate' sufficiently into the private affairs of the patient, but it
also effectively protects the former from being drawn into the transference relation:
'whether it is love or hate the patient projects upon him, he fails to reciprocate in
the expected terms. He remains objective and affectively neutral' (Parsons 1951:
460–1).

This discrepancy between the transference reaction and the realistic role of the
physician provides a crucial point of therapeutic leverage, not simply in psy-
chotherapeutic settings, *but in medical contexts more generally*, whether one is aware
of it or not. Psychotherapy, to the 'militantly anti-psychiatric organic' physician,
Parsons states,

> is like theory to the anti-theoretical empirical scientist. In both cases *he practices it
> whether he knows it or wants to or not*. He may well indeed do it very effectively just
> as one can use language without even knowing it has a grammatical structure. But
> the general conclusion is that a *very important part of non- and pre-psychiatric med-
> ical practice is in fact 'unconscious psychotherapy'* and this could not be true if the
> institutional structure of the physician's role were not approximately what it has
> here been shown to be. (1951: 462, my emphasis)

From this flows the following general conclusion. The sick role and physician role
serve as mechanisms of 'social control' through the 'channelling' of deviance, in this

case illness, thereby avoiding other potentially dangerous possibilities, such as group formation (that is, a deviant 'sub-culture' of the sick). The sick role, in other words, provides both an 'insulating' and a 'reintegrative' function, the significance of which, as we have seen, is greatly enhanced through conscious and unconscious processes of psychotherapy which, in a general sense, may be subsumed under the rubric of the 'art of medicine'. All good medicine, to repeat, involves some degree of psychotherapy. Deliberate psychotherapy, however, is

> *only the tip of the iceberg* which extends above the water. *The considerably larger part is below the surface of the water.* Even its existence has been largely unknown to most psychiatrists, to say nothing of laymen. It consists in certain institutional features of the physician's role in its particular form of meshing with the sick role. (Parsons 1951: 478, my emphasis)

The sick role, in short, is part and parcel of a much larger set of mechanisms embedded in the social system: a 'window', effectively, on a broader set of motivational balances, of which illness is part, extending far beyond the doctor's surgery.

Gerhardt (1979b, 1989) sheds further important light on these issues, delineating what she takes to be two models of illness in the Parsonian paradigm. The 'incapacity model', as she terms it, focuses on illness as a breakdown of role capacity, the aetiology of which is role-related strains due to competitive occupational and other roles, with therapy viewed in terms of the exemptions and duties of the sick role. The 'deviance' model, on the other hand, views illness as motivated deviance from the norm to conform with role expectations, the aetiology of which is related to repressed dependency needs which act as unconscious motivation to become ill, with therapy conceived as a four-stage process of social control. 'Unconscious psychotherapy', within this latter model, moves from *permissiveness* to *support,* to *denial of reciprocity* (selective rewarding), to *manipulation of rewards* (reinforcement): a process in which unleashed dependency needs are re-repressed and superego controls restored en route to recovery (Gerhardt 1979b: 238). These two models, therefore, may be characterized as *structural* and *psychodynamic* explanations of illness, respectively. They may be reconciled, Gerhardt suggests, by virtue of the fact that they focus on 'different stages of the illness process, and may be seen as complementary rather than alternative' (1979b: 238). For Gerhardt, moreover, there has been a tendency to mistake the structural incapacity model for Parsons's deviance model of illness, thereby over-simplifying the paradigm and resulting in much misplaced criticism (see also Gerhardt 1989).

What, then, of the salience and significance of psychodynamic processes in current *medical practice*, and the relevance of psychoanalytical insights and unconscious processes for *medical sociology* today? Certainly Parsons's insights, on the first count, appear both accurate and prophetic, particularly in the light of developments in areas such as general practice. Armstrong (1979, 1983, 1984), for example, draws attention to the reconstruction of aspects of the general practitioner's role from the

1950s onwards, particularly through the work of Balint (1957), in which the importance of the GP as 'friend, guide and counsellor' was continually stressed. 'Emotional illness, stress, psychotherapy', it was argued, 'were integral elements of any general practice' (Armstrong 1983: 81). In this way, the 'patient's view', centred on new forms and techniques of 'biographical medicine', was very much (back) on the agenda (see also Chapter 1). The function of the doctor, Armstrong explains,

> was to listen and form a relationship – not with a passive object but a patient as subject. The examination of the psycho-social thus functioned as a mechanism for seeking and treating the patient as subject. The discovery of the 'relationship' between doctor and patient and the importance assigned to it, assumed a coming together of subjects whose behaviour and attitudes would mutually affect one another. (1983: 81)

The 'unique' qualities of the patient, therefore, and the links between diagnosis, biography and treatment, gave the consultation an *intrinsically therapeutic role*:[3] though not, it appears, unproblematically so, given the disparity between 'theory' and 'practice' (see, for example, May et al. 1996). It is not simply the patient who has come into new subjective or biographical view, however, but the doctor too, albeit in a largely disembodied fashion. The disembodied, disinterested 'clinical gaze', Gothill and Armstrong (1999) state, in true Foucauldian fashion, was initially trained on the patient's body, with the doctor's view indistinguishable from the collective 'body' of professional peers. As the web of relationships described above became more complex and diffuse, in contrast, a new entity arose: a doctor with an individual 'self', containing an instrument – the 'doctor's mind' – to examine the newly formulated 'patient's mind'. This, however, these authors stress, only implicated aspects of the doctor's *subjectivity* relevant to the consultation, thereby remaining a largely *disembodied* viewpoint despite its extension beyond the former dispassionate eye of the clinical gaze. This triad of entities (patient's body, patient's mind, doctor's mind), of course, strongly implies a fourth. To date, nonetheless, 'the anatomy and physiology of the subjective "doctor's body" is yet to be fully elaborated' (1999: 10). The doctor's body instead is a sort of

> proto-space, into which can be projected the existential pain of patients and the organisational strain of the health care system upon which conflict between the personal and the professional can be played out. Its shadow can sometimes be seen in the form of a communicating object . . . on the video monitors of its colleagues. Its presence is also indirectly suggested in expanding accounts of the vulnerability of doctors. When their health is threatened by abstract entities like 'mental illness', 'stress', 'substance abuse' and even 'suicide', doctors, unlike patients, have no terrain, no physicality upon which these external agents act. Their distress can only be defined in terms of their inability to work; yet accounts of doctor's pathology seem strangely incomplete without an analysis of the effect of this work on their own bodies. (Gothill and Armstrong 1999: 10)

Disembodied or not, the stresses and strains of health care professionals, including risks of violence and abuse, are increasingly apparent. West for example, in his tellingly entitled book *Doctors on the Edge* (2000), highlights how medics and medicine, in many ways, are in 'poor health'. His study of twenty-five GPs working in difficult inner-city areas shows poor morale and defensiveness; racism which blights the career of many 'minority' doctors; inadequacy of initial training and feelings of impotence; and the impact of patients' disturbances on the emotional health and well-being of doctors themselves in a profession where mental health issues, for doctors and patients alike, have a low priority. Many GPs, moreover, felt on the 'edge of their profession' vis-à-vis specialist, hi-technology medicine. Their stories, in this respect, revealed the dangers of neglecting emotions, both their own and those of their patients, in medical practices and beyond.[4]

Turning now to the second main issue raised concerning the relevance of psychoanalytic insights and unconscious processes for medical sociology, the picture here is equally complex, if not contradictory. On the one hand, writers such as Figlio (1987) and Lupton (1997b) call for a medical sociology or sociology of health and illness which incorporates understandings of subjectivity derived from psychoanalytic writings, with particular reference to the medical consultation and illness experience. A sensitive and sympathetic return to Parsons – alongside other writers on the psychodynamics of the medical encounter such as Stein (1985) – is indeed appropriate on this count. Lupton (1997b) goes further in fact, arguing not only that Foucauldian thought reprises in many ways some of the themes of Parsonian thought (given a similar interest in the voluntary taking up of societal imperatives), but that there is much value in bringing together Foucauldian and theoretical psychoanalytical perspectives on subjectivity in ways that go beyond the therapeutic emphasis on the use of psychoanalysis in favour of a more critical approach. The contradictory nature of desires and imperatives, she rightly argues, is integral to the understanding of humans as social beings. It is important for current debates on the potential of human agency and resistance, therefore, including those arising from Foucauldian critiques, to recognize this

> contradiction and ambivalence at the heart of subjectivity and the potentially disruptive nature of desire and the unconscious. The psychoanalytic perspective goes some way to providing a theoretical basis for the emergence of resistance to social norms and expectations. *Individuals are viewed as actively participating in their own domination as well as resisting it, disrupting as well as conforming to convention because of emotional investments, desires and phantasies that they themselves may be unable fully to articulate.* (1997b: 576, my emphasis)

Without some degree of understanding of the psychoanalytic processes involved, Lupton contends, sociologists of health and medicine will be 'unable fully to analyse the continuing complexities of the doctor/patient relationship, the medical encounter and the illness experience' (1997b: 577). Psychoanalysis, moreover, not only provides potentially valuable insights into (Kleinian) processes such as *projection*, *introjection* and *splitting* (of the 'good'/ 'bad' variety)[5] by doctors and patients alike, it can also, as we saw in Chapter 1, be turned on the sociological imagination itself in more or less fruitful or 'playful' ways (cf. Craib 1988, 1995, 1997).

Caution is needed here, however, suggesting perhaps the need for a somewhat more *tempered* response to the sociological merits of psychoanalysis. Pilgrim (1998), for example, raises a number of important points in this respect in his rejoinder to Lupton (1997b). Psychoanalysis, he notes, indeed had a 'fair airing' within social science, rather than sociology *per se*, throughout the twentieth-century. What is needed, therefore, is for psychoanalysis to be 'appraised not praised'. Whilst the illuminating contribution of groups such as the Frankfurt School is important to acknowledge, the 'problems of psychoanalysis-as-social-science should also be critically estimated' (1998: 542). Of particular note in this respect is its 'doctor-centred authoritarianism' – psychoanalysis *itself* is a version of medical work – its imperialistic stance towards subjectivity, its lack of internal coherence, and its tendency towards psychological reductionism: all of which, Pilgrim suggests, makes it a 'rather dubious starting point for medical sociologists' (1998: 542). Viewed in these terms, alleged sociological neglect or ignorance of psychoanalytic matters may not simply be well founded but a carefully considered stance.

What this boils down to, then, in part at least, is a struggle between those advocates of a 'psychoanalytic sociology' and those, like Pilgrim, who favour instead a 'sociology of psychoanalysis', and a defence of the irreducible social and material dimensions of life.[6] Here we return to debates raised at the beginning of this book (Chapter 1) concerning the 'limits' of sociology, like all other disciplines and forms of knowledge (including psychoanalysis itself), and the differing directions in which any such realization, for better or worse, might lead: a debate in short, fittingly perhaps, without closure.

Consumerism, trust and the medical encounter: the ties that bind?

It is at this particular juncture that the following pertinent question arises: how do the issues discussed previously square with the supposed advent of *consumerism* in health care? Is the nature of the medical encounter itself being transformed in this context, and if so, with what consequences for whom? Certainly it is possible to point toward various policy initiatives which are moving things in this direction. Developments in the British health care context, for example, from the Thatcher years onwards, have increasingly ushered in consumerist themes, including the Patient's Charter. These approaches and initiatives are echoed on the other side of the globe in countries such as Australia and New Zealand (Lupton 1997c), as well as on the other side of the Atlantic in the marketized American health care complex.

Such a policy, as already noted, is very much in line with New Right thinking in which an emphasis on self-reliance and individual choice, exercised through the marketplace, is seen as a viable, if not desirable, 'solution' to the supposed 'dependency culture' of the Welfare State, injecting a new competitive edge or ethos into a 'flabby' health care system. Consumerism is not, however, confined to the New Right agenda. It resonates too with New Left thinking where paternalistic welfare agencies are likewise criticized (Gabe and Calnan 2000: 255). New Labour itself, indeed, in many ways, has built upon rather than reversed previous Conservative policies in the new, so-called '*modern*', '*dependable*' National Health Service (DoH 1997, 2000). Patient rights and responsibilities, therefore, as consumers of health care and informed citizens, are high on the political agenda. The underlying assumption here, as Lupton points out, is of a rational reflexive agent, or dispassionate, calculating subject, who is encouraged to: (i) resist paternalism or medical dominance; (ii) actively evaluate health care sciences; (iii) voice complaints through the appropriate channels; and (iv) 'shop around' (potentially at least) should the 'commodity' which health care is fast becoming not prove to be up to scratch (1997c: 373–4; see also Henderson and Petersen 2002 for an exploration of the diverse meanings and manifestations of consumersism in health care).

These issues, in turn, feed into a broader series of so-called 'challenges' to medicine in the current climate, from new forms of 'managerialism' to the rise in medical litigation, and from medicine 'on trial' in the media to the role of self-help groups, and the growing popularity of various alternative and complementary therapies (Gabe et al. 1994). For some (US scholars), this has prompted suggestions, given the changing market situation and working practices of medicine, that a (neo-Marxist) process of *de-skilling* or *proletarianization* is taking place (Mckinlay 1988; McKinlay and Arches 1985). For others, it is the assault on medicine's knowledge base and professional authority that matters most, particularly from the informed consumer in the digital era of information-based society – factors which suggest a (neo-Weberian) process of *de-professionalization* (Haug 1973, 1988).[7]

We are living, according to writers such as Giddens (1990, 1991), in the era of late or high modernity, where reflexivity permeates every facet and feature of our lives. Not simply is knowledge contested and divergent in its implication, but trust itself must continually be won, retained until further notice, in the face of growing risks and uncertainties, if not radical doubt. The world, we are told, is increasingly populated by 'clever' people, who are 're-skilling' in the face of abstract systems and forms of expertise, aided and abetted by the surfeit of information and the pluralization of (lifestyle) options and choices in late modernity. The body and self, in similar fashion, are increasingly incorporated into these internally referential systems of late modernity, themselves becoming reflexive themes or projects in health as elsewhere (see, for example, Williams and Calnan 1996a and Chapter 2 of this volume). A 'congruence', therefore, exists between the notions of the consumerist patient and the reflexive actor of late modernity: 'both are understood as actively calculating, assessing and, if necessary, countering expert knowledge and autonomy with the objective of maximizing the value of services such as health care' (Lupton 1997c: 374).

Is this, however, an accurate picture of the nature and dynamics of health care at the dawn of the new millennium? On the one hand, it seems, there are reasons to think so, at least as far as the *rhetoric* of consumerism is concerned. The *reality*, nonetheless, is somewhat different: a complex if not messy affair. This is so for many reasons. First, at the policy level, it is clear that users of health care have not, as Gabe and Calnan (2000) comment, found themselves 'empowered' through such developments. Whilst an increase in information about certain aspects of health and health care is evident, there still remains a considerable *asymmetry* between patients and providers. The growth of new managerialism, likewise, has not empowered users greatly. Managers, in conjunction with doctors, still have the final say in any rationing decisions taken. Patients, furthermore, continue to rely on GPs to act as 'proxy consumers' who organize health care on their behalf (Gabe and Calnan 2000: 269). 'Shopping around' in this 'supermarket' or consumerist model of health care, therefore, is unlikely on a number of counts, including continuing user preferences for doctors' decision-making responsibilities in the context of illness and the insufficient bases to date to 'empower' users as individuals or groups (Gabe and Calnan 2000: 269). 'Dependency', indeed, both in the public and private sectors of health care, appears a fundamental characteristic of the medical encounter, regardless of the mode of provision (Gabe and Calnan 2000: 271). People, it seems, for all the rhetoric, do not really see or position themselves as 'consumers' or characterize doctors as purveyors of a 'commodity' (Lupton et al. 1991).

These points, in turn, are augmented in the light of the previous discussion concerning the emotionally charged nature and dynamics of the medical encounter and the conscious and unconscious processes contained therein for patients and doctors alike. Lupton (1996, 1997c), for example, in an illuminating empirical study, highlights the importance most people continue to place upon the *affective* aspects of health care. Whilst the notion that the medical profession is subject to more criticism than before was generally endorsed by her Australian respondents, most people still nonetheless articulated respect for doctors and faith in medical science – even amongst those expressing a consumerist discourse. Dependency, moreover, echoing the above points, was found to be a critical feature of the illness experience and the medical encounter, militating against the full adoption of the consumerist position, which itself rests on a problematic division between mind and body. The privileged representation of the patient, *qua* reflexive autonomous consumer, in other words,

> simply fails to recognise the *often unconscious, unarticulated dependence that patients may have on doctors*. This representation also tends to take up the mind/body separation in its valorizing of rational thought over affective and embodied response. It is as if 'the consumer' lacks the physically vulnerable, desiring, all-too-human body which is the primary object of medical care. (Lupton 1997b: 380, my emphasis)

Trust relations in medical encounters, from this perspective, are always charac-terized by ambivalence, anxiety, uncertainty and a sense of risk because this relationship characteristically entails a 'high degree of vulnerability and dependency' (Lupton 1996: 167). Allowing oneself to be cared for, in this respect, 'involves emo-tions of comfort and reassurance', which at one and the same time generate 'emotions of dependence and anxiety' (1996: 167). Herein lies the final paradox, namely that consumerism may *exacerbate* rather than assuage anxiety in the health care context. Far from alleviating the vulnerability and anxiety accompanying such dependence, that is to say, 'the continuing emphasis upon autonomy, individualism and distrust in consumerist discourse may only serve to generate further uncer-tainty and vulnerability' (1996: 170). Lay people, in short, may pursue both the ideal-type 'consumerist' and 'passive patient' subject positions *simultaneously* or *var-iously* depending on the context in question. Either way, a one-sided emphasis on consumerism fails to account for the complexity of medical encounters and the changeable/chargeable nature of desires, emotions and needs contained therein (Lupton 1997c).

As for broader issues surrounding the alleged proletarianization or de-professionalization of medicine, such pronouncements, to say the very least, are somewhat premature: hypotheses or trends for the future perhaps, as their expo-nents stress, but little more as yet. Lupton's (1997c, 1997d) work again is revealing here, derived from interviews with a cross-section of both the lay populace and doctors themselves. When invited to reflect on the changing role and status of doc-tors in contemporary Western society, for example, lay people were extremely variable in their negative comments, oscillating back and forth between support and criticism of doctors (Lupton 1997c). Even those expressing strong dislike of doctors often went on to mention their gratitude on particular occasions when doctors had helped them or their families. 'Good' qualities of the doctor, in this respect, included an ability to listen and *communicate* well, demonstrating empathy and providing comfort and support when appropriate. Medical *expertise* was also valued, but this meant different things to different people (Lupton 1997c: 376–7). The biomedicine versus alternative therapies contrast, in keeping with these views, was not in fact conceptualized in this way, people instead adopting a hierarchy of resort (alternative therapy *after* orthodox medicine), often combining both *simultaneously* (1997c: 377): findings which echo those of other studies (see, for example, Sharma 1996).

Lupton's findings also suggest a high level of awareness and sensitivity to changes felt by doctors themselves, particularly with respect to public perceptions of their profession. Doctors, it was agreed, were not quite as 'omnipotent' as perhaps they once were (Lupton 1997d: 490). This, however, was not necessarily viewed nega-tively or with hostility. Doctors, in general, supported a diminution in their 'god-like' status, preferring instead a more realistic set of expectations about what they could offer their patients. Some, indeed, were highly supportive of patients who requested more information, and had attempted to render the medical encounter less formal – sometimes, interestingly enough, 'in the face of patient resistance' (Lupton 1997d: 491).[8] Smith (2001), in this respect, goes further, proposing nothing short of a 'new contract' in which doctors and patients agree that: (i) death, sickness and pain, are part of life; (ii) medicine has limited powers, particularly to solve social problems; (iii) doctors don't know everything, they need decision-making and psychological support; (iv) we're in this together; (v) patients can't leave problems to doctors; (vi) doctors should be open about their limitations; and (vii) politicians should refrain from extravagant promises and concentrate on reality (see also Smith 2002).

The de-professionalization and proletarianization debates have their limits then, to repeat, as these and other findings suggest (Calnan and Williams 1995), not least in glossing over the complex dynamics of the medical encounter and the ambivalence, tensions and paradoxes this reveals at the micro- and macro-sociological levels of analysis. It is, therefore, from this perspective, a question not of doctors, the state or patients 'gaining' power from or over each other, but of a dynamic series of 'interpersonal negotiations of power centred on the ethic of professional practice' (Lupton 1997d: 493). Viewed in this light, the *de*-professionalization debate may itself be profitably recast along the lines of '*re*professionalization', whereby professional power is *constantly negotiated* at the level of everyday practice, as well as at the level of policy and organizational structure (Lupton 1997d: 493).[9] These are issues we shall return to towards the end of this chapter, when questions of health and healing in the twenty-first century are (re)considered more fully. For the moment, however, it is to a broadening of these emotional terms of reference beyond the traditional confines of the medical encounter, and the gendered implications of doing so, that we now turn.

Gender, health care and the emotional division of labour

Gender has been a muted theme in this chapter until now. It is clear, however, that any adequate engagement with issues of caring, and the emotion work it entails, must inevitably address its gendered dimensions. Stacey, for example, provides a classic formulation of these issues in her essay 'The division of labour revisited, or overcoming the two Adams' (1981), the implications of which extend far beyond the (formal) health care arena. Sociological analysis of the division of labour in health care, she argues, has been impeded by limitations in the general 'malestream' sociological theories of the division of labour, which fail to reconcile theories of production and the social control of workers (taking Adam Smith as a common point of reference) with theories of reproduction and the social control of women (which all began with Adam and Eve). It is only as a result of the 'urgent insistence of feminists' indeed, Stacey notes, that the 'problematic nature of the social order related to reproduction has been recognised' (1981: 172). The analysis of the gender order in any complex society, in this respect, inevitably raises questions to do with the division of society into public and domestic domains (Stacey 1988: 8). This is particularly important in health care, given that many of the tasks performed straddle the domestic and public domains and involve ideologies associated with both. It is important, therefore, contra traditional male-centric theories, to include not simply paid work, but the unwaged work both of carers and patients – themselves important health workers of sorts (Stacey 1988: 6–10).

Caring, Graham (1983) argues, is experienced by women as a 'labour of love', whose form and content, *qua* work role, is shaped and continually reshaped through intimate social and sexual relationships. It is as such the medium through which women gain admittance into the private world of the home and the public world of the labour market, marking the point at which 'capital and gender intersect': 'It is through caring in an *informal* capacity – as mothers, wives, daughters, neighbours, friends – and through *formal* caring – as nurses, secretaries, cleaners, teachers, social workers – that women enter and occupy their place in society' (Graham 1983: 30).[10]

The formal sphere of health care, as Stacey (1988) puts it, is a 'male-dominated gender order'. Professions, in this respect, are themselves very much gendered projects (Davies 1996, 2002; Witz 1992). Important changes have undoubtedly occurred here in recent times: a growing number of women now enter the professions, for example, with considerable public debate concerning equal opportunities and barriers to women's advancement. It is not so much the *exclusion* of women from professional work, however, Davies points out, but rather their routine *inclusion* in ill-defined 'support roles' which, through the 'adjunct work' they involve, facilitate and rest upon a masculinist construction/vision of professional work – evident in the '*fleeting encounter*' – that fails to recognize its partial and dependent character (1996: 633; see also Pringle 1989 and Putnam and Mumby 1993). Some of this adjunct work is 'technical, specialized and detailed', some of it concerns 'coping with emotions and the embodied and particular character of patients'. Almost all, nonetheless, is 'done by women' (Davies 1996: 671).[11] Even for women doctors, moreover, the gender order is still apparent, with female representation in the upper echelons of the medical career structure far from equal to that of men (Riska and Wegar 1993).

Nursing provides a paradigmatic example of these issues and the gendered dilemmas they entail. Nicky James (1989, 1992), for example, in a detailed observational study of a hospice, shows how the formula 'care = organisation + physical labour + emotional labour' captures important components of 'carework'.[12] An instructive point of comparison and contrast is drawn here between women's domestic carework and that of the hospice nurse. Family care, James notes, has provided an important model for hospice care. Domestic and workplace care, however, differ in the flexibility with which individualized responses can be made. This itself is compounded in the workplace setting of the hospice (which replicates hospital labour divisions) through a *task*-oriented division of labour: one which is incompatible with the 'family' model of domestic carework. Physical labour, in fact, is very much the priority in the hospice, despite the emphasis on 'holistic care', serving as a 'framework' which has primacy over emotional labour and 'organizing' – one which the philosophies of 'teamwork' and 'total care' are unable to erode (James 1992: 500). Emotional labour, in this respect, remains largely informal and 'grafted on' to the dominant biomedical, physical system (1992: 503). The concept of 'total care', nonetheless, also needs to be questioned, James warns, bringing both 'benefits and harm': an 'extension' in effect of 'medicine's territory further' (1992: 505; see also May 1992 on questions of 'knowing' the patient and patient 'resistance' in nursing work).

Lawler (1991), in similar fashion, questions these notions of 'holistic' nursing practice in her 'behind the screens' account of 'nursing, somology and the problems of the body'.[13] The notion of 'holistic practice', she notes, has been 'philosophized', 'theorized' and 'proselytized' by nursing writers since the 1970s: an approach promoted in the belief that personalized and individualized care is best facilitated in this way via the 'nursing process' and other such terms (1991: 216). It also, of course, provides an avenue through which nursing can move away from the dominant medical model, emphasizing instead the 'whole patient', and raising its professional status in the process. This, however, Lawler shows, is not necessarily grounded in empirical work or practice (*practical* know-how, that is to say, rather than *abstract* knowledge). It is, moreover, a very 'clean' image of nursing in which the body care and dirty aspects of nurses' work (which are considerable) disappear, replaced instead by neologisms and euphemisms. This period in nursing, therefore, can be seen as an attempt 'to both overcome the "problem of the body" in an occupation of dirty workers who deal with the messy details of physical being, and so to scientize and sanitize nursing knowledge and practice' (Lawler 1991: 216). In contrast to these 'imposed' models, Lawler shows nurses' practice in a more 'somological' way which 'integrates *lived experience* with the object body'. Somology, in other words, is a 'composite perspective developed from what is regarded by nurses as relevant. It can be holistic but need not be, it is fundamentally person-related . . . and it is context-bound. It is a view *developed in practice*. It is a *way of knowing which is different from abstract knowledge*' (1991: 216, my emphasis).

These bodily themes and emotional dilemmas are further illustrated in Meerabeau and Page's (1998) study of the drama and (in)dignity of cardio-pulmonary resuscitation (CPR) work in nursing. Again the seemingly tenuous relationship between taught (CPR) *theory* and the *reality* of nursing practice is highlighted: a situation in which the responsibilities of the nurse are significant and the assumption of 'appropriate' emotions all-important. Unsurprisingly perhaps, the role of anxiety in inhibiting performance is considerable in such contexts, with reactions *after the event* ranging from 'sadness to laughter, from emotional outpouring to tight-lipped professional control' (1998: 308). As before, however, the difficulties, dangers and draining nature of this emotion work become 'submerged beneath the business of body work and the practicalities of "getting the job done"' (1998: 308). Uncertainty, unpredictability and proximity to death, nonetheless, result in unique tensions classified in terms of 'good' or 'bad', 'success' or 'failure', 'desirable' or 'undesirable'. The medicalized moves (during resuscitation), from life to death and back again, in this respect, require

> feelings and actions that befit the moment, the see-saw between indignity in CPR and dignity with last offices providing key examples. Issues of power and control over the body in both its living and dead states weave their way throughout as resuscitation spans the field of ethical, moral, spiritual, physiological, professional and economic debates. *Nurses surely deal with both the sacred and the profane.* (Meerabeau and Page 1998: 309, my emphasis)

The emotional costs of such labour, as this suggests, may prove particularly difficult to bear. Pam Smith, for example, commenting on one student nurse's experience in a paediatric ward (where she became particularly involved with a young girl with cancer and her family), has the following comments to make:

> Like Hochschild's flight attendants, she must induce or suppress her own feelings, some would say subordinate them, to make others feel cared for and safe, irrespective of how she feels herself. She learns through 'trial and error' to 'switch off' and 'forget about work' when she goes home. But is this through surface acting to the point that she can no longer remain involved with patients other than at a superficial level, at risk of becoming detached and alienated? Or can she learn through experience and systematic training to recognize and use her feelings to remain therapeutically involved both for herself and for the patient? (1992: 15)

Faced with such dilemmas, nurses may indeed be viewed as something akin to emotional 'juggler' and 'synthesizers' (Bolton 2001). Raising the profile of emotional care, however, Smith warns, far from resolving these dilemmas, may in fact put the nurse at risk of 'increasing her anxiety by removing the protection provided by task-orientated care' (1992: 10): a point which returns us to criticisms of the nursing process raised previously (see also Menzies's [1960] psychoanalytic study of nursing practice).[14]

A key issue underpinning much of the discussion so far, readers will note, concerns the management of one emotion in particular: namely anxiety. De Swaan's (1990) study of affect management in a cancer ward, for example, is particularly revealing here, highlighting the 'defence' strategies of patients and medical staff alike. Anxieties abound in such contexts, de Swaan shows, requiring careful management, particularly with respect to that scarce and precious commodity 'attention as *support*'. One strategy, echoing Menzies's classic study (1960), concerns the *displacement* or *translation* by medical staff of emotional and relational difficulties into organizational terms – difficulties, that is to say, of *task* orientation and instruction (de Swaan 1990: 41). Patients, de Swaan observes, show a similar mechanism of displacement, albeit to a stronger degree, 'somatizing' their discontent, translating it into physical complaints, demanding action in terms of treatment. The medical treatment itself, in this context, acquires a 'sedative function' helping patients 'push aside their anxieties and worries for the time being' (1990: 33).

Alternatively, patients may keep their concerns to themselves, remaining silent about their troubles for fear that articulating them may make matters worse, thereby raising anxiety levels still higher (1990: 43). 'Being strong' in this respect is not simply viewed as a moral virtue, it is also (in hospital folklore) seen to influence the very course of the illness itself: an 'unrefuted', 'half-concealed', 'pseudo-medical' idea which serves a purpose (1990: 45; cf. Parsons's [1951] discussion of magic). Patients' anxious complaints, when they materialize, may also be avoided in a variety of ways by medical staff, from appearing vaguely absent-minded or otherwise preoccupied with medical or administrative concerns, to active displays of 'imperative cheerfulness', 'compelling jest' and 'overt censure' (1990: 45). The 'strong patient', therefore, is matched by the 'imperturbable doctor', the affect management of one supporting the other in the reciprocal control of emotions. Medical imperturbability nonetheless, de Swaan insists, in the last analysis, is inspired by identification with the patient:

> It is for their sake. The restraint is reassuring and it also conveys a cue to patients to keep themselves in check. The forceful control of emotions has its parallel in the strong limitation of affect between higher and lower staff ranks. The relations of authority in the hospital also imply that the doctors and head nurses hide their vexation and fatigue in front of nurses, and that nurses, in turn, rein in their indignation and anxiety towards their superiors. (1990: 47–8)

Not all support, however, as we have seen, is conveyed explicitly through emotional assistance. Basic nursing care, embodied and expressed in such seemingly simple tasks as the washing of a dilapidated patient, may equally at times 'comfort and reassure'. The nurse who can 'stand the sight' of the patient, who can deal with their 'wounds and lumps', it is claimed, can also 'liberate' them, however temporally, from their 'isolation' (de Swaan 1990: 48). In highlighting these and many other emotion-related issues in such settings,[15] de Swaan puts his finger on a key paradox: that it is precisely because so many emotions remain hidden or unspoken that the idea takes hold that this 'wordless emotion is indeed unbounded' (1990: 49). What so many people really 'blame' doctors for, moreover, is 'that they *need* them' (1990: 56, my emphasis).

This, in turn, raises a further paradox. Whilst patients' bodies may be 'objectified' in various ways in formal health care settings, particularly by doctors, the process of providing a dependent patient with 'total body care' may also engender a situation in which the patient's body becomes, to some extent at least, *assimilated* into or merged with the carer's own sense of self. Lawton, for example, in her study of 'the dying process', found that when family members reflected upon their personal experiences of caring for a patient at home, the *intersubjective* and *intercorporeal* impact of that patient's deterioration became very evident (2000: 106). A new corporeal unit, in other words, may be formed in these interactional moments of care, in which the selfhood of the carer is 'located and experienced within two bodies simultaneously (the carer's and the patient's) . . . hence the carer's self extends into the body of the "dependent" patient she or he is tending to or moving around' (2000: 108). The 'communicative' body (Frank 1991a), in this sense, may be truly intersubjective and intercorporeal, for moments at least.

What we have here, in summary, is a complex, if not contradictory, picture of the criss-crossing trends and dilemmas which characterize the gendered nature of care, itself a multi-dimensional phenomenon, spanning the public and domestic domains. Emotion work and emotional labour, in such contexts, embody and express these gendered dilemmas, for recipients and providers of care alike, including: (inter)corporeal relations and the vicissitudes of 'deep' and 'surface' acting; tensions between the 'lived' and 'objectified' body; the (in)visibility and (de)valuation of such efforts; the dignities and indignities this entails; and the pros and cons of moves towards 'holistic' patient-centred care. Writing about the emotional dynamics of nursing in the rationalizing context of contemporary US health care, Olesen and Bone raise a series of pertinent questions here for future sociological research discussion and debate:

> Will the newly redesigned organization of work require new or different emotional competencies? Is the labour-intensive work of providing emotional support during illness being replaced with stylized performances of hospitality and routinized niceness? As service workers experience labour speed-ups and are required to do more faster, how might emotions be felt and expressed differently? When individuals confront restructuring of emotional work, do flexible emotionalities emerge, replacing earlier, more uniform emotional standards? What adaptations of expression and communication of feelings transpose during the emotional nano-seconds of the brief and efficient encounter between nurse and patient in the managed-care environment? For some nurses, emotional involvement is considered one of the rewards of care-giving work. Does renewed professional interest in caring and empathy represent efforts of nurses to reclaim this role, holding firm to traditional emotional turf? (1998: 321)

The gendered dynamics of care, in short, both formal and informal alike, raise an ongoing series of dilemmas and debates as to the 'fate' of emotions and embodiment in the 'rationalizing' climate of our times. A further important point arises here, however, namely that any adequate analysis of the gender dynamics of emotion work and emotional labour should, in doing so, be alive to the pitfalls of perpetuating the 'emotional' woman/'unemotional' man stereotype, whether celebrated or bemoaned (see, for example, Lupton 1998a; Williams 2001b). Things indeed, without in any way contradicting the foregoing analysis, are more complex than that, including the *concealing* as well as the *revealing* of emotion, and the management of emotions (as Parsons amongst others reminds us) in such highly charged settings as the medical encounter. It is not simply then, from this viewpoint, a question of the

gender of those doing the tasks, but the gendered construction of the tasks themselves that matters. We may also, in keeping with these comments, caution against
too strong a focus on emotion work itself (vis-à-vis other forms of work), given the
risk, intentionally or otherwise, of perpetuating the very divisions from which we are
trying to escape.[16] From these discussions and debates, it is but a short step to
broader questions of ethics.

Facing up to (bio)ethics: bodies, illness and care(ss)

How do the foregoing concerns translate into questions of ethics/the ethics of
embodiment? Has the (modernist) notion of ethics founded on reason and universal duty run its course? And if so, how should we proceed in this ambivalent if not
aporetic light? A digression into more general debates on ethics and the body is
required at this point, as a backdrop to the themes which follow.

We are, at the dawn of the twenty-first century, experiencing something of a
resurgence or revitalized concern with ethics and the body, both in sociology and in
society at large. Sociology, to be sure, has always been a moral enterprise. Debates on
ethics and debates on bodies, nonetheless, are themselves in need of greater recon-
ciliation or integration. The body, Russell (2000: 102) comments, figures as both a
generator of ethical issues – through (prenatal) genetic screening, abortion, surrogate
motherhood, cloning, cosmetic surgery, transsexuality, euthanasia, and so on – and
a site for *embodied ethics*: ethics, that is to say, 'lived' and articulated in and through
bodies (see also Smart 1996).

This, in turn, raises a complex series of issues concerning the 'fate' of ethics and
the various projects it spawns in contemporary Western society: itself the subject of
much debate. For some writers, such as Giddens (1990, 1991), the reflexive project
of self in late modernity takes place in the context of routines largely devoid of ethical content or moral meaning. Others point instead to the growing imbrication of
ethics and *aesthetics* in consumer culture, which the ethical body experiences and
expresses: an aesthetic ethics or 'art of existence' in which the 'good' and the 'beautiful' are combined anew (Featherstone 1995; Foucault 1987, 1988a, 1988b).
Maffesoli (1996) goes further, however, highlighting what he takes to be other, more
tribal or *collective* currents of emotional renewal and communalized empathy as an
antidote to the *individualized, rationalized, disenchanted* world and its (morally bank-
rupt) contractarian mentality (see Chapter 2). Views, then, differ considerably on
these matters, as one might expect, perhaps, in these ambivalent times. For Bauman
(1993), indeed (himself critical of Maffesoli's 'episodic', 'inconsequential' neo-tribes),
this takes us to the very heart of the matter. A postmodern ethics, he insists – one
characterized by *disbelief* in the possibility of a *universal* and '*objectively* founded'
ethics – must inevitably confront the fact that humans are morally *ambivalent* (a
non-ambivalent morality is therefore an existential impossibility) and that moral

phenomena are inherently 'non-rational' (since they are only moral if they precede the calculative means–end formula).[17]

To fully appreciate the embodied implications of these issues, however, we must turn to Levinas (1985; see also Cohen 1986 and Hand 1989), upon whom Bauman himself draws much inspiration in his own postmodern ethics. To engage with Levinas, as Smart (1996) puts it, is indeed to face up to ethics through 'facing the body': a process, that is to say, where ethical and moral concerns are articulated and expressed *with* the body. The philosophical complexities of Levinas's thought, particularly his pre-ontological stance on ethics, should not delay us here. What is most important, for our purposes, is his insistence: that (i) ethics is *first philosophy* in the sense that it precedes or lies beyond ontology (being) and epistemology (knowledge); (ii) that ethics involves an (infinite) responsibility for other human beings; and that (iii) it is the alterity of the *Other*, embodied in the *face*, which commands us as ethical subjects – subjecting the subject, in effect, to the 'subjection of response', which itself for Levinas is the very 'meaning of meaning' and the 'event of ethics' encountered in the 'face-to-face' (Cohen 1985: 12). As Levinas puts it:

> I analyse the inter-human relationship as if, in proximity with the Other . . . his [*sic*] face, the expressive in the Other (*and the whole human body is in this sense more or less face*), were what *ordains* me to serve him. *The face orders and ordains me.* Its signification is an order signified . . . this order is the very signifyingness of the face. (1985: 97–8, my emphasis)

Ethics, from this viewpoint, emerge from *facing the other*, a radical alterity which disturbs the complacency of being through *responsibility in proximity*. Here we revisit, from a new critical vantage point, the shallow moral waters of an ethics of self, or an aesthetic stylization of life, fashioned in the fashionable (self-consumed) world of consumer culture. Goffman's fleeting world of face-to-face encounters and self-centred concerns is likewise rendered problematic (Smart 1996). For Levinas, in contrast, it is our responsibility for the other which is crucial, occurring as the 'moral height' of the other person over me *qua* being (Cohen 1985: 10). From here it is only a short step to related embodied matters to do with *love*, *touch* and *caress* (Russell 2000): issues, in the hands of feminist writers such as Irigaray (1986), which challenge the dominant masculine ordering of the senses in which sight (the most distant of the senses) is privileged. Touch makes it possible, Irigaray states, to 'wait, to gather strength, so that the other will return to caress and reshape, from within and without, flesh that is given back to itself in the gestures of love . . . *The caress does not try to dominate a hostile freedom*' (1986: 232–3, my emphasis).

What, then, of the (bio)ethics of medicine and health care? What embodied issues and agenda does this signal with or without the help of Levinas? For postmodern writers such as Nicholas Fox (1999, 2000), what this amounts to is nothing short of a wholesale rethinking of the politics and ethics of care. His reference points in this venture, as noted in previous chapters, encompass a diverse array of thinkers, from Foucault to Derrida, Deleuze and Guattari to Cixous (though Levinas is strangely missing). The realm of professionalized health care, Fox asserts, has become something of a 'vigil'. The *vigil* of care, in Foucauldian terms, from this viewpoint, is the disciplinary technology which, through discourses of professionalism and theory, 'fabricates and inscribes' those receiving care, closing down possibilities for other relations to flourish. This, moreover, is reflected in the discourses of carers themselves (both lay and voluntary), whose work extends far beyond the clinical gaze, into the clients' homes and private lives (Fox 2000: 337). This construction of a discipline of power/knowledge (or 'care-as-discipline'), in other words, entails 'a technology of surveillance, the *vigil* of care which is the continual subjection of carer's clients, and increasingly, all aspects of the environment in which they live, to the vigilant scrutiny of carers, and the consequent fabrication and perpetuation of subjectivities as "carer" and "cared-for"' (Fox 2000: 335).

Caring, however, Fox stresses, also contains another possibility, which embraces resistance to this disciplining *qua* vigil. Fox, in this respect, draws on Cixous's (1986) distinction between the 'Proper' and the 'Gift'. The *proper*, he argues, relates to aspects of the vigil: a masculine realm, in Cixous's terms, of property, possession, identity and dominance. The *gift* of care, in contrast, which Cixous formulates as feminine, pertains to issues of '*generosity, trust, confidence, love, commitment, delight* and *esteem*': a giving without any expectation of return (Fox 2000: 338). The force and value of this distinction, Fox explains – tied as it is to his broader commitment to go 'beyond health' (see Chapters 1 and 2) – lies in the possibility/promise that things could indeed be different. In particular, it offers the potential for an

> *ethics* and *politics* of engagement based on a celebration of difference not of identity . . . The *proper* is a possessive relationship, constantly requiring of its object that it behaves in certain ways, that it is defined (as 'patient', 'nurse', 'carer'), and repeats the patterns of those who have been objects of its discourse previously. Substituting *gift* relationships changes everything. We engage with others now as others, not as those with whom we might wish to identify. Definition is replaced with metaphor and allusion, analysis and theory with poetics and expression, professional care by love and the celebration of difference. (Fox 2000: 338)

One may ponder here (as before) the merits of Fox's case, particularly his commitment to the Deleuzo-Guattarian Body-without-Organs, and the extent to which he all too readily writes off prevailing forms of health care in the process (see Chapter 1). A fairer assessment perhaps, is that Fox, in taking this line, points to the ethical tensions and dilemmas of care – including the possibility, as Bauman puts it, that the 'moral impulse to care for the Other, when taken to the extreme, leads to . . . domination and oppression' (1993: 11). The possibility also arises, as Smart's contrast between Goffman and Levinas reveals, that professional *training*, whereby a caring concern for the other is a 'skill to be acquired, a discipline to be taught, learnt and examined', reduces morality to something of a Goffmanesque performance or side-show in which *moral concern* with moral matters, in a Levinasian sense, is pretty much absent (Smart 1996: 72).

Fox's 'gesture' towards feminist theory, however, together with Levinas's own ('male-identified') ethics, are both found wanting in Shildrick's (1997) 'leaky' post-modern recuperation of women, bodies and (bio)ethics. What emerges, she asks, when rigid, self-contained notions of identity and difference no longer provide the grounds for moral discourse? Steering a considered path through feminist debates on the new reproductive technologies and the limits of conventional (bio)ethics – in particular its privileging of (male) autonomy, control and identity – Shildrick attempts to recover a feminist post-structuralist ethics that goes beyond or overspills prevailing binary terms: divisions which effect closure, positioning women outside moral discourse or agency. This ethic, she suggests, is to be found in the notion of *leaky bodies* and *boundaries*, which *undermine ontological or epistemological closure*. The leaky body in illness, in this respect, finds its counterpart in the Derridean leaky *logos*. Questions of relativism again loom large here, *but* Shildrick insists, the issue is not so much that concepts of 'freedom, rationality and equality' have no place at all, simply that we should always acknowledge the 'specificity' and 'insta-bility of boundaries and distinctions' (1997: 212). Then and only then, it seems, can participants to a decision work towards a 'solution' in full acceptance of its *contingent* rather than absolute character. Relativism, from this viewpoint, is not the inevitable or irretrievable abyss some have claimed: the 'anything goes' motto does not in fact follow. This strand of postmodern feminism, moreover, 'insists on the significance of embodiment', turning away from the 'value-resistant and free-floating abstraction of an ultimately ir-responsive postmodernism', asserting instead that it is 'not at all immaterial' (Shildrick 1997: 216). At stake here, in other words, is a radical rethink-ing of the 'ethical moment'. What matters, we are told, both in bioethics and for the ethical affirmation of the feminine more generally, is that

> an acceptance of the *leakiness* of bodies and boundaries speaks to the necessity of an *open* response. The open within the same is far more than a metaphor for the reproductive potential of women's bodies; it is an expression of the discursive interplay between all bodies and all subjects. Where modernist morality directs itself to the other as alien, as simply different, postmodernist feminism relocates the ethical moment as the response to the intimate other, never fully and finally sepa-rate, yet always non-identical in multiple ways to the self. (1997: 217, my emphasis)[18]

This, as Shildrick acknowledges, is above all an 'ethics of risk' (1997: 212). Risk indeed, as Frank (2000) comments, is inherent in all illness and treatment. Leakiness, moreover, is itself a 'risky condition', one which bureaucratic modes of rationaliza-tion seek to eliminate. Bioethicists, faced with these 'dilemmas', scramble to the aid of medicine, seeking to 'repair leakiness rather than developing a standpoint based on it' (Frank 2000: 391). The autonomy paradigm, in this respect, for patient and physician alike, 'belongs to a world that few people live in' and 'few ever really enjoyed' (Frank 2000: 393). People, it seems, want 'more from society than a fading promise of autonomy . . . but they also do not want to give up the real gains – the protections and occasional entitlements – made in the name of autonomy. The dilemma of bioethics after autonomy is the dilemma of contemporary social life' (Frank 2000: 393–4).[19] We are back here, in short, face to face with the contradictions of life and living in these ambivalent times: issues it seems we must ourselves face up to (see also Frank 2003).

A final important strand in these debates remains to be aired: one, quite literally, to do with the voicing of these concerns themselves through a 'narrative bioethics'. Medicine, Frank comments, may well need Levinas: physicians, it seems, all too often 'speak *about* patients (under various categories) rather than *to* them' (2000: 393). A narrative bioethics, it is ventured – one in which the witnessing of suffering through both telling and listening to stories is morally central – would contribute much to these debates and their evolving agendas (Frank 1995, 1997). Like illness, David Morris (1998) argues, narrative is a biocultural phenomenon, situated at the 'crossroads' of biology and culture (see also Morris 1991), which in turn implies a need to 'understand the stories that shape the individual experience of illness and the art that shapes the stories we tell' (1998: 256). Telling and listening to stories, thinking *with* stories, is a *moral occasion* for Frank, involving opportunities, reflection and change through a process of 'becoming'. As wounded, people may be *cared for*, but as storytellers, Frank insists, 'they care for others'. Through their stories, 'the ill create empathic bodies between themselves and the listeners. These bonds expand as the stories are retold . . . the circle of shared experience widens. Because *stories can heal*, the wounded healer and wounded storyteller are not separate, but are different aspects of the same figure' (Frank 1995: xii, my emphasis). Rather than simply *translate*, *reduce* or *reject* these stories in favour of dominant biomedical or rationalist discourses, therefore, the goal instead is very much grounded in *moral reflection* and *personal change* set in motion by these stories of illness and the wounded bodies to which they speak.

A narrative bioethics, Morris claims, provides the chance to explore a variety of contexts in which *emotions* 'play a valuable, even crucial, role in moral thought and action, supplementing and perhaps even modifying the power of reason' (1998: 259; see Blasi 1998, however, on the question of emotions and moral motivation). *Dialogue*, like emotion, is also an everyday affair that narrative bioethics places in a 'new moral light'. A narrative bioethics, in this respect, requires that physicians know '*why* to listen, *how* to listen, and what to listen *for*': skills which themselves are inconceivable without some knowledge, intuition or learning of dialogics (Morris 1998: 265). A final feature of narrative bioethics, for Morris, involves a shift away from abstract principles and 'megawatt, life-and-death, technology-driven emergencies' into the *ordinary* and the *everyday*, thereby redressing the increasingly 'big' issues of conventional bioethics (1998: 265). A narrative bioethics, from this viewpoint, may chose to focus on smaller, more manageable questions that the media preoccupation with megawatt issues tends to render invisible. It can thus help us *reclaim* for moral knowledge an entire area of medical practice that, because it is invisible, seems almost devoid of ethical implications. It can offer us an ethical understanding of the everyday world that may prove crucial in the experience of illness. (1998: 265)[20]

Greco's (2001) work on alexithymia, ethics and self casts further light on these issues, adding another important twist to these (emotion-centred) debates. Alexithymia – which, she shows, is a socioculturally specific construct, with para-digmatic potential in the broader field of psychosomatic medicine – quite literally means 'without words for emotions'. More specifically, it refers to a difficulty in identifying and describing feeling; difficulty in distinguish feelings and bodily sensations of emotional arousal; difficulty constructing imaginative processes; and an externally orientated cognitive style (Greco 2001: 473). The story Greco tells does not stem, however, from the experience of ill people themselves, but from the interpretations of clinicians – an expert narrative, in effect, albeit one not wholly aligned with the voice of biomedicine. On the one hand, what we have here, to use Hyden's (1997) terminology, is a narrative *about* illness. On the other hand, what this speaks to is narrative *as* illness: a 'faulty narrative' which itself may play 'a role in the pathogenesis of unspecified diseases' (Greco 2001: 485). What is particularly interesting, nonetheless, Greco stresses, is that this expert narrative also implies a *prescription*, given the very nature of the condition in question, to become 'sub-jectively reflexive, to refuse narrative colonization and to elaborate a unique self-story' (2001: 486). This, in turn, makes it more difficult to speak of '"surren-der" or "resistance" to the discourse of medicine for, in this case, it is a discourse that no longer demands unquestioning compliance, but rather seems to invite cre-ativity and difference' (2001: 486). Alexithymia, in this regard, evinces a number of interesting variations on some familiar themes within the illness narrative genre, not least the notion of an 'expert-meta-narrative concerning the relative value of different self narratives in relation to the possibility of health and illness' (2001: 484).

Bury (2001) too sounds an important note of caution here. Narratives, he argues, are perhaps more contradictory, if not mundane, than many writers allow. The indi-vidual in pain and distress, moreover, is at times portrayed in 'romantic if not sentimental terms', such that the 'actual relationship in which the individual is embedded may be lost in an overemphasis on positive "personal narratives" that are uncritically reproduced by the sociological author' (2001: 277). The potential of moral narratives for establishing *social distance* as well as personal worth should also not be forgotten (2001: 277). In these and other respects, Bury suggests, claims about the potential of narrative analysis in medicine need to be treated with caution: a challenge not simply for medicine but for sociological analysis itself (see also Brown et al. 1996).

A complex series of moral issues and (bio)ethical debates, to summarize, have been raised here: debates in which (engendered) matters of emotion and embodiment, and the turn to narrative/narrative turn, loom large. The crucial issue in this respect, postmodern or otherwise, is not simply to *rethink* but to *re-embody* ethics within and beyond the health care arena. Facing up to ethics, in short, is indeed an embodied possibility, with or without Levinas on board.

Health care in the twenty-first century: a new medical pluralism?

What, then, of the 'fate' of biomedicine and the future of health care in the twenty-first century? Are we, for instance, entering a new era of medical pluralism?

On the one hand, it seems, returning to earlier debates in this and previous chapters, the medical citadel is under attack from all quarters, including calls and initiatives both inside and outside the profession to put its 'house in order'. Besieged by an incessant tide of policy reforms in the health service, auditing and accountability exercises, league tables and performance measures, scandals over cases of gross professional misconduct – not to mention academic critiques of various sorts, a growing wave of complaints and rising patient expectations – doctors may well be fed up.[21] Scarcely a day goes by, in fact, without some new problems or dilemmas breaking out about the state of the health service or the 'crisis' in medicine. Story upon story, inquiry upon inquiry, promise upon promise, initiative upon initiative, crisis upon crisis, critique upon critique, the attractions of a career in the medical profession are fading fast.

On the other hand, however, the future of biomedicine looks more or less assured. Despite being more critical and informed, people are not in fact, as we have seen, turning their backs on biomedicine: how could they? Medical encounters and health care interactions, furthermore, do not readily lend themselves to the importation of a consumer ethos, as this chapter attests. The medical profession itself, moreover, may be *re-stratifying* in various ways in response to these 'challenges', without any significant loss of overall corporate power (cf. Freidson 1985, 1994): doctors turned managers, 'poachers turned gamekeepers' (Hunter 1992). The de-professionalization and proletarianization theses, then, as noted earlier – despite increasing state and corporate involvement and new intermediary power relations – may be somewhat wide of the mark, suggesting instead a period of 'uncomfortable readjustment', 'reconfiguration' (Gabe et al. 1994) or 're-professionalization' (Lupton 1997d) at the *micro*, *meso* or *macro* levels.

A delicately poised/balanced situation then? Two issues, in particular, are worth addressing more fully here in closing. The first concerns recent attempts by the British medical profession to put its own 'house in order', including the effectiveness and efficiency of the General Medical Council (GMC) itself (for earlier studies of the GMC, see Stacey 1992, 1995). It is time, Sir Donald Irvine (1997a, 1997b) remarked, in an early signal of things to come, for a new agreement between medicine and society: one founded (unsurprisingly perhaps, given his position at the time as President of the GMC) on sound *self*-regulation, which should, he argued, bring the public's and the profession's interests 'successfully together'. All doctors, Irvine stressed, have a duty to maintain good practice, whilst patients themselves must be protected from poor practice. 'Dysfunctional' doctors too should be helped back to practise whenever appropriate, with 'openness' about doctors' performance seen as essential to public trust and confidence. A 'strengthened professionalism', demonstrating good standards of practice and effective mechanisms of self-regulation and openness, is the proposed 'remedy' therefore: the means of securing public trust whilst safeguarding, at one and the same time, the independence of the profession in the face of greater threats of external control (see also Irvine 2001).

These calls have subsequently been taken forward by the GMC through a series of proposals and plans for reform based on consultation with patient and consumer groups, doctors, employers and a wide range of organizations with an interest in their work: proposals which, at the time of writing, the government is now consulting on (see, for example, Dewar and Finlayson 2001; DoH 2002; GMC 2001; GMC 2002b). The preuse details of these reforms need not concern us here, except to say that they promise a more *effective*, *inclusive*, *accountable* and *transparent* GMC which will reduce its size from 104 to 35 members and increase lay membership from 25 per cent to 40 per cent. What is more important, for our purposes, is what they signify: namely, that medicine, in an era where the rhetoric if not the reality of accountability, quality assurance, transparency and the like is high on the agenda (backed up by new NHS organizations such as the National Clinical Assessment Authority and the National Patient Safety Agency, and others with a responsibility for assessing the quality and safety of patient care) is having to move with the times, like it or not. Taken together indeed, in the GMC's own words, this 'represents the most comprehensive and wide-ranging reform of professional regulation since parliament set up the GMC in 1858' (GMC 2002b).

If this suggests one way in which the medical profession is responding to potential challenge, disarming it more or less effectively through consultation exercises and internal reform, then a second, related method concerns something akin to the 'if you can't beat them join them' mentality. This, in many respects, appears to be precisely what is happening in debates over alternative and complementary medicine (CAMs),[22] including moves to so-called *'integrative medicine'*. Here we confront, more directly perhaps than in the first example above, the possibilities and prospects of a 'new' medical pluralism. In many ways of course, as Cant and Sharma (1999) rightly note, a medical pluralism of sorts has been the norm, historically and globally speaking. The dominance of Western biomedicine from the mid-nineteenth-century onwards, in this respect, is itself something of an aberration. A *resurgence* of interest in alternative and complementary therapies from the late twentieth-century onwards, nonetheless, warrants the prefix 'new' with reference to any such pluralism, given the power and dominance of the medical profession.

Approximately half the population of industrialized countries, it is estimated, now use CAMs regularly: education, income, health status themselves being important predictors of usage, alongside gender (with a female predominance). US expenditure on CAMs, for instance, rose in the 1990–7 period from $13 billion to $38 billion a year, with twice as many consultations with CAMs practitioners as with orthodox family doctors (Rees and Weil 2001). In Britain too, as in Australia, all available evidence points to the fact that use of CAMs is now widespread and increasing (Cant and Sharma 1999; House of Lords 2000; *WHICH?* 1986, 1992, 1995).[23] Estimates in 1997, for example, suggest that Britons spend some £75 million a year on aromatherapy, homeopathy and herbal medicines alone: most of this spent by women (Forna 1997).[24] The number of CAMs practitioners in Britain, moreover, is now larger than the number of registered GPs.

Does this amount to a new medical pluralism, however? The answer, it seems, may well be a qualified yes, depending, of course, on the definition of this term 'pluralism' itself. While an ideal-typical pluralism would suggest multiple players on a level playing field, medical pluralism in a postcolonial world, Cant and Sharma note, more usually represents a situation 'where such equality is only apparent' (1999: 4). What we have here, in fact, is a situation in which 'biomedicine is still dominant and still plays a major part in the process by which different therapies are accorded different degrees of legitimacy and prestige' (Cant and Sharma 1999: 195). This, for example, is clearly evident in various British Medical Association reports on CAMs: the tone becoming appreciably less harsh over the years, as strategies have switched from proof of scientific efficacy concerning *alternative* medicine to calls for greater accreditation, competence to practice and patient protection regarding *complementary* or *non-conventional* medicine (BMA 1986, 1993). Regulation, therefore, has become wrapped in a benevolent guise as medicine assumes the moral mantle of patient protector or consumer advocate – a kind of professional shield/guide through a bewildering array of CAMs which serves medical regulatory interests well. This, of course, is not to dismiss such concerns, nor to suggest that these forms of therapy are immune from testing (debates on appropriate methodologies notwithstanding). It is, however, to point to the fact that vested professional interests are at stake, and that a concern with patient or consumer welfare is not the whole story. The recent House of Lords Report (2000) on CAMs, in this respect, provides the latest chapter in this long-running story, recommending *inter alia*: (i) the need for greater regulation and accreditation of practitioners; (ii) that NHS patients should have greater access to CAMs (if a therapy gains a critical mass of evidence to support its efficacy over and above the 'placebo effect'); (iii) that certain treatments offer 'real' benefits; and (iv) that more money should be spent on testing the claims of CAMs (proposing a ten-year strategy of 'pump priming' funds).

It is in this context that notions of '*integrated*' or '*integrative*' medicine come to the fore, shedding further light on these trends, tensions and debates. The term 'integrated' or 'integrative' medicine (the latter is more frequently used/better recognized in the United States than in the United Kingdom) can refer to almost any situation in which CAMs and orthodox medicine relate to one another beyond the level of simple impersonal referral. It can, for example, refer to the use of CAMs or therapeutic techniques by biomedical professionals (Cant and Sharma 1999: 160–1). More specifically, however, it is used to denote *either*: (i) clinics where CAMs and biomedical practitioners collaborate or work alongside one another in a variety of institutional settings and arrangements (most often in the primary health care sector); *or* (ii) the integration of CAMs knowledge into biomedical education (see also Sharma 2002). Much is being made of this in recent years, particularly in the United States. The *British Medical Journal* also devoted considerable space to these matters in its 20 January 2001 issue – one with a telling image of two flamingos on the front cover, their necks entwined, bearing the title 'Integrated Medicine: Orthodox Meets Alternative'. Articles in the education and debate section, for instance, included the need for undergraduate *education* in CAMs in order to familiarize tomorrow's doctors with these therapies (Owen et al. 2001); the need for *regulation* in CAMs (Mills 2001); the problems involved in conducting *research* on CAMs (including recruiting suitable patients and finding appropriate placebos) (Nahin and Straus 2001); and the lessons on integration from the *developing world* (Bodeker 2001). Other short pieces, by various advocates, included such eye-catching headers as: 'Integrated medicine imbues orthodox medicine with the values of complementary medicine' (Rees and Weil 2001); 'Directly studying human healing could help to create a unifying focus in medicine' (Reilly 2001); and 'Teaching complementary medicine offers a way of making teaching more holistic' (Berman 2001).[25]

Again, however, this raises more questions than it answers. Will any such push towards integration, for example, whatever that means and whoever initiates it, lead to greater equality or simply new forms of medical dominance in a more or less subtle guise (old wine in new bottles)? All too frequently it seems, if the current experience of CAMs practitioners in the National Health Service is anything to go by, the situation is more akin to 'bolting on' than truly *integrating* these therapies. This, furthermore, may be at the expense of a considerable dilution of CAMs principles and practices through working in biomedicine's own backyard. Whose interests, therefore, does integration really serve? A related question concerns the issue of knowledge bases. If by integration we mean the inclusion of CAMs modules in the medical curriculum, which itself now is supposedly more interdisciplinary, then, 'yes', developments are already under way (see, for example, Bryden 2001; Owen et al. 2001; Rees and Weil 2001). Is this, however, *integration* or simply *addition/combination*? CAMs modules in current medical curricula, moreover, to the extent that they exist at all, are in large part *optional* rather than *compulsory*: hardly the basis for any widespread integration. More to the point, perhaps, are we dealing here, despite the hype or best of intentions, with 'incommensurable' paradigms?[26] And what, on a more rhetorical note, does this tell us about medicine as currently constituted: a 'disinte- grated' form of practice (Morrell 2001)? 'It is hard to see', Sharma concludes, 'how integration could be a coming together of equally valued systems of knowledge' (2002: 228). At worst, it seems, patients are receiving an 'eclectic' form of medicine. At best, they are benefiting from the 'cross-fertilisation of different traditions of healing and the development of an holistic synthesis' (Cant and Sharma 1999: 184).

To the extent, to summarize, that a 'new' medical pluralism is evident, it is one in which biomedicine still enjoys a dominant position:[27] a 'diversity', that is to say, which itself is 'highly structured' (Cant and Sharma 1999: 195). The expansion of CAMs, moreover, is unlikely to continue indefinitely, if for no other reason than they too will come to experience the 'same kind of funding constraints as biomedi- cine' and the 'same public realization of the limitations to its claims to efficacy' (Cant and Sharma 2000: 437). The gender dynamics (as well as class relations) of these issues should also not be forgotten, given the high proportion of women patients and practitioners, and the premium placed upon feelings and emotions. At present, then, if not for the foreseeable future, CAMs occupy a 'limited', yet 'impor- tant', role in the 'total health care systems of Western societies' (Cant and Sharma 2000: 437).

Conclusions

From the psychodynamics of the sick role to the future of health care in the twenty- first century, this chapter has sought to explore relations between bodies, care and ethics. Emotions again, as we have seen, loom large here, be it in the traditional medical encounter, the gender division of labour in health care, or the flourishing of CAMs in the so-called 'new' medical pluralism: issues, moreover, which themselves call into question any simple, unproblematic notion of the 'emotional' woman and the 'unemotional' man, whether celebrated or bemoaned. Traces or intimations, if not fully fledged expressions, of the communicative body may be found in much of this discussion, particularly with respect to the need for a truly *embodied* ethics. *Facing* up to these issues, and *voicing* such concerns, with or without the help of Levinas, is indeed crucial, if not of first importance, given the limits of existing (bio)ethical paradigms and the need to move beyond them. As for the fate of bio- medicine and the future of health and healing in the twenty-first century, the twin pressures of *regulation* and *integration*, themselves much debated, are very much on the agenda. The stage is set therefore for a truly fascinating unfolding drama, clues to which may well be discerned in previous dress rehearsals (with more or less accomplished performances by medicine); but with many budding scriptwriters, who knows . . .

Notes

1   Parsons, in fact, is indebted in these and other respects to L.J. Henderson, who wrote a paper in 1935 entitled 'Physician and Patient as a social system'.

2   These problems include Parsons's *consensual* (medico-centric) approach to these matters; his formulation of what in effect is a *patient* role which neglects the illness iceberg; the limited applicability of the sick role to *chronic illness* and other conditions such as pregnancy; and his failure to address factors such as *class*, *gender*, *age* and *ethnicity* in medical encounters. We may also question whether illness is deviance given (i) the extent of illness in the community and (ii) the fact that sick role incumbency involves *conformity* rather than deviance. For classic critiques of and extensions to the Parsonian sick role, see, for example, Freidson (1970) and Gallagher (1976). See also Pflanz and Rhode (1970) on the latter theme of illness behaviour as deviance or conformity. In response to his critics, Parsons (1975) claimed: (i) that he had never meant to confine the category of illness to deviant behaviour, though its negative valuations should nonetheless be borne in mind; (ii) that his concerns were not exclusive to cases of acute illness as opposed to chronic illness; and (iii) that, although interaction between doctor and patient is a two-way not a one-way process, it is still basically asymmetrical, because of the physician's expertise and the special fiduciary responsibility this entails for the care of the sick.

3   See May (1992) and Nettleton (1992) for related studies of nursing and dentistry.

4   For another interesting study of doctors as patients and the power dynamics of the medical consultation in this context, see McKevitt and Morgan (1997).

5   *Projection* involves the psychic process of putting or pushing feelings from the inner world into someone else or something in the external world; *introjection* refers to the taking 'in' of something outside oneself, making it part of oneself; whilst *splitting* involves the splitting of the world into 'good' and 'bad' (Craib 1988: 146).

6   As Lupton's (1998a, 1998b) response makes clear, her position here is certainly not one which advocates the colonization of medical sociology or the substitution of its theories by psychoanalytic perspectives. The latter instead provide a *complement* to this extant body of sociological work on health, illness and medicine.

7   For a general discussion of these and related issues, see Coburn and Willis (2000). See also Light (2000) on the sociological character of (changing) health care markets.

8   Whilst female and younger doctors were particularly positive about such changes, the type of medicine doctors practised also appeared to influence their views: specialists, for example (who were also invariably older and male), found little desire on their patients' part to question their authority or judgement.

9   Navarro (1988) takes a different line, arguing that the real power lies with capitalism not medicine, thereby rendering the professional dominance, de-professionalization and proletarianization theses equally problematic. The power and interests of the pharmaceutical industry, we might add, are also important to consider here (Abraham 1995).

10   In what follows I focus primarily on *formal* caring. For a detailed discussion and illuminating recent analysis of informal care, see Heaton (1999). Carers, she argues – given shifts from care in the community to care by the community in the 1970s and the associated development of the discourse of informal care – are simultaneously established as a "relay" of the gaze caring for others under the tutelage of the formal carers, and also as an object of the gaze whose wellbeing is a matter of concern' (1999: 773).

11   For a detailed dicussion of the engendered emotion debate, see Lupton (1998a) and Williams (2001b). See also Fineman (1993, 2000) for many interesting essays on emotion in organizations.

12   Hochschild's (1983, 1998) pioneering work on the 'managed heart', critically appropriated or otherwise, provides a key point of reference in these debates, helping us to 'see things differently' (see also Chapters 3 and 7). We all, of course, engage in emotion *work* or emotion *management* of some sort, revealing or concealing our feelings, as appropriate, in particular contexts and settings. For Hochschild, nonetheless, emotions have increasingly

been 'put to work' as part and parcel of broader transformations in the labour process and the *feminization* of employment practices. Emotional *labour*, from this viewpoint, is very much part of the picture in late capitalism, sustained through a complex web of '*feeling rules*' and commercialized imperatives pertaining to the 'managed heart'. The smiling, friendly, courteous and considerate flight attendant exemplifies these processes, for Hochschild, through both '*surface*' and '*deep*' acting: the former involving a conscious change of outer expression in an attempt to make inner feeling conform to how we appear, the latter requiring a change of feelings from within, so to speak, using a variety of methods, thereby translating 'inner' feeling into 'outer' expressions. See Williams (1998d) for a detailed discussion of Hochschild's work and Wouters (1989) for an Eliasian critique.

13 See also Lawler (1997) for an interesting edited collection of essays on 'the body in nursing'.

14 Menzies's (1960) study of a London hospital was designed to investigate some of the reasons for student drop-out in nurse training. A key contributing factor, she suggested, was high anxiety levels, which the *task*-orientated nature of nursing guarded against as an organized *defence* mechanism.

15 De Swaan (1990), for example, discusses various 'exceptional states' such as laughing fits, anxiety attacks and loss of decorum, embodied in the 'house joker', as well as sufferers of 'anxiety hysteria' and the 'senile' and 'demented'.

16 A broader debate on the strengths and weaknesses of the concept of emotion management is beyond the scope of this chapter/book. See, however, Barbalet (1998) and note 12 above.

17 Here we return to the thorny reason–emotion debate; see Chapter 7.

18 Shildrick makes the interesting point here that through the privileging of the doctor as *subject* of knowledge and the patient as *object*, and through the equation of illness with leaky bodies and the anxiety this engenders, the sick become the (feminized) other, with the role of doctors and patients being cast, respectively, as masculine and feminine (1997: 100).

19 Frank also discusses here, in his review essay on bioethics, Tauber's (1999) attempt to incorporate or found a relational Levinasian ethics in medicine; Tauber's take on which Frank questions. 'Levinas', Frank states, 'may require even more of medicine than Tauber acknowledges', given his commitment to the radical alterity of the Other (2000: 392).

20 Mention should be made here of at least two important strides forward in recent years: first the publication of Greenhalgh and Hurwitz's book *Narrative Based Medicine* (1998); second, a subsequent conference on this very theme, organized by the *British Medical Journal* in association with the Royal Anthropological Institute in September 2001 at Homerton College, Cambridge.

21 See, for example, Smith (2001, 2002) and West (2000), discussed earlier.

22 CAMs, it seems, is the current preferred reference, given the 'vexed' question of terminology (Sharma 1992, 1996). Treatments here range from acupuncture to naturopathy, chiropractic to shiatsu, homeopathy to hypnotherapy, osteopathy to reiki. See, for example, the House of Lords (Science and Technology Select Committee) Report on CAMs (2000) for a recent attempt at classification, successful or otherwise.

23 For a useful review of the situation in developing countries, see Bodeker (2001). Cant and Sharma (1999) also provide a useful discussion of lessons from the postcolonial countries.

24 This itself raises questions about new forms of healthicization, commercialization and control in women's lives. See, for example, Forna (1997).

25 One might question here, of course, the benefits of any such 'holistic synthesis'. See Chapter 2.

26 For an interesting discussion of the metaphysics of alternative medicine, see Scott (2003). See also Aakster (1986) for a comparison of concepts in biomedicine and alternative medicine.

27 Developments such as the new genetics, moreover, may provide medicine with its most potent 'trump card' yet (see Chapter 8). To the extent that this threatens a renewed *reductionism*, however, it may promote precisely the opposite effect, strengthening the hand of those 'holistic' therapies for whom the limits of reductionism are all too apparent.

Conclusion: The Challenges Ahead

What conclusions can be drawn from the embodied themes and issues discussed in this book? In part, of course, the answer lies in the conclusions already provided at the end of each respective chapter. It is the challenges ahead, therefore, within and beyond the sociology of health and illness, that I shall focus on here in this brief 'conclusion' to the book, taking these former conclusions as read.

Perhaps the first, ongoing challenge is not so much to bring the body 'back in' (mission more or less accomplished), but to move towards a more fully *embodied* sociology, with implications for sociologists themselves as well as for those whom we seek to study. The body may well be 'back' on the sociological agenda, if 'back' was ever the correct term, but much still remains to be done to fully explore the embodied implications and potential of any such move, including the dormant matter of sleep, particularly when the flesh is all too easily forgotten in a world of signs and symbols. The issue, then, to return to debates raised at the beginning of this book, is to do not so much with a sociology *of* the body (which of course has its place), as with an *embodied* sociology, in health as elsewhere: one in which emotions are accorded a central rather than a peripheral role.

This, in turn, opens up a second key challenge concerning a rethinking of *biology–society* relations and associated divisions in sociology and beyond. Sociologists, to be sure, may be wary of any such enterprise or undertaking given the taint of past biologism or its socio-biological reworkings. The risks, however, may be more apparent than real. There are, as we have seen, many viable alternatives to reductionism available to draw upon, including non-determinist principles of *irreducibility* and *emergence*. Going beyond the biological, to repeat, does not mean leaving it out altogether, or reducing it to mere discourse. Realist agendas provide one more or less promising way forward here, as elsewhere, in keeping with the broader commitment to embodiment raised above (see Archer 1995, 2000, for example).

If *society* rather than sociology (in large part) directs the research agenda, then the imminent worldwide epidemic of AIDS, Gerhardt (1989: 354) ventured in the epilogue of her *magnum opus*, may drastically change the landscape of medical sociology over the ensuing years or decades. The epidemic of AIDS, of course, has not gone away, at least on a global scale. Our increasing Western complacency, moreover, given pharmaceutical breakthroughs such as AZT, may well be shattered as new resistant strains of the virus emerge. Gerhardt's predictions, nonetheless, have been somewhat eclipsed or overshadowed by developments such as the *new genetics*, which may indeed transform the agenda of sociology of health and illness more or less radically over the coming decades. The prospects, as we have seen, are potentially mind-boggling. The hype and overblown promises of the new genetics to date, however, remind us that caution is needed here in evaluating such claims, particularly when the multi-factorial nature of health and illness and its broader structural determinants are taken into account. Herein lies the third key challenge ahead regarding the place and function of sociology in relation to the new genetics. From the social construction of genetic knowledge in lay and professional cultures, to debates on the potential for new genetic forms of discrimination and risk, and from studies of media reportage of the new genetics to questions of bioprospecting, sociologists will doubtless find many roles and niches, not least as disseminators of critiques, debunkers of myths, advocates of deliberative/participatory democracy, and defenders of rights: part and parcel perhaps of a critical (medical) sociology linked to a reinvigorated public sphere, including various social movements as the harbingers of challenge/change (cf. Scambler 2002) . These issues in turn, of course, are themselves part and parcel of the broader array of biotechnological and digitalized possibilities which stretch before us, for better or worse, in this 'Brave New World', post-human or otherwise .

Here we anticipate a fourth key challenge, regarding the *(bio)ethical* dilemmas and agendas this raises: issues in which (medical) sociology must play its part. Existing ethical paradigms have their limits, as we have seen, presaging the search for new ethical positions or moments, including an *embodied ethics/ethics of embodiment*. Facing up to ethics, therefore, is central to an embodied sociology, one which permeates every facet of our lives, from the dilemmas of hi-tech medicine and the corporate interests of biotechnology/biocapitalism, to the all-consuming pleasures (and anxieties) of consumer culture.

This brings me to the fifth challenge I wish to raise in closing. It concerns not simply an ongoing commitment to theorizing and tracking, explaining and tackling (health) *inequalities* in the Western world – themselves, as we have seen, complex, multi-dimensional phenomena which take us (yet again) beyond either/or debates, forging profitable new links with mainstream debates in the process – but the need to place these very issues, and the sociology of health and illness in general, in the context of global debates in this new phase of (disorganized) capitalism. One may well be sceptical of much 'globalony' surrounding *globalization* and *globalism* to date (Cohen and Kennedy 2000). That such debates are now occurring is itself, nonetheless, both timely and instructive. Are we, for example, really witnessing the emergence of a 'global' society? What positive or negative scenarios does this suggest? And who are the winners and losers in any such process? The supposed 'coming together' of the global era may also, paradoxically, provide opportunities for new tensions, conflicts and resentments to arise. Population pressures (expected to increase by 50 per cent by the middle of this century), the flows of tourism, global communications, the rise of transnational producer and consumer relations and the development of new forms of urban and cultural life – these and many other processes affect people within and across nation states and national borders (Cohen and Kennedy 2000). Green battles and green movements, likewise, evince global concerns and global issues pertaining to the environment and the protection of the biosphere: issues which world leaders such as President Bush would do well to heed.

Meanwhile, anti-capitalist protesters have been taking to the streets in recent years, exposing the exploits of the transnational corporations and the brokers of the 'global economy'; relations which can be traced from the export-processing zones and sweat-shops of developing countries to the welcoming air-conditioned, music-piped, high-street stores of the West (Klein 2000; 2002). To this we may add issues of migration, the growth of a refugee 'problem', the tragic loss of human life in famine-prone parts of the world, not to mention the epidemic of AIDS in Africa. We begin the new century, as the outgoing US President Clinton remarked, with half the world's people struggling to survive on less than $2 a day, nearly 1 billion living in chronic hunger. The 'cutting edge' of the new global economy, in this respect, is juxtaposed with amazing numbers of people who still live on the 'razor's edge of survival' (Clinton 2000). The global economy, the information technology revolution, advances in science, democracy not dictatorship, these and many other supposed 'benefits' of the modern world, in other words, exist in tension with the 'burdens' of global poverty, problems of the global environment, and worries about global warming, to mention but a few of the challenges ahead (Clinton 2001).

All these issues carry important implications for health, including, of course, issues of *globalization* and *genetization*, inviting if not demanding medical sociologists to go beyond their traditional (Western) concerns, connecting local, regional and national issues to global debates, if not a global sociology (Cohen and Kennedy 2000). Here again, to repeat the point made earlier, we glimpse the promise and potential of a critical (medical) sociology which, in association with new social movements, provides a timely defence of deliberative democracy, human rights and health/ecological agendas around the globe. There are, to be sure, some promising signs already here, particularly with respect to issues such as the new genetics (including GM foods and GMOs) (Petersen and Bunton 2002) and associated biotechnologies (Clarke et al. 2000). Much remains to be done, nonetheless, on these and other global counts.

I have not mentioned war or terrorism until now, but these too, of course, carry important implications for health and health care on a global scale. From the battles in the Balkans and the horrors of ethnic cleansing, to the military bombings of Iraq and the depleted uranium fall-out left in its wake, and from the troubles of war-torn Kosovo to the ongoing struggles and bloodshed of the Israeli and Palestinian conflict, the scale of human tragedy, misery and unnecessary suffering is truly devastating. Meg Stacey (2002) has spoken elegantly and eloquently to these themes in her reflections on gender, health and healing across the public/private divide. Why, she asks, has medical sociology not taken the health consequences of war on board? 'Maybe the analytical methods of modern science and of logic as practised', she ventures, 'make it easier for us to evade some painful, difficult and dangerous topics. Wars, after all, come under military studies or peace studies, not under the provision of health care of the sociology of medical knowledge' (2002: 279). The closest, it seems, medical sociologists have got to war to date is via the metaphors of battle and military tropes employed by biomedicine in its endless war with disease or the shift from 'combat' to 'codes' through developments such as 'bio-informationalism' and the new genetics (cf. Haraway 1991; Montgomery 1991). There is indeed, Stacey continues, something 'uncannily similar between aspects of modern medicine and modern war: both involve high-precision instruments, application of the latest techno-science and the separation of one problem from all others' (2002: 279). 'Clinical' war, precision bombing (which is not that precise), soldiers with mysterious illnesses, the health consequences of sanctions – many connections can be made. Medical historians have made some profitable inroads here in recent years, addressing the medicalization of war, the militarization of medicine (Harrison 1996) and the broader relations between war, medicine and modernity (Cooter et al. 1998, 1999). Should medical sociology follow suit?

These issues appear all the more pressing in the aftermath of 11 September 2001: events, quite literally, which transformed the global landscape in tragic and horrifying ways. The implications, to be sure, are still unfolding in what is now dubbed the new, so-called 'war' on terrorism. The threat or risk of bio-terrorism, for example, is now high on the agenda – from anthrax attacks/scares, to the spectre of smallpox or Marburg disease martyrs (Miller et al. 2001). What we have here, in other words, remote or otherwise, is the possibility of a new era of *calculated* contagion or *deliberate* disease, including genetically spliced super-bugs, with public health implications around the globe: from smart bombs to smart bugs indeed. The World Health Organization, for instance, is clearly taking this threat seriously, whilst nations around the world review current security, surveillance and disaster management procedures, including public health measures, with a healthy injection of funds for the bio-defence industry. The risks of bio-terrorism, in short, are *both* real and exaggerated (Miller et al. 2001), with important paradoxes to ponder; not least that past success in eradicating diseases such as smallpox, render us all the more *vulnerable* to their reintroduction now (Fuller 2002: 1.6.) Again, medical sociology is well placed to contribute to these debates, including the 'epidemics of fear' they unleash (Showalter 1997; Strong 1990), as we think the unthinkable in these uncertain times (Williams 2001c).

As for the future of medical power and professional dominance, the challenges ahead are many and varied. Doctors may well be 'unhappy' – beset on all sides, with health care systems such as the NHS on the 'sick' if not 'critical' list, despite the recent pledge of increased funds – but medical power and dominance is still, it seems, very much intact (albeit in reconfigured, re-packaged ways): all the more effective for being so, perhaps, in the so-called 'new medical pluralism'? This, in turn, suggests a continuing need on the part of sociologists themselves to return to, if not rethink, prevailing notions of professional power and dominance in a changing world: part and parcel of the ongoing debate between medicine and sociology. The imperialist charge, to be sure, may be somewhat wide of the mark here, but revisiting it from time to time is instructive nonetheless, not least for the (reflexive) issues it raises in relation to sociological critiques themselves. The relays between medicine and sociology, in short, are complex, if not mutually reinforcing. This, perhaps, is no bad thing.

The sociology of health and illness, to conclude, is a flourishing sub-discipline which has truly come of age: no mere handmaiden to medicine, nor the poor relation of mainstream sociological theory (if ever it was). With a foothold in the interdisciplinary medical curriculum (GMC 2002a), and a more or less full-bodied (if not embodied) engagement with many other key issues pertaining to medicine, health and society in the new millennium, the future looks bright with some promising directions ahead. Not so much 'challenges', then, but opportunities for the taking.

References

Aakster, C.W. (1986) Concepts in alternative medicine. *Social Science and Medicine*, 22, 2: 265–73.

Abraham, J. (1995) *Science, Politics and the Pharmaceutical Industry*. London: UCL Press.

Acheson, Sir D. (chair) (1998) *Independent Inquiry into Inequalities in Health*. London: The Stationery Office.

Albrow, M. (1990) *Max Weber's Construction of Social Theory*. London: Macmillan.

Alderson, P. (2000) *Young Children's Rights: Exploring Beliefs, Principles and Practice*. London: Jessica Kingsley.

Alexander, N.J. (1995) Future contraceptives. *Scientific American*, September: 104–8.

Alfredsson, L., Karasek, R. and Theorell, T. (1982) Myocardial infarction risk and the psychosocial work environment. *Social Science and Medicine*, 16: 463–7.

Alvarez, A. (1995) *Night*. London: Vintage.

Anderson, R. and Bury, M. (eds) (1988) *Living with Chronic Illness: the Experience of Patients and Their Families*. London: Unwin Hyman.

Anderson, W.F. (1995) Gene therapy. *Scientific American,* September: 96–8b.

Andrews, H. and House, A. (1989) Functional dysfonia. In G.W. Brown and T.O. Harris (eds) *Life Events and Illness*. London: Unwin Hyman.

Annandale, E. (1998) *The Sociology of Health and Medicine: a Critical Introduction*. Cambridge: Polity Press.

Annandale, E. and Hunt, K. (1990) Masculinity, femininity and sex: an exploration of their relative contribution to explaining gender differences in health. *Sociology of Health and Illness*, 12: 24–46.

Annandale, E. and Hunt, K. (eds) (2000) *Gender Inequalities in Health*. Buckingham: Open University Press.

Anthias, F. (2001) The concept of 'social division' and theorising social stratification: looking at ethnicity and class. *Sociology*, 35, 4: 835–54.

Arber, S. and Ginn, J. (1991) *Gender and Later Life: a Sociological Analysis of Resources and Constraints*. London: Sage.

Arber, S. and Ginn, J. (1995) *Connecting Gender and Ageing: a Sociological Approach*. Buckingham: Open University Press.

Arber, S. and Ginn, J. (1998) Health and illness in later life. In D. Field and S. Taylor (eds) *Sociological Perspectives on Health, Illness and Health Care*. Oxford: Blackwell Scientific.

Archer, M. (1995) *Realist Social Theory: the Morphogenetic Approach*. Cambridge: Cambridge University Press.

Archer, M. (2000) *Being Human: the Problem of Agency*. Cambridge: Cambridge University Press.

Archer, M., Bhaskar, R., Collier, A., Lawson, T. and Norrie, A. (eds), (1998) *Critical Realism: Essential Readings*. London: Routledge.

Ariès, P. (1962) *Centuries of Childhood*. London: Jonathan Cape.

Ariès, P. (1976) *Western Attitudes Towards Death and Dying: From the Middle Ages to the Present*. London: Marion Boyars.

Ariès, P. (1981) *The Hour of Death*. London: Allen Lane.

Aristotle (1957) *On the Soul, Parva Naturalia, On Breath*. London: William Heinemann.

Arksey, H. (1998) *RSI and the Experts: the Construction of Medical Knowledge*. London: UCL Press.

Armstrong, D. (1979) The emancipation of biographical medicine. *Social Science and Medicine*, 13A, 1: 9–12.

Armstrong, D. (1983) *Political Anatomy of the Body*. Cambridge: Cambridge University Press.

Armstrong, D. (1984) The patient's view. *Social Science and Medicine*, 18: 737–44.

Armstrong, D. (1986) The problem of the whole-person in holistic medicine. *Holistic Medicine*, 1: 27–36.

Armstrong, D. (1987) Silence and truth in death and dying. *Social Science and Medicine*, 24, 8: 651–8.

Armstrong, D. (1995) The rise of surveillance medicine. *Sociology of Health and Illness*, 17, 3: 393–404.

Arney, W.R. and Neill, J. (1982) The location of pain in childbirth. *Sociology of Health and Illness*, 7: 109–17.

Artaud, A. (1988) *Selected Writings* (edited with an intro by S. Sontag). Berkeley: University of California Press.

Aubert, V. and White, H. (1959a) Sleep: a sociological interpretation I. *Acta Sociologica*, 4, 2: 46–54.

Aubert, V. and White, H. (1959b) Sleep: a sociological interpretation II. *Acta Sociologica*, 4, 3: 1–16.

Ayers, R. (1999) Serene and happy and distant: an interview with Orlan. *Body & Society*, 5, 2–3: 171–84.

Backett-Milburn, K. (2000) Children, parents and the construction of the 'healthy body' in middle-class families. In A. Prout (ed.) *The Body, Childhood and Society*. Basingstoke: Macmillan.

Baker, P. (2001) The international men's health movement. *British Medical Journal*, 323: 1014–15.

Bakhtin, M. (1968) *Rabelais and his World*. Cambridge, MA: MIT Press.

Balint, M. (1957) *The Doctor, His Patient and the Illness*. London: Pitman.

Balsamo, A. (1992) On the cutting edge: cosmetic surgery and the technological production of the gendered body. *Camera Obscura*, 28: 207–37.

Balsamo, A. (1995a) Forms of technological embodiment: reading the body in contemporary culture. *Body and Society (Cyberspace, Cyberbodies, Cyberpunk)*, 1, 3–4: 215–38.

Balsamo, A. (1995b) *Technologies of the Gendered Body: Cyborg Women*. Durham, NC: Duke University Press.

Banks, I. (2001) No man's land: men, illness, and the NHS. *British Medical Journal*, 323: 1058–60.

Barbalet, J. (1998) *Emotion, Social Theory and Social Structure*. Cambridge: Cambridge University Press.

Barbour, R. (2001) Sub-fertility, science and superstition: confronting paradoxes. Paper presented at the BSA Medical Sociology Group Conference, 21–3 September, University of York.

Barnes, C. and Mercer, C. (1996) Introduction: exploring the divide. In C. Barnes and G. Mercer (eds) *Exploring the Divide: Illness and Disabiity*. Leeds: The Disability Press.

Baszanger, I. (1998) *Inventing Pain Medicine: From Laboratory to the Clinic*. New Brunswick, NJ, and London: Rutgers University Press.

Battersby, C. (1993) Her body/her boundaries: gender and the metaphysics of containment. In A. Benjamin (ed.) *Journal of Philosophy and the Visual Arts: the Body*. London: Academy Group Ltd.

Battersby, C. (1998) *The Phenomenal Woman: Feminist Metaphysics and the Patterns of Identity*. Cambridge: Polity Press.

Baudrillard, J. (1993/1976) *Symbolic Exchange and Death*. London: Sage.

Baum, F. (2000) Social capital, economic capital and power: further issues for a public health agenda. *Journal of Epidemiology and Community Health*, 54: 409–10.

Bauman, Z. (1991) *Modernity and Ambivalence*. Cambridge: Polity Press.

Bauman, Z. (1992a) *Mortality, Immortality and Other Life Strategies*. Cambridge: Polity Press.

Bauman, Z. (1992b) Survival as a social construct. *Theory, Culture and Society*, 9, 1: 1–36.

Bauman, Z. (1993) *Postmodern Ethics*. Oxford: Blackwell.

Beck, U. (1992) *Risk Society: Towards a New Modernity*. London: Sage.

Beck, U. (1995) *Ecological Politics in the Age of Risk*. Cambridge: Polity Press.

Beck, U. (1997) *The Reinvention of Politics: Rethinking Modernity in the Global Order*. Cambridge: Polity Press.

Beck, U. and Beck-Gernsheim, E. (1995) *The Normal Chaos of Love*. Cambridge: Polity Press.

Belloc, N.B. and Breslow, L. (1972) Relationship of physical health status and health practices. *Preventive Medicine*, 1: 409–21.

Bendelow, G. and Williams, S.J. (1995) Transcending the dualism? Towards a sociology of pain. *Sociology of Health and Illness*, 17, 2: 139–65.

Bendelow, G., Williams, S. and France, A. (1998) *Beliefs of Young People in Relation to Health, Risk and Lifestyles (End of Project Report: Mother and Child Health Programme, NHS South Thames Executive)*. Centre for Research in Health, Medicine and Society, University of Warwick.

Benton, T. (1991) Biology and social science: why the return of the repressed should be given a (cautious) welcome. *Sociology*, 25, 1: 1–29.

Berger, P. (1967) *The Sacred Canopy: Elements of a Sociological Theory of Religion*. New York: Anchor Books.

Berkman, L.S. and Breslow, L. (1983) *Health and Ways of Living: the Almeda County Study*. Fairlawn, N.J: Oxford University Press.

Berliner, H.S. and Salmon J.W. (1980) The holistic alternative to scientific medicine: history and analysis. *International Journal of Health Services*, 10, 1: 133–47.

Berman, B.M. (2001) Complementary medicine and medical education: teaching complementary medicine offers a way of making teaching more holistic. *British Medical Journal*, 322: 121–2.

Bhaskar, R. (1998) Philosophy and scientific realism. In M. Archer, R. Bhaskar, A. Collier, T. Lawson, and A. Norrie (eds) *Critical Realism: Essential Readings*. London: Routledge.

Biggs, S. (1999) *The Mature Imagination: Dynamics of Identity in Midlife and Beyond*. Buckingham: Open University Press.

Birke, L. (1999) *Feminism and the Biological Body*. Edinburgh: Edinburgh University Press.

Blane, D., Davey Smith, G. and Bartley, M. (1993) Social selection: what does it contribute to social class inequalities in health? *Sociology of Health and Illness*, 15, 1: 1–15.

Blasi, A. (1998) Emotions and moral motivation. *Journal for the Theory of Social Behaviour*, 29, 1: 1–19.

Blaxter, M. (1976) *The Meaning of Disability*. London: Heinemann.

Blaxter, M. (1983) The causes of disease: women talking. *Social Science and Medicine*, 17: 59–69.

Blaxter, M. (1990) *Health and Lifestyles*. London: Routledge.

Blaxter, M. (2000) Class, time and biography. In S. Williams, J. Gabe and M. Calnan (eds) *Health, Medicine and Society: Key Theories, Future Agendas*. London: Routledge.

Bloom, B.R. and Trach, D.D. (2001) Genetics and developing countries. *British Medical Journal*, 322: 1006–7.

Bloor M., Samphier M. and Prior L. (1987) Artefact explanations of inequalities in health: an analysis of evidence. *Sociology of Health and Illness*, 9, 3: 321–64.

Bluebond-Langer, M. (1978) *The Private Worlds of Dying Children*. Princeton, NJ: Princeton University Press.

Bluebond-Langer, M., Perkel, D. and Goertzel, T. (1991) Paediatric cancer paitents' peer relationships: the impact of an oncology camp experience. *Journal of Psychosocial Oncology*, 9, 2: 67–80.

BMA (British Medical Assocation) (1986) *Alternative Therapy: Report of the Board of Science and Technology*. London: BMA.

BMA (British Medical Assocation) (1993) *Complementary Medicine. New Approaches to Good Practice*. Oxford: Oxford University Press/BMA.

Bodeker, G. (2001) Lessons on integration from the developing world's experience. *British Medical Journal*, 322: 164–7.

Boden, S. and Williams, S.J. (2002) Consumption and emotion: *The Romantic Ethic* revisited. *Sociology* 36, 3: 493–512.

Bolton, S.C. (2001) Changing faces: nurses as emotional jugglers. *Sociology of Health and Illness*, 23, 1: 85–100.

Bordo, S. (1993) *Unbearable Weight: Feminism, Western Culture and the Body*. Berkeley: University of California Press.

Boseley, S. and Campbell, D. (2001) First human embryo cloned. *The Guardian*. 26 November: 1.

Boston Women's Health Collective (1973) *Our Bodies Ourselves*. New York: Simon and Schuster.

Botting, B. (2002) Overview: children. In ONS *Social Trends No. 32*. London: The Stationery Office.

Bourdieu, P. (1977) *Outline of a Theory of Practice*. Cambridge; Cambridge University Press.

Bourdieu, P. (1978) Sport and social class. *Social Science Information*, 17: 819–40.

Bourdieu, P. (1984) *Distinction: a Social Critique of the Judgement of Taste*. London: Routledge.

Bourdieu, P. and Wacquant, L. (1992): *An Invitation to Reflexive Sociology*. Cambridge: Polity Press.

Bransen, E. (1992) Has menstruation been medicalized? Or will it ever happen? *Sociology of Health and Illness*, 14, 1: 98–110.

Breggin, G.R. and Breggin, P. (1994) *Talking Back to Prozac*. New York: St Martins Press.

Breggin, P. (1993) *Toxic Psychiatry*. London: HarperCollins.

Broom, D. and Woodward, R.V. (1996) Medicalization reconsidered: toward a collaborative approach to care. *Sociology of Health and Illness*, 18, 3: 357–78.

Brown, B., Nolan, P., Crawford, P. and Lewis, A. (1996) Interaction, language and the 'narrative turn' in psychotherapy and psychiatry. *Social Science and Medicine*, 43, 11: 1569–78.

Brown, G.W. and Harris, T.O. (1978) *The Social Origins of Depression: a Study of Psychiatric Disorder in Women*. London: Tavistock.

Brown, G.W. and Harris, T.O. (1989a) Summary and conclusions. In G.W. Brown and T.O. Harris (eds) *Life Events and Illness*. London: Unwin Hyman.

Brown, G.W. and Harris, T.O. (eds) (1989b) *Life Events and Illness*. London: Unwin Hyman.

Browne, A. (2000) How sleep can save your life. *Observer*, 29 October: 12.

Brunner, E. (1996) The social and biological basis of cardiovascular disease in office workers. In E. Brunner, D. Blane and R.G. Wilkinson (eds) *Health and Social Organization*. London: Routledge.

Bryan, J. and Clare, J. (2001) *Organ Farm. Pig-to-Human Transplants: Medical Miracle or Genetic Time Bomb?* London: Carlton Books.

Bryden, H. (2001) Commentary: special study modules and complementary and alternative medicine – the Glasgow experience. *British Medical Journal*, 322: 157–8.

Bunton, R., Nettleton, S. and Burrows, R. (eds) (1995) *The Sociology of Health Promotion: Critical Analyses of Consumption, Lifestyle and Risk*. London: Routledge.

Burton, L. (1975) *The Family Life of Sick Children*. London: Routledge and Kegan Paul.

Bury, M. (1982) Chronic illness as biographical disruption. *Sociology of Health and Illness*, 4, 2: 167–82.

Bury, M. (1986) Social constructionism and the development of sociology. *Sociology of Health and Illness*, 8, 2: 137–69.

Bury, M. (1988) Meanings at risk: the experience of arthritis. In R. Anderson and M. Bury (eds) *Living with Chronic Illness: the Experience of Patients and their Families*. London: Unwin Hyman.

Bury, M. (1991) The sociology of chronic illness: a review of research and prospects. *Sociology of Health and Illness*, 13, 4: 451–68.

Bury, M. (1996) Defining and researching disability: challenges and responses. In C. Barnes and G. Mercer (eds) *Exploring the Divide: Illness and Disability*. Leeds: The Disability Press.

Bury, M. (1997) *Health and Illness in a Changing Society*. London: Routledge.

Bury, M. (2000) Health, ageing and the lifecourse. In S. Williams, J. Gabe and M. Calnan (eds) *Health, Medicine and Society: Key Theories, Future Agendas*. London: Routledge.

Bury, M. (2001) Illness narratives: fact or fiction? *Sociology of Health and Illness*, 23, 3: 263–85.

Bury, M. and Holme, A. (1991) *Life After Ninety*. London: Routledge.

Busfield, J. (1996) *Men, Women and Madness: Understanding Gender and Mental Disorder*. London: Macmillan.

Busfield, J. (2002) The archaeology of psychiatric disorder: gender and disorders of thought, emotion and behaviour. In G. Bendelow, M. Carpenter, C. Vautier and S. Williams (eds) *Gender, Health and Healing: the Public/Private Divide*. London: Routledge.

Buytendijk, F.J.J. (1950) The phenomenological approach to the problem of feelings and emotions. In M.C. Reymert (ed.), *Feelings and Emotions (The Mooseheart Symposium in Cooperation with the University of Chicago)*. New York: McGraw Hill.

Bytheway, B. (1995) *Ageism*. Buckingham: Open University Press.

Callahan, D. (1987) *Setting Limits: Medical Goals for an Aging Society*. New York: Simon and Schuster.

Callon, M. (1986a) The sociology of an actor-network: the case of the electric vehicle. In M. Callon, J. Law and A. Rip (eds) *Mapping the Dynamics of Science and Technology*. London: Macmillan.

Callon, M. (1986b) Some elements of a sociology of translation: domestication of the scallops and the fisherman of St Brieuc Bay. In J. Law (ed.) *Power, Action and Belief: a New Sociology of Knowledge? (Sociological Review Monograph 32)*. London: Routledge and Kegan Paul.

Calnan, M. (1987) *Health and Illness: the Lay Perspective*. London: Routledge.

Calnan, M. and Williams, S.J. (1995) Challenges to professional autonomy in the United Kingdom? The perceptions of general practitioners. *International Journal of Health Services*, 25, 2: 219–41.

Campbell, C. (1987) *The Romantic Ethic and the Spirit of Modern Consumerism*. Oxford: Blackwell.

Cant, S. and Sharma, U. (1999) *A New Medical Pluralism? Alternative Medicine, Doctors, Patients and the State*. London: UCL Press.

Cant, S. and Sharma, U. (2000) Alternative health practices and systems. In G. Albrecht, R. Fitzpatrick and S. Scrimshaw (eds) *Handbook of Social Studies in Health and Medicine*. London: Sage.

Carpenter, M. (2000) Reinforcing the pillars: rethinking gender, social divisions and health. In E. Annandale and K. Hunt (eds) *Gender Inqualities in Health*. Buckingham: Open University Press.

Carricaburu, D. and Pierret, J. (1995) From biographical disruption to biographical reinforcement: the case of HIV-positive men. *Sociology of Health and Illness*, 17, 1: 65–88.

Cartwright, L. (2000) Reach out and health someone: telemedicine and the globalization of health care. *Health*, 4, 3: 347–77.

Casper, M.J. (1995) Fetal cyborgs and technomoms on the reproductive frontier: which way to the carnival? In C.H. Gray (ed.) *The Cyborg Handbook*. New York/London: Routledge, 1995.

Chadwick, E. (1965/1842) *The Sanitary Conditions of the Labouring Population of Great Britain: Report 1842*. Edinburgh: Edinburgh University Press.

Chapman, J. (2001) Scientists warn over fatal flaws in cloning. *Daily Mail*. 6 July: 37.

Charlton, B. (1993) Medicine and post-modernity. *Journal of the Royal Society of Medicine*, 86: 497–9.

Charmaz, K. (1987) Struggling for a self: identity levels of the chronically ill. *Research in the Sociology of Health Care*, 6: 283–321.

Cherniavsky, E. (1993) (En)gendering cyberspace in Neuromancer: postmodern subjectivity and virtual motherhood. *Genders*, 18: 32–46.

Christensen, P.H. (1993) The social construction of help among Danish children: the intentional act and actual content. *Sociology of Health and Illness*, 15, 4: 488–502.

Christensen, P.H. (2000) Childhood and the cultural constestation of vulnerable bodies. In A. Prout (ed.) *The Body, Childhood and Society*. Basingstoke: Macmillan.

Cixous, H. (1986) Sorties. In H. Cixous and C. Clément (eds) *The Newly Born Woman*. Manchester: Manchester University Press.

Clarke, A.E. (1995) Modernity, postmodernity and reproductive processes, ca 1890–1990, or 'mommy where do cyborgs come from anyway?' In C.H. Gray (ed.) *The Cyborg Handbook*. London: Routledge.

Clarke, A.E., Fishman, J.R., Fosket, J.R., Mamo, L. and Shim, J.K. (2000) Technoscience and the new biomedicalization: Western roots, global rhizomes. *Science Sociales et Santé*, 18, 2: 11–42.

Claus, L. (1983) The development of medical sociology in Europe. *Social Science and Medicine*, 17, 1: 591–7.

Clinton, B. (2001) The Presidential Visit: Remarks by the President to the community of the University of Warwick, 14 December. <http: //www.clinton.warwick.ac.uk/clintonspch.html>.

Clinton, B. (2001) The struggle for the soul of the 21st century. Richard Dimbleby Lecture, 14th December. London: BBC. <http: //www.bbc.co.uk/arts/news_comment/dimbleby/clinton>.

Coburn, D. (2000a) Income inequality, social cohesion and the health status of populations: the role of neoliberalism. *Social Science and Medicine*, 51: 135–46.

Coburn, D. (2000b) A brief response. *Social Science and Medicine*, 51: 1009–10.

Coburn, D. and Willis, E. (2000) The medical profession: knowledge, power, and autonomy. In G. Albrecht, R. Fitzpatrick, and S. Scrimshaw (eds) *The Handbook of Social Studies in Health and Medicine*. London: Sage.

Cochrane, A. (1972) *Effectiveness and Efficiency: Random Reflections on the Health Service*. London: Nuffield Provincial Hospital Trust.

Cockerham, W.C. (1995) *Medical Sociology* (Sixth Edition). Englewood Cliffs, NJ: Prentice Hall.

Coe, J. (1997) *The House of Sleep*. Harmondsworth: Penguin.

Cohen, L. (2001) The other kidney: biopolitics beyond recognition. *Body & Society*, 7, 2–3: 9–29.

Cohen, R. and Kennedy, P. (2000) *Global Sociology*. Basingstoke: Macmillan.

Cohen, R.A. (1985) Translator's introduction. In E. Levinas, *Ethics and Infinity*. Pittsburgh: Duquesue University Press.

Cohen, R.A. (ed.) (1986) *Face-to-Face with Levinas*. Albany, NY: State University of New York Press.

Cohen, S. and Syme, S.L. (eds) (1985) *Social Support and Health*. New York: Academic Press.

Cole, T., Achenbaum, W.A., Jackobi, P. and Kastenbaum, R. (eds) (1993) *Voices and Visions of Aging: Toward a Critical Gerontology*. New York: Springer.

Collins, R. (1990) Stratification, emotional energy, and the transient emotions. In T.J. Kemper (ed.) *Research Agendas in the Sociology of Emotions*. New York: State University of New York Press.

Connell, R.W. (1987) *Gender and Power: Society, the Person and Sexual Politics*. Cambridge: Polity Press.

Connell, R.W. (1995) *Masculinities*. Cambridge: Polity Press.

Connor, S. (2002) Pigs cloned with organs designed for human transplants. *The Independent*, 3 January: 2.

Conrad, P. (1992) Medicalization and social control. *Annual Review of Sociology*, 18: 209–32.

Conrad, P. and Gabe, J. (1999) Introduction: sociological perspectives on the New Genetics: an overview. *Sociology of Health and Illness*, 21, 5: 505–16.

Conrad, P. and Jacobson, H. (2003) Enhancing biology: cosmetic surgery and breast augmentation. In S.J. Williams, L. Birke and G. Bendelow (eds) *Debating Biology: Sociological Reflection on Health, Medicine and Society*. London: Routledge.

Conrad, P. and Schneider, J.W. (1980) Looking at levels of medicalization: a comment on Strong's critique of the thesis of medical imperialism. *Social Science and Medicine*, 14: 75–9.

Cook, S. (2001) Chain of evidence. *The Independent (Magazine)*, 23 June: 22–5.

Cooper, W. (1987) *No Change: a Biological Revolution for Women*. London: Arrow Books.

Cooter, R., Harrison, M. and Sturdy, S. (eds) (1998) *War, Medicine and Modernity*. Stroud: Sutton Publishing.

Cooter, R., Harrison, M. and Sturdy, S. (eds) (1999) *Medicine and Modern Warfare*. Amsterdam–Atlanta, GA: Randolphi.

Corbin, J. and Strauss, A.L. (1987) Accompaniments of chronic illness changes in body, self, biography and biographical time. *Research in the Sociology of Health Care*. 6: 249–81.

Corea, G. (1985) *The Mother Machine*. New York: Harper and Row.

Coren, S. (1996) *Sleep Thieves*. London: Simon and Schuster.

Cornwell, J. (1984) *Hard-Earned Lives*. London: Tavistock.

Coward, R. (1989) *The Whole Truth*. London: Faber and Faber.

Craib, I. (1988) *Psychoanalysis and Social Theory: the Limits of Sociology*. Hemel Hempstead: Harvester Wheatsheaf.

Craib, I. (1994) *The Importance of Disappointment*. London: Routledge.

Craib, I. (1995) Some comments on the sociology of emotions. *Sociology*, 29, 1: 151–8.

Craib, I. (1997) Social constructionism as social psychosis. *Sociology*, 31, 1: 1–15.

Craig, T. (1989) Abdominal pain. In G.W. Brown and T.O. Harris (eds) *Life Events and Illness*. London: Unwin Hyman.

Crawford, R. (1980) Healthism and the medicalization of everyday life. *International Journal of Health Services*, 10: 365–88.

Crawford, R. (1984) A cultural account of 'health': control, release and the social body. In J.B. McKinlay (ed.) *Issues in the Political Economy of Health Care*. London: Tavistock.

Crawford, R. (1994) The boundaries of self and the unhealthy other: reflections on health, culture and AIDS. *Social Science and Medicine*, 38, 10: 1347–66.

Crawford, R. (1999) Transgression for what? A reply to Simon Williams. *Health*, 3, 4: 350–66.

Crawford, R. (2000) The ritual of health promotion. In S. Williams, J. Gabe and M. Calnan (eds) *Health, Medicine and Society: Key Theories, Future Agendas*. London: Routledge.

Crompton, R. (1998) *Class and Stratification* (2nd Edition). Cambridge: Polity Press.

Crossley, N. (1998) Emotions and communicative action. In G. Bendelow and S.J. Williams (eds) *Emotions in Social Life: Critical Themes and Contemporary Issues*. London: Routledge.

Crossley, N. (2000) Emotion, psychiatry and social order: a Habermasian approach. In S. Williams, J. Gabe and M. Calnan (eds) *Health, Medicine and Society: Key Theories, Future Agendas*. London: Routledge.

Crossley, N. (2001) *The Social Body: Habit, Identity and Desire*. London: Sage.

Crossley, N. (2003) Prozac nation and the biochemical self: a critique. In S.J. Williams, L. Birke and G. Bendelow (eds) *Debating Biology: Sociological Reflection on Health, Medicine and Society*. London: Routledge.

Crow, L. (1996) Including all of our lives: renewing the social model of disability. In C. Barnes and G. Mercer (eds) *Exploring the Divide: Illness and Disability*. Leeds: The Disability Press.

Cunningham-Burley S. and Backett-Milburn, K. (eds) (2001) *Exploring the Body*. Basingstoke: Palgrave.

Damasio A.R. (1994) *Descartes' Error: Emotion, Reason and the Human Brain*. New York: Putnam.

Dannenfeldt, K.H. (1986) Sleep: theory and practice in the late Renaissance. *The Journal of the History of Medicine and Allied Sciences*, 41: 415–41.

Daudet, A. (2002/1930) *In the Land of Pain*. London: Jonathan Cape.

Davidson, J. (1999) A phenomenology of fear: Merleau-Ponty and agoraphobic life-worlds. *Sociology of Health and Illness*, 22, 5: 640–60.

Davies, C. (1996) The sociology of professions and the profession of gender. *Sociology*, 30, 4: 661–78.

Davies, C. (2002) What about the girl next door? Gender and the politics of professional self-regulation. In G. Bendelow, M. Carpenter, C. Vautier and S. Williams (eds) *Gender, Health and Healing: the Public/Private Divide*. London: Routledge.

Davis, K. (1994) *Reshaping the Female Body: the Dilemmas of Cosmetic Surgery*. London: Routledge.

Davis, K. (1998) Pygmalions in plastic surgery. *Health*, 2, 1: 23–40.

Davison, C., Davey Smith, G. and Frankel, S. (1991) Lay epidemiology and the prevention paradox: implications for coronary candidacy and health education. *Sociology of Health and Illness*, 13, 1: 1–19.

Davison, C., Frankel, S. and Davey Smith, G. (1992) The limits of lifestyle: reassessing "fatalism" in the popular culture of illness prevention. *Social Science and Medicine*, 34, 6: 675–85.

de Beauvoir, S. (1972) *Old Age*. London: Weidenfeld and Nicolson.

de Botton, A. (1997) *How Proust Can Change Your Life*. London: Vintage Books.

de Botton, A. (2000) *The Consolations of Philosophy*. London: Hamish Hamilton.

Deitch, J. (1992) *Post-Human*. Amsterdam: Idea Books.

Deleuze, G. and Guattari, F. (1984) *Anti-Oedipus: Capitalism and Schizophrenia I*. London: Athlone Press.

Deleuze, G. and Guattari, F. (1988) *A Thousand Plateaus: Capitalism and Schizophrenia II*. London: Athlone Press.

Dement, W.C. (1972) *Some Must Watch, Whilst Some Must Sleep: Exploring the World of Sleep*. New York: W.W. Norton & Co.

Dement, W.C. with C. Vaughan (2000) *The Promise of Sleep: The Scientific Connection between Health, Happiness and a Good Night's Sleep*. New York/London: Delacourt Press/Macmillan.

Denny, E. (1996) New reproductive technologies: the views of women undergoing treatment. In S.J. Williams and M. Calnan (eds) *Modern Medicine: Lay Perspectives and Experiences*. London: UCL Press.

Denzin, N.K. (1984) *On Understanding Emotion*. San Francisco: Josey Bass.

de Sousa, R. (1990) *The Rationality of Emotion*. Cambridge, MA: MIT Press.

de Swaan, A. (1990) *The Management of Normality: Critical Essays in Health and Welfare*. London: Routledge.

Dewar, S. and Finlayson B. (2001) Reforming the GMC: current proposals make a muddle of the possibilities for radical change. *British Medical Journal*, 322: 689–90.

d'Houtaud, A. and Field, M.G. (1984) The image of health: variations in perception by social class in a French population. *Sociology of Health and Illness*, 6, 1: 30–60.

Dickens, P. (2000) *Social Darwinism*. Buckingham: Open University Press.

Dickens, P. (2001) Linking the social and natural sciences: is capital modifying biology in its own image? *Sociology*, 35, 1: 93–110.

DoH (Department of Health) (1997) *The New NHS – Modern and Dependable*. London: The Stationery Office.

DoH (Department of Health) (1998) *Our Healthier Nation: A New Contract for Health*. London: The Stationery Office.

DoH (Department of Health) (1999) *Saving Lives: Our Healthier Nation*. London: The Stationery Office.

DoH (Department of Health) (2000) *The NHS Plan*. London: The Stationery Office.

DoH (Department of Health) (2002) *Reform of the General Medical Council: A Paper for Consultation*. <http://www.doh.gov.uk/gmcreform.htm>

Douglas, M. (1966) *Purity and Danger: an Analysis of the Concepts of Pollution and Taboo*. London: Routledge and Kegan Paul.

Douglas, M. (1970) *Natural Symbols: Explorations in Consmology*. London: The Cresset Press.

Doyal, L. (2001) Sex, gender and health: the need for a new approach. *British Medical Journal*, 323: 1061–3.

Drever, F., Fisher, K., Brown, J. and Clark, J. (2000) *Social Inequalities* (2000 Edition). London: The Stationery Office.

Duster, T. (1990) *Back Door Eugenics*. London/New York: Routledge.

Edwards, R. (1981) Mental health as rational autonomy. *The Journal of Medicine and Philosophy*, 6: 309–22.

Eisenstein, Z. (1994) Writing hatred on the body. *New Political Science*, 30–1: 15–22.

Ekirch, A. R. (2001) Sleep we have lost: pre-industrial slumber in the British Isles. *American Historical Review*, April: 343–86.

Elias, N. (1978/1939) *The Civilizing Process: Vol. I: the History of Manners*. Oxford: Blackwell.

Elias, N. (1982/1939) *The Civilizing Process: Vol. II: State Formations and Civilization*. Oxford: Blackwell.

Elias, N. (1985) *The Loneliness of Dying*. Oxford: Blackwell.

Elias, N. (1991) On human beings and their emotions: a process sociological essay. In M. Featherstone, M. Hepworth and B.S. Turner (eds) *The Body: Social Process and Cultural Theory*. London: Sage.

Elias, N. and Dunning E. (1986) *The Quest for Excitement: Sport and Leisure in the Civilizing Process*. Oxford: Blackwell.

Elstad, I.J. (1998) The psycho-social perspective on social inequalities in health. *Sociology of Health and Illness*, 20, 5: 598–618.

Elster, J. (1999) *Alchemies of the Mind: Rationality and the Emotions*. Cambridge: Cambridge University Press.

Emery, J. and Hayflick, S. (2001) The challenge of integrating genetic medicine into primary care. *British Medical Journal*, 322: 1027–30.

Engels, F. (1987/1849) *The Condition of the Working Class in England*. Harmondsworth: Penguin.

Estes, C. (1979) *The Aging Enterprise*. San Francisco: Jossey Bass.

Estes, C. (1991) The new political economy of aging: introduction and critique. In M. Minkler and C. Estes (eds) *Critical Perspectives on Aging: The Political and Moral Economy of Growing Old*. New York: Baywood.

Estes, C. and Minkler, M. (1984) *Readings in the Political of Aging*. New York: Baywood.

Ettorre, E. (1999) Experts as 'storytellers' in reproductive genetics: exploring key issues. *Sociology of Health and Illness*, 21, 5: 539–59.

Evans, D. (1997) Michel Maffesoli's sociology of modernity and postmodernity: an introduction and critical assessment. *The Sociological Review*, 45, 2: 221–43.

Evans, J.P., Skrzynia, C. and Burke, W. (2001) The complexities of predictive testing. *British Medical Journal*, 322: 1052–6.

Fagerhaugh, S. (1975) Getting around with emphysema. In A. Strauss and B. Glaser (eds) *Chronic Illness and the Quality of Life*. St Louis, MO: Mosby.

Fairhurst, E. (1998) 'Growing old gracefully' as opposed to 'mutton dressed as lamb': the social construction of recognising older women. In S. Nettleton and J. Watson (eds) *The Body in Everyday Life*. London: Routledge.

Falk, P. (1994) *The Consuming Body*. London: Sage.

Faludi, S. (1999) *Stiffed: The Betrayal of Modern Men*. London: Chatto and Windus.

Farnell, R. (1999) In dialogue with 'posthuman' bodies: interview with Stelarc. *Body & Society*, 5, 2–3: 129–47.

Featherstone, M. (1991) The body in consumer culture. In M. Featherstone, M. Hepworth and B.S. Turner (eds) *The Body: Social Process and Cultural Theory*. London: Sage.

Featherstone, M. (1995) *Undoing Culture: Globalization, Postmodernism and Identity*. London: Sage.

Featherstone, M. (1999) Body modification: an introduction. *Body & Society*, 5, 2–3: 1–13.

Featherstone, M. and Burrows, R. (1995) Cultures of technological embodiment: an introduction. *Body & Society*, 1, 3–4: 1–19.

Featherstone, M. and Hepworth, M. (1991) The mask of ageing and the postmodern lifecourse. In M. Featherstone, M. Hepworth and B.S. Turner (eds) *The Body: Social Process and Cultural Theory*. London: Sage.

Featherstone, M. and Hepworth, M. (1998) Ageing, the lifecourse and the sociology of embodiment. In G. Scambler and P. Higgs (eds) *Modernity, Medicine and Health: Medical Sociology Towards 2000*. London: Routledge.

Featherstone, M. and Wernick, A. (eds) (1995) *Images of Ageing: Cultural Representations of Later Life*. London: Routledge.

Figlio, K. (1987) The lost subject in medical sociology. In G. Scambler (ed.) *Sociological Theory and Medical Sociology*. London: Tavistock.

Fineman, S. (ed.) (1993) *Emotion in Organizations*. London: Sage.

Fineman, S. (ed.) (2000) *Emotion in Organizations* (2nd Edition). London: Sage.

Finkel, M. (2001) Complications. *New York Times (Magazine)*, 27 May: 26–33, 40, 52, 59.

Flanagan, O. (2000) *Dreaming Souls*. Oxford: Oxford University Press.

Foley, S. (2002) PPL stock soars on knock-out piglets. *The Independent*, 3 January: 15.

Forna, A. (1997) Is therapy making fools of women? *The Independent on Sunday* (Real Life Section), 2 November: 1.

Foster, T. (1993) Meat puppet or robopath? Cyberpunk and the question of embodiment. *Genders*, 18: 11–31.

Foucault, M. (1971) *Madness and Civilization*. London: Tavistock.

Foucault, M. (1973) *The Birth of the Clinic*. London: Tavistock.

Foucault, M. (1987) *The Uses of Pleasure: The History of Sexuality (Vol. 2)*. Harmondsworth: Penguin.

Foucault, M. (1988a) Technologies of the self. In L.H. Martin, H. Gutman and P.H. Hutton (eds) *Technologies of the Self: a Seminar with Michel Foucault*. London: Tavistock.

Foucault, M. (1988b) *The Care of the Self: The History of Sexuality (Vol. 3)*. Harmondsworth: Penguin.

Fox, N.J. (1993) *Postmodernism, Sociology and Health*. Milton Keynes: Open University Press.

Fox, N.J. (1999) *Beyond Health: Postmodernism and Embodiment*. London: Free Association Books.

Fox, N.J. (2000) The ethics and politics of caring: postmodern reflections. In S.J. Williams, J. Gabe and M. Calnan (eds) *Health, Medicine and Society: Key Theories, Future Agendas*. London: Routledge.

Fox, R.C. (1977) The medicalization and demedicalization of American society. *Daedalus*, 106: 9–22.

Fox, R.C. (2000) Medicial uncertainty revisited. In G. Albrecht, R. Fitzpatrick and S. Scrimshaw, (eds) *The Handbook of Social Studies in Health and Medicine*. London: Sage.

Fox, R.C. and Swazey, J. (1992) *Spare Parts: Organ Replacement in American Society*. New York: Oxford University Press.

Frank, A.W. (1991a) For a sociology of the body: an analytical review. In M. Featherstone, M. Hepworth and B.S. Turner (eds), *The Body: Social Process and Cultural Theory*. London: Sage.

Frank, A.W. (1991b) From sick role to health role: deconstructing Parsons. In R. Robertson and B.S. Turner (eds) *Parsons: Theorist of Modernity*. London: Sage.

Frank, A.W. (1992) Twin nightmares of the medical simulacrum: Jean Baudrillard and David Croneberg. In W. Stearns and W. Chalouplea (eds), *Jean Baudrillard: the Disappearance of Art and Politics*. London: Macmillan.

Frank, A.W. (1995) *The Wounded Storyteller: Body, Illness and Ethics*. Chicago/London: University of Chicago Press.

Frank, A.W. (1997) Illness as moral occasion: restoring agency to ill people. *Health*. 1, 2: 131–48.

Frank, A.W. (2000) Social bioethics and the critique of autonomy. *Health*, 4 3: 378–94.

Frank, A.W. (2003) The bioethnics of biotechnology: alternative claims of Posthuman futures. In S.J. Williams, L. Birke and G. Bendelow (eds) *Debating Biology: Sociological Reflections on Health, Medicine and Society*. London: Routledge.

Frankenberg, R. (1990) Review article: Disease, literature and the body in the era of AIDS – a preliminary exploration. *Sociology of Health and Illness*, 12, 3: 351–60.

Franklin, S. (2001a) Sheepwatching. *Anthropology Today*, 17, 3: 3–10

Franklin, S. (2001b) Culturing biology: cell lines for the new millenium. *Health*, 5, 3: 335–54.

Freidson, E. (1970) *Profession of Medicine*. New York: Dodd, Mead.

Freidson, E. (1985) The reorganization of the medical profession. *Medical Care Review*, 42, 1: 11–35.

Freidson, E. (1994) *Professionalism Reborn*. Cambridge: Polity Press.

Freund, P.E.S. (1990) The expressive body: a common ground for the sociology of emotions and health and illness. *Sociology of Health and Illness*, 12, 4: 452–77.

Freund, P.E.S. (1998) Social performances and their discontents: reflections on the biosocial psychology of role-playing. In G. Bendelow and S.J. Williams (eds) *Emotions in Social Life: Critical Themes and Contemporary Issues*. London: Routledge.

Freund, P.E.S. (2001) Bodies, disability and spaces: the social model of disability and disabling spatial organizations. *Disability and Society*, 16, 5: 689–706.

Fries, J. (1980) Ageing, natural death and the compression of morbidity. *New England Journal of Medicine*, 303: 130–5.

Fries, J. (1989) The compression of morbidity: near or far? *The Milbank Quarterly*, 67, 2: 208–32.

Fukuyama, F. (2002) *Our Posthuman Future*. London: Profile Books.

Fuller, S. (2000) The coming biological challenge to social theory. Unpublished paper, University of Warwick.

Fuller, S. (2001) Looking for sociology after 11 September. *Sociological Research Online*. <http://www.socresonline.org.uk/6/2/fuller.html>

Fuller, S. (2002) Will sociology find some new concepts before the US find Osama bin Laden? *Sociological Research Online*. <http://www.socresonline.org.uk/6/4/fuller.html>

Gabe, J. and Calnan, M. (2000) Health care and consumption. In S. Williams, J. Gabe and M. Calnan (eds) *Health, Medicine and Society: Key Theories, Future Agendas*. London: Routledge.

Gabe, J., Kelleher, D. and Williams, G.H. (eds) (1994) *Challenging Medicine*. London: Routledge.

Gadamer, H.-G. (1996) *The Enigma of Health*. Cambridge: Polity Press.

Gallagher, E. (1976) Lines of reconstruction and extension in the Parsonian sociology of illness. *Social Science and Medicine*, 10: 207–18.

Game, A. and Metcalfe, A. (1996) *Passionate Sociology*. London: Sage.

Gerhardt, U. (1979a) Coping and social action: theoretical reconstruction of the life-event approach. *Sociology of Health and Illness*, 1, 2: 195–225.

Gerhardt, U. (1979b) The Parsonian paradigm and the identity of medical sociology. *Sociological Review*, 27, 2: 229–51.

Gerhardt, U. (1989) *Ideas About Illness: an Intellectual and Political History of Medical Sociology*. London: Macmillan.

Giddens, A (1979) *Central Problems in Social Theory*. London: Hutchinson.

Giddens, A (1990) *The Problems of Modernity*. Cambridge: Polity Press.

Giddens, A (1991) *Modernity and Self-Identity*. Cambridge: Polity Press.

Giddens, A (1992) *The Transformation of Intimacy: Love, Sexuality and Eroticism in Modern Societies*. Cambridge: Polity Press.

Giddens, A (1994) *Beyond Left and Right*. Cambridge: Polity Press.

Giddens, A (1999) *Runaway World: How Globalisation is Shaping our Lives*. London: Profile Books.

Gilleard, C. and Higgs, P. (1998) Ageing and the limiting conditions of the body. *Sociological Research Online*. <http: //www.socresonline.org.uk/3/4/4.html>

Gilleard, C. and Higgs, P. (2000) *Cultures of Ageing: Self, Citizen and the Body*. London: Prentice Hall.

Gilman, S. (1999) *Making the Body Beautiful: a Cultural History of Aesthetic Surgery*. Princeton NJ: Princeton, University Press.

Glaser, B.G. and Strauss, A.L. (1965) *Awareness of Dying*. Chicago: Aldine.

Glaser, B.G. and Strauss, A.L. (1967) *The Discovery of Grounded Theory*. Chicago: Aldine.

Glaser, B.G. and Strauss, A.L. (1968) *Time for Dying*. Chicago: Aldine.

Glassner, B. (1989) Fitness and the postmodern self. *Journal of Health and Social Behaviour*, 30: 180–91.

Glassner, B. (1995) In the name of health. In R. Bunton, S. Nettleton and R. Burrows (eds) *The Sociology of Health Promotion: Critical Analyses of Consumption, Lifestyle and Risk*. London: Routledge.

Gleik, J. (2000) *Faster: the Acceleration of Just About Everything*. London: Abacus.

GMC (General Medical Council) (2001) *Protecting Patients: a Summary Consultative Document*. London: GMC. <http://www.gmc-uk.org/consultation/default.htm>

GMC (General Medical Council) (2002a) *Tommorow's Doctors: Recommendations on Undergraduate Medical Education*. London: GMC.

GMC (General Medical Council) (2002b) *The new GMC.* <http://www.gmc-uk.org/home.htm>

Goffman, E. (1959) *The Presentation of Everyday Life.* New York: Doubleday Anchor.

Goffman, E. (1967) *Interaction Ritual: Essays on Face-to-Face Behaviour.* New York: Doubleday Anchor.

Goldstein, D.E. (2000) 'When ovaries retire': contrasting women's experiences with feminist and medical models of menopause. *Health,* 4, 3: 309–23.

Goleman, D. (1996) *Emotional Intelligence: Why It Can Matter More Than IQ.* London: Bloomsbury.

Goodall, J. (1999) An order of pure decision: un-natural selection in the work of Stelarc and Orlan. *Body & Society,* 5, 2–3: 149–70.

Gordon, S. (1990) Social structural effects on emotions. In T. Kemper (ed.) *Research Agendas in the Sociology of Emotions.* New York: State University of New York Press.

Gorer, G. (1955) The Pornography of Death. *Encounter,* 5 October: 49–53.

Gorer, G. (1965) *Death, Grief and Mourning in Contemporary Britain.* London: Cresset.

Gothill, M. and Armstrong, D. (1999) Dr. No-body: the construction of the doctor as an embodied subject in British general practice 1955–97. *Sociology of Health and Illness,* 21, 1: 1–12.

Graham, H. (1983) Caring: a labour of love. In J. Finch and D. Groves (eds) *A Labour of Love: Women, Work and Caring.* London: Routledge and Kegan Paul.

Graham, H. (ed.) (2000a) *Understanding Health Inequalities.* Buckingham: Open University Press.

Graham, H. (2000b) The challenge of health inequalies. In H. Graham (ed.) *Understanding Health Inequalities.* Buckingham: Open University Press.

Gray, C.H. (2002) *Cyborg Citizen.* London: Routledge.

Gray, C.H. Mentor, S. and Figueroa-Sarriera, H.J. (1995) Introduction. Cyborgology: constructing knowledge of cybernetic organisms. In C.H. Gray with the assistance of H.J. Figueroa-Sarriera and S. Mentor (eds) *The Cyborg Handbook.* London: Routledge.

Greco, M. (2001) Inconspicuous anomalies: alexithymia and ethical relations to the self. *Health,* 5, 4: 471–92.

Green, J. (1997a) Risk and the construction of social identity: children's talk about accidents. *Sociology of Health and Illness,* 19, 4: 457–79.

Green, J. (1997b) *Risk and Misfortune: the Social Construction of Accidents.* London: UCL Press.

Greenhalgh, T. and Hurwitz, B. (eds) (1998) *Narrative Based Medicine: Dialogue and Discourse in Clinical Practice.* London: BMJ.

Greer, G. (1991) *The Change: Women, Ageing and the Menopause.* Harmondsworth: Penguin.

Grice, A. (2002) Thinking the unthinkable is the only way to defuse the pensions timebomb. *The Independent,* 24 May: 6.

Griffith, F. (1999) Women's control and choice regarding HRT. *Social Science and Medicine,* 49: 469–81.

Grosz, E. (1994) *Volatile Bodies.* Bloomington/Indianapolis: Indiana University Press.

Gubrium, J.F. (1993) Voice and context in a new gerontology. In T. Cole, W.A. Achenbaum, P. Jackobi and R. Kastenbaum (eds) *Voices and Visions of Aging: Toward a Critical Gerontology.* New York: Springer.

Habermas, J. (1984) *The Theory of Communicative Action (Vol. I): Reason and the Rationalization of Society.* Cambridge: Polity Press.

Habermas, J. (1987) *The Theory of Communicative Action (Vol. II): Lifeworld and System: A Critique of Functionalist Reason (Transl. T McCarthy.* Cambridge: Polity Press.

Haire, D. (1978) The cultural warping of childbirth. In J. Ehrenreich (ed.) *The Cultural Crisis of Modern Medicine.* New York: Monthly Review Press.

Hakki Onen, S., Alloui, A., Gross, A., Eschallier, A. and Dubray, C. (2001) The effects of total sleep deprivation, selective sleep interuption and sleep recovery on pain tolerance in healthy subjects. *Journal of Sleep Research,* 10, 1: 35–42.

Hand, S. (ed.) (1989) *The Levinas Reader.* Oxford: Blackwell.

Haraway, D. (1991) *Simians, Cyborgs and Women.* London: Free Association Books.

Haraway, D. (1997) Modest_Witness@Second_Millenium: FemaleMan©_Meets_OncoMouse™. London: Routledge.

Harden, J., Scott, S., Backett-Milburn, K. and Jackson, S. (2000) Can't talk, won't talk: methodological issues in researching children. *Sociological Research Online*, 5, 2. <http://www.socresonline.org.uk/5/2/harden.html>

Harrison, M. (1996) The medicalization of war – the militarization of medicine. *Social History of Medicine*, 9: 267–76.

Hart, G. and Carter, S. (2000) Drugs and risk: developing a sociology of HIV risk behaviour. In S.J. Williams, J. Gabe and M. Calnan (eds) *Health, Medicine and Society: Key Theories, Future Agendas*. London: Routledge.

Haug, M. (1973) Deprofessionalization: an alternative hypothesis of the future. *Sociological Review Monograph (No. 20)*. University of Keele.

Haug, M. (1988) A re-examination of the hypothesis of physician de-professionalization. *Milbank Memorial Fund Quarterly*, 66, supplement 2: 48–56.

Heaton, J. (1999) The gaze and the visibility of the carer: a Foucauldian analysis of the discourse of informal care. *Sociology of Health and Illness*, 21, 6: 759–77.

Heideggar, M. (1962) *Being and Time*. Oxford: Blackwell.

Heller, A. (1990) *Can Modernity Survive?* Cambridge: Polity Press.

Henderson, L.J. (1935) Physician and patient as a social system. *New England Journal of Medicine*, 212, 2 May: 819–23.

Henderson, S. and Petersen, A. (eds) (2002) *Consuming Health: The Commodification of Health Care*. London: Routledge.

Hepworth, M. and Featherstone, M. (1998) The male menopause: lay accounts and the cultural reconstruction of midlife. In S. Nettleton and J. Watson (eds) *The Body in Everyday Life*. London: Routledge.

Hepworth, M. (1998) Ageing and the emotions. In G. Bendelow and S.J. Williams (eds) *Emotions in Social Life: Critical Themes and Contemporary Issues*. London: Routledge.

Herzlich, C. (1973) *Health and Illness: a Social and Psychological Approach*. London: Academic Press.

Higgs, P. and Jones, I. (2003) Ultra-Darwinism and health: the limits of evolutionary psychology. In S. Williams, L. Birke and G. Bendelow (eds) *Debating Biology*. London: Routledge.

Higgs, P. and Scambler, G. (1998) Explaining health inequalities: how useful are concepts of social class? In G. Scambler and P. Higgs (eds) *Modernity, Medicine and Health: Medical Sociology Towards 2000*. London: Routledge.

Hirst, M. and Metcalfe, J. (2001) Tinkering with nature. In B. Davey, T, Halliday and M. Hirst (eds) *Human Biology and Health: An Evolutionary Approach*. Buckingham: Open University Press.

Hobson, J.A. (1989) *Sleep*. New York: Scientific American Library.

Hochschild, A.R. (1983) *The Managed Heart: the Commercialization of Human Feeling*. Berkeley: University of California Press.

Hochschild, A.R. (1994) The commercial spirit of intimate life and the abduction of feminism: signs from women's advice books. *Theory, Culture and Society*, 11: 1–24.

Hochschild, A.R. (1998) The sociology of emotion as a way of seeing. In G. Bendelow and S.J. Williams (eds) *Emotions in Social Life: Critical Themes and Contemporary Issues*. London: Routledge.

Hockey, J. and James, A. (1993) *Growing Up and Growing Old: Ageing and Dependency in the Lifecourse*. London: Sage.

Hoe, L. (2001) Prozac Nation: Features. *The Sunday Times*, 2 September: 4.

Hogle, L.F. (1995) Tales from the crypt: technology meets organism in the living cadaver. In C.H. Gray (ed.), *The Cyborg Handbook*. London: Routledge.

Hogle, L.F. (1999) *Recovering the Nation's Body: Cultural Memory, Medicine, and the Politics of Redemption*. New Brunswick, NJ: Rutgers University Press.

Holtzman, N.A. and Marteau, T. (2000) Will genetics revolutionize medicine? *The New England Journal of Medicine*, 343, 2: 141–4.

Horgan, T. (1999) *Undiscovered Minds: How the Brain Defies Explanation*. London: Weidenfeld and Nicolson.

House of Lords (2000) *Complementary and Alternative Medicine*. London: The Stationery Office.

Hughes, B. and Paterson, K. (1997) The social model of disability and the disappearing body: towards a sociology of impairment. *Disability and Society*, 12, 3: 325–40.

Hume, D. (1969/1739–40) *A Treatise of Human Nature*. Harmondsworth: Penguin.

Hunter, D. (1992) Doctors as managers: poachers turned gamekeepers? *Social Science and Medicine*, 35, 4: 557–66.

Hunter, D. (1996) Rationing and evidence-based medicine. *Journal of Evaluation in Clincal Practice*, 2: 5–8.

Huxley, A. (1982/1932) *Brave New World*. Harlow: Longman.

Hyden, L.C. (1997) Illness and narrative. *Sociology of Health and Illness*, 19, 1: 48–69.

Idzikowski, C. (2000) *Learn to Sleep Well: Proven Strategies for Getting to Sleep and Staying Asleep*. London: Duncan Baird Publications.

Illich, I. (1974) Medical nemesis. *The Lancet*, i (11 May): 918–22.

Illich, I. (1975) *Medical Nemesis*. London: Calder and Boyars.

Illsley, R. (1955) Social class selection and class difference in relation to still-births and infant deaths. *British Medical Journal*, 2, 1,520–4.

Irigaray, L. (1986) The fecundity of the caress. In R.A. Cohen (ed.) *Face-to-Face with Levinas*. Albany, NY: State University of New York Press.

Irvine, D. (1997a) The performance of doctors. I: professionalism and self-regulation in a changing world. *British Medical Journal*, 314: 1540–2.

Irvine, D. (1997b) The performance of doctors. II: maintaining tood practice, protecting patients from poor performance *British Medical Journal*, 314: 1613–5.

Irvine, D. (2001) *The Public and the Medical Profession: a Changing Relationship*. The Lloyd Roberts Lecture, Royal Society of Medicine. London: General Medical Council.

Jackson, J. (1994) Chronic pain and the tension between the body as subject and object. In T.J. Csordas (ed.), *Embodiment and Experience: the Existential Ground of Culture and Self*. Cambridge: Cambridge University Press.

Jacobus, M., Keller, E.F. and Shuttleworth S. (eds) (1990) *Body/Politics: Women and the Discourse of Science*. London: Routledge.

Jaggar, A. (1989) Love and knowledge: emotion in feminist epistemology. In S. Bordo and A. Jaggar (eds), *Gender/Body/Knowledge: Feminist Reconstructions of Being and Knowing*. New Brunswick, NJ/London: Rutgers University Press.

James, A. (1993) *Childhood Identities: Self and Social Relationships in the Experience of the Child*. Edinburgh: Edinburgh University Press.

James, A. (1998) Children, health and illness. In D. Field and S. Taylor (eds) *Sociological Perspectives on Health, Illness and Health Care*. Oxford: Blackwell Scientific.

James, A. (2000) Embodied being(s): understanding the self and the body in childhood. In A. Prout (ed.) *The Body, Childhood and Society*. Basingstoke: Macmillan.

James, A. and Prout, A. (1993) *Constructing and Reconstructing Childhood*. Basingstoke: Falmer Press.

James, A. , Jenks, C. and Prout, A. (1998) *Theorizing Childhood*. Cambridge: Polity Press.

James, N. (1989) Emotional labour. *Sociological Review*, 37: 15–42.

James, N (1992) Care = organisation + physical labour + emotional labour. *Sociology of Health and Illness*, 14, 4: 488–509.

James, O. (1998) *Britain on the Couch: Treating a Low Serotonin Society*. London: Arrow.

James, W. (1932/1909) *The Pluralistic Universe*. New York: Longmans, Green.

James, W (1956/1897) The sentiment of rationality. In *The Will to Believe and Other Essays in Popular Philosophy*. New York: Dover Publications.

Jenkins, R. (1992) *Pierre Bourdieu*. London: Routledge.

Jenks, C. (1996) *Childhood*. London: Routledge.

Jewson, N. (1976) The disappearance of the sick man from medical cosmologies: 1770–1870. *Sociology*, 10: 225–44.

Jobling, R. (1988) The experience of psoriasis under treatment. In R. Anderson and M. Bury (eds) *Living with Chronic Illness: the Experience of Patients and Their Families*. London: Unwin Hyman.

Johnson, H.M. (1931) *Bodily Positions in Restful Sleep*. New York: The Simmons Company.

Johnson, H.M., Swan, T.H. and Weigand, G.E. (1930) In what positions do people sleep?, *Journal of the American Medical Association*, 94: 2058–62.

Johnson, M. (1987) *The Body in the Mind: the Bodily Basis of Meaning, Imagination and Reason*. Chicago: University of Chicago Press.

Joralemon, D. (1995) Organ wars: the battle for body parts. *Medical Anthropology Quarterly*, 9, 3: 335–56.

Kai, J. and Hedges, C. (1999) Minority ethnic community participation in needs assessment and service development in primary care: perceptions of Pakistani and Bangladeshi people about psychological distress. *Health Expectations*, 2: 7–20.

Karesek, R. and Theorell, T. (1990) *Healthy Work: Stress, Productivity and the Reconstruction of Working Life*. New York: Basic Books.

Karlsen, S. and Nazroo, J.Y. (2001) Identity and structure: rethinking ethnic inequalities in health. In H. Graham (ed.) *Understanding Health Inequalities*. Buckingham: Open University Press.

Katz, S. (1996) *Disciplining Old Age: the Formation of Gerontological Knowledge*. Charlottesville/London: University Press of Virginia.

Kawachi, I., Kennedy, B.P., Gupta, V. and Prothrow-Smith, D. (1999) Women's status and the health of women and men: a view from the States. *Social Science and Medicine*, 48, 1: 21–32.

Kear, A. and Steinberg, D.L. (eds) (1999) *Mourning Diana: Nation, Culture and the Performance of Grief*. London: Routledge.

Kellehear, A. (1984) Are we a 'death-denying' society? A sociological review. *Social Science and Medicine*, 18, 9: 713–23.

Kelleher, D. (1988) *Diabetes*. London: Routledge.

Kelly, D. (1980) *Anxiety and Emotions*. Springfield, IL: Charles C. Thomas Publishers.

Kelly, M. (1991) Coping with an ileostomy. *Social Science and Medicine*, 33, 2: 115–25.

Kelly, M. (1992a) Self, identity and radical surgery. *Sociology of Health and Illness*, 14, 3: 390–415.

Kelly, M. (1992b) *Colitis*. London: Routledge.

Kelly, M. (1996) Negative attributes of self: radical surgery and the inner and outer lifeworld. In C. Barnes and G. Mercer (eds) *Exploring the Divide: Illness and Disability*. Leeds: The Disability Press.

Kelly, M. and Field, D. (1994) Comments on the rejection of the biomedical model in sociological discourse. *Medical Sociology News*, 19: 34–7.

Kelly, M. and Field, D. (1996) Medical sociology, chronic illness and the body. *Sociology of Health and Illness*, 18, 2: 241–57.

Kelly, M. and Field, D. (1998) Conceptualising chronic illness. In D. Field and S. Taylor (eds) *Sociological Perspectives on Health, Illness and Health Care*. Oxford: Blackwell Scientific.

Kemper, T.J. (1990) Themes and variations in the sociology of emotions. In: T.J. Kemper (ed.), *Research Agendas in the Sociology of Emotions* New York: State University of New York Press.

Kerr, A. and Cunningham-Burley, S. (2000) On ambivalence and risk: reflexive modernity and the new human genetics. *Sociology*, 34, 2: 283–304.

Kerr, A. and Shakespeare, T. (2002) *Genetic politics: From Eugenics to Genome*. Cheltenham: New Clarion Press.

Kirk, D. and Tinning, R. (1994) Embodied self-identity, healthy lifestyles and school physical education. *Sociology of Health and Illness*, 16, 5: 600–25.

Kirwan-Taylor, H. (2001) Snooze control. *Sunday Times* (style supplement), 13 May: 31.

Klein, N. (2000) *No Logo*. London: Flamingo.

Klein, N. (2002) *Fences and Windows*. London: Flamingo.

Kleinman, A. 1988: *The Illness Narratives: Suffering, Healing and the Human Condition*. New York: Basic Books.

Kohli, M. (1988) Ageing as a challenge for sociological theory. *Ageing and Society*, 8, 4: 368–94.

Kramer, P. (1993) *Listening to Prozac*. Harmondsworth: Penguin.

Kroker, A. and Kroker, M. (1988) *Body Invaders: Sexuality and the Postmodern Condition*. Basingstoke: Macmillan.

Kübler-Ross, E. (1969) *On Death and Dying*. London: Tavistock.

Laing, R.D. (1965) *The Divided Self*. Harmondsworth: Penguin.

Langer, R. and Vacanti, J.P. (1995) Artificial organs. *Scientific American*, September: 100–3.

Laslett, P. (1996/1989) *A Fresh Map of Life: the Emergence of the Third Age*. London: Weidenfeld and Nicolson.

Latour, B. (1987) *Science in Action: How to Follow Scientists and Engineers Through Society*. Cambridge, MA: Harvard University Press.

Latour, B. (1993) *We Have Never Been Modern*. Hemel Hempstead: Harvester Wheatsheaf.

Lawler, J. (1991) *Behind the Screens: Nursing, Somology and the Problem of the Body*. South Melbourne: Churchill Livingstone.

Lawler, J. (ed.) (1997) *The Body in Nursing*. South Melbourne: Churchill Livingstone.

Lawrence, C. and Benedixen, K. (1992) His and hers: male and female anatomy in anatomy texts for US medical students 1890–1989. *Social Science and Medicine*, 35, 7: 925–34.

Lawton, J. (1998) Contemporary hospice care: the sequestration of the unbounded body and 'dirty dying'. *Sociology of Health and Illness*, 20, 2: 121–43.

Lawton, J. (2000) *The Dying Process: Patients' Experience of Palliative Care*. London: Routledge.

Lazarus, R. (1984) Thoughts on the relations between emotion and cognition. In K.R. Scherer and P. Ekman (eds) *Approaches to Emotion*. Hillsdale, NJ/London: Lawrence Erlbaum Associates.

Lazarus, R. and Lazarus B.N. (1994) *Passion and Reason: Making Sense of our Emotions*. New York: Oxford University Press.

Leder, D. (1990) *The Absent Body*. Chicago: University of Chicago Press.

Lee, N. (2001) *Childhood and Society: Growing Up in an Age of Uncertainty*. Buckingham: Open University Press.

Lewis, A. and Lindsay, G. (2000) *Researching Children's Perspectives*. Buckingham: Open University Press.

Levinas, E. (1985) *Ethics and Infinity*. Pittsburgh: Duquesue University Press.

Light, D.W. (2000) The sociological character of health-care markets. In G. Albrecht, R. Fitzpatrick and S. Scrimshaw (eds) *The Handbook of Social Studies in Health and Medicine*. London: Sage.

Lloyd, G. (1993) *The Man of Reason: 'Male' and 'Female' in Western Philosophy*. London: Methuen.

Lock, M. (2001) The alienation of body tissue and the biopolitics of immortalized cell lines. *Body & Society*. 7, 2–3: 63–91.

Locker, D. (1983) *Disability and Disadvantage: the Consequence of Chronic Illness*. London: Tavistock.

Lofland, J. (1978) *The Craft of Dying: the Modern Face of Death*. Beverly Hills: Sage.

Longino, C.F., Jr and Murphy, J.W. (1995) *The Old Age Challenge to the Biomedical Model*. New York: Baywood Publishing Co.

Lowenberg, J. and Davis, F. (1994) Beyond medicalization-demedicalization: the case of holistic health. *Sociology of Health and Illness*, 16, 5: 579–99.

Lupton, D. (1994) *Medicine as Culture: Illness, Disease and the Body in Western Societies*. London: Sage.

Lupton, D. (1995) *The Imperative of Health*. London: Sage.

Lupton, D. (1996) 'Your life in their hands': trust in the medical encounter. In V. James and J. Gabe (eds) *Health and the Sociology of Emotions*. Oxford: Blackwell.

Lupton, D. (1997a) Foucault and the medicalisation critique. In A. Petersen and R. Bunton (eds) *Foucault, Health and Medicine*. London: Routledge.

Lupton, D. (1997b) Psychoanalytic sociology and the medical encounter: Parsons and beyond. *Sociology of Health and Illness*, 19, 5: 561–79.

Lupton, D. (1997c) Consumerism, reflexivity and the medical encounter. *Social Science and Medicine*, 45, 3: 373–81.

Lupton, D. (1997d) Doctors on the medical profession. *Sociology of Health and Illness*, 19, 4: 480–97.

Lupton, D. (1998a) *The Emotional Self*. London: Sage.

Lupton, D. (1998b) Psychoanalytic sociology and the medical encounter: a reply to Pilgrim. *Sociology of Health and Illness*, 20, 4: 545–7.

Lupton, D. and Chapman, S. (1995) 'A healthy lifestyle might be the death of you': discourse on diet, cholesterol and heart disease in the press and among the lay public. *Sociology of Health and Illness*, 17, 4: 477–94.

Lupton, D., Donaldson, C. and Lloyd, P. (1991) *Caveat emptor* or blissful ignorance? Patients and the consumerist ethos. *Social Science and Medicine*, 33, 5: 559–68.

Lupton, D., McCarthy, S. and Chapman, S. (1995) 'Panic bodies': discourses on risk and HIV antibody testing. *Sociology of Health and Illness*, 17, 1: 89–108.

Lynch, J. (1985) *The Langauge of the Heart: the Human Body in Dialogue.* New York: Basic Books.

Lynch, J.W., Davey Smith, G., Kaplan, G.A. and House, J.S. (2000a) Income inequality and mortality: importance to health of individual income, psychosocial environment, or material conditions. *British Medical Journal*, 320: 1200–4.

Lynch, J.W., Due, P., Muntaner, C. and Davey Smith, G. (2000b) Social capital – is it a good investment strategy for public health? *Journal of Epidemiology and Community Health*, 54: 404–8.

Lyon, M. (1994) Emotion as mediator of somatic and social processes: the example of respiration. In W.M. Wentworth and J. Ryan (eds) *Social Perspectives on Emotion*, Vol. 2. Greenwich, CT: JAI Press.

Lyon, M.L. (1996) C. Wright Mills meets Prozac: the relevance of 'social emotion' to the sociology of health and illness. In V. James and J. Gabe (eds) *Health and the Sociology of Emotions*. Oxford: Blackwell.

Lyon, M.L. (1997) The material body, social processes and emotion: 'Techniques of the Body' revisited *Body & Society*, 3, 1: 83–101.

Lyon, M.L. (1998) The limitations of cultural constructionism in the study of emotions. In G. Bendelow and S.J. Williams (eds) *Emotions in Social Life: Critical Themes and Contemporary Issues*. London: Routledge.

McGovern, K. (1994) Applications of virtual reality to surgery. *British Medical Journal*, 380: 1054–45.

McGovern, K. and McGovern, L.T. (1994) Virtual clinic: the future is now. *Virtual Reality World*, March/April: 41–4.

Macintyre, S. (1997) The Black Report and beyond: what are the issues? *Social Science and Medicine*, 44 (6): 723–46.

Macintyre, S., Hunt, K. and Sweeting, H. (1996) Gender differences in health: are things as simple as they seem? *Social Science and Medicine*, 42: 617–24.

McKeown, T. (1976) *The Role of Medicine*. London: Nuffield Provincial Hospital Trust.

McKevitt, C. and Morgan, M. (1997) Anomalous patients: the experiences of doctors with an illness. *Sociology of Health and Illness*, 19, 5: 644–67.

McKinlay, J.B. (1988) Introduction. *Milbank Memorial Fund Quarterly*, 66 (supplement 2: Special issue on the changing character of the medical profession), 1–9.

McKinlay, J.B. and Arches, J. (1985) Towards the proletarianization of physicians. *International Journal of Health Services*, 15: 161–95.

McNeil, M., Varcoe, I. and Yearley, S. (eds) (1990) *The New Reproductive Technologies*. London: Macmillan.

MacSween, M. (1993) *Anorexic Bodies*. London: Routledge.

Maffesoli, M. (1996) *The Time of the Tribes: the Decline of Individualism in Mass Society*. London: Sage.

Marinoff, L. (2000) *Plato Not Prozac*. London: HarperCollins.

Marmot, M., Rose, G., Shipley, M. and Hamilton, P.J.S. (1978) Employment grade and coronary heart disease in British Civil Servants. *Journal of Epidemiology and Community Health*, 32: 244–9.

Marmot, M., Davey Smith, G., Stansfield, S., Patel, C., North F. and Head, J. (1991) Health inequalities among British civil servants: the Whitehall II study. *Lancet*, 337: 1387–93.

Marteau, T. and Lerman, C. (2001) Genetic risk and behavioural change. *British Medical Journal*. 322: 1056–9.

Martin, E. (1987) *The Woman in the Body*. Milton Keynes: Open University Press.

Martin, E. (1994) *Flexible Bodies: the Role of Immunology in American Culture from the Age of Polio to the Age of AIDS*. Boston: Beacon Press.

Martin, E. (2000) Flexible bodies: science and a new culture of health in the US. In S. Williams, J. Gabe and M. Calnan (eds) *Health, Medicine and Society: Key Theories, Future Agendas*. London: Routledge.

Martin, J., Meltzer, H. and Eliot, D. (1988) *OPCS Surveys of Disability in Great Britain. Report 1: The Prevalence of Disability Among Adults*. London: HMSO.

Mattison, R., Lingarde, F., Nilsson, J.A. and Theorell, T. (1990) Threat of unemployment and cardiovascular risk factors: longitudinal study of quality of sleep and serum cholesterol concentrations in men threatened with redundancy. *British Medical Journal*, 301: 461–6.

Mauss, M. (1973/1934) Techniques of the body. *Economy and Society*, 2: 70–88.

May, C. (1992) Nursing work, nurse's knowledge and the subjectification of the patient. *Sociology of Health and Illness*, 14, 4: 472–87.

May, C., Dorwick, C. and Richardson, M. (1996) The confidential patient: the social construction of therapeutic relationships in general medical practice. *Sociological Review*, 44, 2: 187–203.

Mayall, B. (1996) *Children, Health and the Social Order*. Buckingham: Open University Press.

Mayall, B. (1998a) Towards a sociology of child health. *Sociology of Health and Illness*, 20, 3: 269–88.

Mayall, B. (1998b) Chidren, emotions and daily life. In G. Bendelow and S.J. Williams (eds) *Emotions in Social Life: Critical Themes and Issues*. London: Routledge.

Mayall, B., Bendelow, G., Barker, S., Storey, P. and Veltman, M. (1996) *Children's Health in Primary Schools*. London: Falmer Press.

Meek, J. (2001) A lease on life. *The Guardian (Weekend)*, 30 June: 21–32.

Meek, J. (2002) Designer baby gets go-ahead. *The Guardian*, 23 February: 1.

Meek, J. and Scott, K. (2002) Dolly hobbles back into the limelight. *The Guardian*, 5 January: 3.

Meerabeau, L. and Page, S. (1998) 'Getting the job done': emotion management and cardiopulmonary resuscitation in nursing. In G. Bendelow and S.J. Williams (eds) *Emotions in Social Life: Critical Themes and Contemporary Issues*. London: Routledge.

Melbin, M. (1978) Night as frontier. *American Sociological Review*, 43, 1 (Feb.): 3–22.

Melbin, M. (1989) *Night As Frontier: Colonizing the World After Dark*. London: Macmillan.

Mellor, P. and Shilling, C. (1993) Modernity, self-identity and the sequestration of death. *Sociology*, 27, 3: 411–32.

Mellor, P. and Shilling, C. (1997) *Re-forming the Body: Religion, Community and Modernity*. London: Sage.

Meltzer, H., Gill, B., Petticrew, M. and Hinds, K. (1995) *The Prevalence of Psychiatric Morbidity Amongst Adults Living in Private Households*. London: OPCS.

Menzies, L.I. (1960) A case study of social systems of defence against anxiety: a report on a general hospital. *Human Relations*, 13, 1: 95–121.

Merleau-Ponty, M. (1962) *The Phenomenology of Perception*. London: Routledge.

Meštrović, S.G. (1997) *Postemotional Society*. London: Sage.

Miller, J., Engelberg, S. and Broad, W. (2001) *Germs: Biological Weapons and America's Secret War*. New York: Simon and Schuster.

Mills, S. (2001) The regulation of complementary and alternative medicine. *British Medical Journal*, 322: 158–60.

Mishler, E.G. (1989) Critical perspectives on the biomedical model. In P. Brown (ed.) *Perspectives in Medical Sociology*. Belmont, CA: Wadsworth.

Mishler, E.G. (1990) The struggle between the voice of medicine and the voice of the lifeworld. In P. Conrad and R. Kern (eds) *The Sociology of Health and Illness: Critical Perspectives*. New York: St Martins Press.

Monaghan, L. (2001) Looking good, feeling great: the embodied pleasures of vibrant physicality. *Sociology of Health and Illness*, 23, 3: 330–56.

Montgomery, S.L. (1991) Codes and combat in biomedical discourse. *Science as Culture*, 2, 3, 341–91.

Moody, H.R. (1992) Gerontology and critical theory. *The Gerontologist*, 32, 3: 294–5.

Moody, H.R. (1995) Ageing, meaning and the allocation of resources. *Ageing and Society*, 15: 163–84.

Moore, L.J. and Clarke, A.E. (2001) The traffic in cyberanatomies: sex/gender/sexualities in local and global formations. *Body & Society*, 7, 1: 57–96.

Morgan, D.H.J. (1993) You too can have a body like mine: reflections on the male body and masculinities. In S. Scott and D.H.G. Morgan (eds) *Body Matters*. London: Falmer Press.

Morrell, D. (2001) Integrated medicine is not new (letters). *British Medical Journal*, 322: 168–9

Morris, D. (1991) *The Culture of Pain*. Berkeley: University of California Press.

Morris, D. (1998) *Illness and Culture in the Postmodern Age*. Berkeley: University of California Press.

Morris, T.V. (1998) *If Aristotle Ran General Motors: The New Soul of Business*. New York: Henry Holt and Co.

Muntaner, C. and Lynch, J. (1999) Income inequality, social cohesion, and class relations: a critique of Wilkinson's neo-Durkheimian research programme. *International Journal of Health Services*, 29, 1: 59–81.

Myles, J. (1984) *Old Age in the Welfare State: the Political Economy of Public Pensions*. Lawrence, KS: University Press of Kansas.

Nahin, R.L. and Straus, S.E. (2001) Research into complementary and alternative medicine: problems and potential. *British Medical Journal*, 322: 161–4.

Navarro, V. (1975) The industrialization of fetishism or the fetishism of industrialization? A critique of Ivan Illich. *Social Science and Medicine*, 9: 351–63.

Navarro, V. (1980) Work, ideology and science: the case of medicine. *Social Science and Medicine*, 14: 191–205.

Navarro, V. (1988) Professional dominance or proletarianization? Neither. *International Journal of Health Services*, 19, 311–14.

Navarro, V. (1994) *The Politics of Health Policy: the US Reforms 1980–1994*. Oxford: Blackwell.

Navarro, V. (ed.) (2002) *The Political Economy of Social Inequalities: Consequences for Health and Quality of Life*. New York: Baywood Publishing Co. Inc.

Nazroo, J.Y. (1997a) *The Health of Britain's Ethnic Minorities: Findings from a National Survey*. London: Policy Studies Insitute.

Nazroo, J.Y. (1997b) *Ethnicity and Mental Health: Findings from a National Community Survey*. London: Policy Studies Institute.

Nazroo, J.Y. (2001) *Ethnicity, Class and Health*. London: Policy Studies Insitute.

Nettleton, S. (1992) *Power, Pain and Dentistry*. Buckingham: Open University Press.

Nettleton, S. and Watson, J. (1998) *The Body in Everyday Life*. London: Routledge.

NSF (National Sleep Foundation) (2001) Sleep in America Poll results <www.sleepfoundation.org>.

NSF (National Sleep Foundation) (2002) Sleep in America Poll results <www.sleepfoundation.org>.

Nussbaum, M. (1992) Human functioning and social justice: in defence of Aristotelian essentialism. *Political Theory*, 20, 2: 202–46.

Oakley, A. (1984) *The Captured Womb*. Oxford: Blackwell.

Oakley, A., Bendelow, G., Barnes, J., Buchanan, M. and Hussain, O. (1995) Health and cancer prevention: knowledge and beliefs of children and young people. *British Medical Journal*, 310: 1029–33.

Oatley, K. and Jenkins, J.M. (1996) *Understanding Emotions*. Oxford: Blackwell.

(OECD) Organization for Economic Co-operation and Development) (1995) *Ageing in OECD Countries (Social Policy Studies No. 20)*. Paris: OECD Publications.

Olesen, V. and Bone, D. (1998) Emotions in rationalizing organizations: conceptual notes from professional nursing in the USA. In G. Bendelow and S.J. Williams (eds) *Emotions in Social Life: Critical Themes and Contemporary Issues*. London: Routledge.

Oliver, M. (1990) *The Politics of Disablement*. London: Macmillan.

Olson, L.K. (1982) *The Political Economy of Aging: the State, Private Power and Social Welfare*. New York: Columbia University Press.

O'Neill, J. (1985) *The Five Bodies: the Shape of Human Society*. Ithaca, NY/London: Cornell University Press.

ONS (Office of National Statistics) (2002) *Social Trends No. 32*. London: The Stationary Office.

Owen, D.K., Lewith, G. and Stephens, C.R. (2001) Can doctors respond to patients' increasing interest in complementary and alternative medicine? *British Medical Journal*. 322: 154–8.

Pakulski, J. and Waters, M. (1996) *The Death of Class*. London: Sage.

Parsons, E. and Atkinson, P. (1992) Lay constructions of genetic risk. *Sociology of Health and Illness*, 14, 4: 437–55.

Parsons, E. and Atkinson, P. (1993) Genetic risk and reproduction. *Sociological Review*, 41: 679–706.

Parsons, T. (1951) *The Social System*. London: Routledge and Kegan Paul.

Parsons, T. (1964) *Social Structure and Personality*. London: Free Press.

Parsons, T. (1975) The sick role and the role of the physician reconsidered. *Milbank Memorial Fund Quarterly*, 53, 3: 257–78.

Parsons, T. (1978) *Action Theory and the Human Condition*. New York: Free Press.

Paterson, K. (2001) Disability studies and phenomenology: finding a space for both the carnal and the political. In S. Cunningham-Burley and K. Backett-Milburn (eds) *Exploring the Body*. Basingstoke: Palgrave.

Petersen, A. and Bunton, R. (2002) *The New Genetics and the Public's Health*. London: Routledge.

Pflanz, M. and Rhode, J.J. (1970) Illness: deviant behaviour or conformity? *Social Science and Medicine*, 4: 645–53.

Phillipson, C. (1982) *Capitalism and the Construction of Old Age*. London: Macmillan.

Phillipson, C. (1998) *Reconstructing Old Age: New Agendas in Social Theory and Practice*. London: Sage.

Pilgrim, D. (1998) Medical sociology and psychoanalysis: a rejoinder to Lupton. *Sociology of Health and Illness*. 20, 4: 537–44.

Pinder, R. (1996) Sick-but-fit or fit-but-sick? Ambiguity and identity at the workplace. In C. Barnes and G. Mercer (eds) *Exploring the Divide: Illness and Disability*. Leeds: The Disability Press.

Place, B. (2000) Constructing the bodies of ill children in the intensive care unit. In A. Prout (ed.) *The Body, Childhood and Society*. Basingstoke: Macmillan.

Pole, C., Mizen, P. and Boulton, A. (1999) Realising children's agency in research: partners and participants? *International Journal of Social Research Methodology*, 2, 1: 39–54.

Popay, J. (1992) 'My health is alright, but I'm just tired all the time': women's experience of ill health. In H. Roberts (ed.) *Women's Health Matters*. London: Routledge.

Popay, J. (2000) Social capital: the role of narrative and historical research. *Journal of Epidemiology and Community Health*, 54: 401.

Porter, R. (1997) *The Greatest Benefit to Mankind: a Medical History of Humanity*. London: Fontana Press.

Pound, P., Gompertz, P. and Ebrahim, S. (1998). Illness in the context of older age: the case of stroke. *Sociology of Health and Illness*, 20, 4: 489–506.

Prendergast, S. (2000) 'To become dizzy in our turning': girls, body-maps and gender as childhood ends. In A. Prout (ed.) *The Body, Childhood and Society*. Basingstoke: Macmillan.

Prendergast, S. and Forrest, S. (1998) 'Shorties, low-lifers, hard nuts and kings': boys and the transformation of emotions. In G. Bendelow and S. Williams (eds) *Emotions in Social Life: Critical Themes and Contemporary Issues*. London: Routledge.

Prigg, M. (1998) Robots try their hand at surgery. *The Sunday Times*, 15 February: 7.

Pringle, R. (1989) *Secretaries Talk: Sexuality, Power and Work*. London: Verso.

Prior, L. (1989) *The Social Organization of Death*. London: Macmillan.

Prout, A. (1986) 'Wet children' and 'little actresses': going sick in primary school. *Sociology of Health and Illness*, 8: 765–89.

Prout, A. (1989) Sickness as a dominant symbol in life course transitions: an illustrated theoretical framework. *Sociology of Health and Illness*, 11, 4: 336–59.

Prout, A. (2000a) Childhood bodies: social construction and translation. In S. Williams, J. Gabe and M. Calnan (eds) *Health, Medicine and Society: Key Theories, Future Agendas*. London: Routledge.

Prout, A. (2000b) Childhood bodies: construction, agency and hybridity. In A. Prout (ed.) *The Body, Childhood and Society*. Basingstoke: Macmillan.

Putnam, L.L. and Mumby, D.K. (1993) Organizations, emotions and the myth of rationality. In S. Fineman (ed.) *Emotion in Organizations*. London: Sage.

Radden, M.H. (1985) *Madness and Reason*. London: George Allen and Unwin.

Radley, A. (1989) Style, discourse and constraint in adjusting to chronic illness. *Sociology of Health and Illness*, 11, 3: 230–52.

Radley, A. (1999) The aesthetics of illness: narrative, horror and the sublime. *Sociology of Health and Illness*, 21, 6: 778–96.

Radley, A. and Green, R. (1987) Chronic illness as adjustment: a methodology and conceptual framework. *Sociology of Health and Illness*, 9, 2: 179–207.

Rawdon Wilson, R. (1995) Cyber(body)parts: prosthetic consciousness. *Body & Society*, 1, 3–4: 239–59.

Ray, L. (2001) Introduction to the rapid response to September 11. *Sociological Research Online*. <http://socresonline.org.uk/introduction.html>.

Rees, L. and Weil, A. (2001) Integrated medicine imbues orthodox medicine with the values of complementary medicine. *British Medical Journal*, 322: 119–20.

Reilly, D. (2001) Enhancing human healing: directly studying human healing could help to create a unifying focus in medicine. *British Medical Journal*, 322: 120–1.

Riessman, C.K. (1989) Women and medicalization: a new perspective. In P. Brown (ed.) *Perspectives in Medical Sociology*. Belmont CA: Wadsworth.

Rifkin, J. (1998) *The Biotech Century: How Genetic Commerce Will Change the World*. London: Phoenix.

Riska, E. and Wegar K. (eds) (1993) *Gender, Work and Medicine: Women and the Medical Divison of Labour*. London: Sage.

Ritzer, G. (1995) *The McDonaldization of Society: an Investigation into the Changing Character of Contemporary Social Life*. London: Sage.

Robinson, I. (1988) *Multiple Sclerosis*. London: Routledge.

Robinson, I. (ed.) (1994) *Life and Death under High Technology Medicine*. Manchester: Manchester University Press.

Rose, G. (1995) *Love's Work*. London: Chatto and Windus.

Rose, H. (1994) *Love, Power and Knowledge: Towards a Feminist Transformation of the Sciences*. Cambridge: Polity Press.

Rose, H. and Rose, S. (eds) (2000) *Alas Poor Darwin: Arguments Against Evolutionary Psychology*. London: Jonathan Cape.

Rose, N. (1990) *Governing the Soul: the Shaping of the Private Self*. London: Routledge.

Rose, S. (1997) *Lifelines: Biology, Freedom and Determinism*. Harmondsworth: Penguin.

Rose, S. (2002) Review: F. Fukuyama, Our Posthuman Future. *The Guardian* (Review),1 June: 14.

Rowland, R.A. (1985) A child at any price? *Women's Studies International Forum*, 8, 6: 539–46

Rowland, R.A. (1992) *Living Laboratories: Woman and the Reproductive Technologies*. London: Pan Macmillan.

Russell, R. (2000) Ethical bodies. In P. Hancock, B. Hughes, E. Jagger, K. Paterson, R. Russell, E. Tulle-Winton and M. Tyler *The Body, Culture and Society*. Buckingham: Open University Press.

Sabo, D. and Gordon, D. (eds) (1995) *Men's Health and Illness: Gender, Power and the Body*. London: Sage.

Sackett, D.L., Richardson, W.S., Rosenberg, W. and Haynes, R.B. (1997) *Evidence-Based Medicine: How to Practise and Teach EBM*. London: Churchill Livingstone.

Saltonstall, R. (1993) Healthy bodies – social bodies: men's and women's concepts and practices of health in everyday life. *Social Science and Medicine*, 36, 1: 7–14.

Sapolsky, R.M. (1991) Poverty's remains. *Science*, 31: 8–10.

Sartre, J.-P. (1969) *Being and Nothingness*. London: Routledge.

Sartre, J.-P. (1971/1939) *Sketch for a Theory of the Emotions*. London: Methuen.

Sassen, S. (2002) Towards a sociology of information technology. *Current Sociology*, 50, 3: 365–88.

Sawicki, J. (1991) *Disciplining Foucault: Feminism, Power and the Body*. London: Routledge.

Sayer, A. (1997) Essentialism, social constructionism and beyond. *The Sociological Review*, 45, 3: 453–87.

Sayer, A. (2000) *Realism and Social Science*. London: Sage.

Scambler, G. (ed.) (1987) *Sociological Theory and Medical Sociology*. London: Tavistock.

Scambler, G. (1989) *Epilepsy*. London: Routledge.

Scambler, G. (ed.) (2001) *Habermas, Critical Theory and Health*. London: Routledge.

Scambler, G. (2002) *Health and Social Change: A Critical Theory*. Buckingham: Open University Press.

Scambler, G. and Higgs, P. (1999) Stratification, class and health: class relations and health inequalities in high modernity. *Sociology*, 33, 2: 275–96.

Scheff, T.J. (1990) *Microsociology: Discourse, Emotion and Social Structure*. Chicago/London: University of Chicago Press.

Scheper-Hughes, N. (2001a) Bodies for sale – whole or in parts. *Body & Society*, 7, 2–3: 1–8.

Scheper-Hughes, N. (2001b) Commodity fetishism in organs trafficking. *Body & Society*, 7, 2–3: 31–62.

Scheper-Hughes, N. and Lock, M. (1987) The mindful body: a prolegemonon to future work in medical anthropology. *Medical Anthropology Quarterly*, 1, 1, 6–41.

Schilder, P. (1950) *The Image and Appearance of the Human Body*. New York: International Universities Press, Inc.

Schneider, J.W. (1985) Social problems theory: the constructionist view. *Annual Review of Sociology*, 11: 209–29.

Schneider, J.W. and Conrad, P. (1981) Medical and sociological typologies: the case of epilepsy. *Social Science and Medicine*. 15A: 211–19.

Schneider, J.W. and Conrad, P. (1983) *Having Epilepsy: the Experience and Control of Epilepsy*. Philadelphia: Temple University Press.

Schwartz, B. (1970) Notes on the sociology of sleep. *Sociological Quarterly*, 11, Fall: 485–99.

Scott, A. (2003) A metaphysics for alternative medicine: 'Translating' the social and the biological worlds. In S.J. Williams, L. Burke and G. Bendelow (eds) *Debating Biology: Sociological Reflections on Health, Medicine and Society*. London: Routledge.

Scott, J. (2000) Class and stratification. In G. Payne (ed.) *Social Divisions*. Basingstoke: Macmillan.

Seale, C. (1995) Heroic death. *Sociology*, 29, 4: 597–613.

Seale, C. (1998) *Constructing Death: the Sociology of Dying and Bereavement*. Cambridge: Cambridge University Press.

Secretary of State for Health (1999) *Saving Lives: Our Healthier Nation*. Cm 4386. London: The Stationery Office.

Seidler, V. (1994) *Unreasonable Men: Masculinity and Social Theory*. London: Routledge.

Sennett, R. (1998) *The Corrosion of Character: The Personal Consequences of Work in the New Capitalism*. London: Norton.

Shakespeare, T. (1995) 'Back to the future'? New genetics and disabled people. *Critical Social Policy*, 44, 5: 22–35.

Shakespeare, T. (1999) Losing the Plot? Medical and activist discourses of contemporary genetics and disabled people. *Sociology of Health and Illness*, 21, 5: 669–88.

Shakespeare, T. (2003) Rights, risks and responsibilities: new genetics and disabled people. In S.J. Williams, L. Birke and G. Bendelow (eds) *Debating Biology: Sociological Reflections on Health, Medicine and Society*. London: Routledge.

Shakespeare, T. and Erickson, M. (2000) Different strokes: beyond biological determinism and social constructionism. In H. Rose and S. Rose (eds) *Alas Poor Darwin: Arguments Against Evolutionary Psychology*. London: Jonathan Cape.

Shapiro, C.M. (ed.) (1994) *The ABC of Sleep Disorders*. London: BMJ Publications.

Sharma, U. (1992) *Complementary Medicine Today*. London: Routledge.

Sharma, U. (1996) Using complementary therapies: a challenge to orthodox medicine? In S.J. Williams and M. Calnan (eds) *Modern Medicine: Lay Perspectives and Experiences*. London: UCL Press.

Sharma, U. (2002) Integrated medicine: an examination of GP-complementary practitioner collaboration. In G. Bendelow, M. Carpenter, C. Vautier and S. Williams (eds) *Gender, Health and Healing: the Public/Private Divide*. London: Routledge.

Sharp, L.A. (1995) Organ transplantation as a transformative experience: anthropological insights into the restructuring of the self. *Medical Anthropology Quarterly*. 9, 3: 357–89.

Shaw, G.B. (1946/1911) *The Doctor's Dilemma*. Harmondsworth: Penguin.

Shaw, I. (2002) How lay are lay beliefs?, *Health*, 6, 3: 287–99.

Shaw, M., Dorling, D., Gordon, D. and Davey Smith, G. (1999) *The Widening Gap: Health Inequalities and Policy in Britain*. Bristol: The Policy Press.

Shaw, M., Dorling, D. and Mitchell, R. (2002) *Health, Place and Society*. London: Prentice Hall.

Shildrick, M. (1997) *Leaky Bodies and Boundaries: Feminism, Postmodernism and (Bio)Ethics*. London: Routledge.

Shilling, C. (1993) *The Body and Social Theory*. London: Sage.

Shorter, E. (1997) *A History of Psychiatry: From the Era of the Asylum to the Age of Prozac*. New York: John Wiley.

Showalter, E. (1987) *The Female Malady*. London: Virago.

Showalter, E. (1997) *Hystories: Hysterical Epidemics and Modern Culture*. London: Picador.

Siegrist, J., Peter, R., Junge, A., Cremer, P. and Seidel, D. (1990) Low status, high effort at work and ischaemic heart disease: prospective evidence from blue-collar men. *Social Science and Medicine*, 31: 1127–34.

Skultans, V. (1999) Narratives of the body and history: illness in judgement on the Soviet past. *Sociology of Health and Illness*, 21, 3: 310–28.

Slouka, M. (1995) *War of the Worlds: the Assault on Reality*. London: Abacus.

Smaje, C. (1995) *Health, 'Race' and Ethnicity*. London: King's Fund Institute.

Smaje, C. (1996) The ethnic patterning of health: new directions for theory and research. *Sociology of Health and Illness*, 18: 139–71.

Smaje, C. (2000) A place for race? Medical sociology and the critique of racial ideology. In S. Williams J. Gabe and M. Calnan (eds) *Health, Medicine and Society: Key Theories, Future Agendas*. London: Routledge.

Smart, B. (1996) Facing the body – Goffman, Levinas and the the subject of ethics. *Body & Society*, 2, 2: 67–78.

Smith, P. (1992) *The Emotional Labour of Nursing*. London: Macmillan.

Smith, R. (2001) Why are doctors so unhappy? *British Medical Journal*, 322: 1073–4.

Smith, R. (2002) Oh NHS, thou art sick. *British Medical Journal*, 324: 127–8.

Sontag, S. (1978) *Illness as Metaphor*. Harmondsworth: Penguin.

Soper, K. (1992) *What is Nature?* Oxford: Blackwell.

Spector, M. and Kitsuse, J.I. (1977) *Constructing Social Problems*. Menlo Park, CA: Cummings.

Springer, C. (1991) The Pleasure of the Interface, *Screen*, 32, 3: 303–23.

Stacey, M. (1981) The divison of labour revisited, or overcoming the two Adams. In P. Abrahams, R. Deem, J. Finch and P. Rock (eds) *Development or Diversity: British Sociology 1950–1980*. London: Allen and Unwin.

Stacey, M. (1988) *The Sociology of Health and Healing*. London: Unwin Hyman.

Stacey, M. (1995) The British General Medical Council: from Empire to Europe. In T. Johnson, G. Larkin and M. Saks (eds) *Health Professions and the State in Europe*. London: Routledge.

Stacey, M. (1992) *Regulating British Medicine: The GMC*. Chichester: John Wiley.

Stacey, M. (2002) Concluding comments. In G. Bendelow, M. Carpenter, C. Vautier and S. Williams (eds) *Gender, Health and Healing: the Public/Private Divide*. London: Routledge.

Stacey, M. and Homans, H. (1978) The sociology of health and illness: its present state, futures and potential for health research. *Sociology*, 12: 281–307.

Stanworth, M. (ed.) (1987) *Reproductive Technologies: Gender, Motherhood and Medicine*. Cambridge: Polity Press.

Stein, H. (1985) *The Psychodynamics of Medical Practice: Unconscious Factors in Patient Care*. Berkeley: University of California Press.

Steinberg, D.L. (1990) The depersonalization of women through the administration of '*in vitro* fertilization'. In M. McNeil, I. Varcoe and S. Yearley (eds), *The New Reproductive Technologies*. London: Macmillan.

Steinberg, D.L. (2000) 'Recombinant bodies': narrative, metaphor and the gene. In S. Williams, J. Gabe and M. Calnan (eds) *Health, Medicine and Society: Key Theories, Future Agendas*. London: Routledge.

Stelarc (1999) Parasite visions: alternate, intimate, involuntary experiences. *Body & Society*, 5, 2–3: 117–27.

Straus, R. (1957) The nature and status of medical sociology. *American Sociological Review*, 22: 200.

Strauss, A.L. and Glaser, B. (eds) (1975) *Chronic Illness and the Quality of Life*. St Louis, MO: Mosby.

Strong, P.M. (1979a) Sociological imperialism and the profession of medicine: a critical examination of the thesis of medical imperialism. *Social Science and Medicine*, 13A: 199–215.

Strong, P.M. (1979b) *The Ceremonial Order of the Clinic: Parents, Doctors and Medical Bureaucracies*. London: Routledge and Kegan Paul.

Strong, P.M. (1990) Epidemic psychology: a model. *Sociology of Health and Illness*, 12, 3: 249–59.

Sunday Times Magazine (1998) The 'Viagravation' of society. 6 September: 48–52.

Swain, J., Finklestein, V., French, S. and Oliver, M. (eds) (1993) *Disabling Barriers – Enabling Environments*. London: Sage.

Synnott, A. (1993) *The Body Social: Symbolism, Self and Society*. London: Routledge.

Szreter, S. (1988) The importance of social interaction in Britain's mortality decline – 1850–1914: a reinterpretation of the role of public health. *Bulletin of the Society for the Social History of Medicine*, 41: 1–37.

Tarlov, A.R. (1996) Social determinants of health: the sociobiological translation. In D. Blane, E. Brunner and R.G. Wilkinson (eds) *Health and Social Organization: Towards a Health Policy for the 21st Century*. London: Routledge.

Tauber, A.I. (1997) *The Immune Self: Theory or Metaphor?* Cambridge: Cambridge University Press.

Tauber, A.I. (1999) *Confessions of a Medical Man: an Essay in Popular Philosophy*. Cambridge, MA/London: MIT Press.

Taussig, M. (1980) Reification and the consciousness of the patient. *Social Science and Medicine*, 14B: 3–13.

Taylor, B. (1993) Unconsciousness and society: the sociology of sleep. *International Journal of Politics, Culture and Society*, 6, 3: 463–71.

Thacker, E. (1999) Performing the technoscientific body: RealVideo surgery and the anatomy theatre. *Body & Society*, 5, 2–3: 317–36.

Thoits, P. (1995) Stress, coping, and social support processes: where are we? What next? *Journal of Health and Social Behaviour* (extra issue): 53–79.

Tober, D.M. (2001) Semen as gift, semen as good: reproductive workers and the market in altruism. *Body & Society*, 7, 2–3: 137–60.

Tomas, D. (1995) Feedback and cybernetics: reimaging the body in the age of cybernetics. *Body & Society*, 1, 3–4: 21–43.

Townsend, P. (1981) The structured dependency of the elderly: the creation of social policy in the twentieth century. *Ageing and Society*, 1, 1: 5–28.

Townsend, P. and Davidson, N. (1980) *Inequalities in Health: the Black Report*. Harmondsworth: Penguin.

Trigg, R. (1970) *Pain and Emotion*. Oxford: Clarendon Press.

Turner, B.S. (1992) *Regulating Bodies: Essays in Medical Sociology*. London: Routledge.

Turner, B.S. (1993) *Max Weber: From History to Modernity*. London: Routledge.

Turner, B.S. (1995) *Medical Power, Social Knowledge* (2nd Edition). London: Sage.

Turner, B.S. (1996/1984) *The Body and Society* (2nd Edition). London: Sage.

Ussher, J. (1991) *Women's Madness: Misogyny or Mental Illness?* London: Harvester Wheatsheaf.

Van Gennep, A. (1960/1909) *The Rites of Passage*. Chicago: University of Chicago Press.

Van Straten, M. (1996) *The Good Sleep Guide*. London: Trafalgar Square.

Verbrugge, L. (1985) Gender and health: an update on hypotheses and evidence. *Journal of Health and Social Behaviour*, 26: 156–82.

Vrancken, M. (1989) Schools of thought on pain. *Social Science and Medicine*, 29, 3: 435–44.

Wadsworth, M.E.J. (1991) *The Imprint of Time: Childhood History and Adult Life*. Oxford: Oxford University Press.

Wadsworth, M.E.J. (1997) Health inequalities in the life course perspective. *Social Science and Medicine*, 44, 6: 859–70.

Wainwright, M. (2002) Dozing driver who caused 10 deaths gets five years. *The Guardian*, 12 January: 1.

Wajcman, J. (2002) Adressing technological change: the challenge to social theory. *Current Sociology*, 50, 3: 347–63.

Waldby, C. (1997) The body in the digital archive: the Visible Human Project and the computerisation of medicine. *Health*, 1, 2: 227–43.

Waldby, C. (2000) *The Visible Human Project: Informatic Bodies and Posthuman Medicine*. London: Routledge.

Walker, A. (1980) The social creation of poverty and dependency in old age. *Journal of Social Policy*, 9, 1: 45–75.

Walker, B.G. (1985) *The Crone: Women of Age, Wisdom and Power*. San Francisco: Harper & Row.

Walter, T. (1995) *The Revival of Death*. London: Routledge.

Walter, T. (1999) *The Mourning for Diana*. Oxford: Berg.

Walter, T., Littlewood, J. and Pickering M. (1995) Death in the news: the public invigilation of private emotion. *Sociology*, 29, 4: 574–96.

Watson, J. (2000) *Male Bodies: Health, Culture and Identity*. Buckingham: Open University Press.

Wearing, B., Wearing, S. and Kelly, K. (1994) Adolescent women, identity and smoking: leisure experience as resistance. *Sociology of Health and Illness*, 16, 5: 626–43.

Webster, A. (2002) Innovative health technologies and the social: redefining health, medicine and the body. *Current Sociology,* 50, 3: 443–57.

Wei Leng, K. (1996) On menopause and cyborgs: or, towards a feminist cyborg politics of the menopause. *Body & Society*. 2, 3: 33–52.

Weiner, C. (1975) Tolerating the uncertainty: the burden of rheumatoid arthritis. In A.L. Strauss and B. Glaser (eds) *Chronic Illness and the Quality of Life*. St Louis: Mosby.

West, L. (2000) *Doctors on the Edge*. London: Free Association Books.

West, P. (1991) Rethinking the health selection explanation for health inequalities. *Social Science and Medicine*, 32: 373–84.

Westergaard, J. (1995) *'Who Gets What?' The Hardening of Class Inquality in the Late Twentieth Century*. Cambridge: Polity Press.

WHICH? (1986) Magic or medicine? 443–7.

WHICH? (1992) Alternative medicine on trial. 102–5.

WHICH? (1995) Healthy choice? 8–11.

Whitehead, M. (1988) *The Health Divide*. Harmondsworth: Penguin.

Wickham, J. (1994) Future developments. *British Medical Journal* 308: 193–6.

Wilkinson, R.G. (1996) *Unhealthy Societies: the Afflictions of Inequality*. London: Routledge.

Wilkinson, R.G. (1999) Income inequality, social cohesion, and health: clarifying the theory – a reply to Muntaner and Lynch. *International Journal of Health Services*. 29, 3: 525–43.

Wilkinson, R.G. (2000a) *Mind the Gap: Hierachies, Health and Human Evolution*. London: Weidenfeld and Nicolson

Wilkinson, R.G. (2000b) Inequality and the social environment: a reply to Lynch et al. *Journal of Epidemiology and Community Health*, 54: 411–13.

Wilkinson, R.G. (2000c) Deeper than 'neoliberalism': a reply to David Coburn. *Social Science and Medicine,* 51: 997–1000.

Williams, G.H. (1984) The genesis of chronic illness: narrative reconstruction. *Sociology of Health and Illness*, 6, 2: 175–200.

Williams, G.H. (1996) Representing disability: Some questions of phenomenology and politics.

In C. Barnes and G. Mercer (eds) *Exploring the Divide: Illness and Disability*. Leeds: The Disability Press.

Williams, G.H., and Busby, H. (2000) The politics of 'disabled' bodies. In S. Williams, J. Gabe, and M. Calnan (eds) *Health, Medicine and Society: Key Theories, Future Agendas*. London: Routledge.

Williams, R. (1990) *A Protestant Legacy: Attitudes to Death and Illness Among Older Aberdonians*. Oxford: Clarendon Press.

Williams, S.J. (1993) *Chronic Respiratory Illness*. London: Routledge.

Williams, S.J. (1995) Theorising class, health and lifestyles: can Boudieu help us? *Sociology of Health and Illness*, 17, 5: 577–604.

Williams, S.J. (1997) Modern medicine and the uncertain body: from corporeality to hyperreality. *Social Science and Medicine*, 45, 7: 1041–9.

Williams, S.J. (1998a) 'Capitalising' on emotions? Rethinking the inequalities debate. *Sociology*. 32, 1: 121–39.

Williams, S.J. (1998b) Health as moral performance: ritual, transgression and taboo. *Health*, 2, 4: 435–57.

Williams, S.J. (1998c) Emotions, cyberspace and the 'virtual' body: a critical appraisal. In G. Bendelow and S.J. Williams (eds) *Emotions in Social Life: Critical Themes and Contemporary Issues*. London: Routledge.

Williams, S.J. (1998d) Arlie Russell Hochschild. In R. Stones (ed.) *Key Sociological Thinkers*. London: Macmillan.

Williams, S.J. (1999a) Reason, emotion and embodiment: is 'mental' health a contradiction in terms? *Sociology of Health and Illness*, 22, 5: 559–81.

Williams, S.J. (1999b) Transgression for what? A reply to Robert Crawford. *Health*, 3, 4: 367–78.

Williams, S.J. (2000) Chronic illness as biographical disruption or biographical disruption as chronic illness? Reflections on a core concept. *Sociology of Health and Illness*, 22, 1: 40–67.

Williams, S.J. (2001a) Sociological imperialism and the medical profession revisited: where are we now? *Sociology of Health and Illness*. 23, 2: 135–58.

Williams, S.J. (2001b) *Emotions and Social Theory: Corporeal Reflections on the (Ir)Rational*. London: Sage.

Williams, S.J. (2001c) From smart bombs to smart bugs: thinking the unthinkable in medical sociology and beyond. *Sociological Research Online*, 6, 3. <http: //www.socresonline.org.uk/6/3/williams.html>

Williams, S.J. (2002) Sleep and health: Sociological reflections on the dormant society *Health*, 6, 2: 173–200.

Williams, S.J. and Bendelow, G. (1998a) *The Lived Body: Sociological Themes, Embodied Issues*. London: Routledge.

Williams, S.J. and Bendelow, G. (1998b) Malignant bodies: children's beliefs about health, cancer and risk. In S. Nettleton and J. Watson (eds) *The Body in Everyday Life*. London: Routledge.

Williams, S.J. and Bendelow, G. (2000) 'Recalcitrant bodies'? Children, cancer and the transgression of corporeal boundaries. *Health*, 4, 1: 51–71.

Williams, S.J. and Calnan, M. (1994) Perspectives on prevention: the views of general practitioners. *Sociology of Health and Illness*, 16, 3: 372–93.

Williams S.J. and Calnan M. (1996a) The limits of medicalisation: modern medicine and the lay populace in late modernity. *Social Science and Medicine*, 42, 12: 1609–20.

Williams S.J. and Calnan, M. (eds) (1996b) *Modern Medicine: Lay Perspectives and Experiences*. London: UCL Press.

Williams, S.J., Annandale, E. and Tritter, J. (1998) The sociology of health and illness at the turn of the century: back to the future? *Sociological Research Online*. <http: //www.socresonline.org.uk/3/4/williams.html>

Williams, S.J., Gabe, J. and Calnan, M. (eds) (2000) *Health, Medicine and Society: Key Theories, Future Agendas*. London: Routledge.

Wilson, E.O. (1975) *Sociobiology: the New Synthesis*. Cambridge, MA: Harvard University Press.

Witz, A. (1992) *Professions and Patriarchy*. London: Routledge.

Wolf, N. (2001) *Misconceptions: Truth, Lies and the Unexpected on the Journey to Motherhood*. London: Chatto and Windus.

Woods, R.L. (ed.) (1947) *The World of Dreams: an Anthology*. New York: Appleton-Century-Crofts.

World Health Organization (WHO) (1980) *International Classification of Impairments, Disabilities and Handicaps*. Geneva: WHO.

Wouters, C. (1989) The sociology of emotions and flight attendants: Hochschild's *Managed Heart*. *Theory, Culture and Society*, 6, 1: 95–123.

Wynne, B. (2002) Risk and environment as legitimatory discourses of technology: reflexivity inside out? *Current Sociology*, 50, 3: 459–77.

Yoshida, K.K. (1993) Reshaping of Self: a pendular reconstruction of self and identity among adults with traumatic spinal cord injury. *Sociology of Health and Illness*, 15, 2: 217–45.

Young, I.M. (1990) *Throwing Like a Girl and Other Essays in Feminist Philosophy and Social Theory*. Bloomington: Indiana University Press.

Young, M. and Schuller, T. (1991) *Life After Work: the Arrival of the Ageless Society*. London: HarperCollins.

Zajonc, R.B. (1984) The interaction of affect and cognition. In K.R. Scherer and P. Ekman (eds) *Approaches to Emotion*. Hillsdale, NJ and London: Lawrence Erlbaum Associates.

Zimmern, R., Emery, J. and Richards, T. (2001) Putting genetics in perspective. *British Medical Journal*. 322: 1005–6.

Zola, I.K. (1972) Medicine as an institution of social control. *Sociological Review*, 20: 487–503.

Zola, I.K. (1982) *Missing Pieces: a Chronicle of Living with a Disability*. Philadelphia: Temple University Press.

Zola, I.K. (1991) Bringing our bodies and ourselves back in: reflections on a past, present and future 'medical sociology'. *Journal of Health and Social Behaviour*, 32 (March): 1–16.

Index